THE CAMBRIDGE EDITION
OF THE WORKS OF

JANE AUSTEN

JANE AUSTEN IN CONTEXT

Cambridge University Press and the General Editor
Janet Todd wish to express their gratitude to the
University of Glasgow and the University of Aberdeen for
providing funding towards the creation of this edition.
Their generosity made possible the employment of
Antje Blank as research assistant throughout the project.

THE CAMBRIDGE EDITION
OF THE WORKS OF

JANE AUSTEN

GENERAL EDITOR: Janet Todd, University of Aberdeen

VOLUMES IN THIS SERIES:
Juvenilia edited by Peter Sabor
Northanger Abbey edited by Barbara Benedict with Deirdre Le Faye
Sense and Sensibility edited by Edward Copeland
Pride and Prejudice edited by Pat Rogers
Mansfield Park edited by John Wiltshire
Emma edited by Richard Cronin and Dorothy McMillan
Persuasion edited by Janet Todd and Antje Blank
Later Manuscripts edited by Brian Southam
Jane Austen in Context edited by Janet Todd

Watercolour drawing of Jane Austen by her sister Cassandra, dated 1804.

JANE AUSTEN
IN CONTEXT

Edited by
Janet Todd

CAMBRIDGE
UNIVERSITY PRESS

CAMBRIDGE UNIVERSITY PRESS

Cambridge, New York, Melbourne, Madrid, Cape Town, Singapore, São Paulo

Cambridge University Press
The Edinburgh Building, Cambridge CB2 2RU, UK

Published in the United States of America by
Cambridge University Press, New York

www.cambridge.org
Information on this title: www.cambridge.org/9780521826440

First published 2005

Printed in the United Kingdom at the University Press, Cambridge

A catalogue record for this book is available from the British Library

Library of Congress Cataloguing in Publication data
Jane Austen in context / edited by Janet Todd.
p.   cm. – (The Cambridge edition of the works of Jane Austen)
Includes bibliographical references (p. 434) and index.
ISBN-13: 978-0-521-82644-0
ISBN-10: 0-521-82644-6
1. Austen, Jane, 1775–1817 – Encyclopedias.   2. Novelists, English –
19th century – Biography – Encyclopedias.   3. Women and literature –
England – History – 19th century – Encyclopedias.   I. Todd, Janet M., 1942–
II. Title.   III. Series.
PR4036.A283 2005   2005012924
823′.7 – dc22

ISBN-13   978-0-521-82644-0 hardback
ISBN-10   0-521-82644-6 hardback

CONTENTS

Contents

ILLUSTRATIONS

PICTURE ACKNOWLEDGEMENTS

For kind permission to reproduce the images and for supplying
photographs, the editor would like to thank the following libraries
and museums: Syndics of Cambridge University Library (figs. 31,
35, 36, 38); National Portrait Library, London (fig. 2); Rare Book
Collection, University of Florida Libraries (figs. 40, 41); St
Andrews University Library (fig. 29); Torquay Museum, Devon
(fig. 1); V & A Images Victoria and Albert Museum, London
(figs. 34, 37); British Museum, London (fig. 42). The editor would

also like to thank Deirdre Le Faye (figs. 30, 39); Brian North Lee and the Folio Society (fig. 28); C. F. Viveash (figs. 4–24); and the owners of the frontispiece. Every effort has been made to secure necessary permissions to reproduce copyright material in this work, though in some cases it has proved impossible to trace copyright holders. If any omissions are brought to our notice, we will be happy to include appropriate acknowledgements in any subsequent edition.

NOTES ON CONTRIBUTORS

ANTJE BLANK is Research Fellow in the Department of English at the University of Aberdeen. She is the editor of *Hannah Cowley* (London: Pickering & Chatto, 2001) and co-editor, with Janet Todd, of Charlotte Smith's *Desmond* (Peterborough, Ont: Broadview Press, 2001) and of *Persuasion* for the *Cambridge Edition of the Works of Jane Austen*.

PAULA BYRNE is the author of *Jane Austen and the Theatre* (London: Hambledon, 2002) and *Perdita: The Life of Mary Robinson* (London: Harper Collins, 2004). She is editor of *Emma: A Sourcebook* (London: Routledge, 2004).

ROBERT CLARK is Reader in English at the University of East Anglia and editor of the web-based *The Literary Encyclopedia*. He has edited *Emma* for Everyman Paperbacks and the *New Casebook* on *Sense and Sensibility* and *Pride and Prejudice* (Basingstoke: Macmillan, 1994).

EDWARD COPELAND is the author of *Women Writing About Money: Women's Fiction in England, 1790–1820* (Cambridge: Cambridge University Press, 1995). He is co-editor of *The Cambridge Companion to Jane Austen* (Cambridge: Cambridge University Press, 1997) and editor of *Sense and Sensibility* for the *Cambridge Edition of the Works of Jane Austen*.

VALÉRIE COSSY is Lecturer of English Literature and Gender Studies at the University of Lausanne. She is the author of *Jane Austen in Switzerland: A Study of the Early French Translations* (Geneva: Slatkine, 2005) and of several articles on French translations of eighteenth-century English prose novelists.

RICHARD CRONIN is Professor of English Literature at the University of Glasgow. He is the author of *1798: the Year of the Lyrical Ballads* (Basingstoke: Macmillan, 1998) and *The Politics of Romantic Poetry: In Search of the Pure Commonwealth* (Basingstoke: Macmillan, 2000). He is co-editor, with Dorothy McMillan, of *Emma* for the *Cambridge Edition of the Works of Jane Austen*.

ALISTAIR M. DUCKWORTH is Professor Emeritus at the University of Florida. He is the author of numerous publications on Jane Austen, most notably *The Improvement of the Estate: A Study of Jane Austen's Novels*, new edition (Baltimore: Johns Hopkins University Press, 1994).

GERRY DUTTON is a local historian living in Steventon. He is a leading member of the North Waltham, Steventon, Ashe and Deane History Society and runs the North Hampshire Tithe Map Project.

MARKMAN ELLIS is Reader in Eighteenth-Century Literature and Culture at Queen Mary, University of London. He is the author of *The Politics of Sensibility* (Cambridge: Cambridge University Press, 1996), *The Coffee-House: a Cultural History* (London: Weidenfeld and Nicolson, 2004) and co-editor of *Discourses of Slavery and Abolition: Britain and its Colonies* (Basingstoke: Palgrave Macmillan, 2004).

JAN FERGUS is Professor of English at Lehigh University, Pennsylvania. She has published *Jane Austen: A Literary Life* (London: Macmillan, 1991), *Jane Austen and the Didactic Novel* (London: Macmillan, 1983), as well as several essays on aspects of Austen's novels.

PENNY GAY is Associate Professor in the English Department at the University of Sydney. She is the author of *As She Likes It: Shakespeare's Unruly Women* (London: Routledge, 1994), *Jane Austen and the Theatre* (Cambridge: Cambridge University Press, 2002) and has written on Jane Austen film adaptations.

DAVID GILSON was a member of the Committee of the Jane Austen Society (1975–1992). He compiled *A Bibliography of Jane Austen*, corrected edition (Winchester: St Paul's Bibliographies, 1997) and wrote articles for *The Book Collector* and the annual *Report* and the *News Letter* of the Jane Austen Society. He contributed bibliographical introductions to the Routledge/Thoemmes facsimile reprints of *The Novels of Jane Austen* (1994) and *Jane Austen: Family History* (1995).

CHRIS JONES is Senior Lecturer in English at the University of Wales, Bangor. He is the author of *Radical Sensibility: Literature & Ideas in the 1790s* (London: Routledge, 1993) and contributor to *The Cambridge Companion to Mary Wollstonecraft*, ed. Claudia Johnson (Cambridge: Cambridge University Press, 2002).

GARY KELLY is Canada Research Chair in English at the University of Alberta. He is the author of *Revolutionary Feminism: the Mind and Career of Mary Wollstonecraft* (London: Macmillan, 1992) and *Women, Writing, and Revolution, 1790–1827* (Oxford: Clarendon Press, 1993). He is general editor of *Bluestocking Feminism* (London: Pickering & Chatto, 1999) and *Varieties of Female Gothic* (London: Pickering & Chatto, 2002).

THOMAS KEYMER is Elmore Fellow and Tutor in English at St Anne's College, Oxford. He is the author of *Sterne, the Moderns, and the Novel* (Oxford: Oxford University Press, 2002). He is co-editor, with Jon Mee, of *The Cambridge Companion to English Literature, 1740–1830* (Cambridge: Cambridge University Press, 2004) and Henry Fielding's *Tom Jones* (London: Penguin, 2005).

MARGARET KIRKHAM is the author of *Jane Austen, Feminism and Fiction*, new edition (London: Athlone Press, 1997) and of various essays and reviews on Jane Austen.

PETER KNOX-SHAW is Research Associate at the University of Cape Town. He is the author of *Jane Austen and the Enlightenment* (Cambridge: Cambridge University Press, 2004) and has published widely on eighteenth-century and Romantic literature.

CLAIRE LAMONT is Professor of English Romantic Literature at the University of Newcastle. She is editor of Walter Scott's *Chronicles of the Canongate* (Edinburgh: Edinburgh University Press, 2001) for the *Edinburgh Edition of the Waverley Novels*.

MAGGIE LANE has been an executive member of the UK Jane Austen Society since 1991 and is currently serving as Hon. Secretary. She is the author of many books, including *Jane Austen's Family* (London: Robert Hale, 1984), *Jane Austen's England* (London: Robert Hale, 1986), *Jane Austen and Food* (London: Hambledon, 1994) and *Jane Austen's World* (London: Carlton, 1996).

DEIRDRE LE FAYE is the author of numerous books including *Jane Austen, A Family Record*, second edition (Cambridge: Cambridge University Press, 2004), *Jane Austen's Letters*, new edition (Oxford: Oxford University Press, 1995), *Jane Austen's 'Outlandish Cousin', the Life & Letters of Eliza de Feuillide* (London: British Library, 2002), *A Chronology of Jane Austen and her Family* (Cambridge: Cambridge University Press, 2005) and, with John Sutherland, *So You Think You Know Jane Austen?* (Oxford: Oxford University Press, 2005). She is co-editor of *Northanger Abbey* for the *Cambridge Edition of the Works of Jane Austen*.

DEIDRE SHAUNA LYNCH is Associate Professor of English at Indiana University. She is the author of *The Economy of Character: Novels, Market Culture, and the Business of Inner Meaning* (Chicago: University of Chicago Press, 1998). She is editor of *Janeites: Austen's Disciples and Devotees* (Princeton, NJ: Princeton University Press, 2000).

ANTHONY MANDAL is Postdoctoral Research Associate in the Centre for Editorial & Intertextual Research at Cardiff University. He is editor of *Cardiff Corvey: Reading the Romantic Text* and co-editor of *The Reception of British Authors in Europe: Jane Austen* (London: Continuum, 2006).

JOHN MULLAN is Senior Lecturer at University College, London. He is the author of many books, including *Sentiment and Sociability: the Language of Feeling in the Eighteenth Century* (Oxford: Clarendon Press, 1988) and *Eighteenth-Century Popular Culture. A*

Selection (Oxford: Oxford University Press, 2000). He is editor of Daniel Defoe's *The Political History of the Devil* (London: Pickering & Chatto, 2004).

JAMES RAVEN is Professor for History at the University of Essex. He has published widely on book and communications history. Since 1990 he has been directing *The Cambridge Project for the Book Trust*. He is co-editor of *The English Novel 1770–1829: A Bibliographical Survey of Prose Fiction Published in the British Isles* (Oxford: Oxford University Press, 2000).

ALAN RICHARDSON is Professor of English at Boston College, MA. He is the author of *British Romanticism and the Science of the Mind* (Cambridge: Cambridge University Press, 2001), *Literature, Education, and Romanticism: Reading as Social Practice, 1780–1832* (Cambridge: Cambridge University Press, 1994) and *A Mental Theater: Poetic Drama and Consciousness in the Romantic Age* (University Park: Pennsylvania State University Press, 1988).

WARREN ROBERTS is Distinguished Teaching Professor at the University at Albany, New York. He is the author of many books, including *Jane Austen and the French Revolution* (London: Macmillan Press, 1979) and *Jacques-Louis David and Jean-Louis Prieur, Revolutionary Artists: The Public, the Populace, and the French Revolution* (Albany: State University of New York Press, 2000).

NICHOLAS ROE is Professor of English at the University of St Andrews, Scotland. He is the author of *John Keats and the Culture of Dissent* (Oxford: Clarendon Press, 1997) and *Fiery Heart: The First Life of Leigh Hunt* (London: Pimlico, 2005).

PAT ROGERS is DeBartolo Chair in the Liberal Arts, University of South Florida. He is the author of numerous publications, including *The Alexander Pope Encyclopedia* (Westport, CT: Greenwood Press, 2004) and *Pope and the Destiny of the Stuarts* (Oxford: Oxford University Press, 2005). He is editor of *Pride and Prejudice* for the *Cambridge Edition of the Works of Jane Austen*. He is associate editor of *The Oxford Dictionary of National Biography* (Oxford: Oxford University Press, 2004).

DIEGO SAGLIA is Associate Professor of English Literature at the University of Parma. He is the author of *Poetic Castles in Spain: British Romanticism and Figurations of Iberia* (Amsterdam: Rodopi, 2000). He co-edited, with Beatrice Battaglia, *Re-Drawing Austen: Picturesque Travels in Austenland* (Naples: Liguori, 2005).

DAVID SELWYN lives and teaches in Bristol. He is the author of *Jane Austen and Leisure* (London: Hambledon, 1999) and has edited *Jane Austen: Collected Poems and Verse of the Austen Family* (Manchester: Carcanet, 1996), *The Complete Poems of James Austen, Jane Austen's Eldest Brother* (Chawton: Jane Austen Society, 2003) and, with Maggie Lane, *Jane Austen, A Celebration* (Manchester: Carcanet, 2000). He is editor of the Jane Austen Society *Report* and *News Letter*.

BRIAN SOUTHAM is a retired publisher and former academic. His recent publications include *Jane Austen's Literary Manuscripts*, new edition (London: Athlone Press, 2001) and *Jane Austen and the Navy* (London: Hambledon, 2000). He is editor of *Jane Austen's Literary Manuscripts* for the *Cambridge Edition of the Works of Jane Austen* and co-editor of *The Reception of British Authors in Europe*: *Jane Austen* (London: Continuum, 2006).

JANE STABLER is Reader in Romanticism at the University of St Andrews, Scotland. She is the author of *Byron, Poetics and History* (Cambridge: Cambridge University Press, 2002) and a new introduction to *Mansfield Park* (Oxford: Oxford University Press, 2003).

RAJESWARI SUNDER RAJAN is Professorial Fellow of Wolfson College and Reader in English at the University of Oxford. She is the author of *Real and Imagined Women: Gender, Culture and Postcolonialism* (London: Routledge, 1993) and *Scandal of the State: Women, Law and Citizenship in Postcolonial India* (Durham, NC: Duke University Press, 2003). She has edited, with You-me Park, *The Postcolonial Jane Austen* (London: Routledge, 2000).

KATHRYN SUTHERLAND is Professor of Bibliography and Textual Criticism at the University of Oxford. Her recent publications include an edition of *A Memoir of Jane Austen and Other Family Recollections* (Oxford: Oxford University Press, 2002) and a critical study on *Jane Austen's Textual Lives: from Aeschylus to Bollywood* (Oxford: Oxford University Press, 2005).

NICOLA TROTT is Head of the Department of English Literature at the University of Glasgow. She has published widely on writing of the nineteenth century and is co-editor of *1800: The New 'Lyrical Ballads'* (Basingstoke: Palgrave, 2001).

MARY WALDRON is the author of *Jane Austen and the Fiction of her Time* (Cambridge: Cambridge University Press, 1999) and *Lactilla, Milkwoman of Clifton: the Life and Writings of Ann Yearsley, 1753–1806* (Athens, GA: University of Georgia Press, 1996). She has edited George Eliot, *Adam Bede* (Peterborough, Ont.: Broadview Press, 2005).

MICHAEL WHEELER is Visiting Professor at the Universities of Lancaster, Roehampton and Southampton. He is the author of many books, including *Heaven, Hell and the Victorians* (Cambridge: Cambridge University Press, 1994), *Ruskin's God* (Cambridge: Cambridge University Press, 1999) and *Jane Austen and Winchester Cathedral* (Winchester: Winchester Cathedral, 2003).

JOHN WILTSHIRE is Reader and Associate Professor at La Trobe University, Melbourne. He is the author of *Samuel Johnson in the Medical World* (Cambridge: Cambridge University Press, 1991) and *Jane Austen and the Body: 'The Picture of Health'* (Cambridge: Cambridge University Press, 1992). He is editor of *Mansfield Park* in the *Cambridge Edition of the Works of Jane Austen*.

PREFACE

For *Northanger Abbey*, probably the first book she prepared for publication, Jane Austen provided an 'Advertisement' by the 'Authoress', pointing out the quotidian nature of the background and details of her fiction. She was readying the work for publication in 1816 just after the end of the Napoleonic Wars, during the last year of her life, but she had, she declared, completed it in 1803, having actually conceived it even earlier. She wrote:

some observation is necessary upon those parts of the work which thirteen years have made comparatively obsolete. The public are entreated to bear in mind that thirteen years have passed since it was finished, many more since it was begun, and that during that period, places, manners, books, and opinions have undergone considerable changes.

Attuned as she was to 'places, manners, books, and opinions', she knew that fashions and hairstyles had altered in thirteen years and that the muslins in style in 1803 were no longer desired in 1816. (Jane Austen, although not keen on shopping, showed herself in her letters intensely interested in clothes.) She knew that the political and literary scene varied from year to year and that, when the naive and fiction-obsessed Catherine Morland suggests that 'something very shocking indeed will soon come out in London', it is quite reasonable for her to be thinking of Gothic fiction and for her more serious friend Eleanor Tilney to assume that she means riots in London, such as were happening in the 1790s. Praising Jane Austen for subordinating her material 'to principles of Economy and Selection' and declaring 'nothing is dragged in, nothing is superfluous', George Henry Lewes also noted in her books an 'ease of nature, which looks so like the ordinary life of everyday'.[1] The appearance is in part given by the careful, spare use of material objects and literary and political allusions.

This volume of entries on aspects of Jane Austen's life, works and historical context necessarily speaks to the interests of the twenty-first century: it treats nationalism and empire as well as transport and the professions, print culture along with dress and manners, the agricultural background of her life as well as the literary. In David Lodge's *Changing Places* Professor Morris Zapp of Euphoric State University intended to make his academic name by saying everything there was to be said on Jane Austen. There is no such hubristic claim for this volume, which simply aims to suggest ways of looking at the novels through this moment's version of late eighteenth- and early nineteenth-century history and culture. In the entries on Jane Austen's life and times it hopes to indicate how her biography subtly interacts with her novels and in the histories of criticism to show how the criticism has responded to literary movements and fashions.

The volume is divided into three parts, with each section of topics in alphabetic order. A bibliography at the end indicates some of the main works used by the contributors and suggests further reading.

I am grateful to the Universities of Glasgow and Aberdeen for their support of this volume. I should also like to thank the contributors for their co-operation and patience through the editing process and Linda Bree of Cambridge University Press for her gracious encouragement at each stage in the preparation. With her detailed knowledge of Jane Austen's life, Deirdre Le Faye has been an invaluable and generous resource. Most of all I owe gratitude to Antje Blank not only for her tireless editorial work and insistent high standards but also for her unflagging and contagious enthusiasm for the novels of Jane Austen.

Janet Todd
University of Aberdeen 2005

NOTE

1. H. Lewes, *Blackwood's Edinburgh Magazine* 87 (March, 1860), 335.

ABBREVIATIONS

 E: *Emma*
 L: *Jane Austen's Letters*, ed. Deirdre Le Faye, new edition
        (Oxford: Oxford University Press, 1995)
 LF: 'Love and Freindship'
 LS: *Lady Susan*
 MP: *Mansfield Park*
 NA: *Northanger Abbey*
 OED: *Oxford English Dictionary*
 P: *Persuasion*
 P&P: *Pride and Prejudice*
 S: *Sanditon*
 S&S: *Sense and Sensibility*
 W: *The Watsons*

Quotations from Jane Austen's novels are sourced to volume and
chapter and given in brackets, e.g. (*S&S*, 2:3). Quotations from
single-volume works are sourced to chapters or letters, e.g. (*S*, 4).
References to Jane Austen's letters are sourced to dates and given
in brackets after the quotation.

CHRONOLOGY

DEIRDRE LE FAYE

1764

26 April   Marriage of Revd George Austen, rector of
             Steventon, and Cassandra Leigh; they go to live at
             Deane, Hampshire, and their first three children –
             James (1765), George (1766) and Edward (1767) –
             are born here.

1768

Summer   The Austen family move to Steventon, Hampshire.
             Five more children – Henry (1771), Cassandra
             (1773), Francis (1774), Jane (1775), Charles (1779) –
             are born here.

1773

23 March   Mr Austen becomes Rector of Deane as well as
             Steventon, and takes pupils at Steventon from now
             until 1796.

1775

16 December Jane Austen born at Steventon.

1781

Winter   JA's cousin, Eliza Hancock, marries Jean-François
             Capot de Feuillide, in France.

1782

             First mention of JA in family tradition, and the first
             of the family's amateur theatrical productions takes
             place.

1783

             JA's third brother, Edward, is adopted by Mr and
             Mrs Thomas Knight II, and starts to spend time with
             them at Godmersham in Kent.

	JA, with her sister Cassandra and cousin Jane Cooper, stays for some months in Oxford and then Southampton, with kinswoman Mrs Cawley.
1785	
Spring	JA and Cassandra go to the Abbey House School in Reading.
1786	
	Edward sets off for Grand Tour of Europe, and does not return until autumn 1790.
April	JA's fifth brother, Francis, enters the Royal Naval Academy in Portsmouth.
December	JA and Cassandra have left school and are at home again in Steventon. Between now and 1793 JA writes her three volumes of *Juvenilia*.
1788	
Summer	Mr and Mrs Austen take JA and Cassandra on a trip to Kent and London.
December	Francis leaves the RN Academy and sails to East Indies; does not return until winter 1793.
1791	
July	JA's sixth and youngest brother, Charles, enters the Royal Naval Academy in Portsmouth.
27 December	Edward Austen marries Elizabeth Bridges, and they live at Rowling in Kent.
1792	
27 March	JA's eldest brother, James, marries Anne Mathew; they live at Deane.
? Winter	Cassandra becomes engaged to Revd Tom Fowle.
1793	
23 January	Edward Austen's first child, Fanny, is born at Rowling.
1 February	Republican France declares war on Great Britain and Holland.
8 April	JA's fourth brother, Henry, becomes a lieutenant in the Oxfordshire Militia.
15 April	James Austen's first child, Anna, born at Deane.
3 June	JA writes the last item of her *Juvenilia*.

1794

22 February	M de Feuillide guillotined in Paris.
September	Charles leaves the RN Academy and goes to sea.
? Autumn	JA possibly writes the novella *Lady Susan* this year.

1795

	JA probably writes 'Elinor and Marianne' this year.
3 May	James's wife Anne dies, and infant Anna is sent to live at Steventon.
Autumn	Revd Tom Fowle joins Lord Craven as his private chaplain for the West Indian campaign.
December	Tom Lefroy visits Ashe Rectory – he and JA have a flirtation over the Christmas holiday period.

1796

October	JA starts writing 'First Impressions'.

1797

17 January	James Austen marries Mary Lloyd, and infant Anna returns to live at Deane.
February	Revd Tom Fowle dies of fever at San Domingo and is buried at sea.
August	JA finishes 'First Impressions' and Mr Austen offers it for publication to Thomas Cadell – rejected sight unseen.
November	JA starts converting 'Elinor and Marianne' into *Sense and Sensibility*.
	Mrs Austen takes her daughters for a visit to Bath.
	Edward Austen and his young family move from Rowling to Godmersham.
31 December	Henry Austen marries his cousin, the widowed Eliza de Feuillide, in London.

1798

	JA probably starts writing 'Susan' (later to become *Northanger Abbey*).
17 November	James Austen's son James Edward born at Deane.

1799

Summer	JA probably finishes 'Susan' (*Northanger Abbey*) about now.

1800

	Mr Austen decides to retire and move to Bath.

1801

24 January	Henry Austen resigns his commission in the Oxfordshire Militia and sets up as a banker and army agent in London.
May	The Austen family leave Steventon for Bath, and then go for a seaside holiday in the West Country. JA's traditional West Country romance presumably occurs between now and the autumn of 1804.

1802

25 March	Peace of Amiens appears to bring the war with France to a close.
Summer	Charles Austen joins his family for a seaside holiday in Wales and the West Country.
December	JA and Cassandra visit James and Mary at Steventon; while there, Harris Bigg-Wither proposes to JA and she accepts him, only to withdraw her consent the following day.
Winter	JA revises 'Susan' (*Northanger Abbey*).

1803

Spring	JA sells 'Susan' (*Northanger Abbey*) to Benjamin Crosby; he promises to publish it by 1804, but does not do so.
18 May	Napoleon breaks the Peace of Amiens, and war with France recommences.
Summer	The Austens visit Ramsgate in Kent, and possibly also go to the West Country again.
November	The Austens visit Lyme Regis.

1804

	JA probably starts writing *The Watsons* this year, but leaves it unfinished.
Summer	The Austens visit Lyme Regis again.

1805

21 January	Mr Austen dies and is buried in Bath.
Summer	Martha Lloyd joins forces with Mrs Austen and her daughters.
18 June	James Austen's younger daughter, Caroline, born at Steventon.
21 October	Battle of Trafalgar.

1806

2 July   Mrs Austen and her daughters finally leave Bath; they visit Clifton, Adlestrop, Stoneleigh and Hamstall Ridware, before settling in Southampton in the autumn.

24 July   Francis Austen marries Mary Gibson.

1807

19 May   Charles Austen marries Fanny Palmer, in Bermuda.

1808

10 October   Edward Austen's wife Elizabeth dies at Godmersham.

1809

5 April   JA makes an unsuccessful attempt to secure the publication of 'Susan' (*Northanger Abbey*).

7 July   Mrs Austen and her daughters, and Martha Lloyd, move to Chawton, Hants.

1810

Winter   *Sense and Sensibility* is accepted for publication by Thomas Egerton.

1811

February   JA starts planning *Mansfield Park*.

30 October   *Sense and Sensibility* published.

?Winter   JA starts revising 'First Impressions' into *Pride and Prejudice*.

1812

17 June   America declares war on Great Britain.

14 October   Mrs Thomas Knight II dies, and Edward Austen now officially takes surname of Knight.

Autumn   JA sells copyright of *Pride and Prejudice* to Egerton.

1813

28 January   *Pride and Prejudice* published; JA half-way through *Mansfield Park*.

?July   JA finishes *Mansfield Park*.

?November   *Mansfield Park* accepted for publication by Egerton about now.

1814

21 January   JA commences *Emma*.

5 April   Napoleon abdicates and is exiled to Elba.

9 May	*Mansfield Park* published.
24 December	Treaty of Ghent officially ends war with America.

1815

March	Napoleon escapes and resumes power in France; hostilities recommence.
29 March	*Emma* finished.
18 June	Battle of Waterloo finally ends war with France.
8 August	JA starts *Persuasion*.
4 October	Henry Austen takes JA to London; he falls ill, and she stays longer than anticipated.
13 November	JA visits Carlton House, and receives an invitation to dedicate a future work to the Prince Regent.
December	*Emma* published by John Murray, dedicated to the Prince Regent (title page 1816).

1816

Spring	JA's health starts to fail. Henry Austen buys back manuscript of 'Susan' (*Northanger Abbey*), which JA revises and intends to offer again for publication.
18 July	First draft of *Persuasion* finished.
6 August	*Persuasion* finally completed.

1817

27 January	JA starts *Sanditon*.
18 March	JA now too ill to work, and has to leave *Sanditon* unfinished.
24 May	Cassandra takes JA to Winchester for medical attention.
18 July	JA dies in the early morning.
24 July	JA buried in Winchester Cathedral.
December	*Northanger Abbey* and *Persuasion* published together, by Murray, with a 'Biographical Notice' added by Henry Austen (title page 1818).

1869

16 December	JA's nephew, Revd James Edward Austen-Leigh (JEAL), publishes his *Memoir of Jane Austen*, from which all subsequent biographies have stemmed (title page 1870).

1871

JEAL publishes a second and enlarged edition of his *Memoir*, including in this the novella *Lady Susan*, the cancelled chapters of *Persuasion*, the unfinished *The Watsons*, a précis of *Sanditon*, and 'The Mystery' from the *Juvenilia*.

1884

JA's great-nephew, Lord Brabourne, publishes *Letters of Jane Austen*, the first attempt to collect her surviving correspondence.

1922

Volume the Second of the *Juvenilia* published.

1925

The manuscript of the unfinished *Sanditon* edited by R. W. Chapman and published as *Fragment of a Novel by Jane Austen*.

1932

R. W. Chapman publishes *Jane Austen's Letters to her sister Cassandra and others*, giving letters unknown to Lord Brabourne.

1933

Volume the First of the *Juvenilia* published.

1951

Volume the Third of the *Juvenilia* published.

1952

Second edition of R. W. Chapman's *Jane Austen's Letters* published, with additional items.

1954

R. W. Chapman publishes *Jane Austen's Minor Works*, which includes the three volumes of the *Juvenilia* and other smaller items.

1980

B. C. Southam publishes *Jane Austen's 'Sir Charles Grandison'*, a small manuscript discovered in 1977.

1995

Deirdre Le Faye publishes the third (new) edition of *Jane Austen's Letters*, containing further additions to the Chapman collections.

PART I

Life and works

I

Biography

JAN FERGUS

Biographical information on Austen is famously scarce. Most people who read the novels know that she was a clergyman's daughter who grew up in a country parsonage with several brothers and one beloved sister, that she never married and that she died relatively young. They may know that she was born in 1775 (16 December), in tandem with the revolutionary end of the eighteenth century, and did not publish a novel until 1811, six years before her death in a more conservative period.

To give us more than those bare facts, we have few materials. Nothing biographical written before her early death remains, apart from some family letters, including her own that have survived. The greatest number were written to her sister Cassandra, older by three years. Cassandra censored these letters, omitting accounts of illness, unhappiness and apparently Austen's one-night engagement. Although Austen was deeply attached to her family and had as well a number of women friends (generally older), she was closer to Cassandra than to anyone. A great-niece born after Austen's death but who knew Cassandra wrote that 'they were wedded to each other by the resemblance of their circumstances, and in truth there was an exclusiveness in their love such as only exists between husband and wife'.[1] Austen's best friend, Cassandra was also her first critic, reading the novels as she wrote them.

After Austen's death, we must rely for information about her life on her brother Henry's short 'Biographical Notice' published in 1818, and other family materials and reminiscences primarily supplied by nephews and nieces. These established the family legend, reiterated through the nineteenth century and a good part of the twentieth, that Austen was an ideal unmarried domestic woman, the modest, helpful, unassuming product of a large, happy family that formed the centre of her life.

Many full-length biographies of Austen, forced to base themselves on such skimpy or censored sources and on what can be gleaned from the novels and the juvenilia, follow the lead of Austen's nephew James Edward Austen-Leigh. His 1869 *Memoir* offered anecdotal accounts of manners and customs of Austen's period to flesh out and support the family story, and modern biographers too tend to offer social history of Austen's time. But they also include disturbing material that the family legend omits or obscures. They point to distress in Austen's life that was suppressed from the letters, such as her unhappiness at learning she had to leave Steventon, the home of her youth. Alternatively, they focus on family crises and fissures that affected Austen less directly. Austen's second oldest brother was handicapped mentally and farmed out to a neighbouring community. Two other brothers, Frank and Charles, left home early to serve in the navy during the long wars with France; both did well but were often away. Austen herself almost died of typhus at seven, when she and her sister had been sent away to school. A wealthy and unpleasant aunt underwent prosecution for theft. Cassandra's fiancé died of yellow fever in Jamaica. Two of Austen's sisters-in-law died in childbirth. Austen's brother Henry went bankrupt, costing his rich uncle James £10,000 and his wealthy brother Edward £20,000. A cousin's husband was guillotined in France during the Terror. Some biographers, dwelling on such disasters, have gone so far as to embrace an anti-family story: Austen was an embittered, disappointed woman trapped in a thoroughly unpleasant family.

The best way for a biography to avoid being scripted by such polarising views of the family and of Austen herself, and to obtain a more accurate assessment of Austen's life and work, is to examine some aspect of both that the traditions do not emphasise. Considering how important money is in the novels, biographers have paid relatively little attention to the family's and Austen's own finances. Though she did not begin by writing for money, Austen was delighted by her first real earnings: she wrote to her brother Frank to announce that every copy of the first edition of *Sense and Sensibility* had been sold: 'it has brought me £140 – besides the Copyright, if that sh^d ever be of any value. – I have now therefore written myself into £250. [having sold the copyright of *Pride and*

Prejudice for £110] – which only makes me long for more' (*L*, 3–6 July 1813). That is, Jane Austen became a professional writer.

Austen stepped into the role of professional woman writer pioneered by women writers she admired, like Frances Burney, Charlotte Smith and Maria Edgeworth, all of whom published just a couple of generations after women managed to support themselves by writing: Aphra Behn (?1640–89) is usually cited as the first. Austen was trying to succeed, then, by taking advantage of a relatively new and still not fully respectable opportunity for making money that Behn and her successors created for women. Its lack of respectability, at least for those conscious as the Austens were of occupying a position at the margins of gentility, is evident in Austen's refusal to allow her name to be printed as the author of novels published during her life. In other words, what her economic position made necessary – some attempt to earn money – her class position made problematic: to be associated with commerce threatened genteel status. Austen's texts express some of the anxieties and complications of these conditions of her life as a woman in the late eighteenth and early nineteenth century.

Jane Austen was born to parents best described as on the fringes of the gentry. Thanks to the custom of primogeniture, which decreed that land would be passed on undivided to the eldest son or sometimes to a daughter, the gentry were always producing daughters, younger sons and more distant relations who were effectively disinherited, on the fringes, as Austen's novels often witness. Jane Austen's parents George Austen and Cassandra Leigh were in just this position: they had little money and no land themselves. But they did have family and friends with enough property and interest to help them or their children. George's distant relatives educated him for the clergy, and his second cousin Thomas Knight gave him two livings valued at £210 by the time of Jane Austen's birth, along with land to farm. He also took in pupils in her youth, and once he retired in 1801, his income had reached almost £600 a year. His childless benefactor Thomas Knight also adopted George Austen's third son Edward as his heir for Godmersham Park in Kent and Chawton Manor in Hampshire. Edward Austen Knight eventually enjoyed an income greater than Mr Darcy's, nearly £15,000 a year, but he was not at first remarkably generous to his mother and sisters after his father's death in 1805 left them virtually homeless. Still, his initial pledge of £100 a year did almost double his mother's income, and eventually he housed her and his sisters in the cottage at Chawton that has become the Jane Austen museum.

Cassandra Leigh, Jane Austen's mother, had aristocratic connections but only a small fortune that produced an income of £122 a year once her husband died. The real money in her family passed her by and went to male relatives – brother, son and grandson. Cassandra Leigh's childless brother James Leigh-Perrot both married and inherited property, including at last a life interest in the huge ancestral Leigh property of Stoneleigh Abbey. He employed some of his fortune in providing clerical livings and supplementary cash for his namesake James, Jane Austen's oldest brother; the property eventually went to James's son James Edward, Austen's biographer. When her uncle's death in 1817 disclosed that he had left nothing in his will to his sister, Mrs Austen, by then a widow on a small income, Jane Austen – already terminally ill – was deeply distressed and suffered a relapse of her illness.

Austen's youthful writing shows an increasing awareness of the economic realities of life for women on the fringes of the gentry, realities that channel money and land to men, bypassing women like her mother or herself. At first, in her earliest work, class position is often comically dwelt on or elevated: the father of 'Beautifull Cassandra' is 'of noble Birth, being the near relation of the Dutchess of —'s Butler'. But money tends to be ignored or easily obtained, as when Sophia in 'Love and Freindship' filches bank-notes from her uncle's escritoire or is provided with an annuity of £400 a year by her husband's family. Austen wrote this brilliant burlesque of sentimental fiction at fourteen, by which time she had obviously read voraciously in contemporary fiction. Despite altogether two years of formal schooling away from home with her sister, her education was largely self-directed, like Elizabeth Bennet's. Her juvenilia, begun as a family amusement at twelve or even earlier, are preoccupied with comic representations of female power and possibility, as many feminist critical analyses have shown. When Austen began to abandon burlesque, however, money and status became serious issues. Catharine Percival (of 'Catharine, or The Bower', written when Austen was sixteen) associates with the local gentry, but her status is dubious, for though 'As an heiress she was certainly of consequence . . . her Birth gave her no other claim to it, for her Father had been a Merchant.' In situation Catharine is the opposite of Jane Austen, but her two friends the Wynnes are like Jane Austen's own friends the Lloyds or indeed like herself in the future: daughters of a clergyman whose death reduced them 'to a state of absolute dependance on some relations'.

The inequities of patriarchal inheritance pervade Austen's first published novels, *Sense and Sensibility* (1811; drafted from November 1797, from a 1795 novel in letters, 'Elinor and Marianne') and *Pride and Prejudice* (1813; drafted as 'First Impressions', October 1796–August 1797). The early versions of those works, written in her late teens and early twenties, certainly also reflect a preoccupation with the reality and threat of disinheritance of daughters that Ruth Perry's work has revealed as characteristic of eighteenth-century novels in general, and Austen's in particular.[2] When in the 1790s Jane Austen was drafting her first novels, she also began to go to balls, to mix somewhat with the surrounding gentry, to make visits to richer relatives, and the insecurities and ambiguities of her class position as well as her economic future must have been as evident to her as they become to the Dashwoods, disinherited in favour of a great-great-nephew by the owner of Norland, or to Elizabeth Bennet, who will be poverty-stricken at her father's death unless she marries. Female gentility is unstable without marriage or money, as shown by *Emma*'s Miss Bates, who lost the Vicarage that Mr Elton occupies when her own father died.

Marriage was a woman's 'pleasantest preservative from want' (*P&P*, 1:22), as the narrator of *Pride and Prejudice* notes of Charlotte Lucas's predicament. And marriage was a possibility for Austen in her twenties though her lack of fortune made it unlikely. Her sister entered into an engagement by 1795 with a young clergyman unprovided with a living, though he expected one eventually from a patron. The patron did not know of his engagement and took him to an unhealthy climate, where he died in 1797, leaving his fiancée Cassandra his fortune of £1,000. During Cassandra's engagement, Jane Austen at twenty flirted with Tom Lefroy, the nephew of her good friend Anne Lefroy, who sent him away when to her the flirtation looked serious: Tom could not afford to marry a penniless woman. Austen was at the time drafting *Pride and Prejudice*, and it may be that some of the relish Elizabeth

Bennet shows for the flattering attentions of Wickham reflects her own pleasure in Tom's company and their brief mutual infatuation.

Jane Austen lost her beloved birthplace early in 1801, when her father resigned his living to his son and moved to Bath; tradition says that she fainted when she learned of his intention. Like Anne Elliot, then, she was to live in rented lodgings in Bath, and (like her also) she did not care for Bath, leaving after her father's death 'with what happy feelings of Escape!' (*L*, 30 June–1 July 1808). Family tradition also says that after this move, but before her father's death, Jane fell in love with a clergyman whom she met on a trip, who shortly died. What is certain is that at nearly twenty-seven, she was asked in marriage by a gentleman more than five years younger than herself, a brother of some close women friends whom she was visiting, and heir to a good estate in her beloved county of Hampshire: Harris Bigg-Wither. She accepted him then took back her consent the next morning and cut her visit short, returning to Bath. It is a remarkable incident, for she knew that, in refusing him, she was unlikely ever to have a home of her own. Her father was over seventy, and comparative poverty threatened. But as she later wrote to a niece, 'Anything is to be preferred or endured rather than marrying without Affection' (*L*, 18–20 November 1814).

What we know about Jane Austen afterwards comes primarily from the letters, which include interesting details about the publication of her novels from 1811 on but largely chronicle her close connections to family and friends. Particularly from 1809, when she settled in Chawton, the life that can be narrated is her professional life.

The possibility of earning money from writing must have become increasingly important to Austen in the 1790s as the threat of loss of her home loomed, more so once it actually occurred in 1801. Her father spearheaded her first unsuccessful attempt at publication in 1797, writing to the publisher to offer 'First Impressions', the early version of *Pride and Prejudice*. It was still conventional for male relatives of a woman writer to negotiate with publishers, though later on Austen would do so herself, attempting to increase her profits through an association with John Murray. The failure to find a publisher in the 1790s did not discourage Austen. She drafted *Northanger Abbey* in 1798–9 before her move to Bath in 1801 and revised it there, selling the copyright to Benjamin Crosby in 1803 under the title 'Susan'.

James Raven in this volume describes the four publishing options available to Austen: sale of copyright, profit-sharing, subscription, and publication for oneself (on commission). Faced with these options, Austen became increasingly professional in her decisions. Her acceptance of £10 in 1803 for *Northanger Abbey* was the choice of a novice, eager to appear in print at no risk to herself. After Crosby failed to bring out 'Susan', Austen apparently began *The Watsons* – that is, she continued to write. Her father's death in 1805 probably caused her to abandon that project, and some four years later, she wrote to Crosby to ask (in vain) for publication or a return of the manuscript. Then, settled in Chawton in 1809, in the cottage that her brother Edward had finally made available, she exercised a different option: revising *Sense and Sensibility* and publishing it on commission through the London publisher Thomas Egerton. Her brother Henry wrote in his 'Biographical Notice' that she reserved a sum to pay costs if the novel did not sell enough copies to cover the expense of printing it. Where she got this sum is doubtful. Her allowance during her father's lifetime had been only £20 a year for clothes, charities, washing, the expenses of receiving letters, everything. Possibly she set aside money from a legacy of £50 that she had received in 1806, but in any case, she had clearly decided by 1811 to invest in herself, in her own professional success.

Austen risked about £180 by my calculations for printing 750 copies of *Sense and Sensibility*, a small edition but about right for an unknown author in 1811. When it sold out, as we know from the letter to Frank previously quoted, she had earned £140 after the expenses were paid (including Egerton's commission). Unfortunately, before she learned in 1813 how profitable this first novel would be, she had accepted Egerton's offer of £110 for the copyright of *Pride and Prejudice*: 'I would rather have had £150, but we could not both be pleased, & I am not at all surprised that he should not chuse to hazard so much' (*L*, 29–30 November 1812). *Pride and Prejudice* was Austen's most popular novel in her lifetime, reaching three editions, but her sale of the copyright meant it was her least profitable novel to herself. I calculate that Egerton himself made a profit of more than £450 on just the first two editions.

Austen never sold copyright again. She had learned something from this experience. After the success of *Pride and Prejudice*, Egerton certainly offered to buy the copyright of her next novel, *Mansfield Park*, but Austen brought the work out herself, on commission. The edition of (probably) 1,250 copies sold out in six months and yielded the greatest profit she received from any novel published during her lifetime: more than £310. Egerton delayed in bringing out a second edition of *Mansfield Park*, however, and partly as a result Austen turned to John Murray, a more reputable and fashionable publisher: Lord Byron and Walter Scott were among his authors. She negotiated with him first through her brother and then directly when she was dissatisfied. She finally rejected his offer of £450 for the copyrights of *Emma*, *Sense and Sensibility* and *Mansfield Park*. In fact, Murray's offer, though not generous, was about right and represents the remaining value of those copyrights to Jane Austen and her heirs. When Murray brought out *Emma* (1816; actually December 1815) and the second edition of *Mansfield Park* (1816), Austen lost so much money from the latter that she received in her lifetime only about £39 for *Emma*, generally regarded as her greatest work and published in her largest edition, 2,000 copies. She had written it quickly. In the same year that she saw *Mansfield Park* through the press, she began *Emma* on 21 January 1814, and finished it on 29 March 1815. She was clearly at the height of her genius. *Mansfield Park* had occupied her almost twice as long, from February 1811 to June 1813 according to her own memorandum.

Before her dealings with Murray, Austen had invested the profits of her first three published novels in £600 worth of 'Navy Fives', which brought her £30 a year that she allowed to accumulate after her brother Henry's bank failed in 1816. This income was not enough to support a gentlewoman independently. She was saving for the future, I believe for future publication. Though she had finished *Persuasion* in August 1816 (having begun it the previous August), she wrote in March 1817 of its appearing a year later, and at the same time of *Northanger Abbey*, which she had reclaimed from Crosby earlier, being 'upon the Shelve for the present' (*L*, 13 March 1817). It seems likely that she had decided to invest again in herself, to underwrite the publication of these two novels on commission, and was setting money aside as she had earlier in case *Sense and Sensibility* failed. And despite failing health, she began a new novel in early 1817, *Sanditon*. But there was not a future. She died on 18 July.

Despite her increasingly professional publishing choices, Austen's six novels earned only about £1,625 through 1832, including profits from the two published posthumously by Cassandra, her executor and principal legatee. This sum compares unfavourably to the earnings of other contemporary women writers, Maria Edgeworth (more than £11,000) or Frances Burney (more than £4,000). Yet we can see in Jane Austen's continuing to write until four months before her death, and in what I take to be her intentions for future publication, possibly the most poignant evidence of her professionalism.

NOTES

1. [Fanny Caroline Lefroy], 'Is it Just?', *Temple Bar* 67 (February, 1883), 282.
2. See, for example, *Novel Relations: The Transformation of Kinship in English Literature and Culture, 1748–1818* (Cambridge: Cambridge University Press, 2004).

2

Chronology of composition and publication

KATHRYN SUTHERLAND

Despite the slimness of Jane Austen's written fiction production (six completed novels, two fragments of novels, a collection of juvenilia, and a novella-in-letters), it is no easy matter to determine issues of chronology. There are three obvious chronologies: of composition, of redrafting and of publication; and they do not follow unproblematically from each other. For example, until 1870 and the publication of the *Memoir* by her nephew James Edward Austen-Leigh (JEAL), it was assumed, on the basis of the 'Advertisement, by the Authoress' attached to the posthumously published *Northanger Abbey*, that though her latest work to appear in print this was her first completed novel. Austen had written there: 'This little work was finished in the year 1803, and intended for immediate publication.' In pioneering accounts of Austen's fiction, like that by Julia Kavanagh in 1863, a good case is made for *Northanger Abbey*, with its cross-references to a range of contemporary novels and novel writers, as the sophisticated debut of a new voice. But in the *Memoir* JEAL included the copy of a letter written by Jane Austen's father on 1 November 1797 to Thomas Cadell, a noted London publisher, offering the manuscript of a novel in three volumes, 'about the length of Miss Burney's "Evelina".'[1] He conjectures (he has no hard evidence) that this 'must have been' the novel which eventually became *Pride and Prejudice*. Cadell declined to publish sight unseen, but the possibility of a completed version of *Pride and Prejudice* before Austen was twenty-two gives her novel-writing career a different trajectory. Things become more complicated when we realise that *Pride and Prejudice* in its 1797 version was probably further removed from the novel finally published under that title in 1813 than *Northanger Abbey* in 1803 from the version eventually published posthumously in 1818. Three of Austen's six novels (*Sense and Sensibility*, *Pride and Prejudice* and *Northanger Abbey*) led such confusing double lives.

Of enduring significance for how critics have viewed Austen's creative life has been JEAL's more misleading suggestion that the six novels were the products of two distinct and matching creative periods – roughly Austen's early twenties and her late thirties – and that these two periods were divided by a largely fallow interlude of around eight years. This influential interpretation places *Sense and Sensibility*, *Pride and Prejudice* and *Northanger Abbey* as Steventon novels, composed and completed in draft at least by 1799, before the break-up of the family home and the various disruptions of the years lived in Bath and Southampton (1801–9). It further argues that the intense burst of creativity between 1810 and 1817 was the necessary consequence of the recreation in the Chawton years of the emotional and environmental security that Steventon had represented; 'so that', as JEAL asserts, 'the last five years of her life produced the same number of novels with those which had been written in her early youth' (*Memoir*, p. 81). There is still a tendency in criticism to divide the novels into two groups of three – the one group (*Sense and Sensibility*, *Pride and Prejudice* and *Northanger Abbey*) lighter, the other (*Mansfield Park*, *Emma* and *Persuasion*) more psychologically complex – and to ignore or marginalise those writings which remained incomplete and in some cases did not see print until the twentieth century. But another interpretation of the same evidence might be that, with the certain exception of a version of *Northanger Abbey*, sold to a publisher in 1803 under the title 'Susan', all the finished novels were the products of the mature Chawton years, and that this intense period of publication (1811–17) was the culmination of some twenty to thirty years of drafting, redrafting and continued experiment.

One advantage of refusing the bi-partite division of Austen's career is that it brings into focus and creative association the full range of the non-published writings. For there is a further chronology to take into account: that of the fiction which remained in manuscript form. In some cases, these are working drafts left unfinished: *The Watsons* and *Sanditon*. In others, they are fair copies or 'confidential publications':[2] works circulating among family and selected friends, sometimes receiving additions and revisions over a period of years, but which did not (and perhaps were never intended to) see print. The three volumes of juvenilia, but also *Lady Susan* and 'Plan of a Novel' fall into this category. We know from the recollections of one of Austen's nieces, Anna Lefroy, that as 'First Impressions', an early version of *Pride and Prejudice* was just such a confidential publication, read and discussed within the extended Steventon household about 1797 (*Memoir*, p. 158). The three manuscript volumes of juvenilia represent a collected edition for confidential publication and not the original drafts of pieces first composed between *c.*1787 (before she was twelve) and 1793. From internal evidence of handwriting, the earliest entries in *Volume the First* (items 1–11) were transcribed and probably written first; but the earliest dated entry in any of the volumes is 'Love and Freindship' (13 June 1790) in *Volume the Second*; and it is clear from evidence of hand, dating and style that entries were made in both other volumes before *Volume the First* was completed (according to internal dating on 3 June 1793, when she was aged seventeen). As late as 1809–11 items in *Volume the Third* were authorially revised, while further insertions, as late as 1814 (or even, it is conjectured, as late as 1829), to 'Evelyn' and 'Catharine, or the Bower' (originally dated August 1792 in that volume), are in hands other than Jane Austen's – those of her niece Anna Austen (Lefroy after her marriage in November 1814) and her nephew James Edward Austen (later Austen-Leigh), both the children of her eldest and most literary brother James.[3] Since 'Plan of a Novel' was probably written in early 1816, we can see that habits of confidential manuscript circulation continued throughout Austen's career even after conventional print publication became her dominant method.

No manuscript of the six novels is known to survive apart from two chapters of *Persuasion*. Of the manuscripts to survive in fair copies, the bulk, probably including *Lady Susan*, are of early works, though, given the long gestation, rejection for publication and subsequent rewriting of early versions of *Pride and Prejudice* and *Northanger Abbey*, any concept of 'early' must be treated with extreme caution and allowed an elastic longevity. Confusingly, first drafts of *Sense and Sensibility* (as 'Elinor & Marianne'), of *Pride and Prejudice* and of *Northanger Abbey*, cannot be separated easily in time from work done on pieces in the three volumes of juvenilia, especially from late juvenile pieces like 'Catharine' and from the slightly later *Lady Susan*, both of which her niece Caroline Austen believed represented a new and troubling phase of Austen's writing, and accordingly designated the 'betweenities' (*Memoir*, p. 186). At the same time, it should be noted how the early full-length novels were successfully rewritten for the press only during the final intense years of mature writing and publication. With Jane Austen, in other words, there is no seamless division into early, middle and late writing, but instead a vital and unexpected revision of material over a considerable period.

Two manuscript works are especially interesting in any consideration of chronology because they are transitional experiments. One, *Lady Susan*, is an epistolary novella and Austen's most ambitious early work. Probably first drafted in 1794–5, *Lady Susan* was subsequently copied on paper two leaves of which bear an 1805 watermark, and at about the same time a conclusion was added in the authorial third person. Like *Northanger Abbey* (drafted and revised as 'Susan' 1798–1803) and the burlesque playlet *Sir Charles Grandison*, probably written over a period of time from the early 1790s to 1800 and only recently attributed to Austen,[4] *Lady Susan* experiments in recasting literary convention and specifically shares characteristics with items in *Volume the Second*. The second transitional work is *The Watsons*, a rough draft rather than a fair copy, written on paper dated 1803, and probably composed during 1804 when Austen was living in Bath. *The Watsons* is no more than a fragment, the opening section of a projected full-length novel; but it is written with a new realism, and the bleak critical eye Austen here trains upon the surface of small-town society throws a bridge from the more romantically illusioned studies of *Sense and Sensibility* and *Pride and Prejudice* to the darker domestic studies of *Mansfield Park* and *Emma*. Unlike *Sanditon*, cut short by final illness, we do not know why Austen abandoned *The Watsons*, though the conjecture provided by Fanny Caroline Lefroy, daughter of Anna Lefroy, albeit at a distance of eighty years, sounds probable. According to Fanny Caroline, 'Somewhere in 1804 [Jane Austen] began "The Watsons", but her father died early in 1805, and it was never finished.'[5] *The Watsons* is a study in the harsh economic realities of dependent women's lives, but unexpectedly in January 1805 the domestic situation sketched for the Watson girls and Austen's own reduced all-female household threatened a convergence too immediate and painful to deal with in fiction.

We have a valuable document in Cassandra Austen's memorandum of composition of the six published novels, which she may have drawn up soon after Jane Austen's death. It is brief and of such importance as to be worth quoting in full:[6]

First Impressions begun in Oct 1796
Finished in Augt 1797. Publishd
afterwards, with alterations & contractions
under the Title of Pride & Prejudice.
Sense & Sensibility begun Nov. 1797
I am sure that something of the
same story & characters had been
written earlier & called Elinor & Marianne
Mansfield Park, begun somewhere
about Feby 1811 – Finished soon after
June 1813
Emma begun Jany 21st 1814, finishd
March 29th 1815
Persuasion begun Augt 8th 1815
finished Augt 6th 1816
North-hanger Abbey was written
about the years 98 & 99
C.E.A.

Alongside these dates of composition we need to set dates of publication for the six novels: *Sense and Sensibility*, November 1811, with a second edition corrected by Austen advertised on 29 October 1813; *Pride and Prejudice*, 28 January 1813, with two further editions (in ?October 1813 and in 1817) issued without the author's involvement; *Mansfield Park*, 9 May 1814, with a second edition corrected by Austen advertised on 19 February 1816; *Emma*, possibly at the end of December 1815, but with title page dated 1816; *Northanger Abbey and Persuasion* as a four-volume set posthumously in late December 1817, with title pages dated 1818.[7] Four of the novels were lifetime publications, and two appeared within six months of Austen's death. Her name was not printed on any title page, but to *Northanger Abbey* was prefixed a brief 'Biographical Notice' by her brother Henry, in which Jane Austen is publicly named for the first time as the author of the novels. Apart from *Northanger Abbey and Persuasion*, all the novels were published in three-volume sets, though the unauthorised third edition of *Pride and Prejudice* appeared in two volumes. *Sense and Sensibility, Pride and Prejudice* and *Mansfield Park* (1814) were published by Thomas Egerton of Whitehall, not an obvious novel publisher but perhaps chosen because of his earlier connection with James and Henry Austen's Oxford University periodical *The Loiterer*. *Mansfield Park* (1816), *Emma*, and *Northanger Abbey and Persuasion* were published from the more prestigious house of John Murray. Austen sold the copyright of only one novel, *Pride and Prejudice*, all her other fictions being issued on commission: that is, the cost of production and advertising was born by the author, the publisher taking a commission on copies sold retail and to the trade, and the author retaining copyright.

When we combine the details of Cassandra's note with references from Austen's extant letters and with known facts of the contemporary publication history of the novels, certain things become clear. *Sense and Sensibility* and *Pride and Prejudice* must each have taken shape, wholly or partly, in more than one draft, between 1795–8 and 1810–12, by which time the former had been recast from a novel-in-letters and the latter, in Austen's own words, 'lopt & cropt' (*L*, 29 January 1813), and according to her sister Cassandra's later memory altered and contracted. It seems likely that the more radical revision of *Sense and Sensibility* occurred at a second period of drafting in the 1790s, while *Pride and Prejudice* may only have been thoroughly overhauled at the later time (R. W. Chapman pointed out that its action fits in general terms the calendars for 1811–12).[8] This would make a possible 1795 novel-in-letters version of *Sense and Sensibility* Austen's first attempt at a full-length novel, drafted immediately after *Lady Susan*, and suggests that following the drafting of *Pride and Prejudice* in 1796–7, *Sense and Sensibility* was recast in something close to its final form, and more lightly overhauled for publication in 1810–11. As well as extensive revision, *Sense and Sensibility* and *Pride and Prejudice* both underwent a change of title. In the case of *Pride and Prejudice* it is generally assumed that this was because Margaret Holford got into print with a novel entitled *First Impressions* in 1801. But it is worth noting that Austen seems to have found the title she preferred for several of her novels at a late stage in writing; for the posthumously published *Northanger Abbey* and *Persuasion* we have no evidence that these were her chosen titles, and some evidence, in first 'Susan' and then 'Catherine' (for *Northanger Abbey*) and the working title of 'The Elliots' (for

Persuasion) that they were not. The manuscript left unfinished at her death, had, according to Cassandra, the working title of 'The Brothers', and though variously known in the family as 'Sanditon' and the 'Last Work' was only decisively entitled *Sanditon* in 1925; *The Watsons* was so named by JEAL, 'for the sake of having a title by which to designate it'.[9]

Mansfield Park has a recorded gestation and composition period of some three years, from February 1811 to mid 1813, which if correct means that for some months in 1811 Austen had three novels on the go: she was recasting *Pride and Prejudice*, drafting *Mansfield Park* and for one busy month, April 1811, also correcting proofs of *Sense and Sensibility*. Apart from proof correction, we do not know what form or forms creative activity took at any particular moment during this intense period: whether planning new material in more or less detail, revising old drafts or full-scale composition. By January 1813 references in letters suggest *Mansfield Park* was more than half written, but that was two years after Cassandra's vague recollection that it was 'begun sometime about Feby 1811'. Writing to Cassandra, Austen apologises for the unforeseen delay in getting a copy of the newly published *Pride and Prejudice*, issued at eighteen shillings, sent to Steventon. Then, her exuberance breaking through the polite family formalities, she bursts out: '*18^s* – He [Henry or her publisher?] shall ask £1-1- for my two next, & £1-8- for my stupidest of all' (*L*, 29 January 1813). The very particularity of 'my stupidest of all' suggests this is no vague projection or insubstantial boast but that there are three further novels currently on the stocks. *Mansfield Park* was well in hand, though Henry Austen, who acted as his sister's unofficial literary agent, was only introduced to the manuscript in its finished state, complete with volume divisions, on the journey to London to have it published more than a year later in March 1814 (*L*, 2–3 March 1814) Again by Cassandra's late account, *Emma* was 'begun Jany 21st 1814, finishd March 29th 1815', which means that in the early stages of working on the new novel, *Emma*, Austen was also seeing *Mansfield Park* through the press: not an easy division of concentration. But had she already begun to think of *Emma* a year earlier, by January 1813 (is this the implication of 'my next two'), and what about 'my stupidest of all'? Is this a reference to the novel written, by Cassandra's estimate, 'about the years 98 & 99' and brought up to date if not more fully revised before being sent in 1803 to the publishers Crosby and Co. under the title 'Susan'? Austen had asked at least once (in April 1809) to have the unpublished manuscript returned to her, but according to JEAL, it would not be bought back until 1816, after the publication of *Emma* (*L*, 5 April 1809; *Memoir*, p. 106.) However, if her 1809 reference to a second copy of the manuscript was more than a facetious threat, she may at any time after August 1809 have been revising 'Susan' in this second copy for publication as 'Catherine'. Again the change of title was probably the consequence of another novel entitled *Susan* appearing anonymously in 1809.

Then again, if it is possible to conjecture some overlap in the planning of *Mansfield Park* and *Emma*, the same is true for *Persuasion* and the revised 'Catherine', especially if there was only ever one manuscript copy and not two. *Persuasion* was begun on 8 August 1815 and the first draft completed on 18 July 1816 (with a revised ending written by 6 August 1816). It is not until March 1817, in a letter to her eldest niece Fanny Knight, that Austen mentions both *Persuasion* (though not by a title) and 'Catherine'. At this point she thinks of them together because they are short, about the same length, though she also informs Fanny that 'Miss Catherine is put upon the Shelve for the present' (*L*, 13 March 1817). But only five days after this letter Austen dated the last words of the *Sanditon* manuscript, '18 March 1817'. (According to the extant draft, *Sanditon* was begun on 27 January 1817.) *Persuasion*, 'Catherine' and *Sanditon* thus share the years 1816–17, as *Sense and Sensibility*, *Pride and Prejudice* and *Mansfield Park* share 1811–12, as 'First Impressions', 'Elinor and Marianne'/*Sense and Sensibility* and 'Susan' share 1795–9, and as *Mansfield Park* and *Emma* may share 1813.

The precise dates Cassandra Austen fixed for the writing of certain of the novels in her memorandum may derive from pocketbook entries Jane Austen made at the time; they are also supported by her habit of dating her manuscripts at several points as she wrote. But against the certainties afforded by the implied particularity of the moment when pen touched paper, there needs to be set the vaguer and more associative kind of dating by which the novels provide hinterlands or contexts for one another. The overlapping implies something more than the routine expectation that novels by one author will share ingredients, themes and narrative treatment in common; rather it suggests a particular habit of composition, with associated

gestation and even allocation of materials within a broader framework than the individual work. It explains our sense that the novels
enact a process of expansion and repetition, retracing the old ground
and discovering it as new ground. *Mansfield Park* and *Emma* belong
together as mirrored studies of social repression and ennui and
of the relationship between human behaviour and environment,
the psychology of setting. This new interest in setting marks them
off from *Sense and Sensibility* and *Pride and Prejudice*, while according to family tradition, the Heywoods in *Sanditon* were to occupy
the same role as the Morlands in *Northanger Abbey*.[10] Incidents
and themes from the aborted fragment *The Watsons* are transposed
or recycled in *Mansfield Park* and *Emma*, while some critics have
detected links between *The Watsons* and *Pride and Prejudice* and
even 'Catharine' from *Volume the Third*.[11] Perhaps, in that case, *The
Watsons* was not taken up and finished at a later date because it had
been so effectively absorbed elsewhere.

We do not know whether Jane Austen followed a general practice
in writing and what it might have been. Long periods of gestation
and of critical attention post-composition are mentioned within
the immediate family (*Memoir*, p. 138) and can be adduced from
the record of dates: it was not just 'Catherine' that she 'put upon the
Shelve for the present'. The accident of posthumous publication
that coupled together two such apparently different works as
Northanger Abbey and *Persuasion* can on reflection be seen as the
inevitable consequence of a chronology of writing which includes
alongside new ventures the mining over time of manuscript fragments and the revision of earlier completed writings, a pattern
which leaves us with *Sanditon*, her final work, as the sequel to
Northanger Abbey, one of her earliest.

	Composition	Redrafting	Publication
c. 1787–93	*Juvenilia*	Fair copies of juvenilia (*Volume the First, Volume the Second, Volume the Third*)	confidential family circulation of juvenilia
1790–1800	drafting the burlesque play *Sir Charles Grandison*		confidential family circulation of other writings

1794–5	*LS*, a novella in letters		
c. **1795**	'Elinor & Marianne', a novel in letters, earliest draft of *S&S*		
Oct. 1796– Aug. 1797	'First Impressions', earliest draft of *P&P*		(1 Nov. offered to Cadell)
Nov. 1797		recasting 'Elinor & Marianne' as *S&S*	
1798–9	Draft of 'Susan', earliest draft of *NA*		
1803		'Susan' revised for publication	MS of 'Susan' bought by Crosby & Co.
1804	begins and abandons *W*		
1805		fair copy of *LS*, perhaps adding conclusion	
1809			(Apr. JA enquires after MS of 'Susan')
1809–11	some revisions to *Volume the Third*	*S&S* revised for publication	Nov. 1811 *S&S*
1811–12	begins *MP*	*P&P* redrafted for publication	
1813	drafting *MP*	revising *S&S* for edn 2	Jan. *P&P*; Oct. *S&S* (edn 2); *P&P* (edn 2)
1814	begins *E*	seeing *MP* through press	May *MP*
1815	drafting *E*	revising *MP* for edn 2	
	drafting *P*	seeing *E* through press	Dec. *E*

1816	drafting *P*	revisions to	Buys back MS
	'Plan of a Novel'	'Susan', retitled	of 'Susan'
		'Catherine'	Feb. *MP*
			(edn 2)
1817	drafting *S*	'Catherine' 'on	*P&P* (edn 3)
		Shelve'	Dec. *NA*
			('Catherine')
			& *P*

NOTES

1. *A Memoir of Jane Austen and Other Family Recollections*, ed. Kathryn Sutherland (Oxford: Oxford University Press, 2002), p. 105. Following references are included in the text.
2. The phrase is Donald H. Reiman's, in *The Study of Modern Manuscripts: Public, Confidential, and Private* (Baltimore and London: Johns Hopkins Press, 1993).
3. B. C. Southam, 'The Manuscript of Jane Austen's *Volume the First*', *The Library*, 5th series, 17 (1962), 231–7; B. C. Southam, *Jane Austen's Literary Manuscripts: A Study of the Novelist's Development through the Surviving Papers*, new edition (London and New York: Athlone Press, 2001), pp. 1–19; and 'Note on the Text', in Peter Sabor *et al.* (eds.), *Jane Austen's Evelyn* (Edmonton, Alberta: Juvenilia Press, 1999), pp. xvi–xx.
4. Information from Southam, *Austen's Manuscripts*, pp. 136–40.
5. [Fanny Caroline Lefroy], 'Is it Just?', *Temple Bar* 67 (February, 1883), 277.
6. *Minor Works*, ed. R. W. Chapman, revised edition (Oxford: Oxford University Press, 1988), facing p. 242.
7. Details in David Gilson, *A Bibliography of Jane Austen*, corrected edition (Winchester: St Paul's Bibliographies, 1997).
8. 'Chronology of *Pride and Prejudice*', in *Pride and Prejudice*, revised edition, ed. R. W. Chapman (Oxford: Oxford University Press, 1988), p. 401.
9. James Edward Austen-Leigh, *A Memoir of Jane Austen*, second edition (1871), p. 295.
10. Anna Austen Lefroy in a letter to JEAL, 8 August 1862, Hampshire Record Office, MS 23M93/86/3c-118(ii).
11. Mary Waldron, *Jane Austen and the Fiction of Her Time* (Cambridge: Cambridge University Press, 1999), p. 26; Jan Fergus, *Jane Austen: A Literary Life* (Basingstoke and London: Macmillan, 1991), p. 115.

3

Language

ANTHONY MANDAL

In an unsigned review of *Emma* published in 1816, Walter Scott draws particular attention to the domestic realism of the novel's anonymous author, whose fiction he perceives as bearing 'the same relation to that of the sentimental and romantic cast, that cornfields and cottages and meadows bear to the highly adorned grounds of a show mansion, or the rugged sublimities of a mountain landscape'.[1] If this delineation of Jane Austen's style seems commensurate with the author's own often-quoted opinion of her work – 'the little bit (two Inches wide) of Ivory on which I work with so fine a brush' (*L*, 16–17 December 1816)[2] – it also damns her with faint praise. Scott locates her work as part of a new class of fiction that replaces the grandness of the earlier romance forms with 'the art of copying from nature as she really exists in the common walks of life' and 'a correct and striking representation of that which is daily taking place' (*Quarterly Review*, p. 192). The lexicon employed by Scott to define Austen's style is a restricted and feminised one: the story has 'a simple plan', and '[t]he subjects are not often elegant, and certainly never grand', while the author's merit 'consists much in the force of a narrative conducted with much *neatness* and *point*, and a *quiet* yet *comic* dialogue' (*Quarterly Review*, pp. 197, 199, my emphases).

This interpretation, while acknowledging the subtlety of Austen's style, occludes much of the vibrancy and range that her works also evidence. One need only read her *Juvenilia* in order to be struck by the rich and dynamic language that is natural to Austen, and which is rendered only in more nuanced terms in her mature writings. The subject matter of these early writings – illegitimacy, alcoholism, gambling, theft, violence and murder – is reflected in the raw, unmediated language. 'Henry and Eliza' is typical: 'Sir George and Lady Harcourt were superintending the Labours of their Haymakers, rewarding the industry of some by smiles of approbation, & punishing the idleness of others, by a cudgel.' Here, the balanced syntax typical of eighteenth-century prosody (rewarding industry/punishing idleness) is juxtaposed with absurd couplings (smiles of approbation/a cudgel). Similarly, in 'Jack and Alice', we are told that '[i]n Lady Williams every virtue met. She was a widow with a handsome Jointure & the remains of a very handsome face' (ch. 1). In the later and more sustained 'Love and Freindship', the heroine is sylleptically warned by her mother to 'Beware of the unmeaning Luxuries of Bath and of the stinking fish of Southampton' ('Letter 4th'). In her earliest writings, then, Jane Austen's awareness of the comic possibilities of language is evident, adumbrating the more modulated linguistic manoeuvres of the novels themselves.

What becomes clear in reading Austen's oeuvre is her preoccupation with the potential for language to be misused. Misapplications of linguistic conventions by Austen's characters generate much of her ironic humour: a key instance occurs in Henry Tilney's debate with Catherine Morland about appropriate uses of the term 'nice'. When she calls Ann Radcliffe's modish Gothic novel, *The Mysteries of Udolpho* (1794), 'the nicest book in the world', Henry points to the banality of the signifier (*NA*, 1:14). The *OED* records the first usage of the term as Catherine applies it ('agreeable; that one derives pleasure or satisfaction from; delightful') as 1769, whereas Johnson's *Dictionary* of 1755 only includes definitions pertaining to accuracy, precision and fastidiousness. What Henry is drawing attention to here, then, is the slippage of meaning that results from the vagaries of fashionable usage, and, throughout *Northanger Abbey*, attention is repeatedly drawn to the inherent ambiguity of language, especially as employed by Catherine, with her tendency towards hyperbole and repetition. A key instance of this occurs after Catherine's arrival at the abbey, when she and Eleanor have been discussing the death of Eleanor's mother, which leads Catherine to imagine that General Tilney has murdered her: Gothicised language is employed to represent Catherine's inaccurate misrecognitions (*NA*, 2:8). Similarly, in *Sense and Sensibility*, such imprecision occurs in Marianne's resistance to gradations of attachment, which results in her lack of understanding about Elinor's feelings for Edward: 'Esteem him! Like him! Cold-hearted Elinor!

Oh! worse than cold-hearted!' (*S&S*, 1:4) Additionally, the use of foreign and fashionable words is shown to be a voguish affectation, indicative of a certain moral vacuity: into this category fall Mrs Elton's use of 'caro sposo' and its variants, Mr Parker's mention of Sir Edward Denham's proposed 'cottage ornèe' (*S*, 3), and Isabella Thorpe's manifold 'horrids'. The use of an inadequate vocabulary points to an inattentiveness to the ethical boundaries that circumscribe human action – in other words, such a lexical framework denies moral purpose to those who employ it.

Catherine and Marianne's slips are, by and large, those of ingenuous young women yet to learn the ways of the world: those of figures such as Isabella Thorpe and Lucy Steele are of a distinctly less innocent nature. They use language as a social tool, employing the contemporary discourse of sensibility to hide their mercenary natures and grasping ambitions. Soon after meeting Catherine, Isabella tells her new friend that 'I have no notion of loving people by halves, it is not my nature. My attachments are always excessively strong' (*NA*, 1:6). In the same manner, Lucy confides to Elinor that 'I have been always used to a very small income, and could struggle with any poverty for [Edward]' (*S&S*, 2:2). Despite such professions, both Isabella and Lucy sever their engagements to worthy men in favour of more prosperous alternatives. Catherine Morland's movement into adulthood is signalled by her realisation, when reading Isabella's letter, that empty linguistic gestures exemplify empty moral stances: 'Such a strain of shallow artifice could not impose even upon Catherine. Its inconsistencies, contradictions, and falsehood, struck her from the very first' (*NA*, 2:12). Similarly, the liberation from Lucy Steele that enables Edward Ferrars to marry Elinor Dashwood is morally inscribed through a linguistic analysis, in his response to her epistolary style: 'this is the only letter I ever received from her, of which the substance made me any amends for the defect of the style' (*S&S*, 3:13).

Austen's representations of moral nullity acquire a more problematised aspect, however, when the amorality of the speaker is not reducible simply to economic factors. Henry Crawford is clearly attracted to Fanny Price, principally owing to her unimpeachable rectitude; however, he cannot access the appropriate moral lexicon, and is able only to employ the fashionable discourse of the social world. It is with no small irony that we are told: 'Henry Crawford had too much sense not to feel the worth of good principles in a wife, though he was too little accustomed to serious reflection to know them by their proper name' (*MP*, 2:12). Similarly, Edmund Bertram detaches himself from Henry's sister Mary owing to her inability to apply an ethical framework in her analysis of her brother's flight with Maria Rushworth: 'I cannot recall all her words. I would not dwell upon them if I could. Their substance was great anger at the *folly* of each' (*MP*, 3:16). More disconcertingly, Mr Elliot consciously manipulates the discourse of social intercourse to his own advantage (*P*, 2:4). Hence, the social world and its linguistic codes are shown to be essentially untrustworthy, because they allow such duplicity and hypocrisy to be perpetrated easily. By contrast, the private world of conversation and correspondence is demonstrated as offering, both linguistically and morally, the most unambiguous indication of people's true identity.

In her later novels, Jane Austen's concern with the misapplication and manipulation of language acquires a more discernible ideological specificity. A debate between Emma and Knightley concerning Frank Churchill is representative. Emma sympathises with 'what an amiable young man may be likely to feel' in opposing his guardians, to which Knightley rather sternly replies: 'No, Emma, your amiable young man can be amiable only in French, not in English . . . he can have no English delicacy towards the feelings of other people: nothing really amiable about him' (*E*, 1:18). Here, then, a contrast is being drawn which aligns national lexemes with moral qualities, and assumes an ideological context, in which 'English' parochialism accrues a specific moral valency when contrasted with French ambiguousness. Austen's use of 'English/England' throughout *Emma* inflects a specific polemical model, emphasising Englishness as a conceptual, rather than a geographical or linguistic, frame of reference. Emma tellingly perceives the view from Donwell Abbey as 'English verdure, English culture, English comfort' (*E*, 3:6): here, Knightley and Donwell Abbey are both synecdochic of a larger national concept of Englishness, which itself carries overtones of provincialism, honesty and integrity. The significance of Frank's admission to Emma, that 'I am sick of England – and would leave it to-morrow, if I could', is inscribed in morally laden terms, following as it does the extended descriptions of the English values represented by Donwell. Such cultural inflections can be read as part of Austen's ethical system, in which an indefiniteness regarding time and space is indicative of moral ambiguity.

As a solution to the inadequate usage of language, Austen employs a controlled vocabulary of related words, which perhaps carried more weight in her time than they do now, and so are often underrated or misconstrued. Terms such as 'manners', 'amiable', 'duty' and 'prudence' recur frequently throughout her novels, and in combination can be seen as constituent elements in Austen's ethical system. The most significant of these keywords is 'manners', the use of which falls into two categories in Austen's novels. Most simply, it is used descriptively to indicate an appropriate adherence to social codes: 'outward bearing, deportment, or style of address . . . characteristic style of attitude, gesture, and utterance' (*OED*). Into this category fall comments such as those by Emma regarding Mr Elton (*E*, 1:4), while on a broader social scale, we are told that Lady Russell has 'manners that were held a standard of good-breeding' (*P*, 1:2). Moreover, manners can indicate as much about a person's mental constitution as they can about their social countenance: Mrs Croft's manners 'were open, easy, and decided, like one who had no distrust of herself, and no doubts of what to do' (*P*, 1:6), while Mr Collins's 'manners were very formal' – a clear adumbration of his own psychological calcification (*P&P*, 1:13). In the second categorisation, manners move beyond the simply descriptive, functioning as a deliberative formulation which attempts to address the problems of linguistic misapplications and ethical inadequacies: 'Conduct in its moral aspect; also, morality as a subject of study; the moral code embodied in general custom or sentiment' (*OED*). Against the backdrop of Sotherton's disused and morally redundant chapel, Edmund Bertram's pronouncement on manners sounds decidedly Evangelical: 'The *manners* I speak of, might rather be called *conduct*, perhaps, the result of good principles; the effect, in short, of those doctrines which it is [the clergy's] duty to teach and recommend' (*MP*, 1:9). In this passage, one sees Austen making connections between various related signifiers – 'manners', 'principles', 'conduct', 'duty' – through which manners can move from a purely social manifestation of individual behaviour towards a manifesto to be promulgated.

Jane Austen's concern with constructing appropriate linguistic models to reflect social and moral conventions manifests itself in her use and refinement of various stylistic techniques. A fundamental issue in Austen's fiction is the importance of conversation, owing to the fact that a woman's sphere of action was considerably restricted in the nineteenth-century gentry world. *Speaking* in the novels often correlates with *doing*; hence, repetition is always a danger (the Thorpes' vacuous and insipid statements are an obvious example here). As a result, opportunities to talk about new subjects assume a vital significance, and the understated nature of Austen's language consequently belies the moral significance of issues being scrutinised. One can consider the subtly inflected significance of Austen's portrayal of the first meeting between Catherine Morland and Eleanor Tilney (*NA*, 1:10). Austen's presentation of dialogue presents a clear line of development, from her early reliance on the Johnsonian speech-patterns of the eighteenth century to a more sustained and naturalistic style of rendering conversation. For instance, Elinor Dashwood's typical speech rhythm tends towards the aphoristic, the balanced syntax and careful matching of verbs and nouns reflecting her own moral perceptions. When defending Edward to Marianne, Elinor notes, 'The *excellence of his understanding* and his *principles* can be concealed only by that *shyness* which too often keeps him *silent*' (*S&S*, 1:4; my emphases). By contrast, her sister is given to a more declamatory style that occasionally slips into burlesque reminiscent of the *Juvenilia* (consider, for instance, Marianne's effusive farewell to Norland at the end of the fifth chapter). In her later works, this use of both the aphoristic and declamatory styles has receded in favour of modulated combinations of long and short sentences, which reflect the urgency or effusiveness of the speaker. For instance, Austen's description of Knightley's admission of love to Emma captures both more normative speech patterns than those of Elinor or Marianne and Knightley's state of emotional confusion (*E*, 3:13).

This attention to the natural rhythms of the spoken word accounts for the 'dramatic' quality of Jane Austen's writing, with a significant proportion of her narrative consisting of dialogue. Austen's descriptions of her characters' physical attributes tend to be minimal; instead, she allows their moral characters to be revealed through their words: one can think here of Mr Collins's

marriage proposal to Elizabeth, which is in essence a comical soliloquy that reveals both his own high self-regard and his obsequious
deference to Lady Catherine (*P&P*, 1:19). Monologues such as
those of Collins tend to be infrequent, however, and Austen's
usual approach is to employ brisk dialogues between characters,
resulting in a narrative that moves with a tempo reminiscent of
the theatre. Austen's writing can also be seen as dramatic because
characters often cluster in groups, having points of exit and entry.
This use of description as stage direction is typical for Austen,
and is employed from the *Juvenilia* to the later novels. In 'Love
and Freindship', for instance, the response of Laura and her parents to Augustus' knocking at their door is staged in very theatrical terms ('Letter 5th'). The first chapter of *Pride and Prejudice* similarly deploys its principal performers, Mr and Mrs Bennet,
'on stage' in their drawing room, while the participants of the excur-
sion to Box Hill 'separat[e] too much into parties' (*E*, 3:7). Austen's
sustained use of dialogue, with its increasing naturalism, combines
with her specific on-stage placement of characters, in order to provide a dramatic urgency to novels in which not very much actually
happens.

Such dramatic rendering is not the defining aspect of Austen's
style, as the economy and flexibility of her writing exceed purely
theatrical qualities, allowing her to employ an economy of form
to compress events and render speech with a speed that would be
impossible on stage. A representative example is Collins's proposal
to Charlotte, following his rejection by Elizabeth: 'Miss Lucas perceived him from an upper window as he walked towards the house,
and instantly set out to meet him accidentally in the lane. But little
had she dared to hope that so much love and eloquence awaited her
there' (*P&P*, 1:22). Austen is able to utilise disjunction to subvert
meaning and generate ironic gaps between appearance and reality,
between the linguistic surface of statements and the moral substance
of them. Austen's use of ironic disjunction can operate through the
contrast between a seemingly unequivocal narrative statement and
the comic disturbance of its authority which follows – for example,
the opening sentence of *Pride and Prejudice* announces a principal
theme of Austen's fiction, the elision of money and matrimony:
'It is a truth universally acknowledged, that a single man in possession of a good fortune, must be in want of a wife.' Of course,

the real question is whose truth this is and by whom is it universally acknowledged – especially when the aphoristic quality and authoritative tenor of the statement are subverted by the novel's praxis, which shows that it is, in fact, *dependent* women who are in *need* of husbands. Disjunction is also generated through statements made by Austen's characters themselves, which although innocuous-sounding at first, adumbrate subsequent events as the novels unfold. For instance, when viewing Emma's painting of Harriet Smith, Knightley warns her: 'You have made her too tall, Emma' (*E*, 1:6). Initially, then, this can be read as a simple analysis of Emma's skills at portraiture; however, as the novel reaches its conclusion, we discover that – thanks to Emma's meddling – Harriet has transferred her affections from the tenant Robert Martin to the landlord George Knightley. Austen's use of irony once again correlates with her general thesis regarding the ambiguity of language: multiple meanings resonate at different levels, and the reader is consequently discouraged to read words at face value, a lesson which Austen's own heroines must also learn for themselves.

Perhaps Austen's most remarkable stylistic achievement is her subtle and sustained use of free indirect discourse (or free indirect speech), a technique through which the speech or thought-processes of her characters are blended with the narrator's descriptions. Typically, free indirect discourse serves one of two main purposes. In the first case, it can be used to provide economical summaries of conversations, whether made by individual or multiple speakers. One can think here of Frank Churchill's discussion on his first meeting Emma, in which only his questions are enumerated in rapid fashion, conveying his eager (if feigned) interest in Emma's life (*E*, 2:5). Similarly, the confused reactions of the Lyme party following Louisa Musgrove's fall down the Cobb are rendered succinctly in volume 1, chapter 12 of *Persuasion*. Alternatively, the technique is employed to compress an individual's thoughts or speech with dramatic and/or ironic purpose: a key example of this ironic interplay of the technique is the scene between John Dashwood and his wife discussing the disposal of his father's legacy in volume 1, chapter 2 of *Sense and Sensibility*. Austen manages a far more psychologised effect in the 'Everingham' episode that occurs during Henry Crawford's visit to Fanny at Portsmouth, in which he nearly convinces her that he is truly reformed: 'For her approbation, the particular reason of his going into Norfolk at all, at this unusual time of year, was given . . . a somebody that would make Everingham and all about it, a dearer object than it had ever been yet' (*MP*, 3:10). Austen's eschewal of direct speech for free indirect discourse allows the narrative to oscillate between what Crawford has *actually* achieved and perhaps Fanny's belief of what he has *possibly* achieved. Henry initially employs the Evangelical lexicon associated in *Mansfield Park* with Fanny, and terms such as 'welfare', 'industrious', 'merits', 'useful' and 'duty' are associated with his reported speech (we cannot be sure whether these are his words, the narrator's, or even Fanny's). With 'It was pleasing to hear him speak so properly', however, the focus moves significantly from the neutral third person to Fanny's own perspective. Nevertheless, as readers we are now one step ahead of her because of the crucial and almost parenthetical 'This was aimed, and well aimed, at Fanny'. Here is the point of divergence between reader and heroine, emphasised by another bifurcation of meaning: 'he had been *acting* as he *ought* to' – our awareness of the novel's state of affairs is determined by where we place the stress. Despite this brief deviation, Fanny and the reader ultimately achieve a congruence of understanding through the deflating sentence which follows the climactic 'To be the friend of the poor and oppressed!' In a masterstroke, Fanny is brought back to reality when she realises that Henry's report really has been a case of 'acting' for her benefit, and further Evangelical terms are now disturbed and debased: 'assistant', 'utility or charity', 'making Everingham a dearer object than it had ever been yet'. Combining economy of form and incisive irony in this paradigmatic scene, Austen's use of free indirect discourse demonstrates that Henry and Fanny exist in different discursive worlds: he is the consummate performer who adopts the role that suits the circumstances, while Fanny perceives the world in Evangelical absolutes. Once again, Austen's innovatory technique is used to evince a moral framework grounded clearly in the subtle inflections of linguistic interchange.

Writing at a transitional point in the history of the English language, Austen's fiction evidences her concern with the potential for linguistic deterioration in her society, despite Dr Johnson's efforts to stabilise language in his great *Dictionary* of 1755. She sees such slippage in meaning as commensurate with an enfeebling of ethical structures. Additionally, Jane Austen associates this linguistic and moral dissipation with the role that money plays in the marriage market; nevertheless, her fiction is paradoxically saturated with the discourse of economics, to the point that her plots are driven by financial imperatives. Despite this, Austen does attempt to locate a solution by constructing an alternative discourse of 'manners' – a particularly difficult paradigm for the modern reader to come to terms with, given the further linguistic deterioration that has taken place in the intervening two centuries. This search for an appropriate linguistic–ethical system manifests itself on a technical level, in those stylistic achievements and that painstaking attention to detail that have come to be perceived as quintessentially Austenian. What Austen's writing demonstrates, then, is the author's particular attunement to the changing socio-cultural context of Britain at the turn of the eighteenth century, and how this is reflected microcosmically at the linguistic level. Consequently, if her novels seem somehow detached from the ideological debates that were raging during her lifetime, this is owing to Austen's carefully controlled choice of language. As Scott himself said so appositely: 'at Highbury Cupid walks decorously, and with good discretion, bearing his torch under a lanthorn, instead of flourishing it around to set the house on fire' (*Quarterly Review*, p. 196).

NOTES

1. Walter Scott's review of *Emma* in *The Quarterly Review* 14 (October, 1815 [March, 1816]), 200. Subsequent references are included in the text.
2. In an earlier letter, Austen described the 'pictures of domestic Life in Country Villages as I deal in' (*L*, 1 April 1816).

4

Letters

DEIRDRE LE FAYE

At a conservative estimate, Jane Austen probably wrote about 3,000 letters during her lifetime, of which only 160 are known and published. The surviving manuscripts are scattered round the globe from Australia to America; most are in the Pierpont Morgan Library in New York, some in the British Library in London and a few are still in private hands. They are usually written on quarto size paper, folded to form two leaves (i.e. four pages of text), but a few are on octavo sheets or even smaller scraps. As Jane Austen's niece Caroline Austen (1805–80) recalled: 'Her handwriting remains to bear testimony to its own excellence; and every note and letter of hers, was finished off *handsomely* – There was an art *then* in folding and sealing – no adhesive envelopes made all easy – some people's letters looked always loose and untidy – but *her* paper was sure to take the right folds, and *her* sealing wax to drop in the proper place.'[1]

The first of Austen's letters to be published were No. 146 and No. 161(C),[2] some very limited extracts of which were used by her brother Henry in his 'Biographical Notice of the Author', prefixed to the posthumous publication of *Northanger Abbey and Persuasion* in 1817 (*Memoir*, pp. 142–3). Thereafter, it was not until the 1860s, when her nephew, the Revd James Edward Austen-Leigh (JEAL) (1798–1874), was contemplating writing a biography of his aunt, that his elder sister Anna, Mrs Lefroy (1793–1872), suggested: 'Letters may have been preserved, & this is the more probable as Aunt Jane's talent for letter writing was so much valued & thought so delightful amongst her own family circle' (*Memoir*, p. 162).

Jane Austen's sister Cassandra (1773–1845) had indeed preserved many of Jane's letters, and JEAL's sister Caroline confirmed: 'Her letters to Aunt Cassandra (for they were *sometimes* separated) were, I dare say, open and confidential – My Aunt looked them over and burnt the greater part (as she told me), 2 or 3 years before her own death – She left, or *gave* some as legacies to the Neices [*sic*] – but of those that *I* have seen, several had portions cut out' (*Memoir*, p. 174). It would seem that Cassandra's censorship was to ensure that these younger nieces did not read any of Jane Austen's sometimes acid or forthright comments on neighbours and family members who might still be alive later in the nineteenth century (see fig. 1), for before this destruction Cassandra had discussed some of them, during the late 1830s, with one of Admiral Francis Austen's daughters, Catherine (1818–77, later Mrs Hubback), who understood from Cassandra that: '[Jane Austen] always said her books were her children, and supplied her sufficient interest for happiness; and some of her letters, triumphing over the married women of her acquaintance, & rejoicing in her own freedom from care, were most amusing' (*Memoir*, p. 191).

As for the idea of using Jane Austen's letters as the basis of a biography, Caroline Austen was doubtful: 'There is nothing in those letters which *I* have seen that would be acceptable to the public – They were very well expressed, and they must have been very interesting to those who received them – but they detailed chiefly home and family events; and she seldom committed herself *even* to an *opinion* – so that to strangers they could be *no* transcript of her mind – they would not feel that they knew her any the better for having read them' (*Memoir*, pp. 173–4).

Nevertheless, no other documentary evidence for a biography was available, and so the first of the letters to appear in anything like their entirety were those used by JEAL in his *Memoir of Jane Austen*, published in 1869. Even then, he had at his disposal only a very limited quantity, merely those letters which had passed down in his own senior line of the Austen family, plus a few more lent to him by his cousins in the Charles Austen line of descent. When Jane Austen's eldest niece Fanny Knight (1793–1882, later Lady Knatchbull) died after being senile for some years, her son, the first Lord Brabourne, found amongst her effects more than eighty letters from Austen, which he published in two volumes in 1884, as *Letters of Jane Austen*.

In 1906 another five of Austen's letters which had descended in Admiral Francis Austen's family were published by John Hubback and his daughter Edith in their collaborative work *Jane Austen's Sailor Brothers*; and a few years later JEAL's descendants William

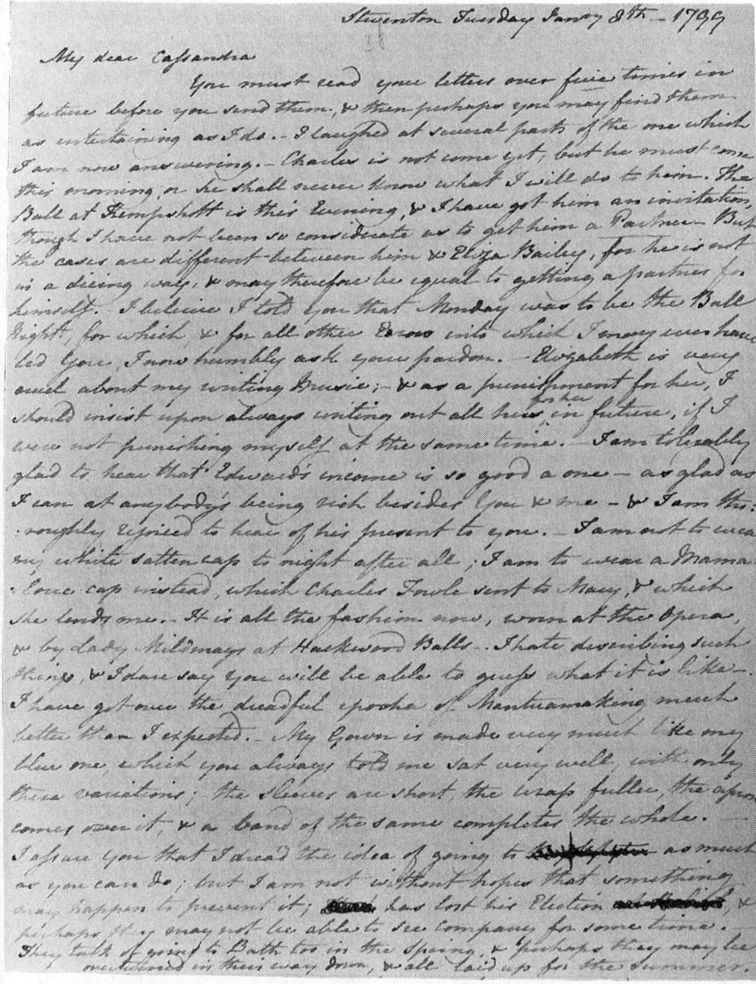

Figure 1. Manuscript letter, Jane Austen to Cassandra, 8 January 1799. Jane Austen made a mildly derogatory reference to their Cooke cousins of Great Bookham, which her sister attempted to obliterate in later years.

and Richard Arthur Austen-Leigh wrote *Jane Austen, her Life and Letters* (1913), and published extracts from a few more letters, including some addressed to Caroline Austen which had not been used in the *Memoir*.

The first 'collected edition' was made by the Austen biographer Brimley Johnson as *The Letters of Jane Austen* (1925), but this reprinted only forty-four of them, selected from the Brabourne volumes, the Hubbacks' *Sailor Brothers* and the Austen-Leighs' *Life*. Further letters belonging to Admiral Charles's last two poverty-stricken spinster granddaughters, the Misses Jane (1849–1928) and Emma Florence Austen (1851–1939) were sold by them in 1925–6. R. W. Chapman published the first proper collection in 1932, giving the complete texts of all the letters then known, and in 1952 he published a second edition, which included another five letters that had surfaced in the intervening twenty years. Since 1952 a few more scraps of letters have come to light, and much more has become known about Austen and her family, hence I compiled a third, and completely new, edition of *Jane Austen's Letters*, published by Oxford University Press in 1995.

In *Northanger Abbey*, Henry Tilney teases Catherine Morland with his provocative statement: 'As far as I have had opportunity of judging, it appears to me that the usual style of letter writing among women is faultless, except in three particulars . . . A general deficiency of subject, a total inattention to stops, and a very frequent ignorance of grammar' (*NA*, 1:3). Austen cannot be accused of the second and third of these faults, but in the past her letters have been criticised for the first reason, 'general deficiency of subject'. This criticism is probably due partly to the way in which her letters have only gradually crept piecemeal into the public domain, and partly to some degree of short-sightedness or tunnel-vision in the critics themselves.

In the *Memoir*, JEAL was apologetic about his aunt's correspondence: 'A wish has sometimes been expressed that some of Jane Austen's letters should be published. Some entire letters, and many extracts, will be given in this memoir; but the reader must be warned not to expect too much from them . . . The style is always clear, and generally animated, while a vein of humour continually gleams through the whole; but the materials may be thought inferior to the execution, for they treat only of the details of domestic life. There is in them no notice of politics or public events; scarcely any discussions on literature, or other subjects of general interest.' (*Memoir*, pp. 50–1)

In 1884 Lord Brabourne made no apology for publishing this family correspondence, but declared: 'the public never took a deeper or more lively interest in all that concerns Jane Austen than at the present moment... This being the case, it has seemed to me that the letters which show what her own "ordinary, everyday life" was, and which afford a picture of her such as no history written by another person could give so well, are likely to interest a public which, both in Great Britain and America, has learned to appreciate Jane Austen ... amid the most ordinary details and most commonplace topics, every now and then sparkle out the same wit and humour which illuminate the pages of *Pride and Prejudice, Mansfield Park, Emma*, etc., and which have endeared the name of Jane Austen to many thousands of readers in English-speaking homes.'[3]

In the preface to his 1932 edition R. W. Chapman gave an explanation, not an apology, for the content of the letters: most of them were addressed to Jane Austen's sister, whose life she shared, hence daily news and family information would obviously need to take priority over other topics; high postal charges would inhibit long discussions on politics, morality or literature, all of which could wait until the sisters were again in each other's company.

He did not enlarge upon the question of postal charges, but they were indeed considerable, and had to be paid by the recipient, not by the sender. First levied in the seventeenth century, charges had risen steadily ever since, with increases during Austen's lifetime in 1784, 1797, 1801, 1805 and again in 1812, when the minimum rate became 4d. for a letter travelling not more than 15 miles, 5d. for 20 miles, 6d. for 30 miles and so on by intermediate stages up to 17d. (1s.5d.) for 700 miles; double rates were payable on two-sheet letters, and fourfold rates on anything heavier.[4] At the end of 1807 Austen noted that, having started the year with £50.15s.0d. in hand, she had spent £3.17s.6½ d. on 'Letters & Parcels';[5] and in 1813 she had to pay 27d. (2s.3d.) for a letter received from brother Francis when his ship was on duty in the Baltic Sea (*L*, 25 September 1813).

R. W. Chapman's explanation did not satisfy the author E. M. Forster, who complained: 'Triviality, varied by touches of illbreeding and of sententiousness, characterises these letters as a whole, particularly the earlier letters . . . Miss Austen's fundamental weakness as a letter-writer . . . [is that] she has not enough subject matter on which to exercise her powers. Her character and sex as well as her environment removed her from public affairs, and she was too sincere and spontaneous to affect any interest which she did not feel. She takes no account of politics or religion, and none of the war except when it brings prize-money to her brothers. Her comments on literature are provincial and perfunctory . . . nothing in her mind except the wish to tell her sister everything . . .'[6] For Forster, Austen was a frivolous, sharp-eyed, hard-hearted young woman, with far too much 'eighteenth century frankness' clinging to her; he thoroughly disapproved of the reference to a bastard child in *Sense and Sensibility*, and thought it quite right that the wording had been toned down in the second edition.

In the second half of the twentieth century, however, as Austen's life and works became the subject of serious study, Lord Brabourne's opinions were proven to be correct. At the present time, literary critics trawl through the letters to pick out every possible hint that can give some clue as to the source of her plots or the origins of her characters, and social historians seek for precise information on the life of the middle-ranking professional classes of the period. Now that the complete texts of Jane Austen's letters, such as do survive at least, are arranged in chronological order, it can be seen that they fall into several clearly defined groups, the style and content of which are appropriate to the recipient. For example, to her brother Francis, away at sea, she sends a bulletin of information about all the family, such as someone away for a long period would need to know: 'Behold me going to write you as handsome a Letter as I can' (*L*, 13 July 1813). No doubt similar letters went to her younger sailor brother, Charles – his diaries note the receipt of a number of letters from Jane, but unfortunately he preserved only the very last of them, that written on 6 April 1817 during her final illness. None of the letters Jane Austen sent to her brother Henry survives, and this is perhaps posterity's greatest loss, for when she wrote to Cassandra on 8 April 1805 she explained: 'I was not able to go on yesterday, all my Wit & leisure were bestowed on letters to Charles & Henry . . .'

As the next generation of nieces and nephews grew up, the letters to Fanny Knight became those of an 'agony aunt' in the modern sense – giving sympathetic advice on affairs of the heart to this motherless teenager: 'Single Women have a dreadful propensity for being poor – which is one very strong argument in favour of Matrimony, but I need not dwell on such arguments with *you*, pretty Dear, you do not want inclination. – Well, I shall say, as I have often said before, Do not be in a hurry; depend upon it, the right Man will come at last' (*L*, 13 March 1817). Anna Lefroy's attempt to write a novel led to the group of letters in which Austen gives practical information and constructive criticism as to how a naturalistic, credible work of fiction should be composed: 'Lyme will not do. Lyme is towards 40 miles distance from Dawlish & would not be talked of there . . . You are now collecting your People delightfully, getting them exactly into such a spot as is the delight of my life; – 3 or 4 Families in a Country Village is the very thing to work on . . .' (*L*, 10–18 August, 9–18 September 1814). There are cheerfully teasing letters to the young JEAL, as he grew from good-natured Winchester College schoolboy into charming Oxford undergraduate: 'One reason for my writing to you now, is that I may have the pleasure of directing to you *Esqre* – I give you Joy of having left Winchester – Now you may own, how miserable you were there; now, it will gradually all come out – your Crimes & your Miseries – how often you went up by the Mail to London & threw away Fifty Guineas at a Tavern' (*L*, 16–17 December 1816) and little joking notes to the much younger Caroline: 'I am sorry you got wet in your ride; Now that you are become an Aunt, you are a person of some consequence & must excite great Interest whatever You do. I have always maintained the importance of Aunts as much as possible, & I am sure of your doing the same now' (*L*, 30 October 1815).

Outside the family, there are chatty letters to her old friends Martha Lloyd and Alethea Bigg, and to Anne Sharp, the one-time governess at Godmersham; crisp business correspondence with Crosby & Co. and John Murray regarding publication, and carefully formal replies to the imperceptive Revd James Stanier Clarke. It is to the latter that Austen writes a self-assessment which has now become most significant for modern literary critics and biographers: 'I am fully sensible that an Historical Romance, founded on the House of Saxe Cobourg, might be much more to the purpose of Profit or Popularity, than such pictures of domestic Life in Country

Villages as I deal in – but I could no more write a Romance than an Epic Poem. I could not sit seriously down to write a serious Romance under any other motive than to save my Life, & if it were indispensable for me to keep it up & never relax into laughing at myself or other people, I am sure I should be hung before I had finished the first Chapter. – No – I must keep to my own style & go on in my own Way; and though I may never succeed again in that, I am convinced that I should totally fail in any other' (*L*, 1 April 1816).

As for her correspondence with her beloved sister Cassandra, Jane herself explains her intentions, in her letter of 3 January 1801: 'I have now attained the true art of letter-writing, which we are always told, is to express on paper exactly what one would say to the same person by word of mouth; I have been talking to you almost as fast as I could the whole of this letter.' To read these letters, even though it is two hundred years since they were written, is the nearest we can come to hearing Jane Austen talk to us as well.

NOTES

1. *A Memoir of Jane Austen and Other Family Recollections*, ed. Kathryn Sutherland (Oxford: Oxford University Press, 2002), p. 171. In addition to reprinting the second (enlarged) edition of the original *Memoir*, this new publication includes Henry Austen's two biographical essays, Caroline Austen's *My Aunt Jane Austen, a memoir*, and Anna Lefroy's *Recollections of Aunt Jane*, together with extracts from other family papers. Subsequent references to this edition are included in the text.
2. *L*, 16–17 December 1816, 28–29 May 1817.
3. Edward, Lord Brabourne, *Letters of Jane Austen* (1884), vol. I, pp. xii–xv.
4. Cyril H. Rock, *Guide to the Postal History Collection, Tottenham Museum* (1938), pp. 14–16; also Frank Staff, *The Penny Post, 1680–1919* (London: Lutterworth Press, 1964), pp. 71–4.
5. Patrick Piggott, 'Jane Austen's Southampton Piano', *Collected Reports* of the Jane Austen Society 3 (1976–85), 146–9.
6. E. M. Forster, *Abinger Harvest* (1936), pp. 156–7.

5

Literary influences

JANE STABLER

In a letter of December 1798 Jane Austen told Cassandra that they were subscribing to a new library. The proprietress had written with the assurance that her collection was not limited to novels, prompting Austen to comment: 'She might have spared this pretension to *our* family, who are great Novel-readers & not ashamed of being so' (*L*, 18–19 December). Mr Austen's taste was liberal, encompassing 'every species of literature', according to Henry Austen's 'Biographical Notice'. The family's enthusiasm for the stage meant that the barn at the rectory at Steventon was fitted up as a theatre and Austen's earliest experiences of English drama was in hearing rehearsals of comedies or farces by writers like Isaac Bickerstaffe, Susannah Centlivre, Hannah Cowley, Henry Fielding, David Garrick and Richard Brinsley Sheridan. Despite her brother's emphasis on serious literature in his memoir Jane Austen was as fond of low comedy and sensational novels as collections of sermons. Theatrical productions helped to populate her work with comic archetypes: rakes, hypocrites, simperers, blusterers, garrulous purveyors of scandal and trivia and grumpy spouses wearily resigned to the incorrigible folly of their partners.

Gothic fiction also found its way into the parsonage: Jane Austen described her father at home in the evening reading *The Midnight Bell* (1798) by Francis Lathom (*L*, 24 October 1798). Isabella Thorpe's enthusiasm for the same story in *Northanger Abbey* (1:6) explains why Mr Austen borrowed it from the library rather than buying it. He did, however, acquire *Arthur FitzAlbini* (1798) a novel by Sir Samuel Egerton Brydges, who had rented the parsonage at Deane. Austen found it odd 'that we should purchase the only one of Egerton's works of which his family are ashamed'. But, she told Cassandra, 'these scruples . . . do not at all interfere with my reading it' (*L*, 25 November 1798). Austen's toleration for those who defied convention was not unlimited, however, and she later discarded a translation of Madame de Genlis's *Alphonsine* (1807). 'We were disgusted in twenty pages . . . it has indelicacies which disgrace a pen hitherto so pure' (*L*, 7–8 January 1807). Mr Austen's library of more than 500 books had to be sold when the family left the parsonage at Steventon and moved to Bath. Despite her glee at exchanging her copy of the oft reissued Robert Dodsley's *A Collection of Poems by Several Hands* (1748–58) for ten shillings, her resentment at the sale and her thwarted attempts to find stimulating reading material when they visited southern coastal resorts comes through in her memory of the library at Dawlish twelve years later as 'particularly pitiful & wretched . . . & not likely to have anybody's publication' (*L*, 10–18 August 1814).

Books were expensive commodities and the Austens' decision to purchase William Cowper's works and James Boswell's *Journal of a Tour to the Hebrides* (1785) and his *Life of Johnson* (1791) in 1798 was carefully calculated. While a subscription to a circulating library cost about a guinea a year, the first edition of Walter Scott's *Marmion* (1808) cost £1.1s.6d in quarto and Austen thought it was 'very generous' (*L*, 10–11 January 1809) of her to send a copy (R. W. Chapman suspects it was probably a later edition) to her brother Charles: it becomes, perhaps, slightly less generous when we recall that she had been disappointed on hearing Scott's poem read aloud the previous year. Reading aloud was an important evening entertainment and – as with the home theatricals – this gregarious practice shaped Austen's art of dialogue. In these live performances Austen's novels and those of her niece, Anna, were tested against traditional English works of fiction – the novels of Samuel Richardson, Henry Fielding, Laurence Sterne and Jonathan Swift.

One of Jane Austen's luxuries in later life would be free range of the library at Godmersham Park. She confided to Cassandra: 'The Comfort of the Billiard Table here is very great. – It draws all the Gentlemen to it whenever they are within, especially after dinner, so that my B^r Fanny & I have the Library to ourselves in delightful quiet' (*L*, 14–15 October 1813). At Chawton Austen belonged to a book club and gloried in its eclectic stock, including 'an Essay on the Military Police & Institutions of the British Empire, by Capt. Pasley of the Engineers' which she found 'delightfully written & highly entertaining' (*L*, 24 January 1813). Her retentive memory and talent for mimicry meant that she effortlessly absorbed other styles, alert to the various responses they provoked in a range of different readers.

Records of book ownership, her writing and family testimonials tell us that Austen knew the poetic tradition of William Shakespeare, John Milton, Alexander Pope, James Thomson, Thomas Gray, Oliver Goldsmith, William Cowper and George Crabbe; she was also familiar with the more recent Romantic legacy of Walter Scott, Thomas Campbell, William Wordsworth and Robert Burns as embraced by Sir Edward in *Sanditon* ('Burns is always on fire', *S*, 7). Austen roamed through the novels of her contemporaries Scott, Charlotte Smith, Jane West, Frances Burney and Maria Edgeworth. The last two were her most immediate literary influences. Austen subscribed to Burney's *Camilla* (1796); ranked Edgeworth above nearly all other authors and joked about Scott as a rival. Like Burney and Edgeworth she blended omniscient narration with Richardson's device of intimate letters to track the evolution of a courtship. Through epistolary exchange, Burney's *Evelina* (1778) follows a young woman's navigation of the traps of English society and the obstacles of embarrassing relatives and unwelcome suitors towards marriage with a worthy aristocrat. Austen found the impeccable Lord Orville unnatural but enjoyed Burney's grotesquely comic characters. In Edgeworth's 'Moral Tale' *Belinda* the heroine learns to recognise false guides and rely on her own judgement. Edgeworth cultivated a strong ethical and practical dimension in her female characters but she was wary of novels as a genre. In *Northanger Abbey* Austen rebukes novelists who degrade 'by their contemptuous censure the very performances, to the number of which they are themselves adding' (1:5): Edgeworth's advertisement to *Belinda* (1801) repudiated the 'folly, errour, and vice . . . disseminated in books classed under this denomination'.

Themes of education and moral development permeated eighteenth-century fictional and non-fictional prose. They underpin Ann Radcliffe's Gothic novels, blended with sensational adventures and descriptions of sublime scenery; they turn up in religious or philosophical dress in periodical literature and conduct guides. Austen declared herself 'pleased' by Thomas Gisborne's *An Enquiry into the Duties of the Female Sex* (1797) (*L*, 24 July 1806) which is to modern ears at least as conservative as the Fordyce sermons inflicted on the Bennet girls by Mr Collins in *Pride and Prejudice* (1:14).

Moral lessons were also drawn from periodical literature, histories and *belles lettres*. Austen's 'History of England' revels in pronouncements which subvert the one-sided authority of historians such as Goldsmith. In *Mansfield Park* Fanny's horizons, like Austen's, are widened by her enthusiasm for travel writing and anti-slavery literature. Biography, like historiography, celebrated great men rather than exposing private vice. The persistent tone of eulogy evidently grated as Austen turned to Southey's *Life of Nelson* (1813): 'I am tired of Lives of Nelson, being that I never read any' (*L*, 11–12 October 1813).

Dr Samuel Johnson was another hero of the age; his appeal as a moralist resides in his good-humoured efforts to secure a stable ethical perspective on human frailty. Austen described a servant who wished to leave her brother Henry's London house as having 'more of Cowper than of Johnson in him, fonder of Tame Hares & Blank verse than of the full tide of human Existence at Charing Cross' (*L*, 3 November 1813). Johnson was no admirer of blank verse and this judgement echoes his response when Boswell remarked on the cheerfulness of Fleet Street: 'Why, Sir, Fleet-street has a very animated appearance; but I think the full tide of human existence is at Charing-cross' (2 April 1775). Johnson's exhilaration at the variety of London life was legendary. He decreed, for example, that a man was in less danger of falling in love indiscreetly in London than anywhere else because the difficulty of deciding between a variety of attractions 'kept him safe'. When Anne Elliot reminds Captain Harville that 'We live at home, quiet, confined, and our feelings prey upon us' (*P*, 2:11), she points to the difficulty women experience in maintaining such a robust outlook although she tries to balance Captain Benwick's dependence on Scott and Lord Byron with 'such works of our best moralists, such collections of the finest letters, such memoirs of characters of worth and suffering . . . as calculated to rouse and fortify the mind' (*P*, 1:11). Johnson was, however, also susceptible to poignant sentiment, particularly the novels of Richardson.

Richardson's novel *The History of Sir Charles Grandison* (1753–4) was an Austen family favourite and, according to Henry Austen, his sister knew the work in minute detail. Richardson's fiction itemises the flux and reflux of emotional turmoil as revealed in the traces of a blush or the broken heel of a shoe. *Grandison*'s heroine, Harriet

Byron, is thrust into the London marriage market, tries to evade the advances of the villainous Sir Hargrave Pollexfen and falls in love with the charitable patrician Sir Charles, who is distracted by his love for a beautiful foreigner. He struggles at great length between different desires and principles and when he eventually asks Harriet to marry him, she is overcome by his magnanimity. Scholars have traced multiple resemblances between *Sir Charles Grandison* and Austen's later works: the growth of Fanny's love for Edmund in *Mansfield Park*, for example, or the episode at Pemberley in *Pride and Prejudice* when Elizabeth is impressed by the housekeeper's esteem for Darcy as a benevolent landlord.[1] Just as significant as these suggestions of direct influence, however, is the versatility of Austen's use of Richardson and her deft transformations of available literary traditions.

Richardson's influence does not stamp Austen's writing in any single way; rather, his novels provided characters, situations, narrative tensions and a consuming fascination with inner life which Austen developed in different contexts. Her youthful dramatic version of *Sir Charles Grandison* is instantly funny as a feat of compression: a seven-volume novel shrinks to five very short acts. Catherine Morland's mother in *Northanger Abbey* 'often reads Sir Charles Grandison' and Isabella Thorpe finds it 'an amazing horrid book' (1:6). In *Sanditon* Sir Edward's character has been malformed by the Richardson school of sentimental novels featuring 'Man's determined pursuit of Woman in defiance of every opposition of feeling & convenience' (*S*, 8). In her letters Austen refers to Richardson's heroines with playful familiarity. When she thanks Cassandra for a long letter she invokes one of them again: 'Like Harriot Byron I ask, what am I to do with my Gratitude? – I can do nothing but thank you & go on' (*L*, 11–12 October 1813). Gentle mockery of Richardson's sensitive virtuous heroines is evident in 'Frederic and Elfrida' when Elfrida hurries into 'a succession of fainting fits' (ch. 5) and 'Love and Freindship' where the heroines 'fainted Alternately on a Sofa' ('Letter the 8th'). This feminine delicacy, like the 'cruel Persecutions of obstinate Fathers' ('Letter the First'), also characterises Sheridan's and Radcliffe's plots.[2]

One of the most obvious features of Austen's early writing is its burlesque mockery of another work through a reproduction of its style in an exaggerated form. In her juvenilia we find merciless skits on literature of sensibility, picturesque conventions, conduct literature and melodrama. Austen's relish of literary parody continued throughout her life. The antidote to *Alphonsine* was Charlotte Lennox's *The Female Quixote* (1752), a work influenced by both Johnson and Richardson. In this novel the heroine, Arabella, is led astray by isolated reading of French romances into a series of social blunders in Bath and London, where she earnestly expects to flee from ravishers. Austen found the book 'quite equal to what I remembered' (*L*, 7–8 January 1807). She praised James and Horace Smith's popular *Rejected Addresses* which caricatured the farcical poetry competition staged around the reopening of the Drury Lane Theatre in 1812; in 1814 she recommended Eaton Barrett's novel *The Heroine, or Adventures of Cherubina* (1813) as 'a delightful burlesque, particularly on the Radcliffe style' (*L*, 2–3 March 1814). Later that year she flippantly projected a parody of Mary Brunton's earnest *Self-Control* (1810), a novel Austen had found 'excellently-meant, elegantly-written' and 'without anything of Nature or Probability in it' (*L*, 24 November 1814; 11–12 October 1813).

In the letters to Cassandra in particular, we can hear the ways in which shared reading nourishes allusive asides between the sisters in the form of private jokes about, for example, the inexperience of provincials in the big city. Borrowing Hannah Cowley's comedy *The Belle's Stratagem* (1780), Austen strikes at renewed plans to visit London: 'I am rather surprised at the Revival of the London visit – but Mr Doricourt has travelled; he knows best' (*L*, 14–16 January 1801).[3] Austen was aware, however, that more consciously learned allusions were an obligatory feature of polite literature. This convention is ridiculed in *Northanger Abbey* when we are given the sum total of Catherine's knowledge via a series of free quotations from Pope, Gray, Thomson and Shakespeare (1:1). Hannah More's parade of classical learning in the title of *Cœlebs in Search of a Wife* (1809) earned Austen's derision: 'in Cœlebs, there is pedantry & affectation. – Is it written only to Classical Scholars?' (*L*, 30 January 1809).

Young ladies were encouraged to peruse improving works of literature through elegant anthologies which selected the 'beauties of' a particular author and omitted anything risqué – this was the age of the bowdlerised Shakespeare. Nevertheless, conduct writers such as Hannah More warned that encounters with extracts alone would result in a superficial mind. *Emma's* Harriet Smith is so superficial that she fails to appreciate even the extracts dutifully read aloud by Robert Martin and tries to introduce him to Radcliffe and Regina Roche (*E*, 1:4). Emma, like Elizabeth Bennet, at least knows that her reading is deficient, and Austen also plays down the extent of her literary expertise. Later in her life she declined a request from James Stanier Clarke, the Carlton House librarian, that she should write about an English clergyman 'Fond of, & entirely engaged in Literature' (*L*, 16 November 1815). Austen insisted that she was unequal to the task, not being 'abundant in quotations & allusions' to classical literature, science and philosophy which were expected in 'Man's Conversation' (*L*, 11 December 1815). Austen does not advertise her reading but she expects readers to be aware of the relevant work's provenance and reputation, surrounding allusions with ripples of irony.

When Maria Bertram invokes the starling's pathetic refrain, 'I cannot get out' from Sterne's *A Sentimental Journey* (1768) (*MP*, 1:10), Austen is having her signal her (un)availability to Henry Crawford through words often extracted in anthologies designed to cultivate female sensitivity and moral worth. Elizabeth Bennet's joke about not wishing to disrupt the party walking at Netherfield ('You are charmingly group'd and appear to uncommon advantage. The picturesque would be spoilt by admitting a fourth', *P&P*, 1:10), is all the more provocative for the readers who know that Gilpin's theory of picturesque groups includes a discussion of the ideal number of cattle. Ostentatious displays of reading are often used to expose a character's weakness. After Lydia's elopement Mary Bennet consoles herself with 'moral extractions' such as Villars's exhortation in *Evelina*: 'Remember, my dear Evelina, nothing is so delicate as the reputation of a woman: it is, at once, the most beautiful and most brittle of all human things' (vol. 2, ch. 8) – at which Elizabeth 'lifted up her eyes in amazement' *(P&P*, 3:5). While she might read sermons and homilies in private, Austen recognises the folly of applying literature directly to life. Fanny Price's quotation of Scott to signal her disappointment at the chapel at Sotherton – 'No signs that a "Scottish monarch sleeps below"' (*MP*, 1:9) suggests an amusing faith in Scott's Gothic window-dressing whereas Austen herself invokes Scott more playfully: "'I do not write for such dull Elves" "As have not a great deal of Ingenuity themselves'" (*L*, 29 January 1813). Mrs Elton exposes her shallowness when she applies the 'charming' lines of Gray's Elegy to the 'charming' Jane Fairfax and later when she echoes Mr Elton's affected reference to Milton's 'L'Allegro' (1645) while recounting small setbacks in their marriage plans: 'he was sure at this rate it would be *May* before Hymen's saffron robe would be put on for us!' (*E*, 2:15, 2:18). Less pretentious and artificial, but just as funny is Miss Bates's garbled gratitude: 'We may well say that "our lot is cast in a goodly heritage"' (*E*, 2:3) where a biblical Psalm is misquoted in a way that brilliantly follows Miss Bates's stream of consciousness from a gift of food to curiosity about a letter.[4]

In this way Austen allows even cherished works to be mangled by less perceptive characters. Henry Austen tells us that Cowper was her favourite moral writer in verse. Cowper's earnest blank verse ranges over conversational sketches of rural life to stern warnings about the corrupting effects of luxury and commerce. Marianne Dashwood and Fanny Price express their inner convictions and integrity through Cowper's poetry, but there is also more than a hint of naive fancy in each. Only Mr Knightley invokes Cowper's poetry with anything like the subtlety of its author. Suspecting a 'private understanding' between Jane Fairfax and Frank Churchill, Mr Knightley is yet wary of 'errors of imagination' and being 'like Cowper and his fire at twilight, "Myself creating what I saw"' (*E*, 3:5). In *Sanditon*, Mr Parker strains to apply Cowper's line on Voltaire to the pretensions of Brinshore to be a seaside resort (*S*, 1). Frequently the energy a character expends in the retrieval of a quotation turns out to be misplaced or ignored by the rest of the party. Reading in Austen's world is supposed to be a sociable activity – either because it instructs the individual in the duties of corporate existence or because it is itself a shared activity. But when Fanny rhapsodises (*MP*, 2:4) or when Marianne and Willoughby idolise the 'same passages' (*S&S*, 1:10), Austen points out varieties of self-centred immolation. Even newspaper reading divides characters in terms of their attention to social obligation. Austen often details snippets from newspapers that have been relayed to her (*L*, 21–22 January

1801). Her male characters, however, use the newspaper as a barrier to shield them from social interaction: in *Mansfield Park*, Edmund and Mr Price both neglect Fanny while they bury themselves in a newspaper; in *Persuasion*, Charles Hayter takes up a newspaper and fails to take little Walter off Anne's back. Taciturn newspaper reading defines Mr Palmer's existence (*S&S*, 1:19).

Scholars have traced myriad influences for Austen's satire but they cannot wholly account for her unforced linguistic precision and her stringent character surveillance. We do not know everything that she read and we cannot always gauge her reaction to a particular work even when she records one. Lady Morgan, for example, is saluted and slighted in the same breath: 'We have got *Ida of Athens* by Miss Owenson; which must be very clever, because it was written as the Authoress says, in three months' (*L*, 17–18 January 1809); Laetitia Matilda Hawkins receives a carefully balanced appraisal: 'very good and clever, but tedious' (*L*, ?late February-early March 1815). Austen's view of Byron is teasingly enigmatic: 'I have read the Corsair, mended my petticoat, & have nothing else to do' (*L*, 5–8 March 1814); and her recommendation of Madame de Staël's *Corinne, or Italy* (1807), a lyrical celebration of female passion, to a deaf, housebound old man in Southampton is similarly inscrutable: 'He has lived in that House more than twenty years, & poor Man, is so totally deaf, that they say he c^d not hear a Cannon, were it fired close to him; having no cannon at hand to make the experiment, I took it for granted, & talked to him a little with my fingers, which was funny enough. – I recommended him to read Corinna' (*L*, 27–8 December 1808). Contemplating the lack of gravitas in *Pride and Prejudice*, Jane Austen acknowledged the literary tradition that she was bypassing: 'an Essay on Writing, a critique on Walter Scott, or the history of Buonaparte' (*L*, 4 February 1813). These non-existent chapters are important. While maintaining a critical distance between 'those enormous great stupid thick Quarto Volumes' (*L*, 9 February 1813) and what she encountered in the 'mere Trash of the common Circulating Library' (*S*, 8), Austen read almost indiscriminately, but wrote with an exacting sense of the narrative voices that needed to be kept at bay as she created a new fiction out of highly important 'Little Matters' (*L*, 9 December 1808).

NOTES

1. See Jocelyn Harris, *Jane Austen's Art of Memory* (Cambridge: Cambridge University Press, 1989), pp. 130–68; Kenneth L. Moler, *Jane Austen's Art of Allusion* (Lincoln and London: University of Nebraska Press, 1968), pp. 105–7.

2. B. C. Southam, *Jane Austen's Literary Manuscripts: A Study of the Novelist's Development through the Surviving Papers*, new edition (London and New York: Athlone Press, 2001), pp. 9–11.

3. Discussed in Paula Byrne, *Jane Austen and the Theatre* (London: Hambledon, 2002), p. 133. Doricourt has completed his Grand Tour and, seeing himself as an experienced cosmopolitan, is somewhat disdainful of provincial England.

4. The Psalm reads: 'The Lord *is* the portion of mine inheritance and of my cup: thou maintainest my lot. / The lines are fallen unto me in pleasant *places*; yea, I have a goodly heritage' (ch. 16, verses 5–6).

6

Memoirs and biographies

DEIRDRE LE FAYE

Some biographers suffer from an excess of source material concerning their subjects, and the resultant biographies are either very large or even run into several volumes. With Jane Austen, the reverse is the case; for many years documentation to confirm even the barest outline of her life remained scanty, so that most biographies were slight and feeble, bulked out with copious quotations from the novels. It was only at the end of the last century that a reasonably complete picture of Austen's life could be seen, based upon original research in family archives and civic records.

The richest source of biographical information is of course Austen's own letters, but these have emerged only gradually, from 1818 right up to the 1980s. During this long period the other main source of information was family tradition – the memories of her siblings and their children, which were eventually written down late in the nineteenth century. But here again, these family comments in many cases did not actually appear in print until the twentieth century.

Apart from Austen's letters, no personal documentation exists. She did not write any memoirs or journals, and although she probably kept the brief pocketbook diaries such as were commonly used by ladies of the period, none of these survives;[1] nor did Cassandra Austen keep any record of her sister's activities. Some of the other Austens kept pocketbooks, and various miscellaneous letters still exist, written by family and friends; these provide useful dating evidence, but (with one or two exceptions) do not give any insights into Austen's character and opinions.

The first introduction of Jane Austen to her readership was made by her brother Henry, in his 'Biographical Notice of the Author', prefixed to the posthumous publication of *Northanger Abbey and Persuasion* in late 1817. By this date Henry had taken Holy Orders and become an enthusiastic cleric of Evangelical views, hence it is understandable that he should end his essay by emphasising his sister's devotion to the Church of England. Apart from this, however, he provided the basic facts of her life, described her appearance and character, spoke of the encouragement she had received within the family to publish the novels she had written for their and her own amusement and quoted briefly from two of her letters.[2]

In 1832 Richard Bentley bought up the copyrights of the novels in anticipation of publishing a complete new edition in his Standard Novels series, and for this Henry Austen sent to Bentley 'a biographical sketch of the Authoress, which is to supersede that already published. I heartily wish that I could have made it richer in detail but the fact is that My dear Sister's life was not a life of event. Nothing like a journal of her actions or her conversations was kept by herself or others . . . Indeed, the farthest thing from her expectations or wishes was to be exhibited as a public character under any circumstances.' Henry also regretted that no professionally executed portrait of Jane had ever been painted. This revised text was now called 'Memoir of Miss Austen', and was updated by the inclusion of two new anecdotes concerning her, as well as quotations from two articles praising her work, recently published in the *Athenaeum* and *The Quarterly Review*.[3]

By the middle of the nineteenth century Austen was being mentioned briefly in volumes of literary criticism – e.g. *Memoirs of the Literary Ladies of England* (1843); W. F. Pollock's article 'British Novelists' in *Fraser's Magazine* (1860); and *English Women of Letters* (1863) – though the information given was based entirely upon the novels and Henry Austen's texts. In 1858 Lord Macaulay had considered writing a biography of the authoress he so greatly admired, but unfortunately never did so (*Memoir*, p. 112).

It was in the 1860s that the three children of Jane Austen's eldest brother, the Revd James Austen – his elder daughter Anna, now Mrs Lefroy (1793–1872), his son the Revd James Edward Austen-Leigh (1798–1874) and his younger daughter Caroline Austen (1805–80) – began to think about composing a biography of their aunt, in response to queries from the ageing original readers of the novels and from younger readers coming to the novels afresh. The last of Jane Austen's siblings, Admiral Francis Austen (1774–1865), was by then very old and frail, and JEAL and his sisters realised that soon they, and one or two of their cousins, would be the only people still alive who had personal knowledge of the writer.

In December 1864 Anna wrote to her brother: 'You have asked me to put on paper my recollections of Aunt Jane, & to do so would be both on your account & her's a labour of love if I had but a sufficiency of material. I am sorry to say that my reminiscences are few; surprisingly so, considering how much I saw of her in childhood, & how much intercourse we had in later years. I look back to the first period but find little that I can grasp of any substance, or certainty: it seems now all so shadowy!' However, memories returned as she wrote, and her letter included anecdotes about Jane Austen's life at Steventon in the 1790s as well as something of the Chawton years. Caroline wrote a long essay recording her childhood memories of visits to Chawton Cottage between 1809–17, upon which JEAL relied quite heavily for his work. He too had his memories, and recalled the family opinion that: 'Cassandra had the *merit* of having her temper always under command, but that Jane had the *happiness* of a temper that never required to be commanded' – an opinion which must have been passed on to him by either his father or his grandmother (*Memoir*, pp. 19, 157–62, 165–82).

A Memoir of Jane Austen was published in December 1869, to coincide with Bentley's new edition of the novels in 1870. Most of JEAL's information had come from Anna and Caroline, with some help from his cousins Cassy Esten Austen (Admiral Charles's eldest daughter), and Catherine Hubback (one of Admiral Francis's daughters). Not surprisingly, the final image of Austen created by JEAL and his sisters is that of a quiet, domesticated, middle-aged maiden aunt, which was how they had known her; no one was left alive who could tell them anything about Jane Austen's younger days.

The *Memoir* was very well received, and in the following year JEAL published a second and enlarged edition, which included the hitherto unknown texts of *The Watsons* and *Lady Susan*, as well as the cancelled chapter of *Persuasion*, a précis of *Sanditon*, and 'The Mystery' as an example of the *Juvenilia*. This second edition has become the basis of all succeeding biographies; but it was still of course information from one side of the family only. JEAL kept all the letters he had received in connection with his work on the *Memoir*, and these were placed in a fine album given him by his children for this purpose. R. W. Chapman saw the album in 1926 and made some typed extracts from a few of the letters; it was lucky that he did so, since the album is now lost, presumed to have been destroyed during the Second World War.[4]

When Jane Austen's eldest niece Lady Knatchbull (formerly Fanny Knight) died in 1882, her son Lord Brabourne found in her house more than eighty letters from Austen, and these he published in two volumes as *Letters of Jane Austen* (1884), with much editorial matter concerning the Kentish families whom Austen knew and mentioned in her correspondence. The *Letters* brought new biographical information to light, redressing the imbalance towards the Austen-Leigh side of the family memories.

In 1885 Austen made her first appearance in the *DNB*, in an article written by Leslie Stephen; and from now on other biographies start to be published, written by non-family authors. These are usually short, frequently inaccurate and highly repetitive, doing no more than paraphrase the information contained in the *Memoir* and the *Letters*. The only useful publication was that by Oscar Fay Adams, of Boston, USA. Adams was the first non-family writer to attempt any original research – he visited England in 1889 to take photographs of the places associated with Austen, and to trace surviving collateral descendants. In 1891 he published *The Story of Jane Austen's Life*, giving new information gained from his researches; and in 1897 he brought out a second edition of his work, this time illustrated by the photographs he had taken during his visit. These are probably the very earliest extant photographs of the houses and other buildings known to Austen.

Another biographer who had local knowledge was Walter Herries Pollock, who published *Jane Austen, Her Contemporaries and Herself* in 1899. He was a barrister and author, who lived in Chawton and knew the Knight descendants living in the Great House, and from them he was able to gain some family anecdotes and see something of their own archive.

The next biographer to attempt original research was Constance Hill, a Londoner. During 1900–1 Hill, accompanied by her artist sister Ellen to do the illustrations, travelled in Austen's footsteps across southern England, and made it her business to interview as many of the collateral descendants as possible. She was allowed to read the three volumes of Austen's *Juvenilia*, and to use other of the family papers, including Caroline Austen's essay originally written for the *Memoir*. The results of her researches were published in 1902, as *Jane Austen, Her Homes & Her Friends*, and Ellen Hill's drawings are valuable as they give the last record of the Austen world in pre-automobile days.

In 1906 John Henry Hubback (1844–1939), one of Admiral Francis's grandsons, collaborated with his daughter Edith in writing *Jane Austen's Sailor Brothers*; they were able to provide some unique anecdotes from their side of the family, and gave much more information about the naval careers of Admiral Francis and Admiral Charles, linking this to Austen's naval scenes in *Mansfield Park* and *Persuasion*. They also reproduced for the first time the only authentic portrait of Jane Austen, the bust sketched in watercolour by Cassandra, which is now in the National Portrait Gallery. This had been inherited by Admiral Charles's daughter Cassy Esten, when she acted as her Aunt Cassandra's executrix in 1845. Many years later J. H. Hubback wrote his own reminiscences, *Cross Currents in a Long Life* (1935), in which he made a few further references to Austen; but unfortunately his memories were by now demonstrably confused and unreliable.

The next family publication was Mary Augusta Austen-Leigh's privately printed biography of her father, *James Edward Austen-Leigh* (1911), for which she used family letters, diaries and other manuscripts. It is of course an account of her father's life, but as his early years overlapped with Austen's later life, and as she talks about his work on the *Memoir*, it provides useful background information towards Austen's own biography.

At last, in 1913, JEAL's son and grandson, William Austen-Leigh, and his nephew Richard Arthur, wrote what was intended to be the first proper biography of their collateral ancestress – *Jane Austen, her Life & Letters, a Family Record*. It subsumed the *Memoir*, Brabourne's *Letters* and the Hubbacks' *Sailor Brothers* – but even so, was still far from giving as complete a picture as was promised by the title. The Austen-Leighs do not seem to have undertaken any research beyond their immediate family circle, and were content to quote arbitrary extracts from Austen's letters without providing much in the way of discursive explanation. Furthermore, in 1920 Mary Augusta Austen-Leigh published her own book, *Personal*

Aspects of Jane Austen, containing information not given in the *Life*, so it was already becoming a little outdated.

The first non-family full-length biography was that written by Elizabeth Jenkins in 1938, *Jane Austen, A Biography*. Jenkins was the first to use properly Chapman's 1932 edition of the collected letters, and was also allowed to see other unpublished family papers in the Austen-Leigh archive. This work was therefore well balanced, as accurate in its facts as was then possible, and placed Jane Austen clearly against the background of her times; it consequently remained the definitive biography for some fifty years to come.

More of the information remaining in the Austen-Leigh archive appeared in print when Richard Arthur Austen-Leigh (RAAL) published *Austen Papers 1704–1856* (1942), a selection of the family manuscripts then in his hands. Unfortunately this work, being privately printed, had only a very limited circulation, and it is difficult today to find a copy. Even more unfortunately, in most cases RAAL – as in the *Life & Letters* – published only extracts of the manuscripts rather than the complete texts. He did not think to publish his grandfather's *Memoir* album, and it was probably about now that it was destroyed in the Blitz.

In the immediate post-war period, R. W. Chapman published *Jane Austen, Facts and Problems* (1948), a small volume which collected together his Clark Lectures at Trinity College, Cambridge, though these in fact had been written unspecified years earlier. In them, he tried to clarify some of the uncertainties now becoming apparent in the various family traditions concerning Austen. In 1953 he issued a *Critical Bibliography*, but did not publish anything more before his death in 1960.

In 1949 the Jane Austen Society was founded, originally with the intention of purchasing the cottage in Chawton where Austen had spent the last years of her life. When the separate Jane Austen Memorial Trust succeeded in buying the property, the Society began instead to encourage research into Austen's life and times, and to publish the results of such researches in its annual reports. In 1952 the Society published in full Caroline Austen's essay *My Aunt Jane Austen*, which showed how much JEAL had relied upon this for his *Memoir*.

For the next twenty years or more biographies became increasingly sterile and inaccurate, as the writers did not seek for fresh information but were content to repeat each other; with the new availability of colour printing, illustrations took the place of text. The tide of modern Austenian studies turned in 1982, when David Gilson published his great *Bibliography of Jane Austen*, covering everything written about her up to 1978, and so providing an invaluable reference source for any modern biographer.

The first full-scale biography since Elizabeth Jenkins's pre-war study was Park Honan's *Jane Austen, Her Life* (1987). This is almost a social history of Austen's life, rather than a biography, as it includes a great deal about the public events of the period, whether or not she was in any way concerned with them; it is certainly inclusive and all-embracing.

In 1989 I published *Jane Austen: A Family Record*; this is a completely revised and updated version of the Austen-Leighs' *Life & Letters*, written at the request of RAAL's heirs. I researched in many hitherto neglected archival sources, and concentrated on collecting all documentary evidence concerning Austen's life, especially those facts recorded in their diaries by family and friends. I did not attempt any 'interpretation' of the facts, preferring to let the Austens speak directly to modern readers. A new edition of this work appeared in 2004, updated to include information which has come to light since the 1980s.

Since 1989 several more biographies have appeared, with as many versions of Austen's character as there are authors. In *Jane Austen, A Life* (1997) Claire Tomalin provided a readable and sympathetic text, seeing Austen as a 'poor relation' carving out a place in gentry society by her own merits. In the same year David Nokes published *Jane Austen, A Life*; in it he claims to have created a 'more lively' version of Austen, seeing her as vain and mercenary, in the style of Mary Crawford. The Canadian novelist Carol Shields, whose own works have been compared to Austen's, provided a discursive, impressionistic sketch in *Jane Austen* (2001), one in Weidenfeld & Nicolson's *Lives* series of short biographies.

In the same period there have been numerous other biographical studies which spotlight some particular aspect of Austen's life and background. Jan Fergus's *Jane Austen: A Literary Life* (1991) concentrates on Austen as an authoress and discusses the publication of her works. The other titles are self-explanatory: George Holbert Tucker's *A History of Jane Austen's Family* (1998); Irene

Collins's *Jane Austen and the Clergy* (1993), which was followed by the same writer's *Jane Austen, the Parson's Daughter* (1998); Maggie Lane, *Jane Austen and Food* (1995); Mavis Batey, *Jane Austen and the English Landscape* (1996); Penelope Byrde, *Jane Austen Fashion* (1999); David Selwyn, *Jane Austen and Leisure* (1999); Brian Southam, *Jane Austen and the Navy* (2000); in 2002 two books entitled *Jane Austen and the Theatre* appeared, one by Paula Byrne and the other by Penny Gay; in the same year I published *Jane Austen's 'Outlandish Cousin', the Life and Letters of Eliza de Feuillide* (2002).

NOTES

1. Patrick Piggott, 'Jane Austen's Southampton Piano', *Collected Reports* of the Jane Austen Society 3 (1976–85), 146–9. Piggott reproduces a chance fragmentary survival – just one page from the back of a pocketbook, giving a summary of Austen's expenditure during 1807.
2. *A Memoir of Jane Austen and Other Family Recollections*, ed. Kathryn Sutherland (Oxford: Oxford University Press, 2002), pp. 135–41.
3. Deirdre Le Faye, 'Jane Austen – New Biographical Comments', *Notes & Queries* 237 (1992), 162–3; also Sutherland (ed.), *Memoir*, pp. 145–54, 258. Subsequent references to the *Memoir* are included in the text.
4. Mary Augusta Austen-Leigh, *James Edward Austen-Leigh, a Memoir by His Daughter* (1911), pp. 264–5. R. W. Chapman's typed extracts from the album are at the National Portrait Gallery, London, in their files on Jane Austen.

7
Poetry

DAVID SELWYN

The handful of poems written by Jane Austen – impromptu, occasional, often arising from games – were the result not so much of the art which produced her novels as of a tradition of family verse-writing inherited from her mother. In 1791 Mrs Austen's cousin Mary Leigh compiled a manuscript volume of family verses composed by herself and various relations in her youth, among them her cousin by marriage, Sir Edward Turner, who, she wrote, was 'almost singular, in encouraging young Women to read' at a period earlier in the century when 'literature in Ladies . . . was little encouraged, less admired, & therefore was seldom seen'.[1] One of the pieces in the collection was a mock-heroic poem in three cantos, dedicated to Sir Edward: clearly inspired by Pope's *The Rape of the Lock*, 'The Adventures of a Pin' includes various episodes set in the London of fashionable beaux and beauties seen through the satirical eyes of three young authoresses. Mary's father, Theophilus, the Master of Balliol, described his niece Cassandra (the future Mrs George Austen) as 'already the poet of the family' at the age of six; and although the remark was presumably intended as a kindly avuncular joke, it turned out to be distinctly prophetic.

No poems written by the young Cassandra Leigh have survived, but the verses she wrote for the entertainment of her family and the boys Mr Austen took into Steventon Rectory to prepare for university reveal a delightful wit and considerable metrical skill. When one of her husband's pupils was absent for an unaccountably long time, she sent him a verse letter tempting him back with satirically couched inducements:

> Then pray thee, dear Sir,
> No longer defer
> Your return to the mansion of learning;
> For we study all day,

> (Except when we play)
> And eke when the candles are burning –
>
> Of Dan: Virgil we say
> Two lessons each day;
> The story is quite entertaining;
> You have lost the best part,
> But come, take a good heart,
> Tho' we've read six, there are six books remaining[2]
>   (*Collected Poems*, pp. 25–6)

Mrs Austen's practical, tolerant outlook on life meant that she had little time for grumblers: when another of the boys complained that she never wrote poems for him, she replied with good-humoured crispness:

> The cheerful Muse
> Does here refuse
> To lend her kind assistance;
> She cannot bear
> A serious air,
> So wisely keeps her distance.
>   (*Collected Poems*, p. 27)

And she took the same unsentimental view of her own troubles. Early in 1804, when they were living at 4 Sydney Place, Bath, she was seriously ill; and in a verse she wrote while recuperating, 'Dialogue between Death and M^rs A:', she comically rounds off a genuine expression of gratitude to her family by introducing the name of the apothecary who has been treating her, to complete the rhyme scheme:

> Says Death 'I've been trying these three weeks or more
> To seize on old Madam here at number four,
> Yet I still try in vain, tho she's turn'd of threescore,
> To what is my ill success oweing'?
> I'll tell you, old Fellow, if you cannot guess,
> To what you're indebted for your ill success;
> To the Prayers of my Husband, whose love I possess,
> To the care of my Daughters, whom Heaven will bless;
> To the skill and attention of BOWEN.
>   (*Collected Poems*, p. 30)

Some of Mrs Austen's verses – riddles, charades, bouts-rimés among them – were written as contributions to family games. In one of these the players had to write a poem in which every line rhymed with the word 'rose', and Jane Austen copied out four attempts (she and her mother often made neat copies of verses that they considered worth preserving). Jane Austen's own offering is a wonderful little sketch of a village labourer in his 'Sunday Cloathes' who, 'As oft with conscious pride he downward throws / A glance upon the ample Cabbage rose / Which stuck in Buttonhole regales his nose', happily goes off to church, where he 'Likes best the Prayers whose meaning least he knows, / Lists to the Sermon in a softening Doze, / And rouses joyous at the welcome close' (*Collected Poems*, p. 22). Edward Austen's wife, Elizabeth, clearly daunted by her clever in-laws, approaches the exercise with misgivings that are justified by the lameness of her efforts: 'Never before did I quarrel with a Rose / Till now that I am told some lines to compose, / Of which I shall have little idea God knows!' (*Collected Poems*, p. 23). Cassandra's verse is, perhaps surprisingly, little better: in a misguided attempt to compare love to the wind, it produces an unfortunate assemblage of glowing bosoms and red noses:

Love, they say is like a Rose;
I'm sure tis like the wind that blows,
For not a human creature knows
How it comes or where it goes.
It is the cause of many woes,
It swells the eyes & reds the nose,
And very often changes those
Who once were friends to bitter foes.
But let us now the scene transpose
And think no more of tears & throes.
Why may we not as well suppose
A smiling face the Urchin shows?
And when with joy: the Bosom glows,
And when the heart has full repose,
'Tis Mutual Love the gift bestows.–
(*Collected Poems*, p. 22)

Mrs Austen's contribution is a very different matter: fresh, witty and assured, she is never more successful than when, at the conclusion, she indulges in a piece of quite triumphant self-deprecation:

> This morning I 'woke from a quiet repose,
> I first rub'd my eyes & I next blew my nose.
> With my Stockings & Shoes I then cover'd my toes
> And proceeded to put on the rest of my Cloathes.
> This was finish'd in less than an hour I suppose;
> I employ'd myself next in repairing my hose
> 'Twas a work of necessity, not what I chose;
> Of my sock I'd much rather have knit twenty Rows. –
> My work being done, I looked through the win*dows*
> And with pleasure beheld all the Bucks & the Does,
> The Cows & the Bullocks, the Wethers & Ewes. –
> To the Lib'ry each morn, all the Family goes,
> So I went with the rest, though I felt rather froze.
> My flesh is much warmer, my blood freer flows
> When I work in the garden with rakes & with hoes.
> And now I beleive I must come to a close,
> For I find I grow stupid e'en while I compose;
> If I write any longer my verse will be prose.
>
> (*Collected Poems*, p. 21)

Though most of Mrs Austen's children contributed to these verse games, only one took the writing of poetry seriously. James, the eldest of the family and subsequently his father's successor as rector of Steventon, wrote verses throughout his life, though he never published any, since they were intended for his own circle – an audience who, as he wrote, 'by partial kindness led, / May deem them poetry, & smile applause'.[3] Prologues and epilogues written for the family theatricals of his youth show a lively humour, as do some of the verses he wrote for his own children; two poems written about his daughter Caroline's cat Tyger are particularly delightful, though they have a robustly unsentimental flavour that is wholly characteristic of the period. Having stolen a mutton steak 'reserved for the author's luncheon', the foolhardy animal is threatened with a dire fate at the hands of the farm bailiff:

> should you hence forth any more
> Be caught within the pantry door,
> You then to *Corbet's* shall be sent,
> (Where for her crimes your sister went)
> And he shall shoot you through the head,
> And strip your skin off when you're dead,
> Arid there your fur, as soft as ermine,
> Shall hang midst mean & vulgar vermin;
> Midst stoats & weazels shall have place,
> A lesson to the tabby race;
> That future cats may warning take
> Nor dare to steal a mutton steak.
>
> (*James Austen*, p. 53)

For the rest, James Austen's poetry is largely concerned with the
north Hampshire country that he loved so much, its features
described with a lyricism derived from Thomson and Cowper, and
often observed with an artist's eye (he had taken drawing lessons
during his years at Oxford), as for example in 'Selbourne Hanger':

> 'Tis sweet on such a day as this,
> To stand upon the precipice;
> And view, at first with dazzled eye
> The landscape's wild variety;
> It's objects here in light displayed
> There half concealed in neutral shade . . .
> Delights it then distinct each part
> To trace; and see with master art
> How Nature works when she designs
> How well each object she combines
> Contrasts her forms, and breaks her lines.
>
> (*James Austen*, p. 46)

Jane Austen's love of Cowper and Crabbe can hardly be said to
have had much influence on her verse, since, unlike her brother, she
wrote mainly short, light pieces, often suggested by domestic matters. There are verses to accompany the gift of a work-bag or some
pocket handkerchiefs; inspiration might come from a headache or
a neighbour's visit to the doctor. Sometimes an assumed voice will
be adopted – that of a little girl welcoming a married uncle and his

bride, or even, in 'Alas! poor Brag', the imaginary speech of a card game; and there are several riddles, including of course Mr Elton's very polished charade in *Emma*.

One day Jane Austen's eye was caught by an announcement in the *Hampshire Telegraph and Sussex Chronicle*: 'Sussex, Saturday, February 23, 1811. On Saturday was married, Mr. Gell, of Eastbourn, to Miss Gill, of Well-street, Hackney.' The item was prominently placed at the head of the left-hand column of the third page of the paper, and one can easily imagine the delight with which she seized on the absurd coincidence of the names, and dashed off an ingenious little joke:

> Of Eastbourn, Mr. Gell
> > From being perfectly well
> Became dreadfully ill
> > For the love of Miss Gill.
>
> So he said with some sighs
> > I'm the slave of your i.s
> Ah! restore if you please
> > By accepting my e.s.–
> > > (*Collected Poems*, p. 14)

There were several autograph copies, so she was obviously sufficiently pleased with it to think it worth circulating. Another play on names was provoked by a Mr Best, who for some reason refused to escort her friend Martha Lloyd to Harrogate; his lack of gallantry drew forth a teasing rebuke, and of course his name was a godsend:

> Oh! Mr. Best, you're very bad
> > And all the world shall know it;
> Your base behaviour shall be sung
> > By me, a tuneful Poet.
> > > . . .
> But if you still refuse to go
> > I'll never let you rest,
> But haunt you with reproachful song
> > Oh! wicked Mr. Best! –
> > > (*Collected Poems*, pp. 5–6)

Where some aspect of the public world can occasionally be glimpsed in the verses – for example a Parliamentary bill to authorise the building of the Weald of Kent Canal, or the court martial of the naval commander Home Riggs Popham – there is also a personal concern: her brother Edward's opposition to the former, and the interest in the latter of a family with strong naval ties. But it is in writing about those to whom she was closest that she is at her most tender. In a verse letter to her brother Francis on the birth of a son, she evokes family memories of *him* as a child:

> Thy infant days may he inherit,
> Thy warmth, nay insolence of spirit; –
> We would not with one fault dispense
> To weaken the resemblance.
> May he revive thy Nursery sin,
> Peeping as daringly within,
> (His curley Locks but just descried)
> With, 'Bet, my be not come to bide.'
>
> (*Collected Poems*, p. 11)

In her one attempt to express her feelings seriously in verse, Jane Austen commemorated her friend Madam Lefroy, who was killed in a fall from a horse on Jane Austen's birthday, 16 December 1804; it was the unhappy coincidence of the date that, four years later, prompted the poem. In the final stanza the connection is at once invoked as ground for some kind of mystical union and rejected as being merely fanciful:

> Fain would I feel an union with thy fate,
> Fain would I seek to draw an Omen fair
> From this connection of our Earthly date.
> Indulge the harmless weakness, – Reason, spare. –
>
> (*Collected Poems*, p. 9)

Jane Austen's own death and burial in Winchester Cathedral were marked in a verse of formal mourning by James:

> Venta! within thy sacred fane
> Rests many a chief in battle slain;
> And many a Statesman great & wise
> Beneath thy hallowed pavement lies.

> ...
> Neer did this venerable fane
> More Beauty, Sense & worth contain
> Than when upon a Sister's bier
> Her Brothers dropt the bitter tear.
>
> (*James Austen*, p. 86)

Her nephew James Edward rose to even greater heights of magisterial piety:

> In Venta's consecrated Pile,
>   Where every swelling note,
> Streams softly down the central Aisle,
>   Oer hallow'd graves to float.
>   ...
> Low in that Awe-inspiring Seat,
>   Thou fair, lamented Maid,
> Where Piety and Genius meet,
>   Right justly wert thou laid.
>   ...
> And een to thee, great change shall be,
>   To make thee quite divine,
> The blood that saved a Magdalen's Soul
>   Was shed alike for thine.[4]

Perhaps a truer and more characteristic memorial can be found in Jane Austen's own last poem, also concerned with Winchester, where she had been taken in her final illness. Reading in the newspaper on St Swithun's Day, 15 July, an announcement of the forthcoming races, she concocted an amusing story about the disgruntled Saint and his visiting of rain upon the townspeople as a punishment for their sporting pursuit:

> ... These races & revels & dissolute measures
> With which you're debasing a neighbouring Plain
> Let them stand – you shall meet with your curse
>   in your pleasures
> Set off for your course, I'll pursue with my rain,

Ye cannot but know my command o'er July,
Henceforward I'll triumph in shewing my powers,
Shift your race as you will it shall never be dry
The curse upon Venta is July in showers.

(Collected Poems, pp. 17–18)

These were her last written words; three days later she was dead.

NOTES

1. British Library, RP 3402 (i), fol. 1.
2. See *Jane Austen: Collected Poems and Verse of the Austen Family*, ed. David Selwyn (Manchester: Carcanet, 1996); the volume contains all known poems by Jane Austen and her mother and a selection of verses by other members of the Austen family. Subsequent references in the text to *Collected Poems* are to this edition.
3. See *The Complete Poems of James Austen, Jane Austen's Eldest Brother*, ed. David Selwyn (Chawton: Jane Austen Society, 2003). Subsequent references in the text are to this edition.
4. Autograph MS in the collection of David Gilson, Esq.

8

Portraits

MARGARET KIRKHAM

There is no good, undisputed portrait of Jane Austen and controversy has developed over what there is. Claudia Johnson's 'Fair Maid of Kent?' article began by asking, 'What did Jane Austen look like?' and concluded that we cannot be at all sure, since 'the only unequivocally authentic image we really have [is] that watercolour depicting Austen from behind, wearing a large bonnet.'[1]

Problems about the portraits arise partly from lack of knowledge about many aspects of Austen's life. As her niece, Caroline Austen, wrote to James Edward Austen-Leigh, when he was preparing his 1870 *A Memoir of Jane Austen*: 'I feel it must be a difficult task to dig up the materials, so carefully have they been buried out of our sight by the past generation.'[2] If Jane Austen's siblings concealed a good deal, the next generation followed suit. Kathryn Sutherland says, 'We now know that her nieces and nephew did not tell us the whole truth about Jane Austen and her family as they knew it.'[3] Once all those of the two generations who had known Austen had died, some information relevant to the portraits was gone for good. It is against this background that questions of authenticity and *image* have to be considered and, where certainty is impossible, degrees of probability assessed.

ORIGINAL PORTRAITS
Cassandra Austen's sketches

The 1804 sketch

This is a watercolour drawing, signed C.E.A. (Cassandra Elizabeth Austen) and dated 1804 (see frontispiece). Identification of the sitter as Jane Austen is confirmed in a letter written by her niece, Anna Lefroy, to James Edward Austen-Leigh in 1862, in which 'a sketch which Aunt Cassandra made of her on one of their expeditions – sitting down out of doors on a hot day, with her bonnet strings untied' is mentioned.[4] It is also probably referred to in a letter of Henry Austen to Richard Bentley in 1832, discussed below. After Cassandra's death, this drawing went, with some letters and other items including the unsigned sketch, to Cassy Esten Austen, eldest daughter of Charles Austen, the youngest of Jane and Cassandra's brothers (*Family Record*, p. 280). It is still owned in the Austen family.

R. W. Chapman did his best for this portrait, saying: 'it shows the graceful outline of a seated lady, and has nothing inconsistent with what is known of Jane Austen's figure' (*Facts and Problems*, p. 214). Not everyone agrees; David Nokes says it offers 'a rear view of a plump, dumpy woman seated on a tuft or stool, gazing away from us into a white blankness'.[5] Claudia Johnson has suggested that this faceless sketch has a wry appropriateness; it: 'reaches us in much the same way as the celebrated irony of her writing does, only by turning away' ('Fair Maid', p. 15).

The unsigned sketch *c.* 1810

This is an unfinished pencil and watercolour portrait of a woman, seated on what looks like a country-made stick-back chair. She wears a cap, from which some sort of headband and curls obtrude. The eyes are dark and penetrating and there is a thin-lipped, unsmiling mouth and a severe expression. She wears a light, short-sleeved and high-waisted dress, the arms and hands, crudely drawn, are crossed in an uncompromising manner and the whole attitude of the sitter appears somewhat confrontational (fig. 2).

Although it is unsigned and undated, there are good reasons for accepting that the artist and the sitter are the same as for the earlier sketch. It was not produced in 1833, when Richard Bentley wanted a portrait for a new edition of *Sense and Sensibility*, the first of the Austen novels to appear in his Standard Novels Series. A letter from Henry Austen to Bentley, dated 4 October 1832, includes the following: 'When I saw you in London, I mentioned that a sketch of her had been taken – on further enquiry, & inspection, I find that it was merely the figure and attitude – The countenance was concealed by a veil – nor was there any resemblance of features intended – It was a "Study".'[6] It looks as though Henry had rashly mentioned the existence of a sketch showing Jane Austen's face, and then had to back down, possibly because Cassandra would not sanction

Figure 2. 'Cassandra Austen's Unsigned Sketch' (*c.* 1810).

publication, or because they jointly decided against it. There is something evasive here, for although the 1804 signed sketch does not show the sitter's face, there is no 'veil', only a large bonnet and some billowing bonnet strings. The inaccuracy may betray a decision to draw a veil over the unsigned sketch. What Henry Austen wrote in his revised 'Biographical Notice', re-entitled 'Memoir of Miss Austen', and published with the new edition of *Sense and Sensibility*, avoids an outright denial that a portrait showing her face existed. All he does is to quote, without comment, from an article by Maria Jewsbury, which had appeared in the *Athenaeum* in 1831: 'So retired, so unmarked by literary notoriety, was the life Miss Austen led, *that if any likeness was ever taken of her, none has ever been engraved*'. An editor's note hardens this into 'No likeness ever was taken of Miss Austen', which has often been taken to mean 'no professional likeness' (*Memoir*, p. 259n, my emphasis), though this is a matter of interpretation. Taking both the letter to Bentley and the guarded wording in the 'Memoir' into account, it seems likely that Henry Austen knew of both sketches, though he was not open about them.

Both sketches were entrusted to Cassy Esten Austen, to whom Cassandra had been close in her later years. Documentation is lacking as to what, if anything, Cassy had been told about them, but she evidently believed this one to be a portrait of Jane by Cassandra, and offered it as such to her first cousin, James Edward Austen-Leigh, when he wanted a portrait for *A Memoir of Jane Austen*, published in 1870 (*Family Record*, p. 280). Its authenticity rests on its having passed directly from Cassandra Austen to one of her nieces, and its acceptance by one nephew and three nieces, all old enough to have known the novelist. What was done with it is discussed below under 'Imaginary portraits'.

Cassandra's unsigned sketch remained in the possession of descendants of Charles Austen until around 1920. It was bought by the National Portrait Gallery in 1948. Why it was not produced or openly referred to in 1832 is not known, but it is easy to see that this portrait does not match the 1833 'Memoir'. The woman depicted here does not look as though she would be entirely 'submissive to criticism', either 'in the bosom of her family', or anywhere else, and she looks perfectly capable of uttering the odd 'hasty, silly or severe expression'. R. W. Chapman did not like this portrait, but many later comments have been more favourable. Helen Denman said, 'Slight and unfinished as it is, it gives the impression that here is a real, unflattering picture of a real person.'[7] The 'testy scepticism, the tough personality, the alertness of the picture by Cassandra' are acknowledged by Margaret Anne Doody and Douglas Murray.[8] The identity of the sitter and artist are not in serious doubt, though how good a likeness Cassandra Austen caught, is. The contrast between the visual image, privately preserved by

Austen's sister, and the verbal image published by her brother, is striking.

The Rice portrait, previously known as the 'Zoffany Portrait'

This is a professional oil painting of an attractive, fashionably dressed girl, whose age is difficult to determine. She has not yet developed a bosom, but has the face and expression of a somewhat knowing adolescent. She looks out at us directly, with dark eyes and a mouth suggesting an amused insouciance. It is a visual image which fits what is known of the young Jane Austen from the irreverent skits she began writing when she was only twelve. As such, it has attracted a number of literary scholars and critics, including Claudia Johnson and Margaret Anne Doody, interested in the authenticity of the Austen image in general. The portrait has now been so widely reproduced and argued over, that it can probably be said to have been incorporated into the image, whether it is actually a likeness of Jane Austen or not.

Documentation about this portrait begins late. There is no known written reference to it before 1880, when its owner at the time, Dr Harding Newman of Magdalen College Oxford, wrote to a friend about his wish to give a 'painting of Jane Austen the novelist by Zoffany to her relative, your neighbour Morland Rice. It is of a girl about fifteen & came into my family, the gift of Col. Austen of Chippington [Kippington] to my mother-in-law, or rather my stepmother; my father's second wife, who was a great admirer of the novelist' ('Literary Portrait', p. 513) The intended beneficiary was John Morland Rice, born in 1823, a grandson of Jane Austen's brother, Edward [Austen] Knight, who received it in 1883. The portrait is still privately owned in the Rice family.

There is no reason to doubt Harding Newman's account of how he came to own the painting, but he was wrong about the artist and may have been wrong about the sitter. There is no record of what Colonel Austen actually said about it when he disposed of it, probably in 1817, more than sixty years earlier. Nor do we know if he was both correctly informed and truthful about it. Once it was returned to family ownership, the painting was speedily accepted as what Harding Newman said it was: 'Jane Austen painted by Zoffany'. It was reproduced by a number of family biographers and others from 1884 until the 1920s. Serious scholarly research had scarcely begun, when in 1932, R. W. Chapman's *Jane Austen's Letters* was published, with Cassandra's rear view sketch as its frontispiece. Chapman writes, 'I have preferred it to the two known portraits of Jane which are familiar' (p. xxxv). No reason is given, but in view of statements made later, it may be inferred that he disliked Cassandra's unsigned sketch and had doubts about the authenticity of the 'Zoffany'. When his *Jane Austen, Facts and Problems* came out in 1948, it included a somewhat bleak Appendix on 'The Portraits'. Chapman had been instrumental in getting the National Portrait Gallery to buy Cassandra's unsigned sketch, but makes clear his dislike of 'this disappointing scratch', and rules out the Rice portrait on the grounds that it 'can be dated by the costume to about 1805 (when Jane Austen was thirty) or later' (pp. 214–15). He avoids discussing weaknesses in the history of the painting, merely saying, 'It had a pedigree (see *Life*, 63)[9] that any layman might think watertight.' The implication, however, is that Chapman thought it had holes in it. He did not specify what they were. To do so would amount to an attack on a family tradition, and Chapman was deferential to the Austen family and its traditions. If the expert opinion of well-accredited art historians was sufficient, nothing else needed to be said. It *was* sufficient, more or less, for nearly half a century. Dissident voices were sometimes to be heard in the annual *Reports* of the Jane Austen Society,[10] but there was no serious dispute about it until the last decade of the century. Since then the Rice portrait has been much publicised and its claims to authenticity reasserted.[11]

Weaknesses in its 'pedigree' are: firstly, the total absence of biographical evidence that Jane Austen ever sat for an expensive professional portrait. This, of course, does not prove that she did not do so, but it is remarkable, if she did, that it is not mentioned in any of the surviving letters, nor any of the biographical writings or extant letters of anyone who had known her. If she was singled out in this way, it would have been an out-of-the-ordinary event, bound to be known and remarked on in her family. A silence of nearly ninety years needs a convincing explanation. The case is different from the secrecy about Cassandra's unsigned sketch, where either the artist's awareness of her limitations, or the unflattering severity of her portrayal, might reasonably account for it. It is possible that an explanation will be found, once further research on the relations between the Kippington and Steventon Austens is published. Secondly, by the time John Morland Rice received the portrait and began to make enquiries about it, everyone in the family who had known Jane Austen was dead, apart from Cassy Esten Austen, and there is no record of her having been consulted. Fanny Caroline Lefroy, Anna's daughter, born in 1820, and regarded by then as the most knowledgeable of the third generation, wrote to her cousin, Mary Augusta Austen-Leigh, in October 1883, 'I never heard before of the portrait of Jane Austen' ('Literary Portrait', p. 513). What she is reported to have said, almost a year later, when she was interviewed by Henry Morland Austen on behalf of the new owner, does not include any clear contradiction of this ignorance. 'She knew before of the painting in your possession' may mean only that she knew of it from about eleven months before the interview. 'Except for one or two difficulties she would have no doubts about its genuineness' implies that she *did* have doubts. What they were is not recorded.[12] Fanny Caroline died a few months later. Such family traditions as there are about this portrait appear to have come into being after 1880.

It is accepted on all sides that the Rice portrait was not painted by Zoffany. George Romney, John Hoppner and Sir Thomas Lawrence have variously been mentioned, but an attribution to Ozias Humphry, who was commissioned to paint a portrait of Jane Austen's great-uncle, Francis Austen of Sevenoaks, is frequently quoted. If Humphry is the artist, the picture must have been painted before 1797, by which time he had become blind. Deirdre Le Faye, who believes that Francis Austen's great-granddaughter, Mary Anne Campion, born in 1797, is the girl depicted, suggests Matthew William Peters as the artist ('Literary Portrait').

The date of the painting is still the decisive issue. Evidence about dating from dress and style has been disputed, but Aileen Ribeiro of the Courtauld Institute, and a long line of other historians of portraiture and costume, have ruled out a date earlier than 1800. Jacob Simon, the present Chief Curator of the National Portrait Gallery, has cited evidence about the date of the canvas, from which he concludes: 'The painting therefore cannot date to before 1801, and probably dates to the period 1801 to 1806 or soon after.'[13]

SILHOUETTES
The Collins silhouette

This is a hollow-cut silhouette showing the right profile of a woman's head. It was found pasted into volume 2 of a second edition of *Mansfield Park* (John Murray, 1816) with a hand-written inscription, 'L'aimable Jane'. Bought by the National Portrait Gallery in 1944, it is tentatively attributed to Mrs Collins, a professional profilist who worked in Bath in the late eighteenth and early nineteenth century, and dated about 1801. Richard Walker, in his 1985 *Regency Portraits*, a catalogue of items in the National Portrait Gallery, says, 'The identity is not absolutely proven', which is certainly the case.

The Lefroy silhouette

Given by Jessie and Louie Lefroy, great-grandnieces of Jane Austen, to Winchester Cathedral, probably in the late 1930s, it shows the left-profile of a woman's head. The nose is decidedly beakier than in the Collins Silhouette. It is inscribed on the back, 'Jane Austin [*sic*] done by herself in 1815'. Deirdre Le Faye, who examined the silhouette in 1995, found the inscription was written in modern blue-black ink and that the handwriting was probably twentieth century. She believes 'that the sitter is the Victorian Miss Jane Austen (1849–1927) and that the silhouette should date to 1895 rather than 1815'.[14]

OTHER ITEMS

These are two drawings, catalogued as portraits of Jane Austen by Christie's in a sale of Godmersham House and its contents in June 1983. They disappeared into private ownership, nothing having been published on them since. It is unlikely, on the evidence available, that the cataloguing was reliable.

There is an amateur watercolour, known as the Stanier Clarke watercolour, of a full-length female figure, pasted into James Stanier Clarke's 'Friendship Book' and publicised by its owner, Richard Wheeler, as a portrait of Jane Austen.[15] Clear evidence supporting this identification has not so far been published.

IMAGINARY PORTRAITS

The Andrews portrait

J. E. Austen-Leigh and his collaborators found Cassandra's unsigned sketch unsatisfactory and commissioned James Andrews of Maidenhead to create a new image of Jane Austen, to be engraved for the 1870 *Memoir*.[16] It was meant to make Aunt Jane presentable to the Victorian public. The Andrews watercolour drawing softens the features and changes the attitude. The arms are no longer crossed defiantly; the eyes have lost their harsh stare, and the stick-like chair of the original is replaced by a later, more expensive-looking one. The Lizars steel engraving completes the process of creating a decently decorous, Victorian Austen: the eyes look larger and still milder, the mouth becomes full-lipped and the expression gentle (fig. 3). Cassy Esten Austen's comment is acute: 'It is a very pleasing, sweet face, – tho', I confess, to not thinking it *much* like the original' (*Family Record*, p. 280). It was, perhaps, an appropriate frontispiece to the *Memoir*. The anachronism of the Andrews portrait strikes even those, like Helen Denman, who think it 'charming' ('The Portraits', p. 342). Claudia Johnson speaks of its 'gruesome quaintness' ('Fair Maid', p. 14).

Improvement of the Cassandra sketch did not stop with Andrews. As early as 1873, 'The Wedding Ring Portrait' was engraved for Evert A. Duyckink's *Portrait Gallery of Eminent Men and Women of Europe and America*. Based on Andrews, it shows a less demure and more elegant Austen, her left arm resting on a large writer's notebook and a wedding ring on her left hand. Her chair is hidden by silk drapery and she seems to have put on a bit of weight. This portrait was used as recently as June 2003 to illustrate a *Guardian* article. The Andrews Austen inspires the lavender-bag and tea-towel Jane of the tourist circuit and, more enjoyably, caricatures like the 'Jane Austen in Hollywood' posted on an Internet site, the Andrews head on a figure in a bikini, lounging in a deck chair beside a swimming pool, with a pile of books at her feet. 'Author and Authenticity' would not have been a bad title for one of them. With digital manipulation of visual images, we are into a new era of imaginary portraits, some of which may be entertaining. The use of forensic techniques (E-Fit likenesses) looks less promising. A bizarre new portrait of Jane Austen, by police

JANE AUSTEN.

Figure 3. The Lizars steel engraving, made from James Andrews's improvement of 'Cassandra's Sketch', published as frontispiece to J. E. Austen-Leigh's 1870 *A Memoir of Jane Austen*.

artist Melissa Dring, can be seen at the Jane Austen Centre in Bath.

NOTES

1. Claudia Johnson, 'Fair Maid of Kent? The Arguments For and Against the Rice Portrait of Jane Austen', *Times Literary Supplement* (13 March 1998), 13–15. Subsequent references are included in the text.
2. Deirdre Le Faye, *Jane Austen: A Family Record*, second edition (Cambridge: Cambridge University Press, 2004), p. 276. Subsequent references are included in the text.
3. *A Memoir of Jane Austen and Other Family Recollections*, ed. Kathryn Sutherland (Oxford: Oxford University Press, 2002), p. xxxiii. Subsequent references are included in the text.
4. R. W. Chapman, *Jane Austen, Facts and Problems* (Oxford: Clarendon Press, 1948), p. 213. Subsequent references are included in the text.
5. David Nokes, *Jane Austen, A Life* (London: Fourth Estate, 1997), p. 246.
6. Deirdre Le Faye, 'A Literary Portrait Re-Examined, Jane Austen and Mary Anne Campion', *The Book Collector* 45:4 (Winter, 1996), 509. Subsequent references are included in the text.
7. Helen Denman, 'The Portraits', in *The Jane Austen Companion*, eds. J. David Grey, A. Walton Litz, Brian Southam (New York: Macmillan, 1986), p. 342. Subsequent references are included in the text.
8. Margaret Anne Doody and Douglas Murray, *A Portrait of Jane Austen* (privately printed, 1995), p. 13.
9. W. and R. A. Austen-Leigh, *Jane Austen, her Life and Letters* (1913).
10. Constance Pilgrim in 1974, Madeleine Marsh in 1985.
11. Doody and Murray, *A Portrait of Jane Austen*; Richard James Wheeler, *The Rice Portrait of Jane Austen* (Sevenoaks: Codex Publications, 1996); Richard James Wheeler and Margaret Hammond, *The Rice Portrait of Jane Austen* (Sevenoaks: Codex Publications, 1997); Marilyn Butler, entry on Jane Austen in *The Oxford Dictionary of National Biography* (Oxford: Oxford University Press 2004), pp. 972–3. For further debates in the *Annual Reports* of the Jane Austen Society see: *Annual Reports* for 1973, 'The Zoffany Portrait', 11–14; *Annual Reports* for 1974, Constance Pilgrim, 'The Zoffany Portrait: a Re-Appraisal', 12–17; *Annual Reports* for 1983, Sir Oliver Millar, 'A Note on

the "Zoffany" Portrait', Gordon Holbert Tucker, 'The Hancock Miniature and Mr Andrews of Maidenhead'; *Annual Reports* for 1985, Madeleine Marsh, 'Ozias Humphry and the Austens of Sevenoaks' and 'The Portrait', 22–29; *Annual Reports* for 1991, Pauline Elliott, 'The Zoffany Portrait'.

12. Wheeler, 'Rice Portrait', pp. 31–2.
13. *Times Literary Supplement* (18 December 1998).
14. Deirdre Le Faye, unpublished notes.
15. *Daily Telegraph* (4 March 1995), 'James Stanier Clarke and his Watercolour Portrait of Jane Austen'.
16. For the artist's first name see David Gilson, *Jane Austen Collated Articles and Introductions* (privately printed, 1998), pp. 100–1.

PART II

Critical fortunes

9

Critical responses, early

MARY WALDRON

The first decade or so of Jane Austen commentary corresponds to a gradual but distinct change in attitude to the novel genre and to novelists; it might be argued that this change was in great measure due to efforts made during the period to analyse and appreciate a somewhat puzzling newcomer to the fictional scene. Reviewers had become accustomed to treating the novels which came under their scrutiny with a degree of contempt; some might be better than others, but they were on the whole hardly worth serious consideration. More than sixty years after Johnson's authoritative statement in *Rambler* 4 there still lingered a necessity for fiction to appear to preach a direct and unequivocal moral lesson in order to be saved from condemnation as, at best, trivial escapism, at worst, moral depravity. On this basis some novels were regarded with respect – those of Frances Burney, for instance, and the early fiction of Charlotte Smith. But a host of later novels seemed opportunistic in their overt appeal to the unthinking mass of readers, and were for this reason often denounced by reviewers. Lachrymose fiction deriving from Rousseau and Mackenzie, ever more sensational Radcliffean Gothic, and, as the conflict with revolutionary France got under way, novels used for political propaganda, both radical and conservative, 'Jacobin' and 'anti-Jacobin', all attracted criticism from some commentators, often on the grounds of improbability or sensationalism. Jane Austen's first published novel could obviously not be charged with either fault; if anything it seemed by comparison rather bland and unexciting. Early reviewers were somewhat at a loss as to how it should be judged.

Sense and Sensibility was advertised as an 'extraordinary novel' in the *Morning Chronicle* in 1811, the year of its publication, and reviewers were aware that they were faced with something unusual, but at first they hardly had the means to take up the challenge. Individual readers, as is evidenced by a mass of informal comment in letters and diaries, were often intrigued and enthusiastic,[1] but more public commentators, though they invariably wrote anonymously, felt it incumbent upon them to be cautious. There is a tentativeness, even diffidence, about the first extant review of *Sense and Sensibility*, published in the *Critical Review* in February 1812, three months after the appearance of the novel, which reflects continuing doubts about the value of fiction in general.[2] The reviewer adopts a tone of patronising condescension which implies that he really has little use for the material he is recommending. 'We are no enemies to novels or novel writers, but we regret, that in the multiplicity of them, there are so few worthy of any particular commendation.' *Sense and Sensibility*, he suggests, is only better than most; a well-written novel can be 'an agreeable lounge . . . from which both amusement and instruction may be derived'; and this one 'happily blends a great deal of good sense with the lighter matter of the piece'. In the process of recommending this 'trifling' story to 'our fair readers' (at this stage novel readers are supposed, quite erroneously, to be exclusively female) he simplifies the novel into a straightforward warning against cads like Willoughby, missing, or ignoring, the complexity of his character and motivation and the subtleties of the interaction between the two sisters.

Another review of *Sense and Sensibility* which appeared in the *British Critic* in May of the same year is even more exclusively concerned with the moral lesson to be gained; the characters of Elinor and Marianne are flattened into lifeless representatives of the opposing virtue and vice apparently inherent in the title: 'Two sisters are placed before the reader, similarly circumstanced in point of education and accomplishments, exposed to similar trials, but the one by a sober exertion of prudence and judgement sustains with fortitude, and overcomes with success, what plunges the other into an abyss of vexation, sorrow and disappointment . . .' Willoughby is again represented as a 'male coquet' with nothing but evil designs on Marianne, and overall the reviewer reduces the novel to the level of heavily didactic stories based on popular conduct books. Towards the end there comes the inevitable assurance of the moral usefulness of 'these volumes' to 'our female friends': 'they may learn from them, if they please, many sober and salutary maxims for the conduct of life'. Both reviewers are well aware that they are dealing with something different and more arresting than the general run of novels, but they are at a loss to explain that difference, except in terms of its value as a fictionalised conduct manual.

These two periodicals also reviewed *Pride and Prejudice* soon after publication in January 1813. There is by this time a perceptible difference of approach – the reviewers are less chary of analysing the novel's impact. The *British Critic* (February 1813) uses words like 'spirit' and 'vigour' and is aware of the complexity, for instance, of Mr Bennet's character. He states without reserve that the novel 'is very far superior to almost all the publications of the kind which have lately come before us'; there is no mention of instruction. To be delighted seems, for this reviewer at least, to be enough.

The *Critical Review* comments on the novel (March 1813) at much greater length, and in a relaxed and relishing style that is conspicuously different from the reviews of *Sense and Sensibility*. But delight is not quite enough; this reviewer edges into traditional literary-critical analysis, approving of the unity of the novel and its dramatic qualities: 'There is not one person in the drama with whom we could readily dispense; – they have all their proper places . . .' He relates Elizabeth to Shakespeare's Beatrice and Wickham to Sheridan's Joseph Surface – an early indication of increasing respect. Still, even he cannot forbear to point out a useful moral: 'the work also shows the folly of letting young girls have their own way'. This comment, however, coming as it does towards the end of the piece, seems almost an afterthought – the statutory reassurance to anxious parents concerned about the trumpeted dangers of novel reading, especially for young girls.

Another notice of *Pride and Prejudice* appeared in the *New Review* of April 1813.[3] It is little more than a hasty plot summary and consciously avoids judgement, leaving readers to 'form their estimate of the author's talents' from an extract from chapter 31 – Elizabeth's challenge to Darcy on the subject of his unsociability.

In 1815 Walter Scott was commissioned by John Murray to review a novel he was about to publish 'by the author of *Pride and Prejudice*', *Emma*. The review appeared anonymously in *The Quarterly Review* in March 1816. Scott chose this opportunity to place Austen's work, including *Emma*, within the novel-writing tradition of the time, not only giving a considered estimate of the quality of her writing, but also taking an important step towards a viable analysis of the contemporary state of fiction.

He argues cogently that until recently 'modern' fiction had not progressed very far beyond the fantasies of old romance. Though the 'hero no longer defeated armies by his single sword, clove giants to the chine, or gained kingdoms' he was still 'expected to go through perils by sea and land, to be steeped in poverty, to be tried by temptation'. As for the heroine, she was 'regularly exposed to being carried off like a Sabine virgin', or if not, 'she had still her share of wandering, of poverty, of obloquy, of seclusion, and of imprisonment, and was frequently extended on a bed of sickness, and reduced to her last shilling before the author condescended to shield her from persecution'. It is easy to identify some of those novels that Scott has in mind here – not only the recent 'Gothic' fiction, but also *Tom Jones*, Frances Burney's *Cecilia*, Charlotte Smith's *Emmeline*, Mary Brunton's *Self-Control* and Burney's last novel *The Wanderer*, amongst many others.

In competition with these, a new kind of novel, Scott says, had 'within the last fifteen or twenty years' been coming into fashion, 'presenting to the reader, instead of the splendid scenes of an imaginary world, a correct and striking representation of that which is daily taking place around him'. But he doubted whether they had succeeded. Though such novelists as West, Hamilton, Edgeworth and others strove to foreground ordinary family life, they on the whole seemed unable to resist heightening the excitement by the inclusion of well-worn stereotypes. Scott perceived that Austen had contrived, exceptionally, to rid her fiction of these. She had, he asserts, 'produced sketches of such spirit and originality, that we never miss the excitation which depends upon a narrative of uncommon events, arising from the consideration of minds, manners, and sentiments, greatly above our own'. The author of *Emma* 'stands almost alone' in this; though he does not say so outright, he clearly perceives her as an original.

This, though, is the extent of his own critical originality, for he flounders somewhat when he attempts to analyse the impact of this fiction, which appears to have so little in the way of story to give reader satisfaction. The best he can do is to recommend its 'precision' – a word he uses several times – and its similarity to 'the Flemish school of painting': 'The subjects are not often elegant, and certainly never grand; but they are finished up to nature, and with a precision which delights the reader.' This is only to say that the novels *entertain* in a different way from their predecessors – there seems to be little appreciation of any serious dimension to the problems which afflict the protagonists. Significantly, he omits all mention of *Mansfield Park*, which he must have known about, probably even read; perhaps the painful dilemmas of Fanny Price simply would not fit the rather static pastoral nature of the fiction as he perceived it. This omission is a strong sign that the puzzle of Austen's achievement had not yet been really confronted. Indeed, Scott finally falls back on the moral issue: 'the youthful wanderer may return from his promenade to the ordinary business of life, without any chance of having his head turned by the recollection of the scene through which he has been wandering' – as much as to say that the novels are harmless, but nothing much more.

But whatever its minor deficiencies, Scott's review must be admired for its honest attempt to escape from some of the dismissive assessments of the past. Not so with other reviews which appeared at about the same time. The reviewer of the *Champion* (31 March 1816)[4] reduces the narrative of *Emma* to a single strand, entirely omitting to mention the Frank Churchill/Jane Fairfax situation and its subtle impact on the assumptions and actions of all the other characters. He admires what he calls the 'light satire' involved in the 'oddities' of Miss Bates and Mr Woodhouse, but he takes John and Isabella Knightley straight and seriously as an 'estimable pair' and actually congratulates the author on having the courage and skill to represent 'unpretending goodness'. It is perhaps too soon to expect a recognition of the peculiar Austen brand of irony, and in any case, this reviewer still needs to identify models for the moral improvement of the reader. In May an anonymous reviewer in the *Augustan Review* complains of the 'remarkable sameness in the productions of this author'. He also, however, finds a good moral: we are to gain from *Emma* a 'rational view of happiness' as grounded in duty and the 'social affections'. He professes to enjoy the humour of Miss Bates and Mr Woodhouse, but remarks devastatingly towards the end that 'we cannot but think that a greater variety of incidents would, in such hands as hers, well supply the place of some of the colloquial familiarity and minuteness to which she has hitherto too much confined herself' – tantamount to a negation of any praise he may have given and asking for a totally different novel. Both these reviews testify to the rising interest in

Austen's work, though there is still considerable uncertainty as to what, if anything, distinguishes it from the ubiquitous fiction of the time.

Five more reviews were published later in the year. In June the reviewer of *Literary Panorama* says virtually nothing about the story except that it 'presents the history of a young lady, who, after allowing her imagination to wander towards several gentlemen . . . fixes them at last on the proper object' – than which nothing could be more inaccurate. He concedes that the story is 'not ill-conceived', but complains, rather obscurely, that the 'gentlemen are rather unequal to what gentlemen should be'. In July the *Monthly Review* is more perceptive, but still very brief. The writer admires the humour and approves of its combination with a useful moral: 'The fair reader may also glean by the way some useful hints against forming romantic schemes'. In default of any real engagement with the way this fiction is operating, the reviewer falls back on instruction as its most valuable object.

In the same month the *British Critic* admires Austen's use of unity of place, marvelling at the way in which she has confined the action to so small a space and yet retained the interest of the reader. In September the *Gentleman's Magazine* reverts to condescension: 'a good Novel is now and then an agreeable relaxation from severer studies'. He admires, though, the preservation of the unities of time and place, and the care taken to make even the minor characters recognisable and real.

So far the reaction of reviewers has been generally more positive than otherwise; a review published in the *British Lady's Magazine and Monthly Miscellany* in September 1816 is sharply challenging. The reviewer pairs *Emma* with Amelia Opie's *St. Valentine's Eve*, giving both novels as examples of the authors' failed attempts to repeat past successes. The author of *Emma*, she says (one supposes that this reviewer is, exceptionally, female), can hardly expect to go on mining the resources of 'country society' and 'middling gentry' for ever. The best she can say of the novel is that it is 'not only readable, but pleasantly so', but would be better if there were considerably less of Miss Bates. She accuses Austen of 'thinking a foolish character will always entertain because it is natural'.

Jane Austen's death in 1817, the posthumous publication of *Northanger Abbey and Persuasion*, and Henry Austen's 'Biographical

Notice' all understandably made a difference to the tone of comment thereafter. But the somewhat hushed respect for the deceased Christian lady writer evoked by her brother's eulogy fortunately did not prevent reviewers of her last published works from beginning to identify some of the distinguishing features of her fiction, as well as finding some fault with it. The reviewer of the *British Critic* of March 1818 considers her 'extremely deficient in imagination'. He considers that she depends 'exclusively on experience'. But he may be the first to light upon Austen's ironic social criticism – 'our authoress never dips her pen in satire; the follies which she holds up to us are, for the most part, mere follies, or else natural imperfections; and she treats them, as such, with good-humoured pleasantry'. Most of this review is concerned with *Northanger Abbey*, which he regards as the better of the two works. He is dubious about the morality of *Persuasion*. Its message seems to him to be that 'young people should always marry according to their own inclinations and upon their own judgement' – his disapprobation of which is absolutely all he has to say.

May 1818 produced another review of *Northanger Abbey and Persuasion* in the *Edinburgh Review and Literary Miscellany*.[5] In direct disagreement with the preceding reviewer this one identifies 'exhaustless invention' in Austen's work; he appreciates without reserve the combination of the recognisable and the surprising in the situations that Austen creates. Curiously – and he is more or less alone in this – he sees her fiction as reverting to an earlier model exemplified in Richardson and Fielding, before public taste had been vitiated, as he saw it, by the sensationalism of Scott and Byron.

So far doubts and reservations had tempered the admiration of most reviewers. These were almost entirely swept away by Richard Whately in *The Quarterly Review* of January 1821. His serious and considered estimate makes most earlier commentary look vague and inconclusive, and sets the tone for later Austen commentary as well as placing the novel form decisively in the mainstream of literature. First quoting part of Scott's 1816 opinion in the same periodical, he goes much further, supplying what Scott may have recognised but does not clearly analyse. Whately relates Austen to acknowledged 'great' writers from Homer to Shakespeare. He invokes Aristotle's dictum that imaginative literature, especially narrative, is more valuable than history and biography, in that it deals with what is probable, rather than actual events, which may have no general application. Readers of novels, he says, are being presented with 'a kind of artificial experience' which is capable of affording them deep insights into human nature. Two things, however, are necessary for success; the probability of the narrative must be absolute – no coincidence or *deus ex machina* can be allowed; and any moral instruction must come obliquely to the reader's consciousness to be effective: 'If instruction', he says, 'do not join as a volunteer, she will do no good service.' He proceeds to compare 'Miss Austin's' work favourably on both counts with that of popular contemporary novelists such as Hannah More and Maria Edgeworth, both of whom, he thinks, sacrifice probability in favour of an 'avowedly didactic purpose'. Unlike them, Austen appears to stand aside and allow readers to 'collect' any moral lessons for themselves, never deviating from the strict probabilities of everyday experience; nor does she set up models ('Miss Austin does not deal in fiends or angels') but shows even Fanny Price to be driven in many ways by 'the influence of strong passion, [which] must alloy the purest mind, but with which scarcely any *authoress* but Miss Austin would have ventured to temper the atheriel materials of a heroine'. In his careful and sensitive analysis of *Persuasion* he goes further: the conclusion of the novel deliberately leaves moral questions unanswered, as they so often are in real life.

In his lengthy and appreciative commentary, Whately identifies what had so far eluded reviewers – that the novel must henceforth be taken seriously; Jane Austen's devotion to the ordinary, recognisable, often chaotic doings of everyday life had shown, perhaps for the first time, how fiction could not only enthral without seeking to astonish, but also enlighten without the need to preach.

NOTES

1. For discussion of this material see Charles Beecher Hogan, 'Jane Austen and her Early Public', *Review of English Studies* 1:1 (1950), 38–54, and William H. Galperin, *The Historical Austen* (Philadelphia: Pennsylvania University Press, 2003), esp. 'Austen's Earliest Readers', pp. 61–75.
2. Unless otherwise indicated, the reviews here cited may be found in their entirety in B. C. Southam (ed.), *Jane Austen: the Critical*

Heritage: Vol. 1: 1811–1870 (London: Routledge & Kegan Paul, 1968).

3. See Nicholas A. Joukovsky, 'Another Unnoted Contemporary Review of Jane Austen', *Nineteenth-Century Fiction* 29 (1974–5), 336–8.
4. See William S. Ward, 'Three Hitherto Unnoted Contemporary Reviews of Jane Austen', *Nineteenth-Century Fiction* 26 (1971–2), 469–77.
5. This review is erroneously attributed to *Blackwood's Edinburgh Magazine* in Southam, *Critical Heritage*, p. 266. See Ward, 'Three Unnoted Reviews', 469n.

10

Critical responses, 1830–1970

NICOLA TROTT

Jane Austen's posthumous reputation depends to an extent on whether her readers belong to the nineteenth or to the twentieth century. On one side of this rough-and-ready divide, Austen is treated primarily as a particular kind of person; on the other, as a controlling sort of idea. By those in the earlier period (the Victorians especially), she is admired for her characters and comedy – the comedy, that is, of social manners. By those in the later, she is important, not because of the characters she creates, but because of the ethos or criticism she offers. The former approach tends to the institution of Janeites; the latter to a reaction against that type of enthusiasm. The first evolves out of the 'Aunt Jane' who was known to her contemporaries and more widely promoted, after her death, by the first major event of her posthumous life, the publication by her nephew Austen-Leigh of the *Memoir of Jane Austen* (1870). The second establishes a resistance to 'Jane', and demands that Austen be regarded, not as a social comedian, but as a morally significant author. For the Leavises – Q. D. and F. R. – Jane Austen is no longer the exquisite watercolourist of society, but beginning to have a critical purchase upon it. It is her 'intense moral preoccupation' – a 'principle of organization' in the work which derives from the 'problems that life compels on her' – that makes her 'a great novelist'.[1]

These changes in attitude seem to be marked by a turn from Life to Work, and from woman to writer. The life-story was tenacious, partly because it emerged only belatedly with the *Memoir*, partly because of a gendered response which linked the liking for Austen to her perceived lack of authorial identity. To notice a writerly aspect was comparatively rare even in 1885, when Leslie Stephen did so in his landmark entry for the *Dictionary of National Biography*. The shift in appreciation coincided with the advent of the modern novel – Woolf, Forster and James all comment – but a critical stance on Austen was acquired, it might be said, just as the criticism of English literature itself became an academic discipline. A lecture of A. C. Bradley's, delivered to the women of Newnham College, Cambridge, and printed in *Essays and Studies* (1911), is 'generally regarded', says B. C. Southam, 'as the starting-point for the serious academic approach to Jane Austen'.[2] This Austen is a 'moralist' as well as a 'humorist', influenced by Johnson on the one hand and 'the drama' on the other. Bradley divides the novels into two groups of three, directs readers also to the letters and unfinished fiction and compares *Pride and Prejudice*, which he prefers, to *Mansfield Park*, which he judges the greater work, for its 'seriousness' and for having 'deeply at heart the importance of certain truths about conduct', while being 'at the same time artistic'.[3] The University of Oxford, where Bradley held a Chair, went on taking Austen seriously: the University Press published in Mary Lascelles's Bradley-inspired *Jane Austen and her Art* (1939) the first full-scale historical and scholarly study; and the highwater-mark came in 1966 with Gilbert Ryle's 'Jane Austen and the Moralists', which attributes to the novelist a 'moral system', 'a secular, Aristotelian ethic-cum-aesthetic' indebted perhaps to Shaftesbury.[4] For Lionel Trilling, writing from the American academy at Columbia, Austen is a moralist still, but of a different kind, one who describes the good place, not – as the Leavisites would have it – one who is on the side of life. Trilling's choice of novel is symptomatic: for him, as for Bradley, it is *Mansfield Park* that matters most – a line of reading that persists right up to the 'incredible moral strength' admired by Tony Tanner in 1968.[5] The earlier favourites, loved for their characters and comedy, had been *Emma* and *Pride and Prejudice*.

The longer term movement in modern Austen criticism leads from Bradley to Butler. While this can also be described as a movement from idealism to historicism, and to that extent be seen as impelled by opposed systems of thought, the understanding of the fiction as fundamentally moral is in fact common to both. If Bradley had to counter the Victorian consensus of Austen as a social comic, Butler saw herself as breaking in upon the 'narrowly aesthetic' Austen who had been extricated from the 'partisan' and directly political engagements by which her conservative fiction was truly energised.[6] Butler's confrontation with Austen's a-historical or amoral appreciators – such as John Bayley, in 'The Irresponsibility of Jane Austen' (*Critical Essays*, pp. 1–20) – is grounded in the ideological debates of the 1790s. Another lasting influence in this sphere has been Alistair M. Duckworth's, in considering Austen's Burkean 'concern over the . . . continuity of the social structure' – for which *Mansfield Park* is once again central – and 'the estate as . . . a metonym for other inherited structures – society as a whole, a code of morality, a body of manners, a system of language'.[7] Together these critics have provided a basis for much of the historical work that has dominated recent criticism. But the role of historicism in Austen criticism itself has a history, stretching back to Marxist readings by Leonard Woolf and David Daiches in the 1940s and on to social accounts by J. F. G. Cornall and Raymond Williams in the 1960s and David Spring in the 1980s.[8] The historical contextualising of Austen in a literary tradition, meanwhile, can be traced to the publication, in 1883, of George Pellew's Harvard Prize Dissertation, and comes to prominence in modern criticism with Ian Watt and Frank W. Bradbrook. Watt attributes the eminence of Jane Austen to her following and surpassing Frances Burney 'in bringing together the divergent directions which the geniuses of Richardson and Fielding had imposed upon the novel', of 'realism of presentation and realism of assessment' or 'of the internal and of the external approaches to character'.[9] Leavis, with a nod in the direction of Lord David Cecil's Leslie Stephen Lecture of 1935, had already made Austen 'the inaugurator of the great tradition of the English novel', which is distinguished from its French or aesthetic equivalent by the 'moral intensity' with which it arbitrates between life and art (*Great Tradition*, pp. 7–9). Internal and external, formal and ideological, aesthetic and moral, these were the rival claims upon the interpretation of Austen for much of the twentieth century.

The great fault-line in nineteenth-century Austen commentary was between Janeites and anti-Janeites. The coinage was apparently George Saintsbury's (*OED*), but the parties emerged ahead of their name, resulting often in the pairing of critic-antagonists, sceptics on one side, devotees on the other. Excesses among the Janeite party, culminating around 1900 in a 'cult' surrounding the 'Legend of St Jane' (Southam, *Critical Heritage*, p. 57), were branded 'Austenolatry' by Leslie Stephen, his sign of *non serviam* before 'the most intolerant and dogmatic of literary creeds'.[10] One difficulty had been to establish Austen's greatness without conceding critical judgement. Exemplary in this regard is her dramatic and in some ways awkward comparison to Shakespeare. The analogy arose, with Macaulay, out of Austen the character-writer, and was both adopted and challenged by George Henry Lewes, who called her, not without a 'sense of incongruity', 'a prose Shakspeare'.[11] So long as considerations of character, and above all 'the rare and difficult art of *dramatic presentation*', were uppermost, Shakespearean Austen carried conviction;[12] but as soon as considerations of literary medium were introduced, feelings of strain became apparent. Lewes's oxymoron tended to divide, then, according to which half of the phrase was being emphasised. It also reflected a recurrent mid nineteenth- to early twentieth-century debate – a debate concerning Jane Austen's literary merit, relative not just to Shakespeare, but to Scott and Turgenev, to Burney and Brontë (Charlotte or, more rarely, Emily), to George Eliot and George Sand.

The Shakespearean tag was shorthand for three further dilemmas about Austen's status: was she poetic as well as prosaic? artistic as well as imitative? universal as well as parochial? To take these in turn. If the prose of life were what was looked for, Austen succeeded admirably; if the poetry, she was found correspondingly deficient. Rarely, attempts were made to combine the two, as in the 'fine poetess of life'. The romantic reaction against 'real' and 'sensible' Miss Austen, fixed by Charlotte Brontë in letters of 18 January 1848 and 12 April 1850, was standardised by Richard Simpson in 1870 – 'Within her range her characterization is truly Shakespearian; but she has scarcely a spark of poetry'[13] – and became the basis for the H. W. Garrod's masculinist 'Depreciation' of 1928.

Secondly, art and imitation. The Shakespearean 'elimination' of the author-function, or its dispersal among Austen's *dramatis personae* (already a feature of Reginald Farrer's classic centenary article for *The Quarterly Review*, July 1917), once had the effect of eliminating also the degree of her novelistic skill or power. For every tribute paid to Austen's artistry, there have been dozens to her representational fidelity, her 'truth to nature' and, implicitly or otherwise, her artlessness. Twentieth-century critics – Vladimir Nabokov, Andrew Wright and Howard S. Babb, to name but three – sought to redress the balance, often through detailed attention to

style or structure. Modern varieties of the 'dramatic' school of criticism, meanwhile, have tended to emphasise the ironist in Austen.
This emphasis, which rather neatly allows both artist and realist
to have her say, has led both to Marvin Mudrick's account of the
coincidence of author and heroine, as observant and potentially
open-minded spectators of life's 'simple' and 'intricate' characters,
and to Wayne C. Booth's alternative assessment, of the author's
divergence from her creation, as testified by the 'Point of View and
the Control of Distance in *Emma*'.[14] On the whole, the truism of
nineteenth-century commentators had been that Austen could do
characters, but not 'plot' (once again, the moderns – for instance,
Malcolm Bradbury[15] – have argued the contrary). By mid-century
there was however a counter-tradition, of Austen as an invisible
artist – one whom the discerning might appreciate, in the 'economy of art' which achieves the highest 'ends' 'by the *least expenditure* of means' or 'the machinery of representation' that is 'almost
wholly concealed from observation'. Lewes even used the phrase
'art for art's sake' of the 'intellectual pleasure' to be derived from
Austen,[16] an indication of how novels once synonymous with a 'likeness to life' might be found surprisingly in tune with the aesthetic
movement, and of how Virginia Woolf might urge *The Common
Reader* to value them for their 'abstract art', an art which 'so varies
the emotions and proportions the parts that it is possible to enjoy
it . . . for itself, and not as a link which carries the story this way
and that'.

Woolf also addresses the third Austenian dilemma, that of the
work's parochial or universal appeal, coming down firmly on the
side of the latter: 'Whatever she writes is . . . set in its relation,
not to the parsonage, but to the universe.'[17] The contrary view,
that she is the sexless spinster of the 'parlour' or the 'parish', has
been taken by all Austenphobes, from Charlotte Brontë to Edward
Fitzgerald, and Mark Twain to H. W. Garrod. On either side of
the argument, there has been widespread agreement that Austen
works within limits. The disagreement arises as to how these are
experienced – briefly, whether hers is the limitation of perfection or
of imprisonment. R. E. Hughes has helpfully and more neutrally
summarised the opposed viewpoints as the 'microscopic' and the
'microcosmic'.[18] The latter has just been illustrated by Woolf, and
there are two metaphors by which critics of the former persuasion

have tended to indicate their position: one is the microscope itself, the other, and more common, is the miniature (a usage which draws on Austen's own famous self-representation, of painting on a 'little bit of ivory'). A major initiative in recent criticism, historicist, materialist or feminist, is that it has largely done away with the assumption of limits, fulfilling the promise which E. M. Forster detected in reviewing the Clarendon edition by R. W. Chapman, of contact between Austen's 'wonderful internal life' and the 'life of facts'.[19]

The nineteenth century quarrelled, or agreed, over a slender critical tradition and a limited set of terms. The twentieth broadened that range of reference, while cohering around the debate pursued by Austen's appreciators and depreciators (overlapping, but not synonymous with, Janeites and anti-Janeites). If there are aspects of latent nineteenth-century commentary that have been vastly expanded, they are to be found in Margaret Oliphant's denial to Austen of 'the simple character it appears at the first glance'; and Richard Simpson's attribution to her of a critical and ironical judgment. Oliphant offered a novelist whose 'limitation' is 'singular' from the 'character' of the author herself, 'full of subtle power, keenness, finesse, and self-restraint'.[20] In this portrait room has been made for both appreciators and depreciators of Austen to notice, not her 'nicely-regulated vein of humour' (as Thomas Henry Lister had it, in the *Edinburgh Review*), but her 'Regulated Hatred', as D. W. Harding notably suggested. A professional psychologist, Harding introduced the biography of Austen to the thinking of Freud, in order to show how the novels find 'means', not for satire exactly, but 'for unobtrusive spiritual survival', or 'for keeping on good terms with people without too great treachery to herself'.[21] All such criticism leads back to the 'fine vein of feminine cynicism' opened by Oliphant, for whom Austen 'has learned to give up any moral classification of social sins, and to place them instead on the level of absurdities'. A 'position of mind . . . essentially feminine' and limited has been made capable of a 'soft' but devastating power, if only of observation (Oliphant, 'Miss Austen and Miss Mitford', p. 294).

If modern criticism after Oliphant sees the back of the complaisant (or complacent) humourist of Victorian England, then modern criticism after Simpson brings to the fore the moral and critical writer of 'didactic' fiction. For Simpson, 'Criticism, humour, irony, the judgment not of one that gives sentence but of the mimic who quizzes while he mocks, are her characteristics.' The 'mimic' is important, in that it establishes the indirect and literary method of Austen which has formed the basis of much twentieth-century work. She 'began, as Shakespeare began, with being an ironical censurer of her [literary] contemporaries'; yet 'manifested her judgment of them not by direct censure, but by the indirect method of imitating and exaggerating the faults of her models'. She also 'schooled herself into an unimpeachable conformity to nature, not by direct imitation of nature, but by looking through, and amusing herself with, the aberrations of pretended imitators'. Sophisticated discussions of Austen's realism,[22] as of her development, have their starting-point here. That Jane Austen 'was a critic who developed herself into an artist' (Simpson, review of *Memoir*, pp. 130–1), that her realism was acquired indirectly through criticism and mimicry, looks forward, not just to textual and formal analysis, but to the modern studies of irony and satire and points-of-view (it was Simpson, not, as is sometimes thought, Bradley, who first noticed the partial sympathy extended to Mrs Norris). For all her heritage value, her aesthetic and class limitations and the scholarship of her eighteenth-century allegiances, the bolder spirits of twentieth-century criticism have worked to ensure that Jane Austen may be seen as 'the first modern novelist' (Leavis, *Great Tradition*, p. 7).

NOTES

1. F. R. Leavis, *The Great Tradition* (London: Chatto & Windus, 1948), p. 7. Subsequent references are included in the text. For Q. D. Leavis, see 'A Critical Theory of Jane Austen's Writings', *Scrutiny* 10 (1941–2), 61–90, 114–42, 272–4; 12 (1944–5), 104–19; and B. C. Southam, 'Mrs Leavis and Miss Austen: The "Critical Theory" Reconsidered', *Nineteenth-Century Fiction* 17 (1962–3), 21–32.
2. B. C. Southam (ed.), *Jane Austen: The Critical Heritage, Vol. 2: 1870–1940* (London: Routledge & Kegan Paul, 1987), p. 233. Subsequent references are included in the text.
3. A. C. Bradley, *A Miscellany* (1929), pp. 42–3, 48, 59.
4. Gilbert Ryle, 'Jane Austen and the Moralists', *Oxford Review* 1 (1966), 5–18.

5. Lionel Trilling, 'In Mansfield Park', *Encounter* 3:3 (September, 1954), 9–19; Tony Tanner, 'Jane Austen and "The Quiet Thing" – A Study of *Mansfield Park*', in *Critical Essays on Jane Austen*, ed. B. C. Southam (London: Routledge & Kegan Paul, 1968), p. 161. Subsequent references to this publication are included in the text.

6. Marilyn Butler, *Jane Austen and the War of Ideas* (Oxford: Clarendon Press, 1975), pp. 3–4.

7. Alistair M. Duckworth, *The Improvement of the Estate. A Study of Jane Austen's Novels*, new edition (Baltimore and London: Johns Hopkins University Press, 1994), pp. 31, xxix.

8. See Joseph Cady and Ian Watt, 'Jane Austen's Critics', *Critical Quarterly* 5 (1963), 49–63; J. F. G. Cornall, 'Marriage and Property in Jane Austen's Novels', *History Today* 17 (December, 1967), 805–11; Raymond Williams, *The English Novel from Dickens to Lawrence* (London: Chatto and Windus, 1970), pp. 18–24; David Spring, 'Interpreters of Jane Austen's Social World: Literary Critics and Historians', in *Jane Austen: New Perspectives*, ed. Janet Todd (New York and London: Holmes & Meier, 1983), pp. 53–72.

9. Ian Watt, *The Rise of the Novel* (London: Chatto and Windus, 1957); Frank W. Bradbrook, *Jane Austen and her Predecessors* (Cambridge: Cambridge University Press, 1966), pp. 296–9.

10. Leslie Stephen, 'Humour', *Cornhill Magazine* 33 (1876), 324–5.

11. Thomas Babington Macaulay, *Edinburgh Review* 76 (January, 1843), 561; George Henry Lewes, *Fraser's Magazine* 36 (December, 1847), 687; *The Leader*, 22 November 1851, p. 1115; *Westminster Review* 58/n.s.2 (July, 1852), 134.

12. *Blackwood's Edinburgh Magazine* 86 (July, 1859), 105.

13. Richard Simpson, review of *Memoir*, *North British Review* 52 (April, 1870), 131. Subsequent references are included in the text.

14. Marvin Mudrick, *Jane Austen: Irony as Defence and Discovery* (Princeton: Princeton University Press, 1952); Wayne C. Booth, 'Point of View and the Control of Distance in *Emma*', *Nineteenth-Century Fiction* 16 (1961–2), 95–116.

15. Malcolm Bradbury, 'Jane Austen's *Emma*', *Critical Quarterly* 4 (1962), 335–46.

16. Lewes, 'The Novels of Jane Austen', *Blackwood's Edinburgh Magazine* 86 (1859) 101–2, 113; W. F. Pollock, *Fraser's Magazine* 61 (January, 1860), 30–1.

17. Virginia Woolf, 'Jane Austen', in *The Common Reader* (1925), p. 175.
18. R. E. Hughes, 'The Education of Emma Woodhouse', *Nineteenth-Century Fiction* 16 (1961–2), 69–74.
19. E. M. Forster, 'Jane, How Shall We Ever Recollect . . .', *The Nation and The Athenaeum* 34 (5 January 1924), 512–14.
20. Margaret Oliphant, 'Miss Austen and Miss Mitford', *Blackwood's Edinburgh Magazine* 107 (March, 1870), 294. Subsequent references are included in the text.
21. Thomas Lister, review of Mrs Gore's *Women As They Are*, *Edinburgh Review* 51 (July, 1830), 450; D. W. Harding, 'Regulated Hatred', *Scrutiny* 8 (1939–40), 346–62.
22. Cynthia Griffin, 'The Development of Realism in Jane Austen's Early Novels', *ELH* 30 (1963), 35–52; A. Walton Litz, *Jane Austen: A Study of her Artistic Development* (Oxford: Oxford University Press, 1967).

11

Critical responses, recent

RAJESWARI SUNDER RAJAN

The present-day scene of Austen criticism is a lively and contentious one, marked by debates between, on the one side, feminist and post-colonial critics who frankly declare their own investments in the revisionary claims of their politics and, on the other, scholars who would counter such appropriation by reading Jane Austen scrupulously along the grain, circumscribing the meaning of her writings within the conditions of possibility generated by her life and times. These recent conversations have, nonetheless, resulted in mutual illumination, a significant interpenetration of methods, and some degree of agreed ground among the contending parties. This evolution has meant not only that the contemporary 'relevance' of (and hence interest in) Austen's work has been vastly enhanced, but also that conventional literary historical research has been pushed into many productive new directions.

One might safely claim, in any case, that the idea of a political Austen is no longer seriously challenged, since the widespread influence of Marilyn Butler's authoritative *Jane Austen and the War of Ideas* (1975) located her in the mainstream of intellectual ideas following the French Revolution. (Butler had not at the time included feminism among the ideas relevant to a reading of Austen's novels, an omission she made up in the introduction to the 1987 edition.) Where Austen stands on a number of contemporary issues – the Revolution, war, nationalism, empire, class, 'improvement', the clergy, town versus country, abolition, the professions, female emancipation; whether her politics were Tory, or Whig, or radical; whether she was a conservative or a revolutionary, or occupied a reformist position between these extremes: these are among the questions with which recent Austen scholarship has been deeply engrossed.

Jane Austen's gender as writer has never been an innocuous issue. For second-wave feminism in the Anglo-American academy engaged in canon battles and arguing for the recuperation of a tradition of *women's writing*, the fact of Austen's being the first major English woman writer led to interest in two questions broadly identifiable as: how might we view her within a category designated as 'women's writing', and how was she shaped by and how did she herself shape different literary histories?

In positing a tradition of 'women's writings' there is a danger of homogenising very different writings within an exclusively gendered concept. This is the case in the thesis of Sandra Gilbert and Susan Gubar's hugely influential book, *The Madwoman in the Attic: The Woman Writer and the Nineteenth-Century Literary Imagination* (1979), which draws an invariant contrast between the 'decorous surfaces' and the 'explosive anger' beneath them in the works of a number of nineteenth-century women writers in England and America, as a result of their authors' need to resort to covert strategies of subversion and opposition. (Compare this with Marilyn Butler's caution that the Austen novel is not 'only a woman's novel', but is *'among other* things a woman's novel').[1] Nevertheless, the attractive and persuasive reading of Austen's work that such a radical feminist approach proposed, like that of several other books written in the 1980s, makes it difficult for us today to regard Jane Austen as anything other than a *woman* writer.

Eschewing essentialising accounts of the 'femininity' of writing, other kinds of feminist criticism have sought an explanation for Austen's writing – its genres, methods, successes and limits – in factors like her own temperament, intellect, education, reading and other influences, as well as in contemporary literary movements and institutions. Placing her within broader intellectual traditions, as well as in the company of women writers, feminist scholars have substantially revised both literary accounts. Austen's stature has in the past meant that other contemporary women writers have been neglected, but more recently it has led to the resurrection of a host of women writers, many of them 'minor', whom we might never have attended to but for our interest in Jane Austen. As a result she has been contextualised in new and interesting ways while other women writers and their genres have been newly revalued.

Feminism's interest in a writer is not necessarily only in establishing if he or she *is* feminist, but also in identifying if and how questions of gender are addressed or occluded in the writer's work, and in exploring the contradictions that gender poses to various forms of narrative resolution. In Austen's case, the question of her feminism has become a central issue for a number of reasons, among them her historical location (her near contemporaneity to Mary Wollstonecraft is not a fact easy to overlook), the centrality of female protagonists in her fiction and the thematic preoccupation with courtship and marriage as the central predicament of women's lives in her novels.

Apart from *The Madwoman in the Attic*, three books appearing in the decade of the 1980s may be said to have established feminist criticism to an extent that there can be no easy going back to any earlier view of an apolitical, or even unqualifiedly 'conservative', Austen, and also in the sense that much subsequent criticism has built upon these seminal works: Julia Prewitt Brown's *Jane Austen's Novels: Social Change and Literary Form* (1979), Margaret Kirkham's *Jane Austen: Feminism and Fiction* (1983) and Claudia L. Johnson's *Jane Austen: Women, Politics and the Novel* (1988). Brown attributed to Austen a 'feminine consciousness' which allowed her to show how 'women find ways to develop and assert their womanhood despite the restrictions placed on them'.[2] In identifying a 'domestic' rather than 'heroic' form of feminism in Austen's novels, Brown offered a comparative historical perspective that considerably clarified this matter for subsequent feminist criticism. Kirkham, in the first major full-length consideration of the question framed explicitly as a historical investigation, identified the parallels between Austen's position on women's rights and Mary Wollstonecraft's, finding in them an identifiably 'Enlightenment' feminism. In her book on Austen Johnson argued, first for the existence of a tradition of women's political novels in the eighteenth century, and, second, for the play in their work of 'flexible' rather than 'partisan' sympathies on various issues including gender distinctions, aligning Jane Austen with these positions. Like other American feminist critics of the 1980s (among them, notably, Mary Poovey),[3] Johnson is also interested in the 'act of [female] authorship' and the strategies of 'indirection' that this demanded at the time. The overview and analysis of feminist approaches in the introduction to Devoney Looser's edited collection, *Jane Austen and the Discourses of Feminism* (1995), consolidates these earlier positions.

The recuperation of Austen's gendered politics in 'other' (non-Western) contexts serves as an interesting supplement to this narrative. Ruth Vanita, writing about the response of female college students in Indian classrooms to the heroines of nineteenth-century English canonical texts, and You-me Park, who discusses a contemporary Korean woman writer whose novels explicitly invoke Austen's marriage plots, provide a cross-cultural perspective on the feminism of Austen's novels that both resonates with and significantly departs from mainstream Anglo-American feminist readings.[4] These invocations of Austen in other places are not a consequence of Austen's 'universal resonance' as might be easily supposed, but reveal instead the conditions of her work's recuperability in different nation-spaces and historical conjunctures. The light thrown on the questions these critics pose about postcolonial 'encounters' or about the adaptability of patriarchy in colonial and neocolonial settings and in the context of the globalisation of Western culture, operates with the full force of the 'supplement' in Derridean terms.

Central to contemporary feminist politics is the interest in sexual politics. The central thematics of heterosexual 'love' in Austen's novels seemingly places them squarely within a conservative acceptance of the normative social institutions of courtship and marriage. But from the very first her readers could not have failed to see that Austen's anti-romantic, pragmatic, frequently satirical representations of romantic love came from the recognition of the middle-class woman's lack of alternatives to marriage. Her privileging of 'good' marriages as narrative resolution (and even as moral imperative) is therefore explicitly edged with a critique of patriarchal social norms. Most contemporary feminist critics foreground this aspect of Austen's critique over the view of her as a conservative in the representation of the social orders of marriage and family.

Radical feminist criticism has sought to find covert but more subversive sexual politics at play in Austen's fiction. Eve Sedgwick in the notorious 'Jane Austen and the Masturbating Girl' (1993) (a title that produced the expected ripples in cultural circles), argues that 'one "sexual identity" that did exist as such in Austen's time, already bringing a specific genital practice into dense compaction with issues of consciousness, truth, pedagogy, and confession, was that of the onanist'. Sedgewick draws upon a Foucauldian history of sexuality to read, in *Sense and Sensibility*, Marianne's nervous breakdown as symptom of masturbatory disorders (and suggests that Edward Ferrars is similarly afflicted). Claudia Johnson provides a different genealogy for 'queering' Austen and highlights a different text. Drawing support from Edmund Wilson's and Marvin Mudrick's early responses, she reads Emma as an 'autonomous and autoerotic' woman, 'susceptible to stirrings of homoerotic pleasure', disdainful of 'heterosexual love' and not constrained by the 'courtship plot'.[5]

The generic classification of Jane Austen's writings as 'domestic fiction' has led to a feminist critical interest in exploring the formal aspects as well as the ideology of such a genre. Nancy Armstrong, for instance, views the centrality of the 'domestic' in nineteenth-century fiction as indication of a significant overall feminisation of bourgeois culture itself while others have come from an opposite direction, noting the tenuousness of the distinction between the 'domestic' and the outside public world, especially since the word 'domestic' refers to affairs of both the national state as well as the household. For example, though the connections between 'domestic realities' and 'imperial fictions' may be actively *disavowed* in *Mansfield Park*, that disavowal is itself, according to Maaja Stewart, an aspect of imperial ideology. In the novel, an idealised domestic space, 'apolitical and noneconomic', bearing no trace of 'the violence intrinsic to imperial power', is privileged over (men's) activities in the outside world.[6]

'Antigua' has become the short-hand reference to the host of questions and controversies generated by Sir Thomas Bertram's journey to the West Indies in *Mansfield Park*, which have also come to represent the sum of so-called 'postcolonial' responses to Austen. This reference to slavery is not by any means a textual crux, so that the fact that 'the silence of the Bertrams' has come to function as such a fraught locus of the novel's meanings is a curious development (in earlier criticism including Butler's, it was the theatricals or the visit to Sotherton which served this purpose). This and a few other scattered references to Sir Thomas Bertram's West Indian concerns in the novel are no more than reported conversations among the characters, with little or no additional authorial commentary that might enable us to judge of their significance for Austen herself.

But precisely this marginalisation and seeming elision of the issue in the novel led Edward Said, in his major book on the culture of imperialism, to invoke *Mansfield Park* with the observation that 'Jane Austen sees the legitimacy of Sir Thomas Bertram's overseas properties as a natural extension of the calm, the order, the beauties of Mansfield, one central estate validating the economically supportive role of the peripheral other.' Said was not of course the first critic to mark the 'Antiguan connection': he himself acknowledges the model of Raymond Williams' argument in *The Country and the City* (1973) for this mapping of geographical spaces in terms of centre and periphery; and the argument about Europe's culture as epiphenomenon of its imperialist enterprises (the slave trade, the colonial plantation, imperial military adventure, territorial conquest) is no more than a Marxist application of the base-superstructure model. The first to research extensively Austen and slavery was Moira Ferguson, who repeatedly criticises Sir Thomas Bertram for 'eurocentrism' (an odd and puzzling term of accusation). Said, however, does not in any vulgar sense *attack* the novel's putative limitations;[7] on the contrary, he even finds historical excuses for what he takes to be Jane Austen's lukewarm position on abolition. He offers instead a sophisticated reading of the novel's political unconscious by invoking the way (great, or canonical) texts can operate against their own grain: such novels are unable to hide 'that other site' (the colony), he maintains, because their qualities of 'formal inclusiveness, historical honesty, and prophetic suggestiveness' perform a revelatory function despite their attempted evasiveness ('Jane Austen and Empire', p. 97).

The critical responses to Said's pronouncements have been many and varied. (Few, however, have been as dismissive as Harold Bloom: 'No one has demonstrated that increased consciousness of the relation between culture and imperialism is of the slightest use whatsoever in learning to read *Mansfield Park*.'[8]) The discussion turns on questions like: what was Sir Thomas doing in Antigua? (quelling slave rebellion, selling his property, overseeing his plantations personally following the changes brought about by the abolition of the slave trade?) What are the real sources of Mansfield's wealth? Does Austen endorse or criticise Mansfield Park values? Fanny Price's admiration of Mansfield? Sir Thomas's behaviour? Is she blind to the sources of Mansfield Park's wealth (the plantation, and therefore slave labour)? or does she implicitly but knowingly condone them? What does the 'dead silence' following the question about slavery mean? One kind of response to Said has led Austen scholars to delve into the author's biography in order to glean her family and other connections to the issue of slavery and the West Indies, and to examine what her remarks and her reading about the subject might reveal; another related mode of scholarship is primarily historical, examining the course of the contemporary debates on slavery, as well as of property, inheritance, land and other forms of wealth at the time; and a third major procedure has been textual, to read the novel's meaning in terms of irony, genre and other clues to authorial intention. Much of this work has served as a valuable addition to Austen scholarship.

Recent feminist and postcolonial concerns have come together over the question of slavery, primarily as it surfaces in *Mansfield Park* and (more obliquely) in *Emma*. The trope of female 'slavery', as critics have shown, circulated in innumerable contemporary texts in descriptions of women's situation, sometimes indicating the sympathies of female abolitionists for the cause, and sometimes subordinating the issue of Caribbean slavery to the fight over women's emancipation in Britain. While acknowledging the historical validity and the value of such readings (though one must confess that the parallels, when relentlessly insisted upon by critics like Ferguson, can strain one's credulity in places), it is also important to preserve the differences – in both degree and kind – between women's subjection based on norms of incipient feminist individualism, and the historical African slave trade whose commodification of labour was predicated on a foundational denial of *human* status to racial others.

Despite this overwhelming attention to *Mansfield Park* and its themes, postcolonial concerns need not be limited to the subject of slavery or European imperialism. It is above all the case that postcolonial criticism brings to reading the English text *different questions*, both theoretical and contextual, rather than narrowly exploring it through the lens of a 'special interest'. The opening up of Austen's world to these questions, and the joining of issue over them by academics everywhere – even to the setting of different agendas for scholarship – can only be regarded as a most welcome development. Clara Tuite's recent *Romantic Austen: Sexual Politics and the Literary Canon* (2002), concerned with how Austen becomes a central figure in the English literary canon, British heritage and global popular culture, may be seen as exemplifying such a trend.

In contrast to the expansiveness of postcolonial, feminist perspectives, we have its contemporary critical response: an explicit eschewing of 'questions of ideology' in Mary Waldron's *Jane Austen and the Fiction of Her Time* (1999), which offers a 'unifying critique of the novel' without either 'straying inappropriately into peripheral historical-cultural detail or insisting on single authoritative readings'.[9] Other books on Austen similarly set out to 'scrutinize, not theorize' her novels (Moreland Perkins, *Reshaping the Sexes in 'Sense and Sensibility'*), or explicitly propose to save her from 'academics, feminists, historical specialists, and would-be radical theorists', restoring her to the domain of the English-speaking common reader.[10] More than any other canonical English writer, Austen is the subject of books by non-specialists, in some cases non-academics, published by mainstream presses. The proceedings of the Jane Austen Society are periodically published as well. But these books are the work of professional, not amateur, scholarship. The historian Warren Roberts's *Jane Austen and the French Revolution*, first published in 1979 and reissued in 1995, is an example of the value and originality of such researches.

Typically the titles of these books link Austen with a particular object of interest and inquiry: Jane Austen *and* food/religion/education/popular fiction/the theatre, as the case may be. Outstanding among these is John Wiltshire's *Jane Austen and the Body: 'The Picture of Health'* (1992), which reflects a newfound interest in the *body*, sexed, medicalised, somatised and constructed in culturally gendered ways. Wiltshire addresses not only theories of the body as sexuality, but more broadly how 'culture is inscribed on the body', locating Austen's work 'at the interface between physiology and culture'. He explores the preoccupation with illness and health in her female (and also some male) characters, and the meanings this yields.[11] *Two* books with the title *Jane Austen and the Theatre* appeared in 2002, indicating the rich potential of this field of research.

All this is to say that Austen scholarship-watching can be an engrossing pastime; but also, more seriously, that 'Austen' is an important locus of English disciplinary studies. The tensions in

Austen criticism between comparative-theoretical perspectives on the one hand, and her reclamation by a canonical-national literary history and traditional scholarship on the other, are marked in some cases by unresolved antagonisms but also in significant instances by signs of a cautious entente.

NOTES

1. Marilya Butler, *Jane Austen and the War of Ideas* (Oxford: Clarendon Press, 1975), p. xxxiii.
2. Julia Prewitt Brown, *Jane Austen's Novels: Social Change and Literary Form* (Cambridge, MA: Harvard University Press, 1979), p. 156.
3. Mary Poovey, *The Proper Lady and the Woman Writer: Ideology as Style in the Works of Mary Wollstonecraft, Mary Shelley, and Jane Austen* (Chicago: University of Chicago Press, 1984).
4. Ruth Vanita, 'Mansfield Park in Miranda House', in *The Lie of the Land: English Literary Studies in India*, ed. Rajeswari Sunder Rajan (Delhi: Oxford University Press, 1992); You-me Park, 'Father's Daughters: Critical Realism Examines Patriarchy in Jane Austen's *Pride and Prejudice* and Pak Wanso's *A Faltering Afternoon* [Hwichongkorinun Ohu]', in *The Postcolonial Jane Austen*, eds. You-me Park and Rajeswari Sunder Rajan (London and New York: Routledge, 2000).
5. Eve Kosofsky Sedgwick, 'Jane Austen and the Masturbating Girl', *Critical Inquiry* 17 (Summer, 1991), 818–37; Edmund Wilson, 'A Long Talk about Jane Austen', in *Classics and Commercials: A Literary Chronicle of the Forties* (New York: Farrar & Strauss, 1950); Marvin Mudrick, *Jane Austen: Irony as Defense and Discovery* (Berkeley: University of California Press, 1952); Claudia L. Johnson, *Equivocal Beings: Politics, Gender and Sentimentality in the 1790s: Wollstonecraft, Radcliffe, Burney, Austen* (Chicago: University of Chicago Press, 1995), p. 195.
6. Nancy Armstrong, *Desire and Domestic Fiction: A Political History of the Novel* (Oxford: Oxford University Press, 1987); Maaja Stewart, *Domestic Realities and Imperial Fictions: Jane Austen's Novels in Eighteenth-Century Contexts* (Athens and London: University of Georgia Press, 1993), pp. 122–3.
7. Edward W. Said, 'Jane Austen and Empire', in *Culture and Imperialism* (New York: Knopf, 1993), p. 79; subsequent references in the text; Moira Ferguson, 'Mansfield Park: Slavery, Colonialism, and Gender', *Oxford Literary Review* 13:1–2 (1991), 118–39.

8. Harold Bloom, *The Western Canon* (London: Papermac, 1995), p. 257.
9. Mary Waldron, *Jane Austen and the Fiction of Her Time* (Cambridge: Cambridge University Press, 1999), p. 13.
10. Roger Gard, *Jane Austen's Novels: The Art of Clarity* (New Haven and London: Yale University Press, 1992), quotation from jacket flap and p. 1.
11. John Wiltshire, *Jane Austen and the Body: 'The Picture of Health'* (Cambridge: Cambridge University Press, 1992), p. 17f.

12

Cult of Jane Austen

DEIDRE SHAUNA LYNCH

In 'The Jane Austen Syndrome', Marjorie Garber – a Shakespeare scholar and self-confessed sufferer from the syndrome her 2003 essay describes – contributes to a long tradition of criticism asserting Jane Austen's kinship with the Bard. It is not only the case that this pair represent English literature's most masterful creators of character and dialogue. Nor for Garber do the similarities end when we acknowledge that Austen and Shakespeare are cultural icons, possessed of, and perhaps cursed by, a celebrity independent of their perceived value as writers. 'More than any other authors I know', she asserts, 'Austen and Shakespeare provoke outpourings of *love.*' That last remark registers the contribution Garber's essay makes to a second venerable strain in Austen's reception history, a tradition of commentary on the ardent identifications that the novels inspire. Jane Austen fosters in her readers, as most other literary giants do not, the devotion and fantasies of personal access that are the hallmarks of the *fan.* For a century, therefore, many a commentator has accompanied his interest in the novels with an interest in the extravagancy of audiences' responses to them – an interest, particularly, in how that heady enthusiasm diverges from the level-headed dispassion that is supposed to define a proper aesthetic response. Thus Henry James in 1905 remarks on the rising 'tide' of Austenian 'appreciation' and finds it, he observes waspishly, to have risen, thanks to the 'stiff breeze of the commercial', 'rather higher . . . than the high-water mark, the highest, of her intrinsic merit'. John Bailey (1864–1931) notes while introducing his 1927 'Georgian Edition' of her fiction 'the extraordinary spread of the cult of Jane Austen' and explains the cult's recruitment successes with a paradox: the passage of time, though putting more distance between her era and readers', has increased the intimacy of the author–reader relation. 'She has ceased to be the 'Miss Austen' of our parents and become our own 'Jane Austen' or even 'Jane'.'[1]

As Bailey implies when he contrasts his parents' generation and his own, the late Victorian period is when readers began thinking of Austen as an author with whom they might be on an intimate, first-name footing – whom they could love rather than merely esteem. An important product of that sense of connection is 'Janeite', the appellation devotees adopted around 1894 to declare that their hearts belonged to Austen and also, as the hint of possessiveness discernible in Bailey's 'our own Jane Austen' suggests, to declare that *she* belonged to *them*.² (The absence in other authors' reception histories of any equivalent to this cosy cognomen is striking. It is hard to imagine admirers of Shakespeare calling themselves *Willies*.) The genesis of this Janeite cult is usually located with the publication in 1870 by Jane Austen's nephew J. E. Austen-Leigh of his *Memoir of Jane Austen*: the first full-length biography and thus the first text to supply a sense of a private personality behind the published books. Certainly, the influence of this familial, insider's view of the novelist helps explain why practices of Austenian appreciation have tended to be focussed, as we shall see, on the institutions of home and domestic privacy, which is to say why, in certain quarters, tours through country houses or the preparation of a '*Pride and Prejudice* dinner party' have become oddly equivalent, as manifestations of Austenian devotion, to novel-reading.

That knowing Austen has from the start involved fantasies of knowing her the way an affectionate family member would may help explain, as well, a phenomenon that will be central to this discussion: the fact that since the Victorian era many admirers of Jane Austen have insisted, their swelling numbers notwithstanding, that there is something private and personal in their admiration. Many have testified, that is, to how their Austen love takes them out of the wider world and into a smaller, more select and closer-knit circle (into a 'loyal tribe', a 'haven' or a 'true lovers' knot' – to cite a few characteristic terms from these testimonies). And yet Austen-Leigh's *Memoir* began proffering this illusion of access to the novelist's private story at the precise historical moment when large claims were being made for the *public* relevance of individuals' aesthetic experiences. 1870 also witnessed the British Parliament's passage of the Education Act that mandated the state-wide establishment of elementary schools. In recognising universal literacy as a national priority, this legislation set in motion new initiatives for the teaching of literature as a national heritage: initiatives (in which Austenians such as Bailey often took the lead) for managing social upheaval with the notion of a changeless, 'classic' Englishness preserved in great books and initiatives for transcoding class difference, so that it would be cancelled by the egalitarian promise embedded in the concept of a shared national heritage and yet refigured simultaneously as the distinction between elite and popular tastes. Indeed, to consider the Education Act together with the *Memoir* (in which Austen-Leigh claims with perverse pride that his aunt's books are too tame for the tastes of 'the multitude')[3] is to see prefigured several of the tensions that have shaped Austen's reception history. These are the tensions between, on the one hand, the work that Jane Austen, or an idea of her, does as sponsor to the social relations defining the literary nation or public and, on the other hand, the work that she does as sponsor to the clannish solidarities defining the *club* – another conspicuous institution in the history of Austenian appreciation. These are also the tensions between a popular audience and an academic one, between readers for whom Austen represents domestic privacy, leisure and sometimes shopping and professional scholars/teachers/readers for whom Austen represents career and a connection to the public sphere.

As it turns out, the unstable semantics of the word that Bailey applies to Austen's admirers – 'cult' – nicely register these disagreements about the kinds of converse that Austen's books promote. According to the *New Shorter Oxford Dictionary*, this previously straightforward word for worship developed a 'derogatory' sense early in the last century and became a designation one might apply to 'a fashionable enthusiasm' or 'a transient fad of an in-group'. By the time Bailey used it, 'cult' had acquired, in other words, a semantic shading that Austen's adherents could exploit in order to distance themselves from those *other* people who, it was proposed, enjoyed Austen in the wrong way and for the wrong reasons – injudiciously, cultishly. This, of course, is the strategy for consolidating one's own position in the cultural hierarchy that James exemplifies when he worries out loud over how an opportunistic 'bookselling spirit' has procured Jane Austen a popular audience.

We shall return later to this drive to discriminate between proper and improper Austenian enthusiasms. However, we would be well advised to first read 'cult' straight and by doing so engage in more depth the intertwining of literary appreciation and religious reverence that shapes Austen-love. Austen's reception history was long influenced by the hagiographic heritage of Victorian-period literary culture and thus by such borrowings from older practices of religious sanctification as also inform, for instance, Thomas Carlyle's proposal in *Heroes, Hero-Worship and the Heroic in History* (1841) that Shakespeare was 'canonised, though no Pope or Cardinal took hand in doing it' or Gerald Massey's 1888 poem in which Shakespeare, 'Our Prince of Peace', goes 'no flag unfurled / To make his conquest of the World'.[4] And there *were* places reserved for women authors within the Victorian sages' temple of culture: those of the saints. In Austen's case, as the artist C. E. Kempe found, even a name had been made ready. The official description of the stained-glass window which Kempe designed and erected in 1900 in Winchester Cathedral (Jane Austen's place of burial) enumerates its figures, who range from St John with his gospel open to the line 'In the beginning was the Word,' to, in the window's head, 'Saint Augustine', 'whose name', we are informed, 'in its abbreviated form is St. Austin'.

The fact that this conflation of a woman novelist and a church father was uncontroversial suggests much about the Victorians' cult of domestic womanhood as well as much, again, about the influence of Jane Austen's nephew-biographer, whose *Memoir* displays few traces of the aunt's wit but many of the writer's clerical office. ('St Aunt Jane of Steventon-cum-Chawton Canonicorum' is one name coined to christen the prim Anglican heroine conjured up in Austen-Leigh's pages; Sutherland, *Memoir*, p. xv.) Yet the records left by less stiff-necked admirers are also dotted with comments ascribing 'divinity' to 'Jane', touting the 'miracle' of the novels and aligning the worshipper's reading experience with ecstatic revelation. From about 1870 to 1940, such exuberant testimonies of faith are staples of Janeite discourse. A 1924 essay by E. M. Forster represents a variation on this theme in observing that 'the Jane Austenite [a category in which Forster included himself] possesses little of the brightness' of his idol and instead, '[l]ike all regular churchgoers . . . scarcely notices what is being said'.[5] Forster's intimation that the content of Janeite rituals may be less significant than the rituals' utility as social emollient – this suggestion that, though perusing the novels might not engender any ideas in the faithful, it does help pack them into the pews – usefully calls attention to the clubbability that has often accompanied Austenians' vaunted sense of spiritual election. The institutions that Austen's admirers have developed to facilitate their camaraderie are, as suggested above, plentiful and run the gamut from the Royal Society of Literature (during the 1920s the Society's mainly male corps of literati shared papers that did much to give Janeite discourse its hothouse flavour); to the mainly female Jane Austen Societies of the United Kingdom (founded 1940), North America (1979), Australia (1988) and elsewhere, whose combined memberships at the present day number far into the thousands; to the California-based Friends of the English Regency, who identify Austen and the founder of the Regency romance genre, Georgette Heyer, as tutelary spirits for their activities, which consist principally in promoting Regency dancing at science fiction conventions.

In regularly publishing updates on the location of 'Relics', early *Reports* of the Jane Austen Society of the UK also drew on an idiom associated with the cult of the saints (with the difference that the earnestness of the *Reports* contrasts sharply with the penchant for camp and preciousness cultivated by a previous Janeite generation). From its beginnings, the Society kept tabs on the quilts, needle cases and other bits and pieces from the Austen family's domestic lives that the Jane Austen Memorial Trust purchased to 'rest' in the 'sanctuary' of Chawton Cottage (Jane Austen's home from 1809 until 1817) and which the Trust had sometimes had to wrest away from American collectors. With the relic that occasioned the fiercest custody battles, a lock of Jane Austen's hair (bought at auction by the American Alberta Hirshheimer Burke in 1946 and afterward donated by her to Chawton), we approach something resembling medieval Christendom's ritual veneration of the remains of its holy men and women.[6] And it is notable that Chawton itself, as the property of the Memorial Trust since 1947, honours not only Austen's memory but also that of Philip John Carpenter, a casualty of the Second World War and son of the Trust's founder. At this place, accordingly – part museum, part souvenir shop, part chapel with reliquaries, part haunted house (an upstairs bedroom is presented just as it would have appeared, or so we are told, while Jane Austen was alive) – the novelist is called upon to perform the saint's work of interceding between the living and the dead whom they mourn.

When the characters in the 2004 best-selling novel by Karen Joy Fowler, *The Jane Austen Book Club*, play a game of 'Ask Austen' and make the novelist their oracle, using a 'Magic 8-Ball' they have filled with quotations as their instrument of divination, they likewise endow her with this power to link the mundane and the transcendent.

Holiday-makers embarking on Austenian tourism continue to invoke the cult of the saints whenever they describe themselves as 'pilgrims' and, striving to follow in the saint's footsteps, create itineraries that take them from Austen's birthplace at Steventon, to Bath (where she lived from 1801 to 1805, and where a Jane Austen Centre has recently been established to market this connection), to Chawton, and then, in the final stage of their journey, to Winchester to lay flowers on the grave. There are additional cultural metaphors organising such itineraries. Certainly, literary tourism promises its participants an enhanced understanding of their beloved authors, on the theory (crucial, too, to biographers' methods) that sharing others' experiences of place increases our affinity with them. But the prime mover in Austenian tourism is often a nostalgic, anglophilic notion of 'heritage': the premise that Chawton, Steventon, Winchester and Bath (joined, following the mid-1990s, by the National Trust properties that had served as settings in the screen adaptations of Austen's novels) permit a kind of time-travel to the past, because they preserve an all but vanished Englishness or set of 'traditional' values. In this scheme, different sectors of 'Jane Austen's world' – tasteful, elegant Bath; picturesque, peaceful Hampshire – represent a refuge from a modernity that supposedly lost its ethical bearings as long ago as the invention of the railway. Star players in recent Austen films, houses have in general been powerful forces in organising Janeite affect. (The origin of the UK Austen Society in 1940 lies in fund-raising done to preserve a then dilapidated Chawton Cottage.) This may demonstrate the influence of a sentimental account of Austen's novels that presents them as means by which readers might *go home again* – to a comfortable, soothingly normal world.[7]

What motivates the homecomings of tourists is often the promise of touching things touched by Jane Austen herself or (by walking Bath's Milsom Street, say, just as Isabella Thorpe did) of making the novels *real*. The tourism business, however, has an interest in making as many places as possible into destinations. In the name of the real and tangible, it conveys its clientele to virtual and invisible destinations. Austenian itineraries may include therefore sites where, in a strict sense, there is nothing for an Austenian to see: for instance, the site where Steventon Rectory was *once*. (In 1869 J. E. Austen-Leigh was already finding it difficult to ascertain its location.) When prior knowledge produces an expected landscape (and when, like the Jane Austenite, in E. M. Forster's essay who basks in the sunshine of the familiar, we need 'scarcely notice' what lies before us), our imaginings about Jane Austen authenticate the place, rather than the other way around. Any engagement with Austen's works involves, of course, an interaction between *her* fictions and the fictions about the writer's personality that the reader, abetted by biographies, perforce authors herself. But in the construction of that imagined territory 'Jane Austen's world', the balance between our authoring and her authoring may have gone off-kilter. As many have noted, Austen movies in the last decade have almost overshadowed the books: Austenians touring country houses turned film sets that Jane Austen never saw inspect exhibits of costumes made for the movies, clothing that nineteenth-century people never wore. But as early as 1902, a guidebook welcomed to 'Austen-Land' all those tourists who communed with Jane Austen's mind and heart, 'whether through her works, her biographies, or her letters'.[8] In the quoted phrase, the conjunction *or* challenges a common understanding of the priorities that should shape audiences' admiration, because it challenges the primacy of what scholars like to call the primary texts. We might all want Jane Austen real in some way, but differ as to which way.

Indeed to academics, many present-day Austenian cultures of appreciation appear alarmingly ready to cast engagement with the texts as just another ritual of appreciation, one only moderately more important than others. Reading, to be sure, does appear rather effete and unsociable when contrasted to more robust ways of performing one's Austenian identifications: i.e., walking the 'Bath of Jane Austen', recreating the 'restrained elegance of Georgian England' in a Manhattan apartment (guidance provided in Susan Watkins's 1996 *Jane Austen in Style*) or wearing period dress while watching other, similarly attired enthusiasts act out imaginary conversations amongst the novels' characters (an activity featuring in many Austen Society programmes, slotted into the schedule right alongside the quiz games and the lectures on the novels' historical contexts). The powerful identifications that Jane Austen compels produce playful attempts to participate in her world, as well as to merge that world with one's own. Thus the Indiana/Illinois chapter of JASNA publicises an upcoming Austen 'birthday tea' in which guests will enjoy 'old-world elegance' and 'raffle baskets that, defying time and space, have been sent by Austen characters to you, their fans'.

Recent analysis of fan cultures emphasises the challenge that such violations of the canons of aesthetic distance pose to professional scholars, whose claim to prestige is validated by their vocation's protocols of dispassion and objectivity. Indeed, amateur cultures of Austenian appreciation – because they are associated with, variously, unbecoming levity, sentimentality, a determination to integrate fiction into life or a conservative nostalgia – bother many academics. Literary scholar Robert Miles observes that 'Almost without exception the vast library of critical works that has grown up around Austen . . . begins with a gallant effort to rescue the writer from the heritage industry or the Janeites.'[9] To some extent, that gallantry appears guided by an unattractive logic of exclusivity that runs like this: since she is my Jane Austen, she cannot be yours too.

Although this essay began by aligning the kinds of worship Shakespeare and Jane Austen have received, his reception history seems unmarked by the episodes of insidership and intolerance that have divided Austen's readerships. Surveying his history, we are hard pressed to find signs of an audience believing that their beloved but imperilled author requires protecting from a cult (in that derogatory sense of the term which has since the early twentieth century been used to police deviations from approved ways of participating in an appreciative audience).[10] It also appears unlikely that there is any equivalent in the history of Bardolatry to the description of Austenian reading that the novelist Katherine Mansfield supplied when, commenting cleverly in 1930 on the pleasure-effects engendered by Austen's irony, she observed that every 'true admirer of the novels cherishes the happy thought that he alone – reading between the lines – has become the secret friend of their author'.[11] This happy thought about the intimacy of the reading situation should, over the years, have become more difficult to credit. By rights, its credibility ought already to have begun to decline at that late nineteenth-century moment when Austen-Leigh's *Memoir* transformed Jane Austen into a popular author and when the Education Act launched a history of civic-minded literacy crusades that would, in new ways, link the consumption of classic novels to the demands of collective civic life. The undiminished enthusiasm of the many cultures of appreciation that pay homage to Austen's works indicates, however – as does, in addition, the ongoing contention over the forms that such homage should take – that we believe it still.

NOTES

1. Marjorie Garber, *Quotation Marks* (New York: Routledge, 2003), p. 203; Henry James, 'The Lesson of Balzac', in *The House of Fiction: Essays on the Novel by Henry James*, ed. Leon Edel (London: Rupert Hart-Davis, 1957), p. 63; John Bailey, *Introductions to Jane Austen*, new edition (1931), pp. 23, 30.

2. Lorraine Hanaway, '"Janeite" at 100,' *Persuasions* 16 (December, 1994), 28–9; Brian Southam, 'Janeites and Anti-Janeites', in *The Jane Austen Handbook*, ed. J. David Grey (London: Athlone Press, 1986), pp. 237–43.

3. *A Memoir of Jane Austen and Other Family Recollections*, ed. Kathryn Sutherland (Oxford: Oxford University Press, 2002), p. 104. Subsequent references are included in the text.

4. See Tricia Lootens, *Lost Saints: Silence, Gender, and Victorian Literary Canonization* (Charlottesville: University Press of Virginia, 1996), pp. 19, 32.

5. E. M. Forster, 'Jane, How Shall We Ever Recollect . . .', *The Nation and The Athenaeum* 34 (5 January 1924), 512. Vivid accounts of the Janeite idiom of divine revelation are provided in Claudia L. Johnson, 'Austen Cults and Cultures', in *The Cambridge Companion to Jane Austen*, eds. Edward Copeland and Juliet McMaster (Cambridge: Cambridge University Press, 1997), pp. 211–26 and in Southam's 'Janeites and Anti-Janeites', as well as in the latter's Introduction to *Jane Austen: The Critical Heritage, Vol. 2: 1870–1940* (London: Routledge & Kegan Paul, 1987).

6. The story of how Mrs Burke, listening to the speakers' bitter complaints about Americans' purchase of Austen relics and of the lock of hair particularly, created a furore at the 1949 meeting of the Jane Austen Society held at Chawton, when she stood

up, declared herself and presented the Society with the lock, has almost passed into legend. When the story is told in the second (1980) number of *Persuasions*, the annual publication of the Jane Austen Society of North America, it almost seems to serve as founding myth for the Society's breakaway origins. Burke's widower, Henry Gershon Burke, was a co-founder of JASNA in 1979.

7. For those attentive to the politics of class and conscious of the history of economic exploitation producing country houses such as Lyme Park (BBC's 'Pemberley'), the notion that this version of the national landscape might represent the authentic home of a normal Englishness is troublesome. See Mike Crang, 'Placing Jane Austen, Displacing England' and Suzanne R. Pucci, 'The Return Home,' in *Jane Austen and Co.*, eds. Suzanne R. Pucci and James Thompson (Albany: State University of New York Press, 2003), pp. 111–30 and pp. 133–55.

8. Constance Hill, *Jane Austen: Her Homes and Her Friends*, p. viii.

9. Robert Miles, *Jane Austen* (Tavistock: Northcote House, 2003), p. 2.

10. The gender politics encoded in Miles's word 'gallantry' and the gender politics that, as Claudia L. Johnson has commented, have ensured that Austen is 'admitted into the canon on terms which cast doubt on her qualifications for entry' but which demonstrate the canon-maker's gentlemanly chivalry, appear pertinent here, *Jane Austen: Women, Politics, and the Novel* (Chicago: University of Chicago Press, 1988), p. xiv.

11. Katherine Mansfield, *Novels and Novelists* (1930), p. 305. Secret friends become a secret society in Rudyard Kipling's 1924 story that helped give the epithet 'Janeite' currency.

13

Later publishing history, with illustrations

DAVID GILSON

Any discussion of the publishing history of Jane Austen's novels after the writer's death in 1817 must, paradoxically, start with foreign publications issued in her lifetime but apparently unknown to her, since it is with these that we see the development of her wider fame, beginning, perhaps surprisingly, in Geneva.

Pride and Prejudice was first published at the end of January 1813, and a series of connected extracts from this novel in French translation appeared in the issues for July, August, September and October of the Swiss monthly periodical *Bibliothèque britannique*, published in Geneva, these extracts being the first appearance of any part of Jane Austen's text in a language other than English. Similar extracts from *Mansfield Park* in French translation appeared in four issues of the same periodical between April and July 1815, while in November 1815 the first complete French translation of *Sense and Sensibility* was issued in Paris in four volumes by Arthus Bertrand under the title *Raison et Sensibilité, ou Les Deux Manières d'Aimer*, the text being adapted by Isabelle de Montolieu. In June 1816 a French version of *Emma* by an unnamed translator was published in Paris by Arthus Bertrand & Cogez, entitled *La Nouvelle Emma, ou Les Caractères Anglais du Siècle*, also in four volumes, and in September 1816 the first French translation of *Mansfield Park* appeared in Paris from J. G. Dentu, still in four volumes, the translator being Henri Vilmain and the title *Le Parc de Mansfield, ou Les Trois Cousines*; also in 1816 the first American edition of *Emma* was published in two volumes by Mathew Carey of Philadelphia. About half of the first French version of *Emma* was reissued in the following year, 1817, in Vienna, with the addition of a hasty conclusion. All early translations and American editions must be assumed to have been issued without the knowledge or authority of the novelist or her heirs, since no family reference to them has been traced.

Figure 4. *L'Abbaye de Northanger* (Paris: Pigoreau, 1824),
frontispiece, vol. 1.

Four years later, in September 1821, Madame de Montolieu's French translation of *Persuasion* was published in Paris in two volumes by Arthus Bertrand under the title *La Famille Elliot, ou L'Ancienne Inclination*; this is notable for being the first published text of a Jane Austen novel to carry the author's name on the title page, and it is also the first illustrated edition of any of the novels, since each volume has an engraved frontispiece by Delvaux after Charles-Abraham Chasselat. In November 1821 the first French translation of *Pride and Prejudice* (apparently by an Englishwoman, Eloïse Perks) was issued in Paris by Maradan in three volumes, entitled *Orgueil et Prévention*, with title pages dated 1822 and not carrying the author's name; a second, entirely different French version of the same novel, with title changed to *Orgueil et Préjugé* and with author and translator not named, was published in Paris and Geneva in four volumes in March 1822 by J. J. Paschoud.

The first German translation of any novel by Jane Austen also appeared in 1822, probably in early summer, when Wilhelm Adolf Lindau's version of *Persuasion* was published in Leipzig in two volumes by Christian Ernst Kollmann, with the author identified as Johanna Austen and the title given as *Anna: Ein Familiengemählde*. The last novel by Jane Austen to appear in French was *Northanger Abbey*, as *L'Abbaye de Northanger*; this translation, by Hyacinthe de Ferrières, was published in Paris in three volumes in about November 1824 by Pigoreau, the author being named as Jeanne Austen. This text has an unsigned engraved frontispiece to the first volume only (albeit illustrating an incident occurring in the second volume, fig. 4). Late in 1827 Madame de Montolieu's 1815 French version of *Sense and Sensibility* was reissued in Paris, although in three volumes, not four, and dated 1828; this reissue has in addition an engraved frontispiece to each volume after Chasselat (fig. 5). The 1821 French translation of *Persuasion* was also reissued in Paris in 1828, each of the two volumes having the same engraved frontispiece as before (fig. 6). Two years later, in 1830, there appeared the second German translation of a novel by Jane Austen, when Louise Marezoll's version of *Pride and Prejudice* was issued in Leipzig by C. H. F. Hartmann in three volumes, under the title *Stolz und Vorurtheil*, with the author's name not given.

No English edition of any novel by Jane Austen had been published since 1818, when in 1831 a letter from the novelist's sister

Figure 5. *Raison et Sensibilité* (Paris: Arthus Bertrand, 1828), frontispiece, vol. 1, by Charles-Abraham Chasselat.

Figure 6. *La Famille Elliot* (Paris: Arthus Bertrand, 1828), frontispiece, vol. 1, by Charles-Abraham Chasselat.

Pickering, pinxt.   Greatbatch, sculpt.

FRONTISPIECE TO "SENSE AND SENSIBILITY," 1833

Then taking a small miniature from her pocket, she added, "To prevent the possibility of a mistake, be so good as to look at this face."

Figure 7. *Sense & Sensibility* (London: Richard Bentley, 1833), frontispiece, by William Greatbatch after, probably, George Pickering.

Cassandra to the London publisher John Murray, dated 20 May, made it clear that the publisher of the second edition of *Mansfield Park* and the first editions of *Emma* and of *Northanger Abbey and Persuasion* was then thinking of reissuing Jane Austen's novels; but no such reissue by John Murray in fact appeared. In August 1832 *Pride and Prejudice* was published in Philadelphia in two volumes by Carey & Lea under the title *Elizabeth Bennet; or, Pride and Prejudice*; the same publishers issued *Persuasion* in November 1832 and *Mansfield Park* in the following month, each title being again in two volumes. Earlier in 1832 the London publisher Richard Bentley had bought the remaining copyrights of all Jane Austen's novels, and he proceeded to issue all six novels in his cheap 'Standard Novels' series of small neat cloth-bound volumes, one novel per numbered volume (except for *Northanger Abbey* and *Persuasion*, which appeared together), retaining the original volume and chapter divisions. These, the first single-volume editions of Jane Austen, are also the first illustrated editions published in England, each having a steel-engraved frontispiece and a second title page with engraved vignette, by William Greatbatch after, probably, George Pickering (fig. 7). As with the frontispieces to the early French translations, the costumes shown are those of the date of actual publication; no attempt was made to represent the costume of the date of each novel's original publication. Bentley issued *Sense and Sensibility*, dated 1833, late in December 1832 or early in January 1833, with, as preface, a rewritten and augmented version of Henry Austen's 'Biographical Notice' of his sister, first published with *Northanger Abbey and Persuasion* in 1818; the remaining novels were all published by Bentley by the beginning of August 1833. In the meantime the Philadelphia publishers Carey & Lea issued *Northanger Abbey* in January 1833, *Sense and Sensibility* in February and the second American edition of *Emma* in July, in each case in two volumes. Bentley's 'Standard Novels' issues were published originally for separate sale, but in October 1833 they were reissued for sale as a set of five numbered volumes in a different binding, the first true collected edition. The separate issues and the collected edition were frequently reprinted, in different binding styles and at various dates until 1869, retaining generally the engraved frontispieces but not always the second title pages with engraved vignettes; in 1870 Bentley published a reset edition of the novels for separate sale, in a larger format, later issues of which retain the engraved frontispieces of 1833, and this edition was many times reprinted up to 1892. The 1870 text setting was also used for the nineteenth century's first attempt at a luxury edition of Jane Austen's novels, Bentley's 'Steventon Edition' of 1882, which was also the first Bentley set to have the novels numbered in the order of their first publication (375 sets printed on handmade paper in brown ink with border rules, uncut, still with the 1833 frontispieces).

From 1833 until 1892 the Bentley edition may be said to lead the field, but other publishers were soon in competition with Bentley on both sides of the Atlantic, before and after the expiry of the copyrights (and on the Continent as well: in 1836 there appeared the first Swedish translation of a Jane Austen novel, a version of *Persuasion* by Emilia Westdahl, published at Nyköping by P. E. Winge, two volumes in one, entitled *Familjen Elliot: Skildringar af Engelska Karakterer*, possibly not from the original English text but from the French version of 1821 and 1828). In 1838 Carey, Lea and Blanchard of Philadelphia reprinted that firm's earlier separate printings of the novels as a collected edition, two volumes in one, printed in double columns, and the same firm (now Carey and Hart) reissued the novels separately, still in double columns (but in single volumes), also in Philadelphia in 1845. Other British firms than Bentley clearly saw profit in publishing Jane Austen and began to issue editions of individual novels from the 1840s onwards. In 1844 H. G. Clarke of London (from this point all publishers named are London firms unless otherwise described) issued *Sense and Sensibility* and *Pride and Prejudice*, each in two small volumes in minute type; in 1846 *Mansfield Park* was published by Simms and M'Intyre in Belfast (the same firm going on to issue *Emma* in 1849 and *Northanger Abbey and Persuasion* in 1850), while in 1848 Wilkins, Carter & Co. of Boston published an edition of *Pride and Prejudice*, which was reissued in 1849, also in Boston, by George W. Briggs. None of these editions carried illustrations. In 1849, too, George Routledge issued separate editions of *Sense and Sensibility* and *Pride and Prejudice* without illustrations, reissuing the two novels in one volume in 1851 with a wood-engraved frontispiece by John Gilbert showing Elizabeth Bennet in a dress of 1851 (fig. 8).

There were soon further foreign editions. In 1855–6 there appeared the first Danish edition of a novel by Jane Austen,

PRIDE AND PREJUDICE.

Figure 8. *Pride & Prejudice* (London: Routledge, ?1870), frontispiece, reprinted from 1851 edition, by John Gilbert.

when a translation of *Sense and Sensibility* by Carl Karup was published in Kjøge in three volumes by L. Jordan for S. Oettinger, under the title *Forstand og Hjerte*. Bunce & Brother of New York issued *Pride and Prejudice* in 1855 and *Sense and Sensibility* in 1856, but the firm was taken over by Derby & Jackson, also of New York, who issued all the novels in 1857 in four volumes (*Sense and Sensibility* and *Persuasion* forming a double volume and *Pride and Prejudice* and *Northanger Abbey* another). This edition has a second, engraved, title page to each volume, incorporating in each case vignettes sometimes, but not always, reminiscent of those of the Bentley 'Standard Novels' issues of 1833, on which they may be based; the plates of its text were reused for further printings by Ticknor and Fields of Boston in 1863, and for undated reprints by Porter & Coates of Philadelphia in the 1870s with the addition of wood-engraved frontispieces (fig. 9). Another foreign edition of the 1850s was a Swedish version of *Emma* under the same title, published in six parts at Linköping in 1857–8 by C. F. Ridderstad, while in 1864 Bernhard Tauchnitz of Leipzig issued the English text of *Sense and Sensibility* in his paperback series 'Collection of British Authors', intended for sale on the Continent of Europe only (the first Continental printing of an English text of a Jane Austen novel), following this with *Mansfield Park* in 1867, *Pride and Prejudice* in 1870, *Northanger Abbey and Persuasion* in 1871 and *Emma* in 1877.

Meanwhile more London editions were appearing. *Mansfield Park*, issued by Routledge in 1857 in the 'Railway Library' series, initiated the style of publication in glazed paper boards (a style later called 'yellowback'), with a wood-engraved illustration on the front board only, not inside the volume; similar editions of *Emma* and of *Northanger Abbey and Persuasion* also appeared from Routledge in 1857. Other Routledge printings were issued in the 1870s and 1880s in illustrated paper wrappers, glazed paper boards or decorated cloth with wood-engraved frontispieces (figs. 10, 11), as in the 'Ruby Series' in the 1870s (a cloth-bound *Sense and Sensibility* in this series also bore the intriguing legend 'Inestimable Stones Unvalued Jewels'); the same firm issued 'Routledge's Edition' in 1883, a reset edition in illustrated glazed paper boards, or in cloth with the same illustration, a wood-engraving, as a frontispiece (fig. 12). The Routledge editions were also reprinted by Richard Edward

FRANK'S LETTER.

Figure 9. *Emma* (Philadelphia: Porter & Coates, [1870s]), frontispiece.

SENSE AND SENSIBILITY.

Figure 10. *Sense & Sensibility* (London: Routledge, *c.* 1875), frontispiece.

EMMA.

Figure 11. *Emma* (London: Routledge, 1870s), frontispiece.

MANSFIELD PARK.   Chap. XXIII.

Figure 12. *Mansfield Park* (London: Routledge, 1883), frontispiece.

King on very poor paper, undated, often with curiously inappropriate illustrations. In 1868 we find the first publication of any work of Jane Austen's apart from the novels, when the novelist's verses in memory of her friend Mrs Anne Lefroy were printed in Sir John Henry Lefroy's privately published *Notes and Documents Relating to the Family of Loffroy*, and in 1870 more minor works were made available in the first edition of the novelist's nephew James Edward Austen-Leigh's *A Memoir of Jane Austen*, issued by Bentley (the lines in memory of Mrs Lefroy, some humorous verses and the burlesque 'Plan of a Novel'). This book's second edition in 1871 added the first publication of *Lady Susan*, *The Watsons*, the so-called 'cancelled chapter' of *Persuasion* and extracts from *Sanditon* (the volume was issued in the format of the 1870 resetting of Bentley's edition of the novels, with its spine misleadingly lettered *Lady Susan &c.*). Further editions of the *Memoir* in the same format were issued in 1872, 1879, 1883 and 1886 as well as in Bentley's 1882 'Steventon Edition' of the novels mentioned earlier, before being reprinted by Macmillan in the same format in 1901 and 1904. The year 1870 was also notable for the reissue by Chapman and Hall of the Bentley 1833 printings of all six novels, in glazed paper boards with an illustration only on the front board (fig. 13).

In 1875 Groombridge and Sons published what I believe to be the first English edition of a Jane Austen novel illustrated with more than just a frontispiece: *Mansfield Park*, illustrated with drawings by A. F. Lydon, reproduced, apparently, lithographically, in tones of purplish grey. These comprise (on stiffer paper than the text) a frontispiece, a decorated title page (in addition to the letterpress title page), and six inserted plates, with figures in the costume of 1875 (fig. 14). This publisher is not known to have issued any other Jane Austen novel.

George Munro of New York published all the novels in 1880–1 in a cheap wrappered series entitled 'The Seaside Library', printed in three columns, with *Lady Susan* and *The Watsons* added in a further issue, while also in 1881 Ward, Lock and Co. issued what was probably the last printing of the novels from the stereotype plates of the 1833 Bentley editions, in glazed paper boards with wood-engraved illustration on the front board, or in cloth.

As we have seen, the last known Bentley printings of the novels were dated 1892; in that year another publisher, J. M. Dent,

Figure 13. *Pride & Prejudice* (London: Chapman & Hall, 1870), spine and front board.

Figure 14. *Mansfield Park* (London: Groombridge, [1875]),
illustration opp. p. 321, by A. F. Lydon.

embarked upon a career of publishing Jane Austen's novels which continued at least until the 1960s. Dent's ten-volume set of the novels published in 1892 is the first, as far as I know, to have any editorial matter (by R. Brimley Johnson), to acknowledge the existence of distinct early editions, and to make any attempt at serious consideration of the text. The illustrations after William Cubitt Cooke (fig. 15), sepia photogravure reproductions of almost monochrome grey-brown wash drawings, three to each volume, are also, as far as I know, the first to attempt (however unsuccessfully) to represent characters in the dress and surroundings, furniture etc. of the dates of composition or first publication of each novel, even if we may now detect an influence of the date of actual publication in some details, as Joan Hassall remarked: 'An artist cannot detach himself from the period in which he lives.'[1] Illustrations in most editions published after 1892 do generally attempt to represent the costume and surroundings of the dates of first publication. This edition offered also a luxury edition of 150 sets printed on handmade larger paper, with superior impressions of the plates. The text of this first Dent edition was reprinted in 1898, again in ten volumes, with new illustrations, six to each volume, by Charles Edmund Brock and his brother Henry Matthew Brock (pen and ink drawings tinted in watercolour and reproduced, rather garishly, by six-colour lithography), with more exact representation of period costumes and interiors than in the 1892 illustrations (fig. 16); the text also reappeared, with only one of the Brock illustrations as a frontispiece to each volume, in the 'Temple Edition' of 1899. The same text setting was again reused in the same publisher's 'Everyman's Library' series of 1906, without illustrations, and with the pagination altered to fit the publication of each novel in one volume. Between 1907 and 1909 Dent published a reset edition of all six novels in the 'Series of English Idylls', with delicately tinted illustrations reproduced by colour half-tone from new watercolour drawings by C. E. Brock alone (fig. 17), twenty-four per volume; these new text settings were used for reprintings of the 'Everyman's Library' editions between 1907 and 1932, again without the illustrations, and were also reissued as a set, with only sixteen of C. E. Brock's illustrations per volume, in 1922. In 1933–4 Dent published a reset edition of the novels in seven volumes, with new illustrations, eight per volume, by Maximilien Vox (fig. 18, printed in colour on

Figure 15. *The Novels of Jane Austen, Mansfield Park* (London: Dent, 1892), illustration opposite p. 179, vol. 1, by William Cubitt Cooke.

Figure 16. *The Novels of Jane Austen, Pride & Prejudice* (London: Dent, 1898), illustration opposite p. 177, vol. 1, by H. M. Brock.

Figure 17. *Pride & Prejudice* (London: Dent, 1907), illustration opposite p. 34, by C. E. Brock.

HE FOUND HIMSELF ON THE STAGE OF A THEATRE,
AND OPPOSED TO A RANTING YOUNG MAN

Figure 18. *Mansfield Park* (London: Dent, 1934), illustration
opposite p. 160, by Maximilien Vox.

a grained paper to reproduce the original rather faint drawings in ink and coloured crayon on linen); this edition is also notable for having in its seventh volume texts of 'Plan of a Novel', *Sanditon*, *The Watsons*, the 'cancelled chapter' of *Persuasion* and *Lady Susan*. But it seems that these new illustrations were not popular, since in a 1945 Dent printing of *Pride and Prejudice*, and in 1950 printings of all six novels, the Vox illustrations were replaced by sixteen of C. E. Brock's colour plates in each volume. The 1933–4 text setting was used for reprints of most volumes in the 'Everyman's Library' series and even for so-called revised editions of titles in that series in the early 1960s.

But we must return to the 1890s. An American twelve-volume set published in 1892 by Roberts Brothers of Boston, and many times reissued by Little, Brown and Company, has photogravure frontispieces to the novels by Edmund H. Garrett (which clearly attempt a period feeling, fig. 19), as well as printing *Lady Susan*, *The Watsons* and the Austen-Leigh *Memoir*, together with seventy-eight of Jane Austen's letters from the Brabourne edition of 1884. But the publication by George Allen in 1894 of an edition of *Pride and Prejudice* with illustrations and decorations by Hugh Thomson (fig. 20) introduces a new style of illustration: line drawings (often printed with the text) by a number of artists of whom Hugh Thomson, the Brock brothers and Chris Hammond (i.e. Christiana Mary Demain Hammond) are the most notable; like the Brock illustrations for the 1898 Dent edition, these make a serious attempt to reproduce the costumes and interior settings of Jane Austen's day, even though the last-named artist in particular cannot escape a strong flavour of the 1890s in her drawings. The 1894 *Pride and Prejudice* was the most elaborately decorated, since the 160 line drawings which Hugh Thomson executed for this volume comprise illustrations in the text, headpieces, tailpieces, ornamental initials and other decorations, including the wholly drawn title page and dedication page. C. E. Brock illustrated *Pride and Prejudice* for Macmillan in 1895 (fig. 21), and Hugh Thomson did the drawings (frontispiece and thirty-nine plates) for each of the remaining novels for the same publisher: *Sense and Sensibility* and *Emma* in 1896, and *Mansfield Park*, *Northanger Abbey and Persuasion* in 1897, all with appreciative introductions by Austin Dobson, while George Allen published editions of *Emma* in 1898 (fig. 22)

Mansfield Park.

Joined the chain and cross and put them round ... *neck. Vol. II. P.49.*

Figure 19. *Mansfield Park* (Boston: Little, Brown, 1898), frontispiece, vol. 2, by Edmund H. Garrett.

Such very superior dancing is not often seen.

Figure 20. *Pride & Prejudice* (London: George Allen, 1894), illustration opposite p. 118, by Hugh Thomson.

'" *No, no; stay where you are.   You are charmingly grouped.*"'

Figure 21. *Pride & Prejudice* (London: Macmillan, 1895),
illustration p. 49, by C. E. Brock.

" My regard for Hartfield is most warm——"   He stopped again, rose again, and seemed quite embarrassed

Figure 22. *Emma* (London: George Allen, 1898), illustration p. 269, by Chris Hammond.

and *Sense and Sensibility* in 1899, and the Gresham Publishing Co. *Pride and Prejudice* in 1900, all three with drawings by Chris Hammond. Other notable publications of the 1890s include the 1895 printing by Spottiswoode of charades by Jane Austen and other members of her family, and the 1898 Grant Richards edition of the novels in ten unillustrated volumes, the 'Winchester Edition' (reissued in 1905–6 by John Grant of Edinburgh, and again by Grant in 1911–12 with two additional volumes, comprising *Lady Susan* and *The Watsons*, necessarily taken from the 1871 *Memoir*, together with Jane Austen's letters, from the 1884 edition). The last translation published in the nineteenth century was a French version of *Northanger Abbey* by Félix Fénéon, written while the translator was in prison on a charge of anarchy; entitled *Catherine Morland*, this was published in instalments in the *Revue Blanche* in 1898, and issued in book form by Editions de la Revue Blanche in 1899.

From the beginning of the twentieth century separate editions are too numerous to record in detail, especially those published in inexpensive series by firms such as Cassell, Nelson, Blackie, Collins and others, including the new feature of annotated texts for schools and colleges, an early example of which is Mrs Frederick Boas's abridged edition of *Pride and Prejudice* from Cambridge University Press in 1910. Some of the cheaper editions have undistinguished illustrations, while others, such as a 1913 Cassell *Pride and Prejudice*, have new drawings by major illustrators, in this case C. E. Brock. There are more collected sets: the unillustrated 'Hampshire Edition' of 1902 (six volumes, published by R. Brimley Johnson), the 'Old Manor House Edition', issued in ten volumes by Frank S. Holby of New York in 1906 (with illustrations by the Brock brothers deriving from the 1898 Dent edition), the Chatto and Windus edition of 1908–9 in ten volumes with rather insipid colour illustrations, ten per volume, by A. Wallis Mills, and the unillustrated 'Adelphi Edition' published in seven volumes by Martin Secker in 1923, its final volume printing *Lady Susan* and *The Watsons*. Also deserving mention are the well-printed texts in Oxford University Press's 'World's Classics' series, small neat cloth-bound volumes, unillustrated and lacking editorial matter but each having appreciative introductions by notable critics, beginning with *Emma* in 1907 and continuing with *Pride and Prejudice* and *Mansfield Park* in 1929, *Northanger Abbey* and *Persuasion* in 1930 and *Sense and Sensibility* in 1931.

The year 1923 also saw the publication of what was to be the standard edition of Jane Austen's novels until the twenty-first century, that with 'the text based on collation of the early editions by R. W. Chapman', published in five volumes by the Clarendon Press, Oxford, with the novel feature of illustrations taken from contemporary sources (fashion plates etc.) in place of imaginative illustrations by artists of the 1920s. The prospectus for this edition claims: 'No illustrated edition has, as this one, illustrations from originals which Jane Austen might have seen. The text is free from modernisation and editorial improvements, while the commentary, appendixes and indexes are free from the intrusion of modernity.' The Chapman edition, one of the earliest critical editions of the writings of any English novelist, retains the original volume divisions and chapter numbering (as very few previous editions since the original editions had done); in each case an introductory note gives the circumstances of composition and publication, while the text is followed by notes (chiefly textual and concerned to give variant readings), indexes of characters and a variety of informative appendixes. The fifth volume has a general index to all six novels (of literary allusions, real persons other than authors and real places); the texts of *Sense and Sensibility* and *Mansfield Park* are based on the second editions and the remaining four titles on the first editions. The text setting of *Pride and Prejudice* is in fact that prepared for a separate edition of this novel published in 1912 by Oxford University Press, edited by Katharine M. Metcalfe (who was to marry R. W. Chapman in 1913); the text setting of *Northanger Abbey* is also that of a separate edition edited by her under her maiden name and published by the Clarendon Press earlier in 1923 than her husband's great edition.

The Chapman edition was reprinted in 1926 in a smaller format, described as 'Second Edition', and again in 1933–4 described as 'Third Edition'; but these are in fact unchanged reprints, although with additions to the notes. The edition was continually reprinted without change to the text, thus keeping its position as an unvarying source of reference. In 1954 R. W. Chapman published as volume 6 of his edition of Jane Austen's writings a complete collection of the minor works, edited from the manuscripts, in seven sections (the three volumes of *Juvenilia*, *Lady Susan*, *The Watsons* and *Sanditon*, 'Plan of a Novel', Opinions of *Mansfield Park* and *Emma*, Verses, Prayers), while a 1965–6 reprinting of the novels had alterations to the notes and appendixes by Mary Lascelles.

The 1920s and following years saw also the first separate print-ings of the minor works, generally unillustrated and edited from the manuscripts. In 1922 the second volume of the *Juvenilia* was published by Chatto & Windus as *Love & Freindship and Other Early Works*, with a preface by G. K. Chesterton, and with colour reproductions on the endpapers of all but one of Cassandra Austen's medallion portraits of kings and queens, illustrating 'The History of England' in the manuscript. *The Watsons* was published in 1923 by Leonard Parsons, with an introduction by A. B. Walkley, the text presumably coming from the 1871 second edition of the *Memoir*. Subsequent separate editions of the minor works are all edited by R. W. Chapman (*Lady Susan* in 1925, *Sanditon* in the same year, 'Plan of a Novel' etc. in 1926, the two chapters of *Persuasion* also in 1926, *The Watsons* in 1927, *Volume the First* in 1933 and *Volume the Third* in 1951, all these being published by the Clarendon Press, Oxford). Another edition of *Lady Susan* published by Philip Earle in 1931 merely reprinted the *Memoir* text, while the Colt Press of San Francisco produced a luxury edition of the *Three Evening Prayers* in 1940. Notable editions of the minor works after the Second World War include the Folio Society's selection with wood-engravings by Joan Hassall, first issued in 1963, B. C. Southam's edition of *Volume the Second*, from the manuscript (also 1963, from the Clarendon Press, Oxford), a facsimile of the entire manuscript of *Sanditon* published in 1975 (Clarendon Press/Scolar Press), a facsimile of the manuscript of *Lady Susan* and of the 1925 printed edition (New York: Garland, 1989), the text and facsimile of the manuscript of the play *Sir Charles Grandison*, attributed to Jane Austen (Burford: David Astor, 1981) and a text of the same edited by Brian Southam (Oxford: Clarendon Press, 1980), *Catharine and Other Writings*, edited by Margaret Anne Doody and Douglas Mur-ray (Oxford University Press, 1993), the facsimile of the manuscript of 'The History of England' (British Library, also 1993), and the editions of separate pieces edited by Juliet McMaster and others, issued by the Juvenilia Press of the University of Alberta from 1992 onwards.

But to return to the 1920s and editions of the novels. In 1927 there appeared a five-volume unillustrated edition of the works with introductions by John Bailey, including *Lady Susan* and *The Watsons*, published by Eveleigh Nash and Grayson, while in 1928 a separate text of *Persuasion* was issued by Gerald Howe with striking illustrations (pencil drawings, lightly colour-washed) by Pearl Binder (fig. 23); this was described as 'The Bath Edition', but no companion volumes ever appeared. Curiously stylised illustrations by Véra Willoughby (reminiscent of Heideloff's *Gallery of Fashion* and printed only in tones of grey, fig. 24) accompanied a text of *Pride and Prejudice* published by Peter Davies in 1929. In 1933 all six novels appeared together in one volume (New York: The Modern Library) for the first time since the Philadelphia edition of 1838, while a notable paperback edition was the 1938 Penguin Books text of *Pride and Prejudice* with wood-engravings by Helen Binyon (fig. 25), in the 'Penguin Illustrated Classics' series. The text of *Pride and Prejudice* issued in 1940 with illustrations by Helen Sewell (line drawings purporting to be imitations of nineteenth-century steel engravings), for members of the Limited Editions Club, began a series of American illustrated limited editions, signed by the illustrators (generally also with a commercial issue by the Heritage Press with fewer illustrations, for the ordinary book buyer), which continued with *Sense and Sensibility* in 1957, also illustrated by Helen Sewell, *Emma* in 1964 illustrated by Fritz Kredel, *Northanger Abbey* in 1971 illustrated by Clarke Hutton and *Persuasion* in 1977 illustrated by Tony Buonpastore. Similarly in England the Book Society issued *Persuasion* in 1944 with delicate illustrations by John Austen (fig. 26, pencil drawings enhanced with watercolour, reproduced by six-colour offset lithography, plus line drawings in the text), with a commercial issue by the Avalon Press; companion volumes were *Northanger Abbey*, 1948, illustrated by Robert Austin, *Sense and Sensibility*, 1949, illustrated by Blair Hughes-Stanton and *Pride and Prejudice*, also 1949, illustrated by B. Gordon Smith (all from the Avalon Press; no separate Book Society issues of the last three have been found).

During the Second World War ordinary reading texts of Jane Austen were hard to come by; after the war, with the lifting of printing restrictions, many publishers found it profitable to reissue the classics. Examples are: Zodiac Press (Chatto and Windus),

Figure 23. *Persuasion* (London: Gerald Howe, 1928), illustration opposite p. 156, by Pearl Binder.

Figure 24. *Pride & Prejudice* (London: Peter Davies, 1929), illustration opposite p. 50, by Véra Willoughby.

Figure 25. *Pride & Prejudice* (Harmondsworth: Penguin Books, 1938), frontispiece, by Helen Binyon.

AN IMAGINARY INVALID

Figure 26. *Persuasion* (London: Book Society, 1944), illustration opposite p. 34, by John Austen.

beginning with *Pride and Prejudice* in 1946 (reissued 1989 by Virago with introductions by Margaret Drabble), Williams & Norgate (an interesting series with introductions by contemporary women authors, beginning with *Persuasion* in 1946, introduced by Angela Thirkell), Nicholas Vane, beginning with *Pride and Prejudice* in 1947, Hamish Hamilton's 'The Novel Library', beginning with *Emma* in 1947 and Macdonald's 'Illustrated Classics' series with attractive, if stylised, illustrations by Philip Gough under the influence of Rex Whistler, beginning with *Emma* in 1948 (fig. 27). Allan Wingate issued all the novels plus *The Watsons* and 'Love and Freindship' in six unnumbered volumes in 1948, while another edition of all the novels was that of Random House, New York, illustrated by Warren Chappell, two volumes, 1950. The Folio Society began its edition illustrated with wood-engravings by Joan Hassall with *Pride and Prejudice* in 1957 (fig. 28), the text being mainly Chapman's; the series was reissued in 1975 with additional illustrations (scraperboard, not wood-engravings), while Penguin Books began its 'Penguin English Library' series of annotated paperback texts with *Persuasion* in 1965, edited by D. W. Harding (the series was later entitled 'Penguin Classics' and also issued in one omnibus volume in 1983), paralleled in America by W. W. Norton's 'Norton Critical Editions' series, of which *Pride and Prejudice*, edited by Donald J. Gray, published in 1966, was the first to appear. After this period inexpensive paperback editions proliferated.

Oxford University Press inexplicably included Jane Austen's novels in its unillustrated 'Oxford English Novels' series (previously restricted to novels by lesser writers long out of print), beginning with *Sense and Sensibility* in 1970, edited with an introduction by Claire Lamont (these texts were reissued in paperback in 1980 in the 'World's Classics' series, and in 1990 with new introductions by Isabel Armstrong and others). A handsome edition of *Pride and Prejudice* illustrated with wash drawings by Isabel Bishop was brought out by E. P. Dutton, New York, in 1976. An English text of *Northanger Abbey* was published in Moscow in 1983 by Raduga Publishers (coupled with a text of Mrs Radcliffe's *The Romance of the Forest*), while in 1985 a limited edition of *Pride and Prejudice* was published by Nottingham Court Press, the 'Godmersham Edition', with line drawings by John Ward originally made in 1948.

Figure 27. *Emma* (London: Macdonald, 1948), frontispiece, by Philip Gough.

Figure 28. *Pride & Prejudice* (London: Folio Society, 1957), frontispiece, by Joan Hassall.

1994 saw the publication of a set of enlarged facsimile reprints of the first editions of the six novels, accompanied by the 1870 *Memoir* and the 1884 edition of Jane Austen's letters, issued by Routledge/Thoemmes Press, to which I contributed bibliographical introductions, while the new 'Penguin Classics' edition, beginning in 1995 with *Northanger Abbey* edited by Marilyn Butler and *Sense and Sensibility* edited by Ros Ballaster, was distinguished by the editorial decision to use the first editions as the base-texts throughout. In 1996 a handsomely produced edition of the novels separately was published (in English) in Cologne by Könemann, while the latest notable editions were those of *Sense and Sensibility* published in 2002 (two separate texts, one edited by Claudia Johnson in the 'Norton Critical Editions' series, New York, and the other edited by Beth Lau in Houghton Mifflin's 'New Riverside Editions', Boston).

Finally, twentieth-century translations, which are very numerous and in many languages. From my book *A Bibliography of Jane Austen*, and from other sources, I have noted versions in Arabic, Bengali, Catalan, Chinese, Czech, Danish, Dutch, Finnish (including *Sanditon* and *The Watsons*), French (including *Juvenilia*), German (including *Lady Susan*, *The Watsons* and *Sanditon*), Greek, Gujarati, Hebrew, Hindi, Hungarian, Icelandic, Italian (including minor works), Japanese, Kannada, Korean, Marathi, Norwegian, Oriya, Persian, Polish, Portuguese, Punjabi, Roumanian, Russian (the first ever Russian translation was one of *Pride and Prejudice* issued in 1967, while a three-volume set of all six novels in Russian, extensively illustrated and annotated, was published in 1988–9), Serbo-Croat, Sinhalese, Slovene, Spanish, Swedish, Tamil, Telugu, Thai and Turkish – as well as the undated and unpublished typescript of a translation of *Pride and Prejudice* into Basic English (now at King's College Library, Cambridge).

NOTE

1. Jane Austen Society, *Report for the Year 1973*, p. 15.

14

Sequels

DEIDRE SHAUNA LYNCH

The sequels, prequels, retellings and spin-offs that Jane Austen's novels have inspired can try the patience and tolerance of the reader who means to be true to her and her example. For one thing, these works are so very numerous. Bibliographies compiled at the end of the 1990s, and currently linked to the website 'The Republic of Pemberley', list over a hundred published books and stories engaging to grant us more of the stylish prose and vivid characterisation that we love in the original. New writers have added to this inventory annually. Never wasting words, practising an exquisite economy on that famous 'little piece (two inches wide) of ivory' that sufficed for her canvas, Austen represents in several accounts of the development of the novel the innovator who trimmed away the flab of the form. Yet through a strange twist of fate she appears to be the cause of verbiage in others. This is the case even though, measured against the other writers who defined the novel for the nineteenth century, Austen wrote very little. There are only the six novels and the two fragmentary beginnings, *The Watsons* (begun and abandoned in 1804) and *Sanditon* (left incomplete at Austen's death in 1817). Speculating on readers' readiness to construe this 'little' that Jane Austen wrote as 'less than enough', the sequel-writers offer us their wares as compensation for that deprivation. None of the novels has escaped becoming grist for their mill.

'Sequel' is a rubric I use loosely in this essay. It covers, for instance, the several books that have provided conclusions for *The Watsons* and *Sanditon*. Following the lead of the bibliographies mentioned above, I also use 'sequel' to label those works which, in either prolonging the novels' action or renarrating it from different perspectives, also transfer their characters into a different generic register – anything from soft-core pornography (as in the 1981 continuation of *Persuasion* entitled *Virtues and Vices*, by the pseudonymous 'Grania Beckford') to fantasy (as in S. N. Dyer's 1996 *Resolve and Resistance*, which imagines a widowed Elizabeth Darcy using Pemberley as the base for a guerrilla movement against Napoleon's occupying army, and learning, with the help of Admiral Nelson, to navigate a fleet of hot-air balloons – 'moon boats' – so as to lead this English resistance to victory). This, of course, is in addition to applying the label to the more numerous books that imagine tamer after-lives for Jane Austen's characters. In the course of demonstrating how the carryings-on of these characters might carry on, the overwhelming majority of Austen sequels preserve Austen's comedy of manners and reduce it to a formula: take 'three or four families in a country village' somewhere in the south of England, some time during the Regency; arrange for strangers to arrive in that neighbourhood, marriageable young men whose ways are vexingly inscrutable; add narrative twists and turns by sending your heroines to balls or Brighton; end with at least one marriage.

Uniformly derivative, this body of material is nonetheless dauntingly diverse. The one generalisation it seems safe to hazard is that it has proven almost impossible to dissociate these attempts to recycle Austen from commercial motives. After all, Austen is good security for publishers' (or film studios') investments. Her audience is ready-made. The author of a sequel is not required, as Jane Austen's contemporary William Wordsworth put it, to create the taste by which he or she (nearly always *she*) is to be enjoyed.

Indeed, the history of Austen sequels – and, in particular, the timing of the up-turns in their production – seems to confirm a cynical understanding of sequel writing as the literati's closest approximation to a get-rich-quick scheme. Continuations of Austen's manuscript fragments begin as a family enterprise in the mid nineteenth century, with the first contributions coming from Jane Austen's nieces: Catherine Hubback (impecunious daughter of Francis, Jane Austen's younger brother), who in 1850 based a tripledecker novel, *The Younger Sister*, on *The Watsons*, and Anna Austen Lefroy (scion of the rival branch of the family headed by Jane Austen's eldest brother James), who evidently some time in the early 1830s began, but did not complete, a continuation of *Sanditon*. The first sequel proper, Sibyl Brinton's *Old Friends and New Fancies*, appears in 1914 – not long, that is, after Henry James issues his famous complaint about the greed of those publishers, editors and producers of 'the pleasant twaddle of the magazines' who find 'dear Jane' so infinitely to their 'material purposes.'[1] The most pronounced upsurge in production of sequels occurs in the late 1990s, timing that suggests, tellingly, that the audience demand these books have recently sought to gratify originated not with a collective rediscovery of the pleasures of Austen's fiction but rather with the 1995 broadcast of the BBC *Pride and Prejudice*. For detractors, the sequels' most irksome aspect might well be how their capitulation to market forces effaces any sense that 'the world of Jane Austen' was ever the creation of a real, distinctive individual. Instead, as sequels spawn sequels (which they do), Jane Austen is more and more thoroughly inscribed into the market's logic of seriality, and her works are more and more thoroughly assimilated to mass-produced Regency Romances – held hostage within a cultural arena organised by the premise that familiarity breeds content, and not contempt.

Of course, the anxieties provoked by the commercialisation of classic literature – anxieties about the fate of originals in capitalism's culture of copies – are nothing new. They fuelled the sociology of culture emerging during Austen's lifetime. By the same token, the sequel itself, far from anomalous, has represented a fundamental element of the history of the novel ever since the form's emergence in the eighteenth century. (After all, Robinson Crusoe, however repentant, could not be allowed to stay at home at the conclusion of Defoe's 1719 novel, but had to undergo 'farther adventures' filling a second and ultimately a third set of volumes.) Bearing this in mind might help us to acknowledge that there are reasons to engage these books – and, in general, the cross-over between classic literature and mass culture they manifest – with some patience and to hold off on accusing their authors of the crime of commercialising Austen. Busy lamenting the sequel writers' impudence and incompetence, their detractors have not got around to exploring why her works appear to have proven more hospitable to sequelisation than those of almost any other novelist.[2] Yet consideration of the last century of para-Austenian literature might illuminate, for instance, what it is about Austen's plotting – particularly in *Emma* and *Pride and Prejudice*, the two novels most often inspiring spin-offs – that awakens these desires for a story that would never come to a definitive end. It might illuminate how Austen's works themselves link the pleasure of stories with the pleasure of stories' nostalgic repetition.

Certainly, disappointment (invariably the counterpart of nostalgic repetition) defines most readers' experience of the Austen sequels. (Despite the regimen of posthumous productivity the sequel writers strive to impose on her, that much longed-for *seventh* Austen novel remains elusive.) And, certainly, there are delights in the original that readers are hard pressed to discover in para-Austenian pages: the bracing pleasures provided by Austen's stinging satire; by the undertone of despondency that haunts her fictions' comedy; by her evident faith in the moral efficacy of art. To assess the pleasures one *can* obtain, it is helpful to follow Betty A. Schellenberg and Paul Budra and distinguish between two kinds of sequels.[3] There is, on the one hand, the kind that pushes past the original ending to recount subsequent events in the story of an evidently unforgettable protagonist: such an approach involves writing beyond the nuptials ending the courtship plot so as to envision, for example, Elizabeth Bennett as a guerrilla insurgent or, less appealingly, as an unhappily barren newly-wed (the role Emma Tennant's 1992 *Pemberley* reserves for her). There is, on the other hand, the kind of sequel that refrains from meddling with the 'happily ever after' conclusion of the original, but arranges other ways to return to the world of the original novel or to what, more expansively, is frequently called 'the world of Jane Austen': such returns may often involve reorganising the story around the viewpoint of a hitherto minor character.

The first sort of sequel brings to the fore, I want to suggest, the pleasures human beings derive from gossip – that imaginative speculation we collaborate in when, on the basis of meagre evidence (chance remarks or scarcely glimpsed gestures), we spin stories about outcomes and consequences, extrapolating in speculative ways that often leave the evidence far behind. The sequels' debt to the rumour-mill is acknowledged with appealing candour when the letter-writing narrator of an early example of this genre, the 1929 'The Darcys of Rosings,' confesses to her correspondent that her husband, 'the Admiral', objects to her 'cackling . . . all over the neighbourhood' (about, for instance, the Wickhams' money troubles).[4] Of course, it is to just such tongue-wagging that we owe the story. Implicitly, readers of sequels in this mode are cast in the roles occupied first by the gossip-hungry residents of Austen's little neighbourhoods of Meryton and Highbury: we too await the latest news of how, as Mr Bennet might put it, our neighbours have been making sport for us.

One has only to recall the 'ingenious animating suspicion . . . with regard to Jane Fairfax, this charming Mr. Dixon, and the not going to Ireland' that relieves Emma Woodhouse from her boredom (*E*, 2:1) to apprehend how rich a resource gossip provides for Austen's fiction. Jane Austen herself, her nephew James Edward Austen-Leigh reported, would, 'if asked, tell us many little particulars about the subsequent career of her people. In this traditionary way we learned that Miss Steele never succeeded in catching the Doctor; that Kitty Bennet was satisfactorily married to a clergyman near Pemberley, while Mary obtained nothing higher than one of her uncle Philips' clerks, and was content to be considered a star in the society of Meriton.' Since its inclusion in Austen-Leigh's 1870 *Memoir* of his aunt, this anecdote has bestowed a seal of authorial approval on sequel-writing – especially as practised by his and his cousins' descendants, who tend to present their special knowledge of the stories' aftermaths as a kind of family legacy.[5] Yet these books that extrapolate from Austen's texts and recount what their heroines do next are generally regarded as dubious enterprises, as reviews attest. It is as if their imaginative flights invariably leave the 'evidence' that Austen's originals had supplied much too far behind them. One of the more high-minded of the sequel-writers, Joan Austen-Leigh (great-granddaughter of James Edward), declares herself an enemy to gossip in the 'Apologia' to her second *Emma* spin-off: she refrains from 'liberties', she says, and leaves the newly-wed Knightley and Emma 'to their well-earned privacy and peace'.[6] However, the sequels' inadequacies may be less a function of their indulgence in prying gossip than a function of a florid taste that often makes their gossiping take a melodramatic turn. The after-lives chronicled in the sequels feature sexual dysfunction, adultery and abductions. Sequel-writers have regaled their audiences with the evil-doings of a con-man from India (in 'The Darcys of Rosings'), of a con-woman from France (in Tennant's *Emma in Love*), or of the swashbuckling smugglers of Hastings (in Alice Cobbett's 1932 continuation of *Sanditon, Somewhat Lengthened*). The consequence is that these narratives often feel like throwbacks to the Gothic and sentimental novels that Austen loved to burlesque.[7] They often feel, in their sensationalism, strangely pre- rather than post-Austenian.

We know that Mrs Elton thought the Knightleys' scheme of residing at Hartfield with Mr Woodhouse 'a shocking plan' that 'would never do' (*E*, 3:17): was she right? We recall that Mr Bennet cautioned his favourite daughter that her 'lively talents would place [her] in the greatest danger in an unequal marriage' (*P&P*, 3:17): was he right? Books such as Rachel Billington's *Perfect Happiness* (1996) and Tennant's *Pemberley* exploit the unsettling undertones one detects in Austen's happy endings and give us pleasure by abetting our prognostications about what, if anything, those undertones foretell. In the second mode of sequelisation, that pleasure, while present, is subordinated to the pleasure of finding that, despite the time that has passed by in the fiction's world and the reader's own world, the everyday lives of Austen's personages continue to go on as usual. Mary Bennet has not left off making moral extracts. Mr Woodhouse still takes his daily constitutionals round the shrubbery. Treated to retellings of Austen's best lines and jokes and demonstrations of the unshakeable staying-power of her comic characters, these books' readers receive a reassuring message about the stability of human personality. Although the sequels' conjectures about what happens next necessarily remind us that time brings changes, books packaged as returns to 'Jane Austen's world' downplay their speculation about unknown futures and play up the comforts of familiarity. It is as if these writers anticipate readers who will resemble Mr Woodhouse in their adherence to routine or resemble Mr Woodhouse's grandsons in asking 'every day for the story of Harriet and gypsies, and still tenaciously [setting Emma] right if she varied in the slightest particular from the original recital' (*E*, 3:3).

They also anticipate readers who like puzzles and quizzes. As several commentators have opined, 'the world of Jane Austen' is frequently viewed through the rose-coloured glasses of nostalgia, mourned as a lost age of placid elegance: confirming this characterisation, the anonymous 'Lady' who continued *Sanditon* in 1975 offers her book as an 'escape' from the 'garishness' of our un-Austenian age and as 'relaxation' in a 'servantless world'.[8] Yet, as constructed by works such as Joan Aiken's *Mansfield Revisited*

(1984) and Julia Barrett's *Presumption* (1993), 'Austen's world' is to a surprising extent defined not only by retrograde longing but also by a kind of postmodern playfulness and predilection for insider joking. This world's architects often take great delight in arranging for the characters from one Austen novel to consort with those from another or in merging details from her fictions with facts from her biography. Brandons keep company with Darcys, and Wickhams with Crawfords; Naomi Royde-Smith's *Jane Fairfax* (1940) reports on the afterlives of characters from Burney's *Evelina*; Jane Austen's aunt's misadventures with lace and the law are in *Presumption* transferred to the Bennet girls' Aunt Philips. The enjoyment offered by such games of recombination, which nonchalantly treat Austen's bits of ivory as so many puzzle pieces, is of a distinctive kind: when we recognise, reading *Mansfield Revisited*, that Lady Bertram's haplessness as she confronts a charade ('can it be a swan? A peacock? An eagle?') is a reprise of Harriet Smith's in *Emma*,[9] we receive gratifying proof that we, at least, are not so clueless. That sense of being in the know is, of course, a boon that Austen herself grants those readers who decipher her allusions to earlier fictions or notice, even before she tells them to, that 'tell-tale compression of the pages' which, in the breezy, proto-postmodern idiom of the final chapter of *Northanger Abbey*, assures them that 'we are all hastening together to perfect felicity' (2:16).

To consider how the sequel balances between such knowingness and that particular form of forgetting called nostalgia, and to think about how the wit that is involved in arranging for Lady Bertram to be reborn as Harriet entails both recognition and surprise, is to realise that the author of the sequel faces a more difficult task than Emma does when she gratifies her nephews with the same old story. That author needs to provide *some* variation on or renovation of the original. She must refrain from simply reconstituting it, even as, paradoxically, she caters to her readers' demand for more of the same. As, over the years, authors have negotiated this conundrum, the minor character who may be remade as a major character has proved highly serviceable. A grown-up Margaret Dashwood, Georgiana Darcy or Susan Price is a new(ish) character who may nonetheless be enrolled in a marriage plot reiterating her siblings' stories. 'Here we go again,' is the relieved (or disgruntled) response of the reader who finds Susan – sister to the now married

Fanny – being described as a girl who exhibits an offensive 'free-dom of manner' and who 'does not improve'; though the words are spoken by Julia Bertram, knowing readers recognise them as vintage Mrs Norris (Aiken, *Mansfield Revisited*, p. 14).

And 'Here we go again' may be just the response Jane Austen solicited. *She* ushered Susan into Mansfield Park and *Mansfield Park* originally; *she* arranged for a cycle to recommence. The evidence of the novels themselves, in other words, suggests that Austen, if not exactly scripting the terms of her future sequelisation, was as happy as her sequel-providers to play with the conventions of narrative teleology and closure. Her narratives often incorporate repetition – the recursive rhythms of everyday life – in ways that stay the forward momentum of the plot and qualify the readers' sense of 'hasten-ing' pell-mell towards 'felicity'. Even in *Pride and Prejudice*, widely considered a model courtship narrative, there is in the third volume a moment when, as Mr Bingley resumes his lease at Netherfield and Mrs Bennet resumes her manoeuvring, Elizabeth thinks with exasperation that time must be going in circles: 'Were the same fair prospect to arise at present, as had flattered them a year ago, every-thing, she was persuaded, would be hastening to the same vexatious conclusion' (*P&P*, 3:11). We should notice, too, as another instance of this unorthodox narratology, that Austen more than once sets up her novels as though they were the sequels to earlier (untold) stories. *Emma* thus *begins* with a wedding and with its heroine congratulating herself (as any author who had just penned her final chapter would) on the fact that she has conducted the love-story of Mr Weston and Miss Taylor to a happy conclusion.

As a genre sequels are, according to Marjorie Garber, at once 'experientially conservative' – bringing out, as I have observed, the Woodhouse in readers, coddling us in our reluctance to counte-nance newcomers – and 'theoretically radical' – challenging, with their own weird postmodern metafictionality, some of the literary tradition's sacrosanct convictions about the boundedness of texts and the mechanisms of narrative closure.[10] Admirers of the origi-nal novels naturally feel affronted by the sequel writers' refusal to give Austen the last word. But cued by their books' 'theoretically radical' nature, the reader might well permit herself some second thoughts – and wonder whether Jane Austen ever believed she would have it.

NOTES

1. Henry James, 'The Lesson of Balzac', in *Jane Austen: The Critical Heritage, Vol. 2: 1870–1940*, ed. B. C. Southam (London: Routledge & Kegan Paul, 1987), p. 230.
2. According to Pamela Licalzi O'Connell, 'A World Without End for Fans of Jane Austen,' *New York Times* (13 January 2000) the novels have proved more hospitable than any other classic literature to writers of fan fiction.
3. *Part Two: Reflections on the Sequel*, eds. Paul Budra and Betty A. Schellenberg (Toronto: University of Toronto Press, 1999), p. 8.
4. E. Barrington (pseud.), 'The Darcys of Rosings', in *'The Ladies!': A Shining Constellation of Wit and Beauty* (1922), p. 241.
5. *A Memoir of Jane Austen and Other Family Recollections*, ed. Kathryn Sutherland (Oxford: Oxford University Press, 2002), p. 119. Francis Austen's great-granddaughter Edith Hubback Brown, writing under her married name, Mrs Francis Brown, published *Margaret Dashwood, or, Interference* in 1929 and *Susan Price, or, Resolution* in 1930. The author biography printed on the dust-jacket of *Pemberley* refers to how Emma Tennant 'grew up . . . hearing about her family's connection to Jane Austen'. For her dust-jackets, Joan Austen-Leigh was photographed with her great-great-great-aunt's writing desk.
6. Joan Austen-Leigh, *Later Days at Highbury* (New York: St Martin's, 1996). *Later Days* indeed permits its audience few glimpses of the Knightleys' wedded life, and those only from a distance.
7. As Judy Simons has pointed out in 'Classics and Trash: Reading Austen in the 1990s,' *Women's Writing* 5:1 (1998); see in particular pp. 35–6.
8. Jane Austen and Another Lady [Marie Dobbs/Anne Telscombe], *Sanditon* (Boston: Houghton Mifflin, 1975), pp. 326–7.
9. Joan Aiken, *Mansfield Revisited* (London: Victor Gollancz, 1984), p. 119. Subsequent references are included in the text.
10. Marjorie Garber, 'I'll Be Back', *London Review of Books* 21:16 (19 August 1999).

15

Translations

VALÉRIE COSSY AND DIEGO SAGLIA

The diffusion on the Continent of Austen's novels in translation began as early as 1813 with the first French translation of *Pride and Prejudice*, soon followed by others in French, German, Danish and Swedish.[1] At first sight cultural variety may well seem to prevent the possibility of considering Austen's reception on the Continent as a whole. But if the close analysis of the different translations constitutes a crucial area of Austen scholarship still largely neglected, general observations drawn from the context of European literature in the nineteenth century are necessary, nevertheless, to help readers come to terms with the baffling idiosyncrasies of the individual texts. This explains the structure of this entry, which will offer some general considerations before focussing on a number of examples in French and German.

The early to mid nineteenth-century panorama of Austen's reception and translation in Europe is generally characterised by gaps and absences, as is well exemplified by the case of Russia. As early as 1816 the journal *Vestnik Evropy* ('The European Herald') published a review of *Emma*, largely drawn from foreign sources rather than from any direct knowledge of the novel. After this early and promising notice, however, Austen disappeared from the Russian literary domain until the 1850s, when the 'anglomaniac' critic Aleksandr Druzhinin mentioned her in an essay about English women writers for the journal *Sovremennik* ('The Contemporary'), an overview that also dealt with Maria Edgeworth, Lady Blessington, Felicia Hemans and the Brontë sisters. Nonetheless, these and other occasional mentions of Austen and her work were not accompanied by translations. The first version of an Austen novel in Russian was published as late as 1967.[2]

Furthermore, one observes that, even in those areas of the Continent where Austen's novels were early available in translation, she herself remained a rather unknown figure as a novelist. Her importance was only gradually recognised and her delayed canonisation was an effect of Anglo-American critical evaluations. As late as 2000 the general editor of her *Œuvres romanesques complètes*, Pierre Goubert, still asserted that Jane Austen is in France 'un auteur méconnu'. He also had to explain for the sake of a general audience why her novels deserved to be included in the prestigious collection of 'La Pléiade' alongside other works of the French and European canon.[3]

This general misapprehension or underestimation of Jane Austen derives in good part from the way her novels were regarded in the nineteenth century as a result of the translations. The main distorting factors in the early diffusion of her work were the relative marginalisation of women writers, but also the predominance of Walter Scott, whose name was synonymous with the 'English' novel for Continental readers. Also, being intensely English, Austen's novels were perceived as 'exotic', so that Continental translators had to make them relevant to local traditions of novel writing and readers' habits. Most often this involved accommodating a local variety of sentimentalism and suppressing Austen's humour.

Notions of cultural appropriation and adaptation are thus crucial to address the earliest translations of Austen's novels. Indeed, early attempts at adapting Austen for European readers did not treat either the author or her works with any special consideration. The novel was a widely consumed literary genre, and Britain, with its abundant production, was an inexhaustible source. In Europe Jane Austen was simply one of the many writers whose works satisfied continental readers' demand for prose fiction.

By 1824, Austen's six novels had all been translated into French, *Pride and Prejudice* three times and *Mansfield Park* twice. Between July and October 1813 the *Bibliothèque britannique* published the first French translation of *Pride and Prejudice* and, between April and July 1815, the first translation of *Mansfield Park*. Each appeared abridged and in four instalments, the proportion of the novel conveyed in translation representing one third of the original. In 1815 the novelist Isabelle de Montolieu signed a 'free translation' of *Sense and Sensibility* and then one of *Persuasion* in 1821. Because of the widespread distribution of the *Bibliothèque britannique* over Europe and because of Isabelle de Montolieu's fame, these can be regarded as the most widely read among the early translations.[4]

The *Bibliothèque britannique* was edited in Geneva by a team of men of letters and their families, directed by the scientist Marc-Auguste Pictet and his brother Charles Pictet de Rochemont, a diplomat and a key figure in the history of the city republic after Waterloo. Like the authors of *Practical Education*, Richard Lovell and Maria Edgeworth, to whom they felt close and whose work they regularly translated, the Pictets dreamed of a well-ordered society united around its middle classes and moving forward thanks to practical progress. Literature was not a priority as such, moral instruction and utility alone justifying the presence of any text in the Pictets' journal. In the context of the *Bibliothèque britannique* fiction was regarded as a potentially didactic genre aimed at an exclusively female audience.

The translations of the *Bibliothèque britannique* make tangible the distance separating a complex novel from conduct literature. They also suggest how liberal Austen's gender politics were. In the case of *Pride and Prejudice*, her heroine and the 'liveliness of her mind' needed drastic trimming to accommodate the editors' definition of suitable reading for dutiful daughters. Their 'Miss Eliza' reveals by contrast the extent to which Lizzy oversteps the limits of proper womanhood through, among other things, her freedom of expression. While the text of the translation focusses exclusively on the central plot of her involvement with Darcy, her verbal exchanges with him are subjected to a process of systematic revision. In the *Bibliothèque britannique* the wit with which these sparkles of truth resist the senselessness of ordinary conversation is replaced by feminine modesty. Elizabeth's boast at the ball – according to which she has 'always seen a great similarity in the turn of [their] minds', because each of them is 'unwilling to speak, unless [they] expect to say something that will amaze the whole room' (*P&P*, 1:18) – is typically the kind of statement that underwent emendation. Her words become: 'Moi, je garde le silence, parce que je ne sais que dire, et vous, parce que vous aiguisez vos traits pour parler avec effet.' The equality of mind which Elizabeth takes for granted is denied and gender distinction introduced. Readers of the Geneva periodical could never know that Darcy actually falls for her 'liveliness of mind' as the translation ends with Mr Bennet's approval of the match in chapter 17, that is, before the words are spelled out in the next chapter. To stop there was a clever editorial choice and shows, paradoxically, the Pictets' good understanding of the implications of chapter 18 for their conception of the novel as a didactic genre. This is the chapter where Austen reviews and dismisses one after the other all the reasons why a good girl should be rewarded with a good marriage. Politeness, beauty, benevolence, sisterly devotion, none of these explains Darcy's love. Within a periodical which praised Frances Burney's *Camilla* for placing women's qualities of the heart above those of their minds (vol. 4, 1797), and which described Mary Wollstonecraft as 'a distorted mind entertaining wrong ideas about subordination and dependence' (vol. 9, 1798), chapter 18 was logically vetoed.

Fanny Price was more in line with the editors' conception of female behaviour. But the translated text of *Mansfield Park* involves a number of structural modifications of the narrative in order to transform the reader's perception of her heroic qualities. Fanny's share of sentimental symptoms – paleness, physical weakness, betrayal of emotions through bodily manifestations of blushing, trembling, weariness or headache – is reflected in the translation. But the status of these symptoms differs. In *Mansfield Park* the narrator invites us to understand them either as natural physical features of Fanny or as attitudes fostered by her deprived position in the Bertram household. Austen repeatedly warns her reader not to mistake them for the novelistic attributes that signal the presence of a heroine. 'Her' Fanny is not one of those 'unconquerable young ladies' one finds in books (*MP*, 3:17, 2:6). Yet this is exactly what she is in the *Bibliothèque britannique*, where her sensibility serves to confirm her heroic status. This shift from the original scepticism of the authorial stance to a prescriptive endorsement of the heroine's sentimental traits is achieved through an alignment of the translated text with the male characters' perception of Fanny: Sir Thomas's, but also Henry Crawford's and Edmund's. The translation generally colludes with Sir Thomas's point of view. His patriarchal authority is left intact thanks to a pattern of cuts and rewriting which reduce the scope of the Antigua connection and present Mrs Norris as the only culprit. Sir Thomas becomes what he is not in Austen's novel: the structural as well as the moral foundation of the text. Entirely constructed by the male gaze, the character of Fanny ends up as an 'unconquerable young lady' indeed, to the extent that the innocent creature of the *Bibliothèque britannique* is not even aware that her feelings for Edmund are not of a sisterly kind. Paradigmatic of the structural shift of the translated text is the suppression of Austen's authorial intervention on behalf of Fanny in chapter 6 of the second volume, a chapter otherwise translated: 'I have no inclination to believe Fanny one of them'. The bond of female solidarity between narrator and heroine is deleted and replaced with the narrative of the patriarch.

The next translation to appear in French was by Isabelle de Montolieu, a very prolific Swiss novelist based in Lausanne and publishing in Paris. The title page of *Raison et sensibilité ou les deux manières d'aimer* announces a 'free translation' by Mme de Montolieu, without any allusion to the 'lady' who authored the original. The preface declares some 'slight changes', 'near the end', clearly an understatement for the profound and numerous changes affecting the plot and the style of *Sense and Sensibility*, but also its genre. The English novel of sensibility conceived by Austen as a metacritical genre, relying on verisimilitude and producing its own critique of sensibility, ended up, under Montolieu's pen, as a French sentimental novel. The sentimental novel was, alongside the Gothic novel, the historical novel and the comic novel, one of the genres defined by the catalogues of the circulating libraries in Restoration France. Montolieu had made a name for herself as the sentimental novelist of the age, coming third in popularity on the librarians' lists of most wanted books behind Mme de Genlis and Walter Scott.[5] By the time she translated *Sense and Sensibility*, her reputation was already firmly established. Austen's novel, consequently, had to accommodate the expectations of her translator's readership, and the 1821 'free translation' of *Persuasion*, indeed, although it bore Jane Austen's name on the title page, was published as volumes 15 and 16 of Montolieu's own *Œuvres complètes*.

In her groundbreaking study of the sentimental novel in France, Margaret Cohen provides an apt context to understand the overall difference between Montolieu's and Austen's conceptions of the genre. As Cohen sees it the French sentimental novel has more affinities with drama, especially tragedy, than with narrative fiction. It is structured around a clear binary opposition and anchored in the Enlightenment rhetoric of duty towards the community *versus* the individual right to happiness. It is also defined by a number of formal features present in Montolieu's novels but absent from those of Jane Austen. Within the French context, the sentimental novel is in conflict with, and is superseded by the realist novel. The sentimental opposition between duty and the right to happiness is then replaced with a plot tracing the progress and success of a male protagonist *against* the social community, negatively conceived as a war of interests.[6] This new map and chronology of the genre in France is helpful not only because it can explain many of Montolieu's interpretative choices but also because it accounts for the lack of recognition of Austen throughout the nineteenth century and to some extent even today in the French-speaking world.

Jane Austen wrote a kind of novel that simply never existed in French. Her work can be understood as a synthesis of liberal sentimentalism and realism. Through Montolieu's translations, which proved, in this respect, very influential, they were incorporated into the sentimental genre that was to be discredited by Stendhal, Balzac and Flaubert and, as far as the canon is concerned, entirely discarded. The rare French critics who were favourable to Austen's work, like Léon Boucher in the *Revue des Deux Mondes* (1878) or Théodore Duret in the *Revue Blanche* (1898), defended her by insisting she was an exclusively realist genius.[7] But her novels do in fact combine elements of sentimentalism and realism both in style and ideology. Austen's heroines are poised between their desire for happiness and their sense of duty towards the community. Yet this emphasis on the heroine's moral choice does not preclude a critical perspective on the repressive nature of social life, Austen focussing simultaneously on inner conflicts and social, cultural or economic factors. Thus, her detailed analysis of the effects of rank and money is incompatible with the sentimental poetics which conditioned the earliest translations of *Sense and Sensibility* and *Persuasion*, while her adherence to the concept of sensibility is alien to the ideology underlying French realist poetics. In this respect we understand also better why the only nineteenth-century translator who took Jane Austen seriously as a challenging author of 'genius' was Félix Fénéon, editor of the *Revue Blanche*, who, in 1898, translated *Northanger Abbey*, the most parodic and least sentimental of the six novels.

In terms of sentimental conventions, one observes Montolieu's propensity to organise her material along a number of binary oppositions and her effacement of realistic references to money or the body, deemed 'vulgaires' by the French aesthetic standards of the early nineteenth century. *Raison et sensibilité* and *La Famille Elliot* are both predicated on a strong binary structure opposing the wise heroine – Elinor and Anne respectively – to a set of corrupt or otherwise undeserving characters whose flaws are expanded and stressed by Montolieu: Robert Ferrars, Lucy Steele and Mrs Willoughby on the one hand, Anne's sisters and the Musgrove girls on the other. In *Sense and Sensibility* a binary structure is, of course, suggested by Austen, but Montolieu turns the difference between the sisters into a radical contrast between duty (Elinor) and the individualistic pursuit of happiness (Marianne, who becomes Maria). The appeal of Montolieu's text is entirely emotional and involves a collusion with Marianne's conception of herself as a sentimental icon. The episode of her illness at Cleveland is in this respect very explicit. In Austen's novel, the heroine's symptoms appear while she is lingering languidly on a sofa, 'with a book in her hand, which she was unable to read', after she has taken a walk in those parts of the park where 'the grass was the longest and wettest' and kept on her 'wet shoes and stockings' (*S&S*, 3:6, 7). Maria is strolling on top of a hill reading Thomson's *Seasons* when she faints, by the 'first step' of a temple of love, on seeing Willoughby and his wife pass by in the distance: 'Elle sent qu'elle est près de mourir, une sueur froide la couvre . . .'

In spite of the kinship between French sentimentalism and melodrama, Montolieu maintained the structural comedy of Austen's endings, but with a major nuance. She is not interested in a comic vein as such, nor does she convey Austen's irony. She even deletes in her translation of the 'Biographical Notice' Henry Austen's reference to his sister's partaking 'largely in all the best gifts of the comic muse'. What is perfunctory and a matter of generic conventions in Austen's conclusions is endowed with the symbolic meaning of a full and complete return to order in Montolieu's. Thus *Raison et sensibilité* does not end simply with the heroine's marriage to Brandon. By the terms of Montolieu's conclusion, Willoughby needs to be thoroughly reformed. He is widowed, free to marry Brandon's stepdaughter, and by the time he remarries and owns his child, the man of the world has turned into a man of feeling: 'je vivrai en philosophe à Haute-Combe entre ma femme et mon enfant,' says he. In *La Famille Elliot* Anne marries Wentworth in due course, but instead of leaving her whereabouts a matter of speculation Montolieu restores her to Kellynch: 'Wentworth acheta une charmante campagne dans ce lieu chéri.' This movement of restoration at the end of Montolieu's translations is typical of the 'idyllic closure' characterising sentimental novels written in Switzerland. These 'Swiss' novels, inspired by Rousseau's Clarens in *La Nouvelle Héloïse*, all rely on the same kind of conclusion: a complete resolution, both aesthetic and moral, whereby every single element of the plot is resolved and errors redeemed within the space of the novel.[8]

The other French translators of *Mansfield Park*, *Emma*, *Pride and Prejudice* and *Northanger Abbey* adhered to a more literal style of translation. Appearing in two waves, in the wake of *Raison et sensibilité* and *La Famille Elliot*, they were marketed according to the generic definitions of library catalogues where they were presented as sentimental or even Gothic (*Northanger Abbey*) novels. As for *Emma*, the preface described it as 'not a novel' but 'un tableau des mœurs du temps' (Gilson, *Bibliography*, p. 161). This indeterminacy about the status of Austen's novels weighed heavily on the French reception of her work throughout the nineteenth century.

The first novel to appear in German was *Persuasion*, translated by W. A. Lindau as *Anna: Ein Familiengemählde* 'von Johanna Austen', for the Leipzig publisher Kollmann in 1822. Lindau was well known as an author of historical novels and a translator from the English. He had made his reputation with a translation in instalments of Scott's *The Antiquary*, published in 1816, that was followed by a series of popular translations from further novels by Scott, Maria Edgeworth, Amelia Opie and Lady Morgan, among others. Although an isolated instance, unlike his several versions from Scott, Lindau's translation of *Persuasion* is also a valuable indication of the degree of simplification and the abolition of cultural specificity undergone by Austen's works in early nineteenth-century translations. Adaptation is in full sight in the transformation of the title and the Germanised version of the author's name, as well as those of the heroine and the entire *dramatis personae*. Lindau replaces geographical names, topographical references or fashionable and familiar addresses with more generic definitions, while he also transforms distances in English miles into indications of

travelling times. Another conspicuous form of adaptation and simplification is the omission of such qualifiers and adverbs as 'particularly' and 'generally', usually associated with distinctively English
expressions of understatement that are not always easily rendered
into other languages. In addition, Austen's examinations of social
intercourse present several difficulties for this German translator,
who, for instance, cannot find satisfactory counterparts for 'gentleman' or 'character'. By the same token, he simplifies the spectrum of English social niceties and discriminations which Austen's
novels highlight through linguistic usage and register, instances
of 'manners' and 'style', references to places and the discourse of
property. This German translation even more drastically reduces
free indirect speech to direct speech; and, although Lindau partly
preserves Austen's irony, in his version the narrator's voice is more
intrusive, and thus more decisively prescribes the reader's construction of the plot. Austen's mobile and multiple anatomy of the
social, as well as intimate, experiences of men and women ultimately becomes a more univocal and easily interpreted picture of
reality.[9]

Nevertheless Lindau's several adaptations and simplifications do
not affect the plot, which was one of the main reasons behind the
choice of Austen's novels for translation and was generally reproduced in all its details. This is also characteristic of the second translation into German, a version of *Pride and Prejudice* published in
1830 in Leipzig by Hartmann with the title *Stolz und Vorurtheil: Ein
Roman frei nach dem Englischen*. The translator was the writer and
magazine editor Louise Marezoll and, as with Lindau's version, hers
is a respectful translation by early nineteenth-century standards. At
the same time, however, as it is 'frei nach dem Englischen' ('freely
[translated] from the English') it betrays again a desire to German-
ise Austen's novel. The practice of adaptation is already visible in
the modifications undergone by the opening sentence which, in
Marezoll's German, reads: 'Nichts ist leichter vorauszusetzen, als
daß ein junger, reicher, unverheiratheter Mann von allen andern
Dingen eine Frau bedarf.' This sentence differs greatly from the
tone of the original: 'wealth' and 'youth' replace Austen's 'possession' and 'good fortune', while the disappearance of 'acknowledged'
abolishes the notion of a universally shared conviction and simplifies Austen's careful examination of social conventions. Like

Lindau, Marezoll is more interested in Austen's plot than her characterisation. She also replaces Austen's skilfully orchestrated free indirect style with direct speech, and tones down such comedic features as the use of understatement by avoiding problematic textual markers such as 'somewhat' or 'rather'. Marezoll's translation rewrites *Pride and Prejudice* as a sentimental, 'love-and-marriage' novel, and intensifies its pathos by greatly reducing the scope of Austen's pervasively ironic outlook. Accordingly, this version simplifies the characterisation of *Pride and Prejudice*, pares down its carefully delineated social distinctions, and does not always reproduce the sparkle of Austen's witty and socially relevant dialogue (Chambers, 'German Translations', pp. 237–43).

The German domain presents phenomena of cultural appropriation and refashioning similar to those seen in Austen's translations and reception in French-speaking countries. Austen's works were translated as sentimental novels with realistic details, social novels, edifying tales or often mere literature of consumption, as is exemplified by the version of *Emma* published in Vienna in 1817 as *La nouvelle Emma* that drastically shortens Austen's original. But Lindau's and Marezoll's German translations are especially interesting because they were reviewed in contemporary literary journals (Gilson, *Bibliography*, pp. 178, 181; Chambers, 'German Translations', pp. 246–9, 408). And these critical examinations do not merely indicate how these versions were received, but also why and to what extent Jane Austen mattered to the German-speaking public. In effect, if reviewers praised Austen for her subtle characterisation and the realistic settings of her scenes and situations, they also couched their appreciations in a sentimental 'language of the heart' that depicts Austen as a representative of late Romantic women's literature. Reviewers thus insisted on notions such as the depth of the feelings portrayed in her narratives, ideas of morality and moral purity ('das Sittlich-Schöne'), domesticity ('Häuslichkeit'), the quotidian and a mixture of 'soft femininity' ('sanfte Weiblichkeit') and 'feeling' ('Gemüth'). The German reviewers employed a lexicon that was similar to the critical language usually applied to women's writings in Britain, especially the tradition of the Romantic poetess of the 1820s and 1830s, yet which more specifically rehearsed the southern German and Austrian *Biedermeier* cultural ideals of homeliness, sentimentalism and religious 'pietism'.[10] Reviewers disseminated an Austen characterised by morality, domesticity and 'sweetness', and based on the translators' simplifications of her language, irony and close observation of culture-specific social realities. The result was a kind of domesticated or 'quietistic' Jane Austen in keeping with mid-century German bourgeois culture.

Similar observations may be extended to the other earliest translations into a European language. A Swedish version of *Persuasion*, entitled *Familjen Elliot*, appeared in 1836 and was probably based on Isabelle de Montolieu's 'free translation' *La Famille Elliot* of 1821. In 1855–6 there appeared a Danish version of *Sense and Sensibility*, *Forstand og Hjerte*, while a Swedish version of *Emma*, simply entitled *Emma*, was published in 1857–8 (Gilson, *Bibliography*, pp. 137–8, 181–6). The fact that these were sporadic and occasional publications confirms that Austen's novels were not chosen by translators for their own literary merit, but rather because of a demand for novels in European cultural contexts that, unlike Britain, did not boast such a rich tradition of novel writing. Indeed, early nineteenth-century German readers demanded English historical novels or romances. Since Austen's works did not fit into either of these categories, they were not systematically translated and were adapted to other popular fictional modes. Later in the century, readers could have formed a more accurate idea of Austen's output thanks to the Leipzig publisher Tauchnitz's English-language editions of *Sense and Sensibility* (1864), *Mansfield Park* (1867), *Pride and Prejudice* (1870), *Northanger Abbey and Persuasion* (1871) and *Emma* (1877), as part of its impressively extensive programme of publications in English aimed at Continental audiences. Before the mid to late twentieth-century burgeoning of translations of Austen, versions were occasional and discontinuous, often deprived of any cultural specificity and modelled on the expectations of foreign readers.

Paradoxically, what was translated in the early nineteenth century was and was *not* Jane Austen. Thus, when seen outside their familiar British context, Austen's works in early nineteenth-century Europe lose their peculiarity within a wide-ranging, rather formulaic tradition of novel writing and consumption. The specificity of Austen's works could be reduced or altogether annulled in order to create texts that corresponded to the cultural imperatives of the translating culture and satisfied the expectations of its readers.

NOTES

1. See section C in David Gilson, *A Bibliography of Jane Austen*, corrected edition (Winchester: St. Paul's Bibliographies, 1997). Subsequent references are included in the text.

2. Gabriella Imposti, 'The Reasons for an 'Absence': Jane Austen's Reception in Russia', in *Re-Drawing Austen: Picturesque Travels in Austenland*, eds. Beatrice Battaglia and Diego Saglia (Naples: Liguori, 2004) pp. 369–76.

3. Jane Austen, *Œuvres romanesques complètes*, ed. Pierre Goubert (Paris: Gallimard, 2000), vol. I, p. xli.

4. See Valérie Cossy, *Jane Austen in Switzerland: A Study of the Early French Translations* (Geneva: Slatkine, 2006). About the *Bibliothèque britannique*, see David Bickerton, *Marc-Auguste and Charles Pictet, the* Bibliothèque britannique *(1796–1815) and the Dissemination of British Literature and Science on the Continent* (Geneva: Slatkine, 1986).

5. Françoise Parent-Lardeur, *Lire à Paris au temps de Balzac, Les cabinets de lecture à Paris 1815–1830* (Paris: Editions de l'Ecole des Hautes Etudes en Sciences Sociales, 1981), p. 172.

6. Margaret Cohen, *The Sentimental Education of the Novel* (Princeton, NJ: Princeton University Press, 1999).

7. Léon Boucher, 'Le roman classique en Angleterre, Jane Austen', *Revue des Deux Mondes*, 3rd series, 29 (1878), 449–67; Théodore Duret, 'Miss Austen', *Revue Blanche* 16 (1898), 278–82. Earlier on, in his account of the English novel 'since Walter Scott', Philarète Chasles had presented Austen as a sentimentalist and dismissed her as one of 'Richardson's granddaughters'. See his 'Du Roman en Angleterre depuis Walter Scott', *Revue des Deux Mondes*, 4th series, 31 (1842), 194.

8. On this rather abundant production see Claire Jaquier, 'L'idylle sensible', *Annales Benjamin Constant* 18–19 (1996), 107–15 and her book *L'Erreur des désirs, Romans sensibles au XVIIIᵉ siècle* (Lausanne: Payot, 1998), esp. ch. 4, devoted to sensibility in Switzerland and to Montolieu. See also Valérie Cossy, 'An English touch: Laurence Sterne, Jane Austen et le roman sentimental en Suisse romande', *Annales Benjamin Constant* 25 (2001), 131–60.

9. See Gilson, *Bibliography*, pp. 176–9, and Helen Chambers, 'Nineteenth-Century German Translations of Jane Austen', in

Beiträge zur Rezeption der britischen und irischen Literatur des 19. Jahrhunderts im deutschsprachigen Raum, ed. Norbert Bachleitner (Amsterdam and Atlanta: Rodopi, 2000), pp. 231–7. Subsequent references are included in the text.

10. See Virgil Nemoianu, *The Taming of Romanticism: European Literature and the Age of Biedermeier* (Cambridge, MA: Harvard University Press, 1984).

PART III

Historical and cultural context

16

Agriculture

ROBERT CLARK AND GERRY DUTTON

To the historian's eye a conspicuous feature of film and televi-
sion versions of Austen's novels is the almost complete absence
of farmers and farm workers. We might think this absence derives
from a 'Heritage' view of the past in which the millions whose labour
supported the great houses of the land are passed over in silence,
but the absence is also evident in Austen's novels, only the relatively
minor character of Robert Martin in *Emma* serving to represent the
most numerous social orders in a period when even the King was
affectionately known as 'Farmer George' and espoused the merits
of the farming life, and when most parish priests were, in the words
of Sir William Scott to the House of Commons in 1802, '*ex officio*
a farmer'.[1] In the nine letters of Jane Austen's parents which still
survive, farming is a constant concern. In one we find Mrs Austen
saying that George Austen 'wants to shew his brother his lands and
his cattle' and rejoicing in her own involvement in dairying: 'I have
a nice dairy fitted up, and am now worth a bull and six cows.'[2] In
another we detect the tone of someone very much in charge of this
aspect of domestic business: 'What luck we shall have with those
sort of cows I can't say. My little Alderney one turns out tolerably
well and makes more butter than we use, and I have just bought
another of the same sort, but as her calf is but just gone, can not
say what she will be good for yet' (*AP*, 26 August 1770). And in a
letter written in the year of Jane Austen's birth, the impression of
a farming family is very clear:

The wheat promises to be very good this year, but we have had a sad
wet time for getting it in, however, we got the last load in yesterday,
just four weeks after we began reaping. I am afraid the weather is not
likely to mend for it rains very much to-day, and we want dry weather
for our peas and oats; I don't hear of any barley ripe yet, so am afraid
it will be very late before harvest is over.   (*AP*, 20 August 1775)

Where Jane Austen's own correspondence is concerned, of the surviving letters from January 1796 to the family's move to Bath in January 1801, a third refer to farming, many of them mentioning John Bond, George Austen's factotum at Cheesedown farm, who was to a degree intimate with the family; Jane Austen on one occasion writes '[My father] & John Bond are now very happy together, for I have just heard the heavy step of the latter along the passage' (*L*, 27–8 October 1798). Taken together, the letters of Mrs Austen and of Jane indicate that the affairs of the farm lapped through the house, much as one would expect of a rural family in these years.

The more we consider these matters, the more they throw into question just how we have tended to understand Jane Austen's early life: on 1 November 1800 she writes 'My mother is very happy in the prospect of dressing a new Doll which Molly has given Anna. My father's feelings are not so enviable, as it appears that the farm cleared 300£ last year.' Early the following year we hear similar notes of financial concern: 'My father is doing all in his power to encrease his Income by raising his Tythes &c, & I do not despair of getting very nearly six hundred a year.' George Austen's revenues from tithes were around £200 p.a. in the 1770s, and Jane's letter implies they were rising towards £600 p.a. by the end of the century, but what usually goes unnoticed is that his farm revenues were around a third of his income, and evidently he had hoped for more (*L*, 3–5 January 1801).

Early in 1801 George Austen decided to retire to Bath, putting his son James in as curate at Steventon and Deane, and retaining the Steventon living and its tithe income in his retirement. As the move was prepared, Jane Austen wrote several letters which indicate that George Austen sold his interest in the remaining years of his lease to a local farmer named Holder. It is usually thought that Austen had been given the Cheesedown lease by Thomas Knight in the 1770s, but the evidence that this was a gift seems no more than family lore and Jane does write as if he is selling his lease. If this is the case, then we must consider how much capital George had invested in his farming activities, such a farm renting for £150–£200 p.a. Cheesedown farm can be readily identified today from maps of 1741 and 1840 and covered 195 acres, to which George added 57 acres of glebe land in the neighbouring parish of Deane, giving him a total of 252 acres and implying an annual expenditure of around £700 in addition to any rental or leasing costs, more than his best hope for tithe income.[3] These considerations have large importance for the family's life since, rather than living in entire security on tithe income, they were exposed to any agricultural misfortune and directly engaged in the most important sector of the British economy.

Austen's farming would have been primarily of the 'sheep-corn' type which is practised extensively in the light heathlands of England, and would have been supplemented with a small amount of cattle farming for beef and dairying. Steventon had been enclosed around 1741 into four modern farms. The arable land would typically have been planted in rotation with wheat, then peas, then oats or barley, with clover underneath to further hearten the soil, perhaps with a fourth year lying fallow, and each of the farms would have maintained sheep flocks, both for the value of the animals and the production of vital manure. The *General View of the Agriculture of Hampshire* (1794) provides a contemporary sketch: 'Towards Basingstoke, the land upon the top of the hills is in general very deep, strong land, with chalk underneath, which produces large crops, particularly in dry season, as it never burns. The usual crops are 1) wheat, 2) pease, 3) oats or barley, with clover.' The *General View* also estimates the sheep population at 185,000 for Hampshire as a whole, nearly one for each human, and notes that 140,000 were sold each year at the Weyhill sheep fair. The parish of Deane (of which George Austen had the living) had 1,300 sheep, and there were 900 in Ashe, another neighbouring parish, figures which constitute the typical range for a Hampshire parish. No figures are given for Steventon, but we may deduce a similar number.[4]

George Austen's farming on his own account was not the limit of his exposure to agricultural economics: his tithes as rector comprised 10 per cent by value of agricultural production in the parish and varied with prices (which were rising strongly in the last years of the century, hence Jane's remark about her father being able to 'raise his tythes'). It follows that *all* of George Austen's revenue, whether from farming or tithes, was derived from the land and related to the market for agricultural products. It also follows that during Jane's Steventon years George Austen's relationship with the local agricultural community cannot have been entirely comfortable: negotiating to raise tithes was a necessary but vexatious part of the parson's relation with his parishioners, even in good times, and in these years in which the agricultural revolution was reaching its apogee there was much alienation between landowners and workers: bad harvests and disruption of trade with the Continent led to huge rises in agricultural prices which were not matched by rises in wages; enclosures were already increasing in the 1780s, but after 1792 landowners found in the French wars a patriotic excuse for completing the conversion of common land into private farms. Over 40 per cent of all Parliamentary enclosure acts were passed during the years of war with France, and 547 were passed 1800–5, almost twenty for each week of the Parliamentary session. Enclosures dispossessed the commoners and converted them to impoverished wage-slaves reliant on Poor Relief. The *General View* noted that 'A considerable quantity of land has lately been enclosed, which increases its value from six shillings to twelve shillings per acre' (p. 11), probably referring to the enclosure of 3,520 acres of Basing Down in 1786–9, an area of roughly two and a half miles (4 km) square through which the thirteen-year old Jane must have passed on her way to shop in Basingstoke. Further afield, Jane Austen's great-uncle, Thomas Leigh of Adlestrop, was a wholesale and vigorous encloser, a fact which she must have appreciated on her visits to him.[5] Commoners who lost their rights through such enclosures became vagrants who had to be returned to their parishes under the Laws of Settlement, relocations which were always unpleasant and usually involved the churchwardens, and at least by implication the parson, as the agencies responsible for implementation of the Poor Law. As Steventon was a closed parish, belonging entirely to the Knight family, and supporting only some thirty families, it is probable that the local effect of the wider catastrophe was not as acutely experienced as elsewhere, but poverty in the neighbouring parishes of North Waltham and Overton – which were open and much more heavily populated – would have led to unpleasant expulsions under the Settlement Acts.[6] As Peter Virgin notes, the church 'according to classic eighteenth-century theory, was a pillar of the constitution; and as such it was part and parcel of the system of law, as well as being the partner – some said the ally – of the state'.[7] Most records of such resettlements have been lost but there is a record of the 'Removal of Elizabeth Armstrong, singlewoman, from Steventon to Old Basing' in 1797, and another from 1816 when 'Robert Rabbits, wife Sarah and children Olliff and Elizabeth were removed from Steventon to Kingsclere'.[8]

The publication of the *General View* itself was symptomatic of the enclosure process. The Board of Agriculture was formed in 1793 and immediately commissioned a series of county reports assessing the agricultural resources the country could call upon in this time of war and propagandising for enclosure as a means of improving outputs. As the wars drove up the price of food and put ideological grist in the mill of capitalists who were bent on enclosure, so even marginal lands became prospects for improvement and this particularly affected downland in Hampshire, much of which would be unwisely enclosed. To quote the *General View* again:

Many parts of the country are well wooded, and adorned with a great number of beautiful seats and villas; but we are sorry to observe such immense tracts of open heath, and uncultivated land, which strongly indicate the want of means, or inclination to improve it, and often reminds the traveller of uncivilized nations, where nature pursues her own course, without the assistance of human art.　　　(p. 10)

Whilst the *General View* tries to appear objective, it is clearly inspired by the aim of promoting 'improvement'. Its view of common land could not be more explicit:

Under this article we shall mention commonable land which belongs to the parishioners in general, which being unenclosed, may be considered as little better than the waste land before mentioned, as it is evident that cultivated land will produce more than that which is totally uncultivated, and left for nature to pursue her own course; and with this disadvantage, that each one is endeavouring to exhaust it of every valuable production, without paying the least attention to its supposed improvement.　　　(p. 31)

The *General View* goes on to identify some 104,845 acres of 'waste' (p. 32) and notes that some of this 'waste' is very productive, but not productive enough: 'King's Clear contains about 1000 acres, upon which young cattle of a good sort are now bred. If this were inclosed it would make good convertible land either for the plough or for feeding, but principally for feeding, and would be worth about 15s per acre' (p. 32). Since the *View* has already equated common land with waste, the encouragement to enclose land which is vital to the livelihoods of the villagers is transparent.

The loss of rights over 'the commonable land which belongs to the parishioners in general' deprived commoners of those small amounts of grazing and arable produce which enabled them to sustain economic independence, leaving them with what they could earn in wages from the large landowners. The price of a loaf of bread rose 600 per cent between the 1780s and 1801, and in the same period agricultural wages rose only about 20 per cent. Already on 17 January 1795 the *Hampshire Chronicle* recorded the acute distress of rural workers and commended the good people of the city for having raised £287 for relief of distress caused by the bad harvest. On 16 March 1795 the same paper carried a report on the continuing distress of the poor due to the high cost of meat and wheat, and on 27 April it reported that on 12 April 500 men of the Oxfordshire militia stationed near Seaford 'notwithstanding the endeavours of the officers had taken arms and with bayonets fixed' seized a vessel laded with flour at Newhaven. The misery was such as to precipitate revolt among the very forces who had been put in arms to defend the rich against the French and revolutionary threat. The harvest of 1795 was no better, and rural misery deepened. On 8 January 1796 when Jane Austen penned her first surviving letter, describing her flirtation with Tom Lefroy at the Harwood ball, it is uncomfortable to note that the poor of Deane were starving in the frost, their possibilities of livelihood much reduced by the enclosure of their common fields in 1773 by an Act of Parliament promoted by Austen's host, John Harwood, and their family friend Henrietta Bramston, and in which George Austen himself had played a modest part.

Indeed, through 1796 the condition of the poor was becoming of national concern, occasioning a vast quasi-governmental report by Sir Frederic Morton Eden, debates in Parliament over the reform of the Poor Law, and a general atmosphere of crisis.[9] Eden himself indicates just what rural poverty could mean when he cites the 'Parochial Report on the State of the Poor' for Petersfield, Hampshire, in October 1795, where the diet of the poor comprised bread and milk for breakfast, bread and cheese for lunch three days a week, bread and cheese for supper every day of the week, the other four meals comprising poor-quality meat. The reality of this diet is revealed when one reads that the allowance of cheese per person per week was half a pound (250g), distributed between the ten meals. Eden's report includes the following commentary in which the smugness of the well-fed baulks at the ungratefulness of the poor:

The Poor are chiefly supported in a work-house, under the superintendence of a standing overseer, who has been in office above 5 years. He does not reside in the house, but attends at meals, provides victuals, and collects the Poor's Rates . . . He pays every proper attention to the wants of the necessitous, and administers the concerns of the parish with fidelity, and discrimination: notwithstanding this, he is disliked by the Poor, and several attempts have been made to burn his house; the gentlemen, however, stand by him, and approve of his proceedings.   (vol. 2, p. 223)

What, then, do we conclude from such contextual information? Firstly, our tendency to see George Austen as primarily a country vicar, secondarily a teacher of genteel pupils and thirdly a bit of a farmer, must be reordered once we appreciate how much money he had tied up in his farm. Because all of his income depended on the price of corn and sheep, he must have stood pretty much as any risk-capitalist does in any petty manufacturing activity, calculating his investments, banking on good luck and trusting his own acumen. Secondly, we must recognise that Jane Austen's lifespan coincided with boom times for rectors' livings: the value of benefices trebled between 1770 and 1800, so Austen was unusually privileged relative to the kind of life rectors had experienced in earlier years, and relative to what would occur in the 1830s. This affluence was a long-term consequence of rising agricultural rents which depended upon enclosure and the application of new scientific and capital-intensive techniques, all of which were given a particular boost by the French wars. Thirdly, that whilst the gentry profited from such a surge in prices and rents, the rural poor were immiserated and driven off the land, creating many kinds of moral dilemmas for the rural clergy who were implicated in their management. Given all these considerations, we have been entirely mistaken to cast George Austen in a dress which might have been more appropriate for a vicar of a later period: he was as engaged in capitalist agricultural activity as any farmer would be today. He may have left much of the day-to-day management to John Bond, or he may have been much more involved than most biographers have thought, but either way he was not living remote from the enormous economic changes which transformed Britain in his lifetime: he was playing his own modest but full role in the drama. It follows that Jane Austen's mentality was formed in a household very much more engaged with the shaping forces of the British economy than in the insulated genteel home that is usually presumed. This realisation enables us to re-evaluate the acuity with which her novels represent the socio-economic transformation of Britain in her lifetime.

NOTES

1. Quoted in Irene Collins, *Jane Austen and the Clergy* (London: Hambledon, 1993), p. 54.
2. Letter from Mrs Austen to Mrs Walter, 6 June 1773, *Austen Papers, 1704–1856*, ed. R. A. Austen-Leigh (1942), p. 29. Subsequent references are included in the text and sourced to *AP*.
3. Arthur Young gives annual costs for a similar farm in Wiltshire in *Annals of Agriculture*, 8 (1787), 64–5.
4. *General View of the Agriculture of Hampshire* (1794), pp. 11–24. Subsequent references are included in the text.
5. *Ibid.*, p. 11. On Adlestrop, see Robert Clark, 'Jane Austen and the Enclosures', in *England's Green and Pleasant Land*, eds. W. M. Verhoeven and Amanda Gilroy (Leuven, NL: Peeters, 2004), pp. 105–24.
6. When the *General View* was revised for its second edition in 1813, it supplied a comprehensive table of parochial population and expenses. Although by this time Jane Austen had moved to Chawton, her brother remained rector of Steventon, where there were 33 families comprising 153 residents and a poor law expenditure of £98 p.a. In the neighbouring parishes of Overton and North Waltham, there were 299 families comprising 1,468 people and an expenditure of £1,155 p.a. Typically, in the 1770s there would have been almost no expenditure for the relief of the poor, but by 1813 many families were receiving as much in poor relief as they were able to make through their labour.

7. Peter Virgin, *The Church in an Age of Negligence: Ecclesiastical Structure and Problems of Church Reform, 1700–1840* (Cambridge: James Clarke & Co., 1989), pp. 15–16.
8. HRO Refs 3M70/56/22 and 19M76/PO5/73.
9. *The State of the Poor, or, An History of the Labouring Classes in England, from the Conquest to the Present Period* (1797). Subsequent references are included in the text.

17

Book production

JAMES RAVEN

Jane Austen wrote and published during a half century in which hundreds of new bookshops and subscription and circulating libraries opened their doors; the volume of book production surged, and print penetrated ever more deeply into British society – to both the delight and horror of contemporaries.

The broader revolution in book production is dramatic: before 1700 up to 1,800 different printed titles were issued annually; by 1830 up to 6,000 – and this is simply a crude title count disregarding the huge increases in the edition sizes of certain types of publication, increases that escalated during the 1820s.[1] Books, print and novels notably contributed to a new age of conspicuous consumption in the late eighteenth and early nineteenth centuries. Book-trade entrepreneurs like Thomas Longman, John Murray, Charles Rivington, Thomas Cadell and George Robinson ranked with Hogarth, Boulton, Watt and Wedgwood as the promoters and beneficiaries of an evolving 'consumer society'. It was not just that printed advertisements and other promotional publications advanced a great range of consumer goods (the subject of much lively social history[2]), but books, magazines and prints themselves became prominent exemplars of the new decencies adorning the homes of propertied men and women.

During Austen's writing career, publishing remained, as it had since the late seventeenth century, dominated by questions of monopoly price-fixing, centralised production and control, technological constraints (and breakthroughs) and the efficiency of distribution networks. The British book production regime was characterised by the extreme variability of the size and price of the printed text, by multiple but modestly sized reprintings of successful titles (instead of ambitious single print runs) and by the manufacture of many non-commercial books where full costs were not always recovered from sale. Above all, the price of new and reprinted books had been modulated for most of the eighteenth century by the effective cartelisation of the trade in which booksellers' protection of reprinting rights maintained monopoly prices in England (although not in Ireland and only ineffectively in Scotland, whose booksellers led the challenge against English claims to perpetual copyright).[3]

The ranks of booksellers fundamentally divided between those who invested and dealt in the ownership of the copyright to publication, and those who either printed, sold or distributed books for the copyholders or who traded entirely outside the bounds of copyright materials.[4] This division endured even after new freedoms to reprint out-of-copyright titles followed legal decisions weakening leading booksellers' monopolistic control of copyright in 1768 and 1774. Further Copyright Acts in 1808 and 1814 imposed new restrictions, sharply reducing the number of titles coming out of copyright. A raft of cheaper reprints contributed to the fourfold increase in publication in the three decades after 1770, but most new in-copyright publications were more expensive than ever and by the 1810s the reproduction of obsolescent literature for lower income book-buyers was renewed (St Clair, *Reading Nation*, chs. 4, 6).

Only at the end of Austen's life did steam-driven paper-making machines and printing presses shatter the principal technological constraint to the expansion of publishing. In the year that *Mansfield Park* was published, *The Times* became the first publication printed by Koenig's new steam press, allowing the printing of 1,000 impressions each hour. The bookseller Charles Knight declared that 'what the printing press did for the instruction of the masses in the fifteenth century, the printing machine is doing for the nineteenth' (Weedon, *Victorian Publishing*, pp. 64–76). It was, however, no overnight revolution and Austen would derive no direct benefits from it. What *The Times* (1814), called 'the greatest improvement connected with printing since the discovery of the art itself' was not widely used until the 1820s.

What the first buyers of Austen's novels did experience was a more competitive and expanding market for books, together with more efficient distributive systems. In 1775, the year of Jane Austen's birth, thirty-one new novels are known to have been published in Britain; in 1811, the year that *Sense and Sensibility* appeared, eighty new titles were published; and in the year after her death, the combined edition of *Northanger Abbey and Persuasion* joined sixty-one other new novel titles with an 1818 imprint. Altogether, British bookseller-publishers issued 2,503 new novels between 1775 and 1818. Output rose sharply before 1800 before a trough in the mid 1810s (with a strong recovery in the 1820s), while the early dominance of the epistolary novel (more than three-quarters of all titles published in 1776) had declined by the 1790s (when Jane Austen penned her novel in letters *Lady Susan*).[5]

It was hardly surprising that all of Austen's novels were first published in London. By the early nineteenth century some 90 per cent of all new British books were published in the capital and the mushrooming numbers of provincial booksellers mostly served not as publishers but as the distribution agents of new books. In the year of Jane Austen's birth only one of the thirty-one new novel titles was not printed in London, and in the year of her death only three of fifty-five. Nevertheless, publishing in Edinburgh and Glasgow advanced during the final third of the eighteenth century, and, after 1800, general book and magazine publication increased in Manchester, Liverpool, Aberdeen, Newcastle, Leeds and other cities.

In order to expand their trade, many novel publishers expertly practised innovative advertising techniques. Advertising was expensive, however, and its cost in newspapers, catalogues and separate notices often proved a shock for authors.[6] In 1816 John Murray II charged Jane Austen £50 for advertising *Emma* in the first nine months of publication, some of which was a charge for advertising in Murray's own catalogue.[7] Small editions also characterised novel publication before and after Austen's lifetime. Most novels were printed in editions of no more than 500. Even some of the most successful titles were issued in editions of 750 or 800. Risk had to be measured carefully. Between 1770 and 1800 about 60 per cent of all novel titles (and in some years, two-thirds) were never reprinted, even in Ireland. Such caution in the novel market contrasts with the monster and repeatedly reprinted editions of successful school and service books of the time. Playbooks reached editions of 2,000 copies or more (and *Emma*, Austen's largest first edition, was also of 2,000). Some histories with proven appeal comprised 4,000-copy editions, but these pall before the huge printings commissioned by Thomas Longman II for staple titles like Watts's *Hymns*, and numerous instruction books, such as an 18,000-copy edition of Fenning's spelling manual.

The production of novels in small editions also enabled artful price setting. Not that printing and typographical flourishes came cheaply – and one production cost, that of paper, proved a further critical variable. The price of the novel increased gradually from the late 1780s until a far steeper acceleration in nominal prices after 1800. What was to be a long-running increase in the price of novels resulted from the increase by about a third in the labour costs of composition and press work between about 1785 and 1810, but, more importantly from the doubling in the price of quality paper between about 1793 and 1801. The average price for a three-volume novel rose from 12s between 1802 and 1805 to 18s between 1813 and 1817.[8] In 1811 Thomas Egerton priced the three-volume *Sense and Sensibility* (printed in an edition of 750) at 15s; the same bookseller sold *Pride and Prejudice* two years later for 18s for the three volumes (as he did *Mansfield Park* the year after that). In 1816, during difficult economic conditions and at the low point in general novel production, John Murray reflected both rising costs and his own higher pricing by selling *Emma*, also in three volumes, for 21s. In 1818 (against a general recovery in economic fortunes) the four-volume set of *Northanger Abbey and Persuasion* retailed at 24s in boards.

In the fashionable novel market, other production decisions followed from high retail pricing. Duodecimo proved the favoured format for popular book production, but octavo was also adopted when booksellers aimed to give publications a certain distinction (even though this format still accounted for only 4 per cent of total novel output in the 1810s). By the 1810s the three-decker (three-volume) novel also began an ascendancy that dominated almost to the end of the century. The greater spacing of text attempted to ensure, at standard pricing per volume, greater returns from retail or from library subscriptions and charges – but it was achieved at great critical cost. Complaints about bloated novels pepper the reviews.

Partly in reaction to hostile critical reviewing, but also as a result of the relationships between publishers and authors, most title pages did not carry the writer's name. Jane Austen continued to use intermediaries in negotiations with publishers and in at least one letter to her would-be-publisher, Crosby, disguised herself as 'Mrs Ashton Dennis' (Fergus, *Jane Austen*, p. 111). Egerton and Jane Austen published *Sense and Sensibility* as 'By a Lady' and the first title pages of all Austen's subsequent novels attributed the work to 'the author of' a named title. Nearly three-quarters of all novels published between 1770 and 1820 were without attribution of author; among these, the vague and often highly dubious tag of 'By a Lady' or 'By a Young Lady' gained special popularity. By the 1790s more than a fifth (21 per cent) of all novel title pages gave named female writers, with an increasing number of women writing under cover of pseudonyms and anonymous title pages.[9] By the 1810s, as Peter Garside concludes, 'the *publication* of Jane Austen's novels was achieved not against the grain but during a period of female ascendancy' (Garside, 'The English Novel', p. 75). It was only in the 1820s that male novelists resumed numerical dominance.

Few authors were beneficiaries of fresh economic opportunities in the book trade.[10] Before the early nineteenth century, very few writers in Britain and certainly very few first-time writers could avoid outright copyright sale, full self-financing (and thus acting as publisher themselves) or deals in which the author bore liability for all losses. Commission agreements whereby the bookseller put up the capital for printing an edition on the understanding that the author would bear any loss, seem to have been very rare – even though these were favoured by Austen. Despite the promotion of new literature as fashionable and expensive delicacies, authors (and especially novelists) also suffered from much poor quality printing. Murray's literary adviser, Gifford, wrote to him in 1815 in praise of *Pride and Prejudice* (sent to Murray by Austen), but found it 'wretchedly printed, and so pointed as to be almost unintelligible'.[11] After *Emma* was published by Murray in December 1815, he issued a second edition of *Mansfield Park* in the new year, improving on the badly printed 1814 Egerton edition. The majority of bookseller-publishers issuing new novels did operate a printing press, but other notable publishers of novels, from the Nobles in the mid eighteenth century to Thomas Norton Longman at the close of the century contracted out the presswork. Egerton used Charles Roworth, a popular printer trading on his own from at least 1799 until 1832 and then with his sons for at least a decade more. Roworth was to print fourteen of the twenty-seven volumes of the various editions of Austen's novels published in her lifetime (Fergus, *Jane Austen*, p. 131). The first editions of both *Pride and Prejudice* and *Mansfield Park* were printed by both Roworth and George Sidney of the Strand, each taking responsibility for different volumes in the set. Murray, publishing *Emma* in 1816, continued to employ Roworth, but again, as was common, shared the work with another printer, in this case J. Moyes of Hatton Garden.

Austen's complaints were shared by almost every writer of her age. Examples of badly executed novel printing are common and evidence of rushed production can be found from almost all booksellers. Jane Austen called Murray, half-jokingly perhaps, a 'rogue', and her own grievances can be set against attempts to defend authors' rights going back to the botched 1710 Copyright Act, Trusler's Society of Authors in the 1760s and then, in Austen's lifetime, the establishment of the philanthropic Royal Literary Fund in 1790. For many authors, if copyright could not be sold outright for a reasonable sum (or at all), then the only options were to fund the costs of publication from their own resources, launch a subscription scheme or attempt to persuade a bookseller to enter a profit-sharing arrangement. Subscription schemes supported much novel publication. A particular attraction for novelists seeking subscribers was an association with an illustrious dedicatee. At Austen's request, *Emma* was sent by Murray to the Prince Regent in order that he might provide the lustre of a royal dedication.

Although it seems that few booksellers turned down a novel if financing were available, it is simply not known how many manuscripts were refused. In 1803 Austen sold *Northanger Abbey* (then titled 'Susan') for £10 outright to Benjamin Crosby of Stationers' Court, in the heartland of the trade. In 1809 after her enquiry, Crosby told her that he considered himself under no obligation to publish and offered the £10 back. Some seven years later Austen finally accepted this and the novel was not published until its posthumous issue with *Persuasion*, in four volumes, by Murray in 1818. Inexperience also ensured that many novelists, like Jane Austen herself, proved maladroit in negotiations. Austen rejected Murray's offer of £450 for the copyrights of *Emma*, *Sense and Sensibility* and *Mansfield Park*, yet ultimately received very little in return for *Emma*, and her sale of the copyright to *Pride and*

Prejudice ensured that Egerton, not she, benefited more from the most popular novel in her lifetime.

Where a novel was 'printed for the author' the bookseller often acted as little more than a vanity press, although in some cases authorial risk-taking did pay off. Of the total number of first editions of novels published in the 1780s and 1790s, 7 per cent were described as 'printed for the author'. These must be minimum figures, when many title pages, such as Mary Robinson's *Widow* of 1794, hide known commission agreements 'on account of the author', where the publisher-writer assumed responsibility for any loss. It was indeed as a question of publishing 'First Impressions' at 'the expence of publishing at the Authors' risk; and what you will advance for the Property of it' that George Austen unsuccessfully approached Cadell and Davies on behalf of his daughter in November 1797 (Fergus, *Jane Austen*, p. 12).

What such unpromising circumstances did was to put heavy responsibility upon authors to choose, in what was largely a buyer's not a seller's manuscript market, the best option for having their work published. Such circumstances explain both Austen's early timidity in relations with booksellers, but also the shrewdness of her commission agreements. Despite her later disappointments over *Pride and Prejudice* and *Emma*, Austen received £140 from her first published work, *Sense and Sensibility*, negotiated through her brother Henry, and for which she had risked £180. Egerton seems to have made about £36 from his 10 per cent commission on sales (Fergus, *Jane Austen*, pp. 16–17, 131). Nevertheless, the combined profits of the four novels published in her lifetime amounted to no more than £700, a decent but by no means a great fortune (Smiles, *A Publisher*, vol. 1, p. 283).

In fact, extraordinary differences appear in the financial rewards of novel writing, especially after 1800. From her contracts securing a share in the returns from later editions of *Camilla* (1796) and *The Wanderer* (1814), Frances Burney gained more than £4,000 (Fergus, *Jane Austen*, pp. 13–15). Maria Edgeworth pocketed £1,050 for her 1812 series, *Tales of Fashionable Life*, and a further £2,100 two years later for her less successful *Patronage*. By contrast, Lane issued advertisements offering from between five and 100 guineas for 'manuscripts of merit', although no one seems to have claimed his top reward. Although the vast majority of the agreements have been lost, we know that, at the top of the range, Cadell and Davies (who rejected Austen's early version of *Pride and Prejudice*) paid Ann Radcliffe £800 for her *Italian* in 1797. Of the fifty or so survivals of agreements the average payment seems to have been about £80, although such estimates rely heavily on the surviving contracts of Longman in the late 1790s, and the Robinsons, known for their relative generosity.

Although more than 600 firms were involved in the publication of novels between 1770 and 1830, many of them were short-lived and during the final quarter of the eighteenth century, four particular firms boosted publication totals: Thomas Hookham, the Robinsons, the long-established Nobles (until 1789) and, from 1775 itself, the newcomer and greatest novel manufacturer of all, William Lane.[12] By the 1790s Lane's 'Minerva Press' published one third of all new novel titles in London, and by the 1810s the firm, directed by A. K. Newman after Lane's retirement, issued almost a quarter of all new fiction titles of the decade. Newman continued the 'Minerva' name until 1820. Minerva writing was rarely distinguished and continuing attacks on circulating libraries and popular novels made the press an easy target. In *Northanger Abbey* the nine 'horrid' novels thrilling the foolish Isabella Thorpe were all authentic titles and six of them were published by Lane.

The further and crucial feature of the businesses founded by Hookham, Lane and then Henry Colbourn (at least until the end of the 1810s) was the extent to which their publishing and retail operations turned on the success of their own circulating libraries and the supply of ready-made fiction and belles-lettres libraries to other booksellers and new proprietors. In 1770 one author, making an optimistic estimate of total edition size, suggested that 400 of every 1,000 copies of novels were sold to circulating libraries.[13] As Austen wrote in 1814, given the high price of new novels, readers were 'more ready to borrow & praise, than to buy' (*L*, 30 November 1814).

For consumers of these novels, possession of a beautiful thing had its own importance. Botched printing was a recurrent disappointment, but well-executed typographical design, distinctive running heads, chapter breaks and page layouts added to the reading experience. Both the high price of new novels and the limits of literacy determined readership boundaries, but these can never be clear cut.

Purchases of non-essential goods depend upon individual taste as much as supply, opportunity, alternative spending attractions and the fundamental level of income. For many, cost bars to new novels were breached by the second-hand market, as well as by library circulation and by other means of acquisition, including gift and simple inheritance. Most aspirants to these 'widening circles' placed a premium on access to the latest literature, and the novel typified modern publication. Many books promoted as typical products of the consumer revolution were also grossly overpriced. Publications reliant not just on literary content but on design and modishness, created fortunes for the most successful of their commercial producers. The other, most obvious feature of the publishing regime negotiated by Jane Austen, was that those who might be deemed the original manufacturers, the authors, largely failed to benefit from the market boom.

NOTES

1. *English Short-Title Catalogue*; A. Weedon, *Victorian Publishing: The Economics of Book Production for a Mass Market, 1836–1916* (Aldershot: Ashgate, 2003), pp. 45–52. Subsequent references are included in the text.

2. J. Alden, 'Pills and Publishing: Some Notes on the English Book Trade 1660–1715', *The Library*, 5th ser., 7 (1952), 21–37; *The Birth of a Consumer Society: The Commercialization of Eighteenth-century England*, eds. N. McKendrick, J. Brewer and J. H. Plumb (London: Europa, 1982); L. Lippincott, *Selling Art in Georgian London: The Rise of Arthur Pond*, (New Haven: Yale University Press, 1983).

3. M. Rose, *Authors and Owners: The Invention of Copyright* (Cambridge, MA: Harvard University Press, 1993); William St Clair, *The Reading Nation in the Romantic Period* (Cambridge: Cambridge University Press, 2004), ch. 1. Subsequent references are included in the text.

4. See G. Walters, 'The Booksellers in 1759 and 1774: the Battle for Literary Property', *The Library*, 5th ser., 29 (1974), 287–311; T. Belanger, 'Booksellers' Trade Sales, 1718–1768', *The Library*, 5th ser., 30:4 (1975), 281–302.

5. Tallies are taken from *The English Novel 1770–1829: A Bibliographical Survey of Prose Fiction Published in the British Isles*,

2 vols., eds. Peter Garside, J. Raven and R. Schöwerling (Oxford: Oxford University Press, 2000).

6. R. M. Wiles, *Serial Publication in England before 1750* (Cambridge: Cambridge University Press, 1957), pp. 149–53; R. Munter, *The History of the Irish Newspaper, 1685–1760* (Cambridge: Cambridge University Press, 1967), pp. 57, 61–6; M. Harris, 'The Management of the London Newspaper Press During the Eighteenth Century', *Publishing History* 4 (1978), 95–112.

7. Jan Fergus, *Jane Austen: A Literary Life* (Basingstoke: Macmillan, 1991). Subsequent references are included in the text.

8. H. Amory, *New Books by Fielding: An Exhibition of the Hyde Collection* (Cambridge, MA: Harvard University Press, 1987), p. 44; P. Garside, 'The English Novel in the Romantic Era' in Garside *et al.*, *The English Novel 1770–1829*, vol. II, p. 93. Subsequent references are included in the text.

9. James Raven, 'The Anonymous Novel in Britain and Ireland, 1750–1830,' in *The Faces of Anonymity: Anonymous and Pseudonymous Publication from the Sixteenth to the Twentieth Century*, ed. R. J. Griffin (Basingstoke: Macmillan, 2003), pp. 141–66.

10. N. Cross, *The Common Writer: Life in Nineteenth-Century Grub Street* (Cambridge: Cambridge University Press, 1985).

11. Gifford to Murray, 29 September 1815, cited in S. Smiles, *A Publisher and his Friends: Memoir and Correspondence of the late John Murray*, (1891), vol. 1, p. 282. Subsequent references are included in the text.

12. James Raven, 'Location, Size and Succession: The Bookshops of Paternoster Row before 1800,' in *The London Book Trade: Topographies of Print in the Metropolis from the Sixteenth Century*, eds. R. Myers, M. Harris and G. Mandelbrote (London: British Library, 2003), pp. 89–126.

13. E. and R. Griffith, *A Series of Genuine Letters Between Henry and Frances*, 6 vols. (1767–70), vol. VI, p. 15.

18

Cities

JANE STABLER

In the year Jane Austen was born, Temple Bar – one of the old gateways to London – still carried what remained of the head of a Jacobite executed in 1746. As the centre of British government, finance and culture, Georgian London was a focus for public displays of all kinds. Fashionable life paraded around the rapidly expanding residential areas of the north and west while in the south and east manufacturing workshops proliferated to supply London's commercial zone. In 1811 the population reached over a million. Austen presents London as a small world and as a metropolis in which it is possible to sink from view. In *Pride and Prejudice* Lydia and Wickham travel to London for 'concealment' and Darcy is only able to hunt them down through the channels of the servant class (3:5, 3:10). Frank Churchill disappears to London to purchase a piano in *Emma* (2:7) and Austen introduces Robert Ferrars as an anonymous male consumer commissioning a pearled toothpick-case in *Sense and Sensibility* (2:11).

Along Pall Mall and Bond Street fashionable ladies did their afternoon shopping (fig. 29); Charles Lamb preferred the lighted shops of the Strand and Fleet Street. He took William Wordsworth to see Bartholomew Fair at Smithfield in 1802 and the older poet's fascinated repulsion at the way everything was 'jumbled up together' captures London as a whole.[1] Summer fairs were set up for trade but their circuses and theatrical side-shows were popular sites of entertainment for all classes. This mingling of occupations is emblematic of the flux and variety of London in Austen's time, when it was an international centre of banking and insurance, and also the home of the gambling clubs or 'hells' in Pall Mall. Theatre and opera flourished alongside the brothels, Turkish baths and fruit market of Covent Garden; the recently founded British Museum, the Royal Academy and the Royal Society fostered the arts and sciences while tea gardens and exhibition halls promoted all manner of musical, mechanical, optical and aerostatic amusements. Under various managers a menagerie existed at the Exeter Exchange in the Strand between 1773 and 1829: John Dashwood is obliged to take little Harry there in *Sense and Sensibility* (2:11); Byron visited it in 1813 and was entranced by the elephant which neatly took his money and removed his hat.[2] The popularity of this sort of London show prompted Austen's description of the city environs as the 'Regions of Wit, Elegance, fashion, Elephants & Kangaroons' (*L*, 11 February 1801).

Jane Austen's visits to her brother Henry's houses in Sloane Street and Hans Place, Chelsea between 1811 and 1815 took her to elegant terraces that had been planned in the 1770s by the architect Henry Holland. Fashionable London concentred on Westminster Palace and St James's, where court patronage and political favours were dispensed. The custom of evening hospitality meant power brokers and businessmen needed a house in London as well as their country retreat. Hill Street, where Admiral Crawford resides in *Mansfield Park*, connects Berkeley Square with the Grosvenor Estate, articulating his influence in high society. Portman Square, Manchester Square and Bedford Square were all laid out between the 1760s and 1780s: they were built for the nobility and gentry, but during Austen's lifetime the commercial classes began to be affluent enough to move in. As Henry Austen found, however, fortunes fluctuated and people and businesses relocated frequently.

Affluence was displayed in the upkeep of family residences and the employment of leading architects such as Holland, Robert Adam and John Nash. They followed the principles of Greek and Roman architecture and their townhouses were delicately neoclassical in design: brick- or stone-fronted, with symmetrical groups of windows, fanlight above the front door and stone steps and iron railings between the house and the pavement. Inside, ornate cornicing, frieze-work, marble fireplaces and wrought ironmongery developed the classical theme of the exterior. Adam enhanced the prestige of Mayfair with his work on Lansdowne House in Berkeley Square (1762–8), Derby House in Grosvenor Square (1773–4) and Home House in Portman Square (1773–6). The Adelphi building (1768–72) brought the Adams firm close to financial disaster, but its completion together with William Chambers's restoration of Somerset House (1776–96) as a Renaissance

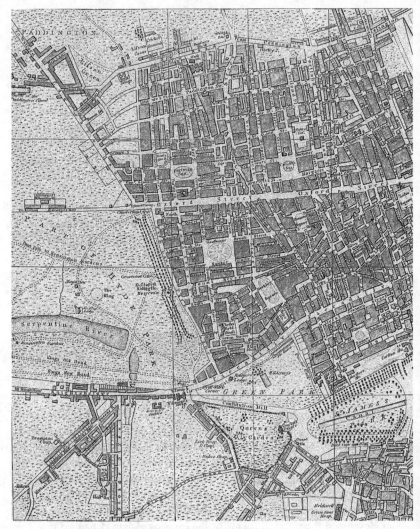

Figure 29. Map of west London from *Modern London; being the History & Present State of the British Metropolis* (1804).

palazzo successfully integrated the wharfs on the north banks of the Thames with the cosmopolitan cultural aspirations of the capital. In Austen's day highly visible port activity signalled the economic prosperity which came from overseas trade.

War was the business of the dockyards at Woolwich, Chatham, Deptford, Sheerness, Plymouth and – of most significance for Jane Austen – Portsmouth. Portsmouth's economic and political importance during Austen's lifetime was due to the wars with France. As it was well connected by road and packet ship, Admiralty couriers from London could reach it in eight hours. Portsmouth was dominated by naval buildings such as the Royal Naval Academy, dating from the early eighteenth century, the Commissioner's House (designed by Samuel Wyatt, 1784–87) and the School for Superior Apprentices (built 1815–17). Sir Samuel Bentham, the Inspector General of Naval Works, initiated schemes to enlarge and deepen the basin and docks, enabling ships to dock without removing their guns.[3] In 1802 Bentham introduced the first bucket ladder steam dredger to deal with Portsmouth's silt problem and a moveable steam engine to help pump water in and out of the docks. At the same time Marc Isambard Brunel (whose more famous son was born in Portsmouth) was developing new block-making equipment to accelerate the refitting of warships. Portsmouth was a beacon of British technological supremacy and its dockyards with their improvements are a tourist attraction for the Londoner, Henry Crawford, in *Mansfield Park* (3:10) as well as being at the sharp end of 'politics' (3:12).

London's exponential growth in the late eighteenth and early nineteenth centuries was enabled by the construction of a network of new turnpike roads, canals and bridges. Westminster Bridge was opened in 1750 and Blackfriars in 1769; Vauxhall Bridge, Waterloo Bridge and Southwark Bridge were all built between 1811 and 1819. In 1756–7 the New Road (or Euston Road) had opened up the important area between Paddington and Islington for residential development to the north of the fashionable centre. After 1807 brilliant gas lighting began to replace oil lamps in the West End of London and paved roads radiated out from the genteel area around Westminster, but dirt accumulated faster than all measures to contain it: cattle were still driven through the streets to and from Smithfield Market until the mid nineteenth century and horse-drawn vehicles added to the labours of the sweepers stationed at street crossings. Smoke from brick kilns and thousands of sea coal fires polluted the air. In 1813 Henry Austen's new home above his offices at No. 10 Henrietta Street appeared to Jane to be 'all dirt & confusion' (*L*, 24 May 1813).

The rapid growth of new buildings along the river and the major roads created a populous metropolis which placed increasing pressure on the political and cultural authority of the court-based establishments in the West End. Soldiers and volunteers drilled regularly on the streets during the Napoleonic Wars. In 1792 Jane Austen's cousin, Eliza, witnessed fighting between soldiers and a mob in central London. Despite Eleanor Tilney's expectation of riot and murder in the capital (*NA*, 1:14), many outlying parishes retained a peaceful village seclusion. Fashionable Richmond counted as a green suburb of London by 1801, and Islington was still 'half rural' when William Wordsworth visited the Sadler's Wells theatre there in 1802. In 1816–17 the households of Leigh Hunt and the Shelleys living in the Vale of Health, Hampstead, felt themselves to be far beyond metropolitan corruption.

Political events changed the London skyline in a number of ways and diverse members of the royal family planted their identities on different parts of London. George III preferred Buckingham House to Hampton Court Palace and Kensington Palace; the latter building fell into disrepair until the Duke of Kent initiated expensive renovations. Kensington Palace was then used as residence for minor royals such as the isolated Princess Caroline, with whom Austen sympathised 'because she *is* a Woman, & because I hate her Husband' (*L*, 16 February 1813). The Prince Regent, who saw himself as a patron of the arts, was keen to foster architectural flamboyance to counter the dreary household economy of his father. As Regent he employed Holland and Nash to recreate Carlton House (1783–1813). It became famous for its garden parties and costly banquets. Jane Austen was invited there in 1815. Nash was later employed to build Buckingham Palace but his greatest scheme in London was the design to connect Regent's Park with Carlton House via Regent's Street (1811–26) with groups of dazzling stucco villas and crescent terraces, blending the architectural patterns of Bath with the landscape of a pleasure garden.

The perverse English enthusiasm for staging social events out of doors and the cultivation of pocket-size gardens to recollect the ideal of the country house while business kept one in town ensured that London's parks were protected from over-development. Like Austen herself in 1811, Elinor in *Sense and Sensibility* enjoys a Sunday walk in Kensington Gardens (3:2) when everything else is closed. The new residential areas preserved 'flowery gardens in vast squares' which impressed Wordsworth, as well as the crowds and noise (*The Prelude*, 7, 134). On the south side of the Thames at Vauxhall and at Ranelagh in Chelsea were famous pleasure gardens. In Austen's time Vauxhall still offered music, fireworks and water-work spectacles, but it had been superseded as an aristocratic resort by Ranelagh (as visited by Lady Delacour in Maria Edgeworth's *Belinda*) with its glittering rotunda for orchestral music and promenading. Outbreaks of rowdy behaviour meant that the gardens lost social cachet: masquerades died out by the 1790s; the Ranelagh rotunda was demolished in 1805 and the Assembly Rooms like Almack's, St James's and clubs or private musical parties at home guaranteed a more exclusive milieu.

When she visited London in 1813–14 Madame de Staël held literary salons which Jane Austen did not wish to attend, but by this time coffee-house and salon gatherings were giving way to public exhibitions, lectures and museums open to anyone who could pay. Francis Jeffrey saw the new enthusiasm for exhibitions as fostering a culture of 'Encyclopedical trifling' among the middle classes.[4] Exhibitions at the Royal Academy, which began in Pall Mall in 1769 and moved to Somerset House in 1781, were a cramped arena of fashionable life. Austen planned to go 'if we have time' in 1813; the same letter records exhibitions of portraits at Spring Gardens and of Sir Joshua Reynolds's paintings at Pall Mall (*L*, 24 May 1813). Painters like Benjamin Haydon crossed the divide between high and low culture by exhibiting huge canvases alongside the circus-like shows in the Egyptian Hall, Piccadilly. This venue was used to display Napoleon's carriage after 1815; it was established by the owner of the Liverpool Museum, whose collection of natural history items Jane Austen viewed in 1811, admitting that her preference for men and women made her more attentive to the company than the sights on display.

Show business flourished around Charing Cross, the Strand, Leicester Square and Piccadilly. Models of Roman ruins or other European cities were hugely popular, as were orreries, phantasmagoria and panoramas such as the 'Battle of Paris' in the purpose-built rotunda in Leicester Square in 1815. Competing with these entertainments, London's theatres during the Regency pandered to the taste for illuminated volcanoes, storms at sea, Miltonic vistas and child prodigies. While his business prospered, Henry Austen owned a box at the Pantheon Opera House in Oxford Street and the Lyceum. Henrietta Street was within easy reach of the Covent Garden and Drury Lane theatres. As patent theatres they held exclusive rights to perform spoken drama as well as providing after-pieces of farce and pantomime with performing animals. The non-patent theatres such as Sadler's Wells, the Lyceum and Astley's amphitheatre were licensed only for musicals or circus shows. Covent Garden (renovated by Holland in 1792) and Drury Lane (upgraded by the Adam brothers in 1775 and Holland in 1791–4) were both rebuilt after fires in 1808 and 1809. Covent Garden was redesigned by Robert Smirke to resemble a Greek temple with portico and coade stone frieze by Flaxman; the new Drury Lane was created by Benjamin Wyatt. The theatres were adopted by the Tories and Whigs in a competition for political patronage of the arts.

By 1800 the granting of twenty royal patents allowed theatres outside London to emulate the glamour of Drury Lane and Covent Garden. Bath's Theatre Royal was licensed in 1768 and its connections with the London stage contributed to the fashionable allure of the city in the eighteenth century. The obvious difference between London and provincial theatres was the size of the buildings: the auditorium of Drury Lane could hold over 3,000 spectators. The smallness of the Theatre Royal at Orchard Street in Bath means that Henry Tilney 'in the opposite box' is actually very close to Catherine when she feels that he is ignoring her.[5] As in London, the auditorium was brightly lit throughout the performance and theatre-going encouraged fashionable, cultural and political pageantry.

When the Austens went to Bath in 1801 it was for the benefit of Mrs Austen's health: the city had plenty of doctors and new medical treatments, including 'electricity', which Edward Austen tried in 1799. The Roman spa had been recreated as a fashionable health resort in the first half of the eighteenth century when the Duke of Chandos, Mrs Austen's great-uncle, used his immense speculative wealth and John Wood's Palladian architecture to redesign the city. Wood and his son arranged successive terraces, circuses and crescents of stone-fronted houses, graced with ionic columns and balustrades. By Austen's day the elegant landmarks of North and South Parade, the Circus (1754), the Royal Crescent (1767–74) and the New Assembly Rooms (1776–71) were all established and the centre had been renovated after the arson and looting of anti-Catholic Rioters in 1780 (witnessed by Frances Burney). Regency Bath's newer fashionable areas were sometimes on damp ground and in close proximity to poorer homes. The question of where to find suitable accommodation was, therefore, rather fraught.

The Austens lodged with the Leigh-Perrots at No. 1 Paragon Buildings and spent weeks walking round a variety of unsuitable or 'putrifying' houses before taking 4 Sydney Place, a newly developed area across the River, between 1801 and 1804 (fig. 30), after which they moved to 3 Green Park Buildings East on the southern outskirts of the city, where Mr Austen died in 1805. Sydney Gardens was designed to rival the attractions of Vauxhall with swings, a bowling green, a labyrinth and evening concerts complete with illuminations and fireworks. Closer to Pulteney Bridge is Laura Place, where Lady Dalrymple stations herself in *Persuasion*. This novel is particularly alert to the changing social nuance of location: Queen Square, where the Austens stayed in 1799, is not regarded as fashionable enough by the Musgrove girls; the Crofts confidently step into the centre of things in Wood's Gay Street, where the Austens lodged briefly while preparing to leave Bath after Mr Austen's death; Sir Walter settles on Camden Place, a new, heavily classical crescent built on the northern heights of the city by John Jelly with rather less impressive views than the Royal Crescent.

In the *New Bath Guide* of 1795, Bath is presented as a 'vortex of amusement'. Fashionable eighteenth-century routines were still adhered to: people visited the Pump Room in the morning then promenaded. Despite the traffic problems mentioned in *Northanger Abbey* (1:7), walking was a favourite pastime. One of Jane Austen's letters from 1799 records the appearance of umbrellas and the moment when 'the Pavements are getting very white again'

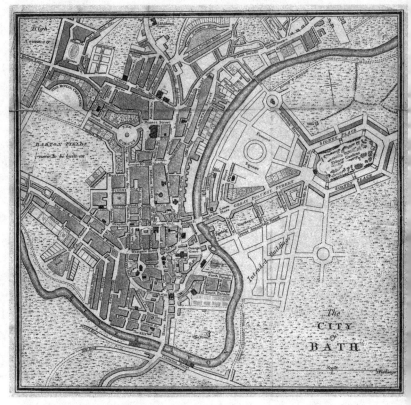

Figure 30. The city of Bath, from *A Guide to all the Watering and Sea Bathing Places* (*c*.1820).

(*L*, 17 May 1799), which means that it is dry enough to walk. After dinner came visits to the theatre or the Assembly Rooms. Traditional ceremony was replaced here by rules of etiquette overseen by the master of ceremonies (who introduces Catherine to Henry Tilney, *NA*, 1:3) which permitted everyone to mix freely. But this mix was one of the reasons for Bath's decline. By the turn of the century Bath was losing its high society glamour; building projects had dwindled. Cheltenham was the new fashionable spa and when not in London the Prince Regent decamped to Brighton, where sea-bathing was the newly fashionable health treatment. In 1816–17

the radical Henry Hunt campaigned in Bath and gathered a substantial petition for Parliamentary reform.[6] This suggests that the
city held a large number of discontented artisans: such a population would inevitably conflict with the ideal of social exclusivity.
As in London, genteel contempt for the mob led to a preference
for private parties over public events and while Catherine Morland
attends a public ball in *Northanger Abbey*, the Elliots' only amusement is in 'the elegant stupidity of private parties': the theatre and
the rooms (where Captain Wentworth is likely to be) are deemed
'not fashionable enough' (*P*, 2:7). All characters, however, converge
on the expensive shops of Milsom Street, still as fashionable as when
General Tilney lodged there in *Northanger Abbey*.

In *Persuasion* it is the network of female characters excluded
from society, connecting the low-rent Westgate Buildings and the
stylish Marlborough Buildings, that exposes the murky business
dealings of Mr Elliot. Anne registers streets thronging with 'news-
men, muffin-men and milk-men, and the ceaseless clink of pattens'
(*P*, 2:2) and her disenchantment with Bath's metropolitan clamour
is often attributed to Austen herself. However, her letter of 1805
which describes the Crescent as 'not crouded enough' (*L*, 8–11
April) paints a slightly different picture and suggests how depress-
ing a once-fashionable city was out of season. As she fumed over
the sale of her father's library in Bath in 1801 and again in London
in 1816 when asking Mr Murray to forward letters to Chawton
'in consequence of the late sad event in Henrietta St', Jane Austen
was aware that however exciting the city could be as a 'Scene of
Dissipation & vice' (*L*, 1 April 1816; 23 August 1796) it was easier
to live on her income in the country.

NOTES

1. William Wordsworth, *The Prelude 1799, 1805, 1850*, eds.
   Jonathan Wordsworth, M. H. Abrams and Stephen Gill (New
   York and London: W. W. Norton & Co., 1979), 7, 691. Subsequent references are included in the text.
2. *Byron's Letters and Journals*, ed. Leslie A. Marchand (London:
   John Murray 1973–94), vol. III, p. 260.
3. See Roger Morriss, *The Royal Dockyards during the Revolutionary
   and Napoleonic Wars* (Leicester: Leicester University Press, 1983),
   pp. 47–9.

4. Cited in Richard D. Altick, *The Shows of London* (Cambridge, MA. and London: Belknap Press, 1978), p. 228. My summary of Regency show land is indebted to this book and also to *The London Encyclopaedia*, eds. Ben Weinreb and Christopher Hibbert (London: Macmillan, 1995).

5. As pointed out by Penny Gay in *Jane Austen and the Theatre* (Cambridge: Cambridge University Press, 2002), p. 9.

6. See R. S. Neale, *Bath 1680–1850. A Social History or A Valley of Pleasure, Yet a Sink of Iniquity* (London: Routledge & Kegan Paul, 1981), pp. 333–4.

19

Consumer goods

DAVID SELWYN

Jane Austen grew up in the last quarter of a century that had seen a remarkable expansion of the British market economy. In *The Wealth of Nations*, published in the year after her birth, Adam Smith examined the relation between wages, production and consumption and, very much in the spirit of the times, advocated the spending of higher incomes and savings in order to perpetuate economic growth. Increasing affluence among the middle classes led to a much greater demand for commodities; and the developments that brought about the Industrial Revolution – availability of raw materials, water power, technical breakthroughs and navigable waterways – enabled it to be met by manufacturers who benefited from conditions that were highly favourable to entrepreneurs. Whilst an important element of this commercial success was a rapid growth in exports, there were still plenty of goods left for the home market; and these were swollen by the large number of imports – more than £12 million worth by 1770 – that the general prosperity made possible. Commodities were brought to Europe from all parts of the globe, and many of them – textiles, sugar, tobacco, for example – gave rise to profitable processing industries; but many were also sold directly to home consumers. Not only tea (expensive at the beginning of the century, less so by the end), coffee, chocolate and spices, but also exotic clothes and furniture were becoming available to the middle classes; and improved transport by means of navigable rivers, canals and turnpike roads, ensured that they were readily obtainable throughout the kingdom. Thus during the reigns of the Georges, particularly that of George III, there was a far wider range of articles of all kinds available for purchase than there had been under the Stuarts; and the average family spent four times as much on them by the end of the century as they had at the beginning.

The fact that things were manufactured does not mean that they were mass-produced, as was to be the case in the nineteenth century:

the craftsman was still predominant, and a screen painted at home by an Elinor Dashwood would not have looked very different from a similar item bought in a shop. What is most significant about the furniture and objects in Georgian houses is the progressive change in taste that they reflected. The heavy oak tables of the previous century had given way to much lighter, more elegant pieces, made in walnut and later satinwood or rosewood, and above all mahogany. They were often oval or round, and leaves could be put in to accommodate more guests at dinner. The pretty Pembroke table, with its side flaps, tapering legs and useful drawer, was a very popular innovation; when one was introduced at Steventon Rectory, Jane Austen reported that her mother had great delight in keeping her money and papers locked up. Sideboards and chests of drawers had serpentine or bow fronts; wood was adorned with elegant brass handles, locks and feet; chairs and sofas were richly upholstered; and beds could be hung and decorated in varying degrees of lavishness to suit the pocket of the owner. Rooms were brightened with colourful wallpapers, pictures, mirrors, elaborate chandeliers and sconces, draped window curtains, patterned carpets, brass fenders, screens, china ornaments; and yet even in the grandest houses many of the rooms had a sense of airiness, as in Miss Darcy's sitting-room at Pemberley, which, to give her pleasure, was 'lately fitted up with greater elegance and lightness than the apartments below' (*P&P*, 3:1). The development of a taste for furniture less heavy and less formally arranged is registered in *Persuasion*, where in the Great House at Uppercross, to 'the old-fashioned square parlour, with a small carpet and shining floor' Henrietta and Louisa are 'gradually giving the proper air of confusion by a grand piano forte and a harp, flower-stands and little tables placed in every direction'. The portraits on the walls seem to be 'staring in astonishment' to see 'such an overthrow of all order and neatness' (*P*, 1:5). It is a similarly atavistic reaction to change, but on the part of a living person, that Emma has to overcome when she introduces a round table to Hartfield.

Throughout the house – the drawing-room, dining-room, library, bedrooms, kitchens, offices, garden buildings – there was a proliferation of objects and gadgets of all kinds; and, with a corresponding increase in the quantity or variety of wearing apparel, personal possessions, reading matter and food, it was inevitable that there should be a huge expansion in the number of shops and ware-houses from which all these goods could be bought, supported by widespread promotion through trade cards and newspaper adver-tisements.

Traditionally, commerce had been carried on at markets and fairs, yet we learn from the census of 1801 that by the end of the eighteenth century there were no fewer than 74,500 shopkeepers and tradesmen in England. Visitors from abroad invariably com-mented on the number and magnificence of the shops, particularly in London; no other city in Europe had anything remotely compa-rable. Drapers accounted for the largest single group; such was the demand for their wares that many of them were specialists – linen drapers, woollen drapers, silk mercers – though in the provinces this was less likely, and in small towns even general shops carried a limited range of drapery and haberdashery. Chandlers, or gro-cers, were also of course numerous, as were butchers, pastrycooks, shoe shops and cabinet makers. Craftsmen such as goldsmiths, jewellers, gunsmiths and carvers-and-gilders established shops for the sale of their own wares; it was possible to find shops special-ising in anything from swords to buttons; and the sophisticated tastes of the time were catered for by perfumers, seedsmen, scien-tific instrument dealers, proprietors of print shops, or booksellers such as James Lackington, who in Finsbury Square sold large num-bers of cheaply priced books in his vast, and rather grandly named, 'Temple of the Muses', which boasted a rotunda gallery and two side rooms for customers who wished to relax and enjoy what he described as a 'literary Lounge' (fig. 31).

Enjoyment was an important aspect of shopping, which became a popular leisure pursuit. In London the most fashionable shops, especially for luxury goods, were in the West End; Oxford Street in particular was very smart, brilliantly lit with oil lamps, its shops staying open until ten o'clock at night. All sorts of attractive goods were enticingly displayed in bright bow-fronted windows, and more were laid out for inspection in the spacious first-floor showrooms of some of the larger establishments. One of the most impressive was Josiah Wedgwood's china warehouse (he did not care to have it described merely as a shop). Having first opened premises in Grosvenor Square in 1765, he was soon looking for somewhere larger and two years later moved to Portland House in Greek Street.

Figure 31. Messrs. Lackington, Allen & Co, the 'Temple of the Muses' on Finsbury-Square, from *Ackermann's Repository of the Arts* for April 1809.

Here there was space to set out dinner services as for a meal, with vases decorating the walls; both displays were changed every few days, to attract visitors back – like other large London shops, it was noted for its social atmosphere. By the time Rudolph Ackermann included a print depicting its first-floor showroom in *The Repository of Arts* in 1809, it had moved again, to York Street, St James's Square, and this is where Jane Austen knew it. Mrs Lybbe Powys, the diarist (and friend of the Austens), noted having gone to Wedgwood's and 'as usual' having been 'highly entertained, as . . . no shop affords so great a variety';[1] yet when Jane Austen went there while staying in London in 1811, it was, as most of her shopping seems to have been, to carry out a 'commission'. When she described another visit in a letter to Cassandra two years later, she had gone because her brother Edward and his daughter Fanny were ordering a dinner set: 'I beleive the pattern is a small Lozenge in purple,' she wrote, 'between Lines of narrow Gold; – & it is to have the Crest' (*L*, 16 September 1813) – pieces of it may still be seen at Chawton today. Jane Austen does not seem to have taken much pleasure in shopping in London, but to have regarded it as a duty she had to perform, often for the benefit of other people. Like any woman, she bought material in drapers' shops, but even those she sometimes found tiresome and time-consuming. In several letters she referred to Wilding and Kent, at Grafton House in New Bond Street, but without any great relish for going there. Describing one visit, when she bought some 'Bugle Trimming' and three pairs of silk stockings, she reported that 'the whole Counter was thronged' and they waited '*full* half an hour' before they could be attended to (*L*, 18–20 April 1811); on another occasion, she expressed her intention of going at 9 o'clock, to 'get [it] over before breakfast', but even then they were there for three-quarters of an hour, 'Edward sitting by all the time with wonderful patience' (*L*, 15–16, 16 September 1813). Layton and Shears was another shop that could be got out of the way before breakfast once Henry Austen had moved into 10 Henrietta Street, Covent Garden, since it was in Bedford House next door. In a letter written on what turned out to be her last time in London, she gave the impression of being thoroughly tired of the whole business of shopping: 'Well – we were very busy all yesterday; from 1/2 past 11 to 4 in the Streets, working almost entirely for other people, driving from Place to Place after a parcel for Sandling [Park] which we could never find, & encountering the miseries of Grafton House to get a purple frock for Eleanor Bridges' (*L*, 26 November 1815).

Traditionally, throughout the country, shops had sold on credit, partly because of the endemic shortage of coins; suppliers extended credit to the shopkeepers and they in turn would allow established customers as long as eight or nine months to pay. But gradually a 'ready money' system was introduced, and this went hand in hand with ticketing, or fixing a price, which of course would be lower than in other shops (it had formerly been the practice to haggle); James Lackington adopted this method at 'The Temple of the Muses'. Credit was still available to customers ordering goods at a distance, though it is interesting that Jane Austen did not know whether that was the case with Layton and Shears: while she was staying at Godmersham and Cassandra was at Henrietta Street, she transmitted an enquiry from Edward's sister-in-law Harriot Moore as to whether they sold material for pelisses, but she added that if it were a '*ready money* house' it would not do, since Harriot could not pay for it immediately (*L*, 3 November 1813).

Besides having the finest shops in Europe, London supplied many of the goods that were offered for sale in the provinces, since its retailers acted as wholesalers for dealers elsewhere. Shopkeepers in the smaller towns and cities would visit London regularly to replenish their stocks, and would return with the latest fashions to attract their customers. After visiting Mrs Rider's haberdashery in Basingstoke, Jane Austen told her sister that she had bought what she had intended to buy, 'but not in much perfection. – There were no narrow Braces for Children, & scarcely any netting silk'; however, she added that Mrs Rider's assistant, Miss Wood, 'as usual [was] going to Town very soon, & [would] lay in a fresh stock' (*L*, 27–8 October 1798) – in much the same way as Mrs Ford in *Emma* has 'a charming collection of new ribbons from town' (*E*, 2:9). Rider's was apparently not a favourite shop; when its proprietor died, Jane Austen commented: 'The Neighbourhood have quite recovered the death of Mrs Rider – so much so, that I think they are rather rejoiced at it now; her Things were so very dear!' (*L*, 21–2 January 1801).

Although pedlars sometimes called at Steventon, selling lace or fabrics, and the village of Oakley, a few miles away, had some shops, including a haberdasher where Jane Austen bought stockings, it was to Basingstoke that the family resorted when making more substantial purchases for the rectory. In common with many of their friends and acquaintances, both Mr Austen and his eldest son James had accounts with John Ring, the cabinet maker, and the firm's books reveal some of their dealings.[2] In March 1792 James Austen married and fitted up Deane parsonage ready for himself and his wife. Helped no doubt by a generous wedding gift from his wealthy father-in-law, General Mathew, he was able to buy good quality furniture, much of it in mahogany, and though he was not extravagant by the standards of more aristocratic customers, the bill of £200.15s.0d. that he ran up during little more than five months was comparatively large for a clergyman. His father was certainly never able to spend so much, and the account for two beds that he bought for his daughters two years later reveals that, whereas James's beds had mahogany posts and cost £2.2s.0d. each, Mr Austen paid little more than half as much for beds with mahogany knobs but only 'Color'd' (i.e. painted) posts; and the 42 yards of blue and white check cotton for the hangings, for which Mr Austen paid £4.4s.0d., were considerably simpler than James's 115 yards of dimity at £13.17s.11d. (It was also at Ring's that on 5 December 1794 Mr Austen paid 12s. for 'a Small Mahogany Writing Desk with a Long Drawer and Glass Ink Stand Compleat', presumably as a birthday present for his daughter Jane; having passed down the family, it is now in the British Library.)

When goods could not be obtained in person, they were ordered and sent by carrier, or possibly delivered by a member of the family. Tallow candles came from Penlington's in Covent Garden, tea from Twining's. Sometimes articles of clothing arrived from a distance: in one letter Jane Austen wrote, 'My father approves his Stockings very highly – & finds no fault with any part of Mrs Hancock's bill except the charge of 3^s.6^d. for the Packing box' (*L*, 25–7 October 1800). Years later, when she was living in Chawton, she wanted to buy a cloak in Alton and having tried to find one at Coleby's, the draper in the High Street, she wrote: 'There was no ready-made Cloak at Alton that would do, but Coleby has undertaken to supply one in a few days: it is to be Grey Woollen & cost ten shillings' (*L*, 29–30 November 1812). There were, however, a number of good cabinet makers in the town; when in 1815 Anna Lefroy was setting up house there, her grandmother Mrs Austen wrote to her: 'You will be able to get many things in the furniture way at Alton. We bought a great deal there.'[3]

At the periods when the Austens stayed – and subsequently lived – in Bath, they had a huge range of shops to hand, and Jane Austen was able to be selective, particularly in the matter of economy. Prices were always a concern. When looking for decorations for a hat on a visit in June 1799, she went to a milliner's near Walcot Church recommended by her aunt, Mrs Leigh Perrot, and wrote 'We have been to the cheap Shop, & very cheap we found it, but there are only flowers made there, no fruit' (*L*, 11 June 1799); later, of course, Mrs Leigh Perrot was accused (but acquitted) of trying to make an economy of her own by stealing a card of lace worth 20s. from Elizabeth Gregory's haberdasher's in Bath Street, probably the same shop in which only two months earlier her niece had seen some gauzes 'at only 4^s a yard' that 'were not so good or so pretty' as her own (*L*, 2 June 1799). When the family moved to Bath in 1801, Jane Austen did not consider it worth bringing much of the furniture, since 'the trouble & risk of the removal would be more than the advantage of having them at a place, where everything may be purchased' (*L*, 3–5 January 1801) – a remark not unlike Mrs Allen's comment that in Bath 'there are so many good shops . . . one can step out of doors and get a thing in five minutes!' (*NA*, 1:3). In the very first letter written after her arrival in the city, she listed approvingly the current prices of produce: 'Meat is only 8^d per pound, butter 12^d & cheese 9 1/2^d'; fish, however, she considered 'exorbitant', a salmon having been sold 'at 2^s: 9^d p^r pound the whole fish', and the cucumber they had not been able to eat on their journey would, she believed, make a 'very acceptable present' for her uncle, Mr Leigh Perrot, since he had 'enquired the price of one lately, when he was told a shilling' (*L*, 5–6 May 1801). Occasionally, however, she would throw caution to the winds: in reply to a query from Cassandra, she wrote 'The 4 Boxes of Lozenges at 1^s.–1^d. – 1/2 per box, amount as I was told to 4^s.–6^d, and as the sum was so trifling, I thought it better to pay at once than contest the matter' (*L*, 21–2 May 1801).

If such cost consciousness brings to mind Mrs Norris, it should be remembered that Jane Austen never endorses extravagance in her characters, and indeed unnecessary expenditure, especially on oneself, is a sign of moral weakness. When Robert Ferrars keeps Elinor and Marianne waiting at the jeweller's counter as he fusses over his order for, of all things, a toothpick case, 'the correctness of his eye, and the delicacy of his taste' exceed his 'politeness', and he merely exhibits 'puppyism' (*S&S*, 11:9).[4] They are in the first-floor showroom of Thomas Gray's shop in Sackville Street (an establishment, incidentally, that had announced its intention of refusing credit and selling only for ready money); Elinor has an impeccable reason for being there, since she is 'carrying on a negociation for the exchange of a few old-fashioned jewels of her mother' (*S&S*, 11:9) and cannot therefore be tainted with the suggestion that she is spending money on herself. Gray's is one of only two real shops in London found in the novels, Broadwood's, where Frank Churchill buys the pianoforte, being the other. In Bath, only Molland's is identified; this was the well-known pastrycook's (so well known that Jane Austen does not even say that it is a pastrycook's) at No. 2 Milsom Street. Otherwise, Anne Elliot finds Admiral Croft critically contemplating the depiction of a boat in the window of an unnamed print-seller higher up Milsom Street; and Charles Musgrove goes off to have 'the sight of a capital gun' simply at 'a fellow's in the market-place' (*P*, 2:11).

The best-known fictional shop in Jane Austen's novels is of course Ford's, 'the principal woollen-draper, linen-draper, and haberdasher's shop united; the shop first in size and fashion' in Highbury (*E*, 2:3). There are obviously other shops, but with the economy characteristic of *Emma*, it more or less stands for all. The description of it as fashionable is gently ironic, in the same way that Frank Churchill's statement that 'every body attends [it] every day of their lives' (*E*, 2:6) is: for important shopping people have to go to Kingston. Yet despite its position of undisputed centrality to the village (from its door, after all, it offers Emma a larger social prospect than she has in the drawing-rooms of her own circle), its function in the novel is still little more than as a location. The only shop that Jane Austen created to exist, as it were, in its own right, to play its part in expressing the meaning of the work, is the library in Sanditon. Situated in the 'short row of smart-looking Houses, called the Terrace' (*S*, 4), it is also a toyshop and sells 'all the useless things in the World that c^d not be done without'; and with a proprietress who has to be 'hurried down from her Toilette, with all her glossy Curls & smart Trinkets' to attend to her customers, it embodies the hollow commercialism that lies at the heart of both the resort and the text. Charlotte Heywood feels herself under the double pressure of being 'among so many pretty Temptations' and of wishing to please Mr Parker, who, 'anxiously wishing to support' the library, has already urged her to buy 'new parasols, new Gloves, & new Broches, for her sisters & herself'. Naturally, she resists, reflecting that 'at two & Twenty there c^d be no excuse for her doing otherwise' (*S*, 6); but at a period in which the production, sale and acquisition of goods had reached unprecedented heights, it was a striking and timely innovation on Jane Austen's part to invoke the lure of rampant consumerism to test her heroine's character.

NOTES

1. Quoted in G. E. Miltton, *Jane Austen and Her Times* (1905), ch. 16.
2. For a detailed discussion of the Austens' accounts at Ring's, see Edward Copeland, '*Persuasion*: The Jane Austen Consumer's Guide', *Persuasions* 15 (1993), 111–23.
3. Deirdre Le Faye, 'Anna Lefroy and Her Austen Family Letters', *Princeton University Library Chronicle* 62:3 (2001), 535.
4. In 1772 Sheridan bought a toothpick case at William Evill's in Bath for £4.4*s.*; the bill is reproduced in Trevor Fawcett's *Bath Commercialis'd* (Bath: Ruton, 2002), p. 119. D. A. Miller deals at length with Robert Ferrars's in *Jane Austen, or The Secret of Style* (Princeton, NJ: Princeton University Press, 2003).

20

Domestic architecture

CLAIRE LAMONT

When Catherine Morland is invited to Northanger Abbey she reflects on the house she was to visit, 'With all the chances against her of house, hall, place, park, court, and cottage, Northanger turned up an abbey' (2:2). A sensitivity to different types of house is typical of Austen's age, as is reflected with a similar vein of humour in the titles of Thomas Love Peacock's works, for instance *Headlong Hall* (1815) and *Nightmare Abbey* (1818), which refer to hall, court, abbey, castle and grange. Austen's list indicates the variety of house types which her characters might experience, a variety which expresses the settled nature of the English counties in which her novels are set. As any house which is at all substantial will usually outlast its first occupants a settled society is likely to show examples of houses of different periods. The different names for house types reflect differences in origin, size and function. They are also in Austen's novels the opportunity for satire on social anxiety or pretension. Mary Crawford is glad to be assured that Mansfield Park justifies its name with 'a real park five miles round' (1:5). Sir William Lucas celebrates his knighthood by moving to a house in the country 'denominated from that period Lucas Lodge' (*P&P*, 1:5).

Two important periods of Austen's own life were spent in villages in Hampshire. Her youth was spent in Steventon Rectory and her last years in a cottage in Chawton. Between these two periods (1801–9) she lived in Bath, Clifton and Southampton. While the sorts of house commonest in these places are present in her novels – the parsonage, cottage and urban house or flat – the best known of the houses in the novels are in the country and are larger, and grander, than these. This has caused commentators to consider the houses which Austen visited. They are many, spread over the southern and south-midland counties of England, and particularly in Hampshire and Kent. An impression of the outside of these houses can be got from the illustrations in Nigel Nicolson's *The World of Jane Austen* (1991). Attention is drawn to the substantial Georgian houses, perhaps a small country house or rectory, rather than to the larger aristocratic houses to which she was a less frequent visitor. One large house, however, should be mentioned: in 1797 Austen's brother Edward, who had been adopted by wealthy relations, became the owner of Godmersham Park in Kent, a Palladian house built in 1732 with later additions, where his sister stayed frequently, giving her experience of life in a large house. Palladianism was the dominant style of great house architecture in the early and mid eighteenth century.

In considering Austen's houses it should be acknowledged that critics, especially if they are architectural historians, have expressed disappointment at the lack of architectural information in her novels.[1] This is caused partly by the paucity of external description of Austen's houses and by the relatively few indications of date. Although Austen gives some details of her older houses, others, and particularly the ones in which the heroines live, are described simply as 'modern'.

The oldest houses in Austen's novels are Northanger Abbey and Donwell Abbey in *Emma*, which are both dispossessed monasteries. Northanger Abbey had 'fallen into the hands of an ancestor of the Tilneys on its dissolution' (2:2), that is the dissolution of the monasteries by Henry VIII in 1536–40. Austen had early experience of such architecture, since she attended for a short time a school in the ruins of Reading Abbey. Her young heroine Catherine Morland, however, sees medieval buildings not through a knowledge of Reformation history – she is ignorant of 'the quarrels of popes and kings' (*NA*, 1:14) – but through the Gothic novel. She is deceived by the architecture of a house which is based on the four sides of a cloister, although it is far less labyrinthine than, for instance, the abbey in Ann Radcliffe's *The Romance of the Forest* (1791). Northanger Abbey is a medieval building altered to secure the comforts of modern living while retaining Gothic features like pointed windows (2:5). In General Tilney's hands it is a place of mental oppression and materialism. Donwell Abbey, by contrast, is presented as positive. In one of the few descriptions of a house from the outside in Austen's novels Donwell is described as 'covering a good deal of ground, rambling and irregular, with many comfortable and one or two handsome rooms' (*E*, 3:6). The reader learns little of the inside of Donwell, except that the house observes the tradition of serving meals indoors at table instead of outdoors as Mrs Elton suggests (*E*, 3:6). Donwell with its fertile gardens is the heir of its monastic origin; its apples and strawberries contrast with the hot-houses in which General Tilney grows pineapples (*NA*, 2:7).

Sotherton Court in *Mansfield Park* is Elizabethan, although it has a late seventeenth-century chapel, recently disused (1:6, 9). It 'is a large, regular, brick building – heavy, but respectable looking, and has many good rooms'. Most of the visit to Sotherton in the novel is concerned with the garden, which is in a formal style inviting improvement. The interior is similarly old-fashioned, being full of furniture 'in the taste of fifty years back' and family portraits that only Mrs Rushworth cares about (*MP*, 1:9). Mavis Batey has pointed out that some of the details of Sotherton are drawn from Stoneleigh Abbey in Warwickshire, which Austen visited in 1806.[2] Whatever its features its new mistress, Maria Rushworth, disregards it in favour of her real choice, a house in Wimpole Street, London (*MP*, 3:9).

The most famous house in Austen's novels is Pemberley in *Pride and Prejudice*. We are not told the age of Pemberley House and readers have been left like Mr Gardiner 'conjecturing as to the date of the building' (3:1). It has been taken to be Elizabethan or Jacobean on account of its having a gallery, a long upstairs room in which it was common to hang pictures (Wellington, 'Houses in Jane Austen's Novels', p. 188). It also has a saloon, which in seventeenth- and eighteenth-century houses was a lofty room for public occasions. Pemberley's saloon seems less grand and its window opening to the ground is a feature of the late eighteenth century's wish to live closer to nature (*P&P*, 3:3).[3] The association of the house with outdoors is increased by its grounds, in which nature and the arts of eighteenth-century landscape gardening have created a series of picturesque scenes inspired by Gilpin. Whatever its age, Pemberley is experienced by the heroine as an eighteenth-century house whose windows allow proper appreciation of the landscape outside. That is consistent with its situation, 'standing well on rising ground' (*P&P*,

3:1). Older houses in Austen are described as low-lying (*NA*, 2:5, *MP*, 1:6, *E*, 3:6). As Mr Parker, in *Sanditon*, remarks, 'Our Ancestors, you know always built in a hole' (4).

It is interesting to note that none of these older houses in Austen's novels is the heroine's home. All are seen only by the visitor. When we turn to the heroine's homes we find that, where the information is given, her heroines live in recently built houses. Barton Cottage, home of the Dashwoods in *Sense and Sensibility*, 'had not been built many years' (1:6); Mansfield Park is 'a spacious modern-built house' and 'modern, airy, and well situated' (1:5, 3:15); Hartfield, the home of Emma Woodhouse, is 'modern and well-built' (*E*, 2:14). What did Austen mean by the term 'modern' in relation to a house? The *OED* gives as its first example of the phrase 'modern-built' applied to architecture Austen's description of Cleveland, the Palmers' house in *Sense and Sensibility*, as 'a spacious, modern-built house' (3:6). Dana Arnold, however, writing of the eighteenth and early nineteenth centuries, says, 'it is not unusual to find references to classically designed country houses as simply "modern".'[4] In such a context classical is opposed to vernacular or baroque. This supports Wellington's conclusion that 'Mansfield Park was . . . a Palladian house dating from the 1730's or 1740's, and was very likely inspired by Godmersham' ('Houses in Jane Austen's Novels', p. 188). None of Austen's recently built houses is in a noticeably fashionable architectural style, for instance the new Gothic pioneered by Horace Walpole at Strawberry Hill and being realised by her contemporary, Walter Scott, at Abbotsford. Only in *Sanditon* do we see actual building taking place, and there the emphasis is on Regency resort planning rather than on the individual house (*S*, 4). Austen's modern houses are somewhere between the grandeur of the Palladian – Lady Catherine de Bourgh's house, Rosings, is 'a handsome modern building' (*P&P*, 2:5) – and what, in the case of lesser houses, we have come to call Georgian.

Domestic architecture is concerned with the interior as much as the exterior of a house. Once again critics – this time perhaps with the rich interiors in Victorian novels in mind – have expressed disappointment at the lack of interior description in Austen's novels. Margaret Lane confessed her 'bewilderment [at finding] that all those interiors of great house and cottage and parsonage which we know so well have been conjured up, so to speak, out of thin air, and very nearly without the aid of description'.[5] While we might agree that Austen does not offer much description, and certainly few set-piece descriptions, she does in the course of her scenes reveal aspects of the interior of the houses in which they take place.

The interior organisation of a house is explicitly described in Austen's novels only when the heroine moves to a new home or visits a house for the first time. Her first published novel, *Sense and Sensibility*, supplies a good example. The Dashwood family, in reduced circumstances, move into a cottage in Devonshire.

As a house, Barton Cottage, though small, was comfortable and compact; but as a cottage it was defective, for the building was regular, the roof was tiled, the window shutters were not painted green, nor were the walls covered with honeysuckles. A narrow passage led directly through the house into the garden behind. On each side of the entrance was a sitting room, about sixteen feet square; and beyond them were the offices and the stairs. Four bed-rooms and two garrets formed the rest of the house.   (*S&S*, 1:6)

These lines, which start as a satire on the romantic view of a cottage, give a clear description of a simple domestic interior. One of the two sitting-rooms (often called parlours) is used for dining, and one can assume that the servants – a man and two women (*S&S*, 1:5) – sleep in the garrets. Because Barton Cottage is small the reader has a clear sense of its interior. These principles of the layout of domestic space, however, hold for most of the other recently built houses in Austen's novels, even those which are much larger and have many more rooms. The houses whose interiors cannot obviously be read according to this plan are her old ones.

An Austen novel proceeds on the assumption that the reader brings to it an understanding of how ordinary English houses of her day commonly function, especially as experienced by the visitor. One enters at the front door into a passage in small houses like Barton Cottage and in larger houses into a hall, sometimes, as in Longbourn House, the home of the Bennets in *Pride and Prejudice*, through a vestibule (3:5). The house will have two storeys, plus attic storey but no basement, and people sleep upstairs. They eat in a dining-room; only light refreshments are served in the drawing-room. Public rooms are on the ground floor, except in urban houses, in which the drawing-room is usually on the first floor, as, for

instance, in Mrs Jennings's London house (*S&S*, 2:4). Hardly any of
her scenes take place in a bedroom; an exception are those associated
with Marianne's heartbreak and subsequent illness in *Sense and
Sensibility*. There are references to nurseries in Mansfield Park and
Hartfield in *Emma* (*MP*, 1:1, *E*, 1:9) but no scene in an Austen
novel is set in a nursery. Likewise no scene is set in a kitchen; it
is an indication of the modest intimacy of Barton Cottage that we
hear that its kitchen fire smokes (*S&S*, 1:14). Although all Austen's
houses are looked after by servants we hear very little about rooms
dedicated to their use, although Mansfield Park rises to the dignity
of a 'servants' hall' (1:12, 15).

The most important domestic spaces in Austen are the public
rooms in which members of the family meet and guests are entertained. They are the dining-room, the drawing-room, and in larger
houses like Longbourn and Mansfield Park, the breakfast-room,
which was often used in the morning for sitting as well as break-
fasting. Dinner is taken in the dining-room in the afternoon. In
the novels the time of dinner varies between 4 o'clock at Barton
Cottage (*S&S*, 1:14, 3:13) and Hartfield (*E*, 1:9) and the more
fashionable 6.30 at Netherfield (*P&P*, 1:8). The time after dinner is spent in the drawing-room. Larger houses could have other
public rooms. A library was usually a public room, as is implied
when Marianne Dashwood, at Cleveland, is described as having
'the knack of finding her way in every house to the library, however it might be avoided by the family in general' (*S&S*, 3:6). In
Pride and Prejudice, however, the library is the particular retreat
of Mr Bennet. Private rooms, distinct from bedrooms, are scarce
in Austen's novels. Mr Bennet's library is balanced by Mrs Bennet's dressing-room; in Mansfield Park two characters have rooms
for their exclusive use, Sir Thomas Bertram and (uniquely among
Austen's heroines) Fanny Price. Sir Thomas's room is the study
of a Member of Parliament and estate owner; Fanny's, the former
school-room renamed the East Room, is a metaphor of her inner
life, being full of books, plants, modest pictures and mementoes
(*MP*, 1:16).

Austen's novels give intense representations of living in the public rooms of fairly large houses. The rooms referred to, and their
relationships, are clearly portrayed in the course of the narrative but
the rest of the house is only vaguely indicated – we are not told the

Figure 32. Smart interior decor, such as the Elliots' Bath property would boast, often reflected classical and Egyptian influence, as shown by Thomas Hope's popular *Household Furniture and Interior Design* (1809).

number of bedrooms or the extent of the 'offices'. We experience a house as family and social life is lived in it, not as an architectural whole. Austen's houses are not all that grand – only Sotherton and Pemberley are country houses big and old enough to be shown to visitors (*MP*, 1:9, *P&P*, 3:1). Mansfield Park might 'deserve to be in any collection of engravings of gentlemen's seats in the kingdom' (1:5), but has no artistic heritage to offer the tourist. Longbourn and Hartfield and the other smaller houses would not achieve even that. They are the houses of the lesser gentry and those whom David Spring has called the 'pseudo-gentry', whose claim to the title, either in the present or the future, is not entirely secure.[6]

Austen's 'modern' houses differ in size, but they share some features. Their public rooms are on the ground floor and their bedrooms are upstairs; the public rooms are segregated (in that they do not lead anywhere else) and they go off a hall from which the main staircase of the house rises. We are not told the date of Longbourn in *Pride and Prejudice* but its interior layout follows this plan, which her old houses do not. Pemberley has an upstairs gallery, and the downstairs rooms in Northanger Abbey and Sotherton are *en suite*, that is, one room leads into another (*NA*, 2:8; *MP*, 1:9). Austen's modern houses all share the interior characteristic of having public rooms on the ground floor, which reflects the late eighteenth-century change whereby the social parts of a house came to dominate at the expense of the private[7] and anticipates the conventions of the bourgeois house with which we are still familiar.

Although many of Austen's houses give an air of permanence the loss of the house, or the threat of it, hangs over all her heroines except Emma. Anne Elliot, in her last novel, *Persuasion*, is, however, alone in being homeless. The novel starts with her father letting out Kellynch Hall to recoup his extravagance, and the house itself is remembered for two features emblematic of what brought him to this pass, its copy of the *Baronetage* lying open on a table (*P*, 1:1) and the quantity of looking-glasses which its tenant, Admiral Croft, had to remove (*P*, 2:13). In place of the old house at the centre of a landed estate the novel offers other possibilities available by renting, a property in a smart street in Bath whose drawing-room boasts walls 'perhaps thirty feet asunder' (*P*, 2:3; fig. 32) and the modest lodging-house where the Harvilles live in Lyme Regis (*P*, 1:11). Although the novel describes the replacing of the traditional aristocracy by the professional classes, represented by the navy, that theme is modified by the presence of another landowning family, the Musgroves. The Musgroves have two houses at Uppercross, both of which show a capacity for moving with the times. Charles and Mary Musgrove live in an old farmhouse which has been altered into a 'cottage' by the addition of a 'viranda, French windows, and other prettinesses' (*P*, 1:5). The Great House, the home of the Musgrove parents, is shown being almost imperceptibly modernised by their children. Visitors are welcomed 'in the old-fashioned square parlour, with a small carpet and shining floor, to which the present daughters of the house were gradually giving the proper air of confusion by a grand piano forte and a harp, flower-stands and little tables placed in every direction' (*P*, 1:5). In Austen's novels the momentum for domestic change is expressed on the part of the women characters by the wish to refurnish the house. For a man whose social aspiration is expressed through domestic architecture the only course is to abandon the old house. Sir Walter Elliot's move to Bath is trumped by Mr Parker in *Sanditon* who, with no financial embarrassment to impel him, abandons the home of his forefathers and builds himself a new house whose name, Trafalgar House, he is already starting to regret (4).

NOTES

1. Gerald Wellesley, Duke of Wellington, 'Houses in Jane Austen's Novels', *Spectator* 135 (1926), 524–5, reprinted in the Jane Austen Society's *Collected Reports 1949–1965* (Alton: Jane Austen Society, 1990), pp. 185–88, subsequent references are included in the text; Nikolaus Pevsner, 'The Architectural Setting of Jane Austen's Novels', *Journal of the Warburg and Courtauld Institutes* 31 (1968), 404–22.

2. Nigel Nicolson, *The World of Jane Austen* (London: Weidenfeld & Nicolson, 1991), pp. 141–4; Mavis Batey, *Jane Austen and the English Landscape* (London: Barn Elms, 1996), pp. 86–8. Stoneleigh had been a Cistercian Abbey and its cloister became a courtyard of the later Elizabethan house. It could, therefore, be cited as an influence on Northanger Abbey, were it not that *Northanger Abbey* is thought to have been substantially written before Austen's visit in 1806.

3. Mark Girouard, *Life in the English Country House* (New Haven and London: Yale University Press, 1978), pp. 100–2, 126–9, 214.

4. *The Georgian Country House: Architecture, Landscape and Society*, ed. Dana Arnold (Stroud: Sutton, 1998), p. 12.

5. Margaret Lane, untitled address to the Jane Austen Society in 1962, in *Collected Reports 1949–1965*, p. 226.

6. David Spring, 'Interpreters of Jane Austen's Social World: Literary Critics and Historians', in *Jane Austen: New Perspectives, Women and Literature*, ed. Janet Todd (New York and London: Holmes and Meier, 1983), pp. 53–72.

7. Girouard, *Life in the English Country House*, pp. 214, 230–1; Philippa Tristram, *Living Space in Fact and Fiction* (London and New York: Routledge, 1989), p. 12.

21

Dress

ANTJE BLANK

Over the four decades of Jane Austen's lifetime, dress styles for women and men altered radically; as always, the 'love of novelty', defined by Beau Brummell as the 'parent of fashion',[1] had much to do with it. But more importantly, changes – in manufacture and in political thought – prompted late eighteenth-century society's move away from brocaded stiffness towards a more natural flowing shape characteristic of the Regency era.

Innovations in cotton spinning technology, such as Crompton's mule of 1770, suddenly enabled the production of high-quality yarn in quantities large enough to satisfy the demands of an already modernised weaving industry. As a result water-powered mills soon supplied cotton and linen fabrics affordable even to the most deprived: registers for the London Foundling Hospital record the cotton garments that abandoned babies were mostly clothed in. The low production costs of cotton fabrics came at a high human price, for mills were run on a factory system that exploited a cheap workforce, chiefly women and children from neighbouring workhouses. Evidence given to a Parliamentary Committee in 1814 revealed that working hours at the notorious Backbarrow mills lasted from five in the morning until eight at night. Printing techniques were also industrialised: block-printing of the 1770s, a step-by-step process which had required separate wooden blocks for every colour and involved much handiwork, was superseded in 1783 by roller-printing utilising machines which produced the distinctive striped designs of the period.

To satisfy the demands of this accelerated textile industry, cotton wool imports to Britain increased exponentially from 6.8 million lbs in 1780 to 99.3 million lbs in 1815. The West Indies, Britain's established supplier, could not keep up with the demand and India, provider of finer varieties of the fibre, proved increasingly unwilling to equip a rival industry. A solution presented itself with the

St Domingo slave uprising in 1791–2, which inflated raw cotton prices and encouraged planters in Carolina and Georgia to cultivate it. By 1802 America had firmly established itself as Britian's largest supplier of cotton wool. And, whereas the exploitation of slave labour on West Indies sugar plantations roused concerns in liberal circles at home, no humanitarian movement comparable to the anti-saccharites questioned Britain's lucrative involvement with the plantation system in the American South. When people grumbled it was more likely a protest against the decline of traditional woollen industries, a result of the eager market for cotton: the 'ladies think no more of woollens and stuffs than of an old almanack' complained one wool merchant.[2] In response regional charities formed, such as the genteel Lincolnshire society organising annual 'Stuff balls' in support of their local woollen manufactures. After one such event in 1791, which guests were made to attend dressed uniformly in woollen fabrics of the same colour, Lady Banks posted textile samples to her correspondents and praised the occasion as 'a charming good Meeting' – though even she had to concede, 'I can't say much for the Manufacture.'[3] Two decades later the technical innovations of the cotton industries became the target of more forceful public rage when workers in Nottinghamshire, Yorkshire and Lancashire stormed factories and destroyed the stocking frames and power-looms that threatened to obliterate their livelihood. The Tory government hit back with a harsh new bill that ruled machine-breaking a capital offence and passed it notwithstanding Lord Byron's impassioned defence of the Luddites.

In the 1780s and 1790s muslins, a variety of delicately woven cotton fabrics so transparent they needed to be worn in multiple layers, became the favoured material for women's gowns. At first the finest muslins came exclusively from India, especially Madras, so that know-all Henry Tilney in *Northanger Abbey* publicises his understanding of the fabric by purchasing 'a true Indian' for his sister at only 'five shillings a yard' (1:3). Domestic manufacturers began to employ expert weavers to try and compete with the imported ware. Scotland was renowned for its good-quality muslins, as was Norwich, from where in 1786 Lady Jerningham proposed bringing a new 'beautiful magnificent gold muslin' for her daughter, which 'everybody is ordering'.[4] Yet on the whole the British muslin industry continued to have difficulties cornering the market for high-quality, expensive cloths. The change was not effected until the beginning of the nineteenth century, when a widespread perception of the decline of the colonial product helped the domestic: *Ackermann's Repository of Arts* for June 1810 concluded that 'for two or three years past, the Indian goods have sunk in the estimation of the public'. Some, like James Maitland, charged the East India Company and its trade monopoly with ruining the Bengal manufactures. To illustrate the former excellence of Indian muslins he told of a luxury variety which, when 'spread upon wet grass' was 'scarcely visible' – so much so that a weaver had been exiled after his cow accidentally ate a precious strip.[5]

With the supply of fine quality muslins on the rise, the popularity of silk waned. It continued to be used especially in formal evening wear but the ban on French silks during the Napoleonic Wars, compounded by the Emperor's decree of 1806 which threatened British trade partners with war and cut off raw silk imports, created a dependence on expensive smuggled ware. More significantly, the war between Britain and France resulted in a swell of patriotic sentiment on either side of the Channel that accorded overblown significance to an individual's choice of fabrics: while the British prided themselves on their colonial empire and domestic cotton manufactures, Napoleon reportedly tore Josephine's embroidered muslin gowns and reintroduced a sumptuous court style to resuscitate the Lyons silk industry.

Muslins could be plain or woven in patterns of stripes, spots or floral sprigs. For evening wear they would be adorned with silver or gold thread embroidery and trimmed with lace or glass beads. Pastel colours like lilac and peach were popular though white was *the* fashion colour throughout the period, from the 1790s when elegant 'Miss Tilney always [wore] white' (*NA*, 1:12) right through the 1810s, when Jane Austen reported to her sister from London that 'They trim with white very much' (*L*, 15–16 September 1813). In the eyes of her young niece, she may have seemed to have 'taken to the garb of middle age unnecessarily soon'[6] but actually Jane Austen was never one to buck a trend: despite some doubts as to the outcome, she decided to have her gown 'trimmed everywhere with white ribbon plaited on, somehow or other' and ordered a '*white* sattin' cap with 'a little white flower perking out of the left ear' to complete the outfit (*L*, 15–16 September 1813).

In the 1780s the emergence of the light, flowing muslins popularised a novel style of women's dress. Worn over several layers of petticoats, the *'robe anglaise'* required voluminous starched muslin kerchiefs, hip-pads and bum rolls to achieve the desired effect of billowing bosom and bell-shaped skirt – the fact that this was widely welcomed as a more 'natural' silhouette speaks volumes about preceding fashions (fig. 33). Equally as popular as the round gown – so called as it was made in one piece – was the wrapping-gown, which Horace Walpole unflatteringly likened to a man's nightgown with a belt: tied at the waist with a wide, often brilliantly coloured, sash that held in place the soft drapes, the style was initially worn as informal morning dress but gradually crossed over into acceptable day wear. Hair fashions were adjusted to suit the more natural look: gone were the unhygienic coiffures of the earlier decades, towering structures crowned with ostrich feathers which had been glued in place by prodigious quantities of goose grease and powder. Thick, copious curls, lightly dusted with hair powder, were now *de rigueur* (fig. 34), preferably accentuated by a wide-brimmed ribboned straw hat, a look that was started by one of Marie Antoinette's pastoral whims: Eliza de Feuillide, updating her cousin Phylly Walter on Versailles fashions, informed her that 'Large Yellow Straw Hats,' such as would be a familiar sight in Kent – 'I believe You may have seen [them] worn by the Hay Makers' – were now 'universally adopted'.[7] Both round and wrapping-gown still required lightly-boned stays though the wide hoops of the previous decades were outmoded. The Georgian court, however, continued to prescribe the cumbersome panier, and, after her arrival in London four years later, Eliza attended a reception at St James's Palace standing, she reported, for two hours 'loaded with a great Hoop of no inconsiderable Weight' (Le Faye, *Outlandish Cousin*, p. 76).

While a fossilised British court clung to tradition, a revolution in France simultaneously did away with royals, aristocrats and the flamboyant dress that had distinguished them. The political move to establish social equality was underpinned by Enlightenment philosophy, which veered between an idealised primitivism yearning for man's 'state of nature' and pragmatic republicanism which espoused classical virtues. Both currents, however, unified in their bloody opposition to luxury. The resulting dress style adopted throughout Paris merged a studied approximation of lower-class

Figure 33. *The Gallery of Fashion* for 1794, showing, on the left, a
double-sleeved muslin round gown and neckerchief. The full
petticoat of spotted muslin on the right is worn with a gown of
red-striped chintz. One hat is of striped sarsenet, the other
accessorised with a red bow and yellow plume.

Figure 34. *The Gallery of Fashion* for July 1796 showing full round gowns. The lady on the left wears her soft powdered curls tucked under a large cap, typical of married and older women. Her companion has accessorised her hair with a sprig of flowers.

practicality with elements of antique simplicity. French radicalisation under the Terror occasioned a patent desire among most British to dissociate themselves from Jacobinical costume and it was only with the establishment in 1795 of a bourgeois Directory that the sexy neo-classical trends slowly filtered through. By the turn of the century British women had taken up dressing *à la grecque* in semi-transparent, narrow-cut muslin gowns which often bared the arms, much of the décolleté, and further accentuated the bosom with a waistline that had moved just underneath the breasts (figs. 35, 36). How much of one's feminine curves was left to the imagination depended on the amount of layering; the most audacious dispensed with corsets altogether and pared down undergarments to the bare minimum of a shift. In 1798 urbane Eliza described the 'uproar' caused in Bath by one pretty officer's wife's skimpy dress: wearing 'only one thick muslin Petticoat and a thin muslin Robe over that, of which the sleeves come only three inches below her shoulders', her 'throat & bosom' were left 'entirely bare', a revealing mode of 'undress' that 'would be remarked even in London', she concluded merrily (Le Faye, *Outlandish Cousin*, p. 154).

Dressing in gossamer fabrics in summer was one thing, but the British weather could prove a health risk to fashion victims like the clergyman Powlett's wife, whom Austen described as being 'at once expensively & nakedly dress'd' in mid-winter (*L*, 8–9 January 1801). To keep cold at bay, outer garments such as spencers, pelisses or shawls gained in popularity. The spencer was a short jacket ending just below the bust, usually made of strong, contrasting colours in either silk or wool. A pelisse was a long-sleeved coat cut on the same lines as the dress, trimmed or lined with furs, often exotic such as leopard, for extra warmth. Large rectangular shawls, especially costly cashmere ones woven in decorative oriental motifs, were especially sought after as they provided possibilities for graceful, classically inspired arrangements. Of course not everyone would have had the option (or self-absorption) of a Lady Bertram to will a relative's hazardous journey to the 'East Indies' that she 'may have [her] shawl' (*MP*, 2:13), so domestic manufactures met the demand with the production of imitation wool shawls mixed with silk – Paisley, in Scotland, set the standard with a pattern still familiar today.

Plate 11 Vol. 2

WALKING COSTUME.

N.5. at ACKERMANN'S REPOSITORY of ARTS & Pub. Aug. 1.st 1809, at 101 Strand LONDON.

Figure 35. *Ackermann's Repository of the Arts* for August 1809, showing a walking dress of fine India muslin and satin spencer with carmelite hood. The girl is wearing a cambric dress and chip hat.

Figure 36. *Ackermann's Repository of the Arts* for August 1811, showing an evening dress consisting of a Grecian round robe made of flowing Indian muslin, worn with a blue satin Roman tunic.

To complement the neo-classical style of dress, hair was now cropped short to frame the face in tight unpowdered curls, either natural, or teased into shape with paper. Small bonnets, caps or turbans, made of satin, velvet or muslin, and trimmed with ribbons, lace veils or swansdown displaced the large straw hats of the previous decades. At the close of the century, artificial fruit trimmings were 'the thing', as Austen reported from Bath, adding she had seen 'Grapes, Cherries, Plumbs & Apricots' sold for the purpose but inclined towards buying a sprig instead as she could not 'help thinking that it is more natural to have flowers grow out of the head than fruit' (*L*, 2 and 11 June 1799).

Even a rigid British court etiquette began to adapt to changing fashions and introduced a bell-shaped hoop which was thought to complement the new style of women's dress. However, a hooped gown belted just underneath the bosom gave even the most slender shape a somewhat bloated appearance. Travelling decked out in prescribed court costume was no slight feat either, though the invention of the revolutionary collapsible hoop added to the wearer's comfort, if not her attractiveness: reporting the arrival of court ladies squeezed into their sedan chairs, the American traveller Louis Simond described 'their immense hoops' folded 'like wings, pointing forward on each side' and concluded bluntly that 'thus cased' they did 'not ill resemble the foetus of a hippopotamus in a brandy bottle'.[8]

The male equivalent of women's revealing dress was the perfectly-tailored suit, popularised by the most influential dandy of the period, Beau Brummell. Blessed with handsome looks and a razor-sharp wit, he held aristocratic society in awe and set the standard for masculine elegance from the Regency onwards: the dark green or blue tailored double-breasted frock coat, set off against the cool whiteness of a linen shirt and starched, meticulously arranged necktie or cravat (fig. 37). He replaced breeches with tight-fitting cream pantaloons which showed off the contours of his leg and teamed them with tasselled Hessian boots. The look of understated perfection was rounded off with lightly coloured gloves – yet where Frank Churchill appears content with the range of 'Men's Beavers' and 'York Tan' provided by Ford's in Highbury, Brummell's were made to order by two tailoring firms, one entrusted

Figure 37. *Le Beau Monde* for May 1807, showing gentleman's evening dress consisting of a dark blue, double-breasted coat. Only the three lower flat gilt buttons were to be buttoned. The look was completed with a high starched necktie, a fine white quilted waistcoat, white silk stockings and breeches tied below the knee.

with the cut of the fingers, the other with the thumbs, to ensure an impeccable fit.

The elegant column-like silhouette of women's Regency costume – though taking the occasional inspiration from exotic realms and foreign folklore (fig. 38) – remained virtually unchanged until about 1815 when the general taste for simplicity gradually gave way to a desire for fussy prints, stiffer fabrics, fuller skirts, puffy sleeves and hems lavishly decorated with bows and ruches (fig. 39). The display of naked arms was also going out of fashion: preparing for a dinner invitation in London in 1814, Austen chose to wear a 'gauze gown' with long sleeves but initially felt insecure about 'how they [would] succeed'. She returned reassured by the hostess 'that they are worn in the evening by many' (*L*, 9 March 1814).

One considerable advantage of cotton textiles was their convenience: even in fashionable pale colours a soiled cotton dress was often salvagable where a silk gown was not. Soap balls, made from lye, animal fat, salt and perfume, were taxed and did not come cheap but a French invention at the end of the eighteenth century allowed the low-cost production of soda and provided a salubrious alternative to that other alkali traditionally credited with cleansing powers: urine. Stubborn stains on luxury fabrics, meanwhile, needed to be treated with other natural detergents: fuller's earth was said to work on grease, lemon juice on ink, butter and hot milk on fruit.

Muslins, however, were sometimes fragile and, as Tilney warns Catherine, likely to 'fray' (*NA*, 1:3) or wash out. Sometimes dyeing could rescue a faded garment, though occasionally the end product turned out worse than the original: after having a gown dyed blue, Austen reported that 'it divided with a Touch' (*L*, 7–9 October 1808). 'Mr Floor', who had ruined her gown with a faulty dye made from either native woad or indigo imported from the West Indies, would very likely also have offered specialist cleaning services for Indian muslins and cashmeres.[9] Large households would often dispatch their washing to a laundry, after recording the individual items on a list similar to the 'washing-bill' mistaken by gullible Catherine for a mysterious Gothic manuscript (*NA*, 2:7). But washing could also be done by the servants: laundry days in gentry and aristocratic households were toilsome and protracted since the infrequency of them was itself a sign of social status indicating

Plate 1. Vol. 6

WALKING DRESS.

No 32 of ACKERMANN'S Repository of Arts, &c. Pub Aug 1811 at 101 Strand LONDON

Figure 38. *Ackermann's Repository of the Arts* for August 1811, showing a high round robe, short capuchin cloak and turban bonnet. The boy is wearing a long-sleeved Indian dimity waistcoat under a trouser jumpsuit and a velvet college cap.

Plate 4. Vol.

Figure 39. *Ackermann's Repository of the Arts* for July 1818, showing a walking dress with puffed sleeves and a lavishly decorated hem. The wide-brimmed hat is accessorised with ribbons in a light pea-green to complement the parasol.

the possession of an ample amount of linen. Hence, once large quantities of washing had piled up, the hiring of outside laundresses often became necessary. Announcing that a new help had been found to undertake their 'Purification', Austen added mischievously, 'She does not look as if anything she touched would ever be clean, but who knows?' (*L*, 27–28 October 1798). This presumed lack of personal hygiene was growing rather rare in the late eighteenth century. Cleanliness, of clothes and one's person, had itself become fashionable: Jane and Cassandra Austen reportedly held 'all untidy ways in great disesteem' (*Memoir*, p. 169) while Beau Brummell, whose ritualistic morning toilette famously took upwards of five hours, decreed categorically 'no perfumes but very fine linen, plenty of it, and country-washing'.[10] Of course the lower classes would have been far from the mind of the period's most illustrious dandy, yet the revolution in the cotton industry also benefited them. Campaigners for social reform such as Francis Place noted the alteration: recalling his childhood in the 1770s when even gentlemen's daughters would wear their quilted petticoats stuffed with wool and horsehair 'day by day until they were rotten, and never were washed', he welcomed the 'great change' in 'improved cleanliness' for all ranks brought about by the 'manufacture of cotton goods'.[11]

During Austen's time, most of women's dress articles were either sewn to order by 'mantua-makers', professional dressmakers, or made at home, often with the assistance of a ladies' maid. At home old garments could serve as patterns; for the latest styles, however, the smartest of one's social circle had to be wheedled into sharing their secrets – as demonstrated when the ambitious Misses Steele persuade Lady Middleton to allow them to copy her modish gowns, no doubt giving rise to that uneasy amalgam of conceit and resentment so astutely captured in Jane Austen's comment to her sister that she was 'pleased with Martha & Mrs Lefroy for wanting the pattern of our Caps' while not being 'so well pleased' with Cassandra for actually giving it to them (*L*, 2 June 1799).

Fabrics were purchased at shops such as Ford's in Highbury, 'woollen-draper, linen-draper, and haberdasher's shop united', where customers like Harriet could dither over plain or figured muslins (*E*, 2:3,9), draped for display in huge swags over doorways and on walls. For the less voluminous Regency styles, seven yards of fabric generally sufficed – though Austen boasted she needed an extra half-yard given that she was a 'tall woman' (*L*, 25 January 1801). Then the cut needed to be chosen and the dressmaker instructed accordingly. To some these decisions seemed more trying than liberating: 'I wish such things were to be bought ready made' an irresolute Austen grumbled (*L*, 24–6 December 1798). Indecisiveness seems to have been no rare occurrence since Place, who himself began his prosperous career as a breeches-maker, complained of the many customers who 'disliked' their garment 'when it was made up': for a man to be a good tailor, he concluded, he 'should be either a philosopher or a mean cringing slave'.[12]

With the growth of consumerism in the late eighteenth century the fashion industry came up with an ingenious way to assist fickle customers: magazines marketing the latest metropolitan trends. The Parisian miniaturist Niklaus von Heideloff, who had fled Jacobin rule, launched the first British magazine solely devoted to fashion in April 1794. His exclusive *Gallery of Fashion* was issued monthly with two aquatint plates, hand-coloured by himself and highlighted with metallic paints. Detailed descriptions of the modish outfits and *de rigueur* accessories accompanied his plates. Other journals such as *La Belle Assemblée* and *Le Beau Monde* followed suit but the most successful venture proved to be *The Repository of Arts, Literature, Commerce* (1806–29): published by the print-seller Rudolph Ackermann, it covered a wide range of cultural topics and included hand-coloured plates and sometimes pattern samples of the latest textiles with addresses where they could be purchased.

Not surprisingly, the fashion industry also found profitable ways to tap into swelled patriotic sentiments. Here, too, the French had set the trend way back in 1789 when miniature replicas of the Bastille carved out of its stone remnants were worn by fashionable ladies as pendants and rings. A decade later in Hampshire, Austen exchanged her mundane white cap for a stylish fez-inspired 'Mamalouc cap' (*L*, 8 January 1799) to celebrate Admiral Nelson's victory over the French in the Battle of the Nile. This bloody fight spawned a lucrative commemorative industry producing patriotic jewellery, fans, ribbons, vinaigrettes and other paraphernalia. Among the most popular accessories were gold anchors engraved with the date of the battle and painted ivory lockets depicting Nelson's heroism and the loyalty of his crew – an emblematic choice considering that little over a year had passed since the successful sailor mutiny at Spithead in spring 1797.

This mushrooming of materialism and conspicuous consumption, fired by a print media that proffered as affordable necessities goods that had once been deemed luxuries, worried middle-class moralists. Vicesimus Knox was concerned over society's increasing obsession with appearance, which he warned would result in 'general ignorance, want of principle, [and] levity of mind and behaviour'.[13] The feminist writer Mary Wollstonecraft was also troubled by the intellectual trivialisation of fashion-conscious women, and even more by the sexual objectification of their bodies. In *A Vindication of the Rights of Woman* (1792) she demanded social change to offer women opportunities to define their self-worth irrespective of their personal attractions – 'surely', she asked, 'she has not an immortal soul who can loiter life away merely employed to adorn her person?' (ch. 2). The moral purport of Austen's fiction (in contrast to her personal delight in fashion evinced in her correspondence) was similarly to depict dress as the concern of, at best, the immature – as is the case of Catherine Morland, who was yet to learn how little the 'heart of man' was 'biassed by the texture of [a] muslin' (*NA*, 1:10) – or, at worst, the vacuous and vulgar. When in 1822 Beau Brummell evaluated the history of costume he, too, lamented the corruption of civilised society though he, in opposition to Knox, Wollstonecraft and Austen, reasoned that a nation 'verges towards its fall' the moment 'utility supersedes beauty' (Brummell, *Male and Female Costume*, p. 121). The decline of Britain he attributed to a trend that would no doubt have delighted them: 'Clever people have greatly increased of late years', he complained, and 'the worst of merely clever people' was 'their indifference about externals'.

NOTES

1. Beau Brummell, *Male and Female Costume*, repr. (1932), p. 124. Subsequent references are included in the text.
2. F. Moore, *The Contrast or a Comparison between our Woollen, Linen, Cotton, and Silk Manufactures* (1782), p. 16. See also Michael M. Edwards, *The Growth of the British Cotton Trade, 1780–1815* (Manchester: Manchester University Press, 1967).

3. Lady Banks on 28 October 1791 and 23 October 1793, in *Dear Miss Heber*, ed. Francis Bamford (1936), pp. 112, 159.
4. *Jerningham Letters*, ed. Egerton Castle (1896), vol. I, p. 37.
5. James Maitland, *An Inquiry into the Practical Merits of the System for the Government of India under the Superintendence of the Board of Controul by the Earl of Lauderdale* (1809), pp. 128–9n.
6. Considering Jane Austen's eager interest in fashion, Caroline Austen's statement that her 'two Aunts were not accounted very good dressers' seems somewhat unconvincing, *A Memoir of Jane Austen and Other Family Recollections*, ed. Kathryn Sutherland (Oxford: Oxford University Press, 2002), p. 169. Subsequent references are included in the text. For an informative study of fashion in Austen's letters and novels, see Penelope Byrde, *Jane Austen Fashion: Fashion and Needlework in the Works of Jane Austen* (Ludlow: Excellent Press, 1999).
7. Eliza to Phylly Walter, 16 May 1780, in Deirdre Le Faye, *Jane Austen's 'Outlandish Cousin', the Life & Letters of Eliza de Feuillide* (London: British Library, 2002), p. 58. Subsequent references are included in the text.
8. Louis Simond, *Journal of a Tour and Residence in Great Britain, during the years 1810 and 1811* (1817), vol. I, pp. 208–9.
9. Jane Ashelford, *Care of Clothes* (London: National Trust, 1997), pp. 8–10, 24.
10. *Harriette Wilson's Memoirs*, ed. Lesley Blanch (London: Folio Society, 1964), ch. 2.
11. British Library Add Ms 27827, ff. 50–1.
12. *The Autobiography of Francis Place (1771–1854)*, ed. Mary Thale (Cambridge: Cambridge University Press, 1972), p. 217.
13. Vicesimus Knox, *Liberal Education: or, a Practical Treatise on the Methods of Acquiring Useful and Polite Learning* (1781), p. 151.

Education and accomplishments

GARY KELLY

As one critic declares, 'All Jane Austen's novels, and many of her minor works, unfinished works and juvenilia, are about education.'[1] They are 'about education', however, in critical and complex ways. Education as usually understood today – schooling in certain skills, practices and bodies of knowledge – formed only part of education as Jane Austen and her contemporaries understood it: a process of socialisation and acculturation based on moral self-discipline and designed to fit the individual for a range of related roles in life, according to sex and rank. Furthermore, during the prolonged national and imperial crisis of Austen's day education became a field of ideological struggle in which the social groups who read Austen's novels – the upper middle class and the gentry – were deeply implicated. Austen's novels are 'about education' because they demonstrate the importance of female education to these social groups and particularly to their material interests in an age of revolutionary change.

Female education had caused increasing concern for over a century. *The Lady's New-Year's Gift; or, Advice to a Daughter* (1688) by George Savile, Marquess of Halifax, was reprinted into the late eighteenth century; François de la Mothe Fénelon's *Traité de l'éducation des filles* (1687) was reprinted several times in English, and enjoyed a revival in Austen's day. Both books prescribe education for moral self-control and social usefulness within family and class. Similar conduct or advice books proliferated after mid-century as female education was implicated in accelerating social change and the national and imperial destiny. The Scottish clergyman James Fordyce's *Sermons to Young Women* (1766), reprinted into the early nineteenth century, advised readers to cultivate femininity for moral reform and leadership in the national cause – Britain had just emerged from the Seven Years' War with France. The English clergyman James Gregory urged a more resolutely middle-class programme in his frequently reprinted *A Father's Legacy to His Daughters* (1774), advising education for domesticity, moral self-discipline and fortitude in married life.

Women writers joined the debate. Early contributions such as Bathsua Makin's *An Essay to Revive the Antient Education of a Gentlewoman* (1677) and Mary Astell's *A Serious Proposal to the Ladies* (1694) were almost forgotten by Austen's day, but Lady Sarah Pennington's *An Unfortunate Mother's Advice to Her Absent Daughters* (1761), which advised education for moral fortitude against the inevitability of female suffering, was reprinted into the early nineteenth century. Twice as popular was Hester Chapone's *Letters on the Improvement of the Mind; Addressed to a Young Lady* (1773), which resumed Makin's and Astell's emphasis on intellectual attainments and moral self-discipline. Such ideas circulated farther in numerous novels of education.[2] One of Jane Austen's favourites was Samuel Richardson's *Sir Charles Grandison* (1753–4), and Félicité de Genlis's *Les Veillées du château* (1784) circulated widely in French and English, but Austen's immediate model was Frances Burney, who developed the form in *Evelina* (1778), *Cecilia* (1784) and *Camilla* (1796). During the Revolutionary and Napoleonic crisis the form became more openly political, with Elizabeth Inchbald's *A Simple Story* (1792), Jane West's *The Advantages of Education* (1793), Robert Bage's *Hermsprong* (1796), Mary Wollstonecraft's *The Wrongs of Woman; or, Maria* (1798), Amelia Opie's *Adeline Mowbray* (1804), Mary Brunton's *Self-Control* (1811) and E. S. Barrett's *The Heroine* (1814). Jane Austen knew most of these.

Such works emphasised moral, ethical and social education,[3] but their underlying concern was women's role in reproducing the dominant economic, social, cultural and political order – the order structuring the world depicted in Austen's novels. In the view of Austen's contemporaries this order was established at the Glorious Revolution of 1688 and consolidated through the long eighteenth century, but was being challenged by radical economic transformation, emergent lower- and middle-class social forces, imperial crisis and global warfare. The dominant order was based on agrarian landed property developed by capitalist practices of investment and improvement and managed by a variety of professions – hence increasing concern with schooling upper- and middle-class boys in professional method and discipline. Jane Austen's brothers received such schooling, two entering the clergy, two the navy, and one the gentry. These professions are central to Austen's novels, and the Austen sisters were educated to be such men's wives – itself considered a profession by many.

For, although women of the classes depicted in Austen's novels were marginalised in this complex economic and social order, they were increasingly thought essential to maintaining it and to need appropriate education for doing so. Property, in the principal form of the landed estate or other forms, was a family concern in both senses – a matter of family interest and a family enterprise. The upper-class family was a corporate entity dependent on landed property to provide the rents underwriting the family's material prosperity and, more important, its status and power. Middle-class families were similarly situated, on a smaller scale. Stability of the family estate across generations was ensured by primogeniture, or inheritance by the first son (rather than division of the estate among all the sons or all the children), and by entailing the estate, in default of a direct male heir, on the nearest male relative. Judging by her novels, Jane Austen had reservations about these practices. Women's interests were entirely subordinated by them, and women had few property rights in or outside marriage. Yet women were necessary to successful transmission of such property from one generation of men to the next in three related ways – biological reproduction, capital investment and social culture – all directed by education.

First, secure generational transfer of property depended on woman's biological ability to bear a male heir, usually with one or two spares for insurance. Failure to produce a male heir could mean transference of the family concern to a distant male relative; such failure underpins the plot of *Pride and Prejudice*, *Emma* and *Persuasion*. Biological ability had to be governed, however, by education that would deter a woman from producing an illegitimate heir, with potentially ruinous contested inheritance. Jane Austen, unlike many contemporary novelists, ignores this possibility to emphasise women's potential moral, intellectual, social and cultural contribution, based on education, to the family estate.

She similarly shifts emphasis in treating women's second major contribution to an estate – bringing capital or property in marriage. All Austen heroines except Emma are almost Cinderellas, bringing to marriage more of the intellectual, moral and cultural capital accumulated through education than the cash or property necessary for what was called 'improvement' of the estate. Improvement was of two related kinds: investment and expenditure. Investment in infrastructure could increase an estate's productivity and rents and thus its ability to sustain its owners' expenditure on socially symbolic conspicuous consumption. Such consumption, from philanthropy to building, from landscaping to literary patronage, constituted a fashion system of intertwined cultural and social distinction. This system was increasingly exploited by entrepreneurs and professionals, however: never before was there such variety and skilful marketing of goods and services, tempting to extravagant consumption and unbalancing the estate and family economy, as Rushworth plans to do in *Mansfield Park*, as Knightley does not do in *Emma* and as Sir Walter Elliot does in *Persuasion*. Austen's novels illustrate the constant challenge of balancing both kinds of 'improvement'.[4] Austen knew that her chosen literary form was itself considered an article of fashionable consumption and condemned not only as such but also for glamorously representing conspicuous consumption and thereby stimulating desire to participate in it. In response, Jane Austen not only makes novel reading, and reading generally, an index of education and thus of character in her novels, but she makes her novels into a process of education for the reader.

In doing so, she accords with the widespread view that education could both appropriately restrain and properly direct dangerous desires of all kinds, for which women were supposed to bear particular responsibility. This is the third major role of female education in the social order Jane Austen knew. Women were widely regarded as instrumental in conspicuous consumption because they were conventionally characterised as creatures of desire, and moralists warned that their fashionable conspicuous consumption might extend to other excesses, including illicit amours, undermining the family estate and indeed the entire dominant order. A wide range of literature depicted these dangers, blamed fashionable female education for exacerbating them and prescribed 'proper' education as the antidote. In Austen's *Mansfield Park* the fashionably educated Bertrams, Rushworths and Crawfords engage in various extravagances, from improper entertainments through reckless estate improvements to an illicit amour, while the properly educated Edmund Bertram and Fanny Price undertake the moral, intellectual and cultural renewal of the estate.

Improvement of the family estate for good or ill was also understood as a microcosm of improvement in the national state. Concern over women's role in the family economy and, by extension, the nation at large, had driven the debate on female education for decades, but never more so than during the unprecedented national and imperial crisis that coincided with Jane Austen's writing career. Equal rights for women were asserted during this debate, linked to women's roles in society, culture and the economy and to differences in male and female education. By Austen's day, many families gave sons a professional education, not only in the middle classes, who depended on intellectual and cultural capital, but also in the gentry, who recognised the usefulness of the knowledge, self-discipline and managerial skills afforded by such education. As social critics from Mary Wollstonecraft to Hannah More pointed out, however, females were excluded from such broad intellectual and moral education and instead trained in what were called 'accomplishments.'

These differed from the other elements in female education – basic schooling, household management and religious instruction. Basic schooling comprised practical skills such as literacy and numeracy – by Austen's day girls were being excluded from the few grammar schools that offered them more advanced schooling.[5] Household management included supervision if not participation in domestic needlework, food preparation, the regular but epic activity of washing-day and care of the sick, the young and the aged.[6] Religious instruction, considered indispensable, inducted the young female into the family's church. Basic schooling occurred at home, sometimes augmented through attendance at day or boarding school; domestic training and religious instruction also occurred at home. Accomplishments, too, could be acquired at home, though usually from governesses and private tutors, perhaps with 'finishing' at a day school or boarding school,[7] such as the one Cassandra and Jane Austen attended at Reading.

Governesses and tutors were freelance employees, governesses living in the family for a small salary and bed and board, tutors visiting and paid per lesson. Novelists from Rousseau on had depicted tutors as romantically dangerous to their female pupils; Austen ignores that possibility. Novelists for the next century would depict governesses as romantically sympathetic;[8] Austen glanced down that road with Jane Fairfax, but she represents governesses as the subordinate creatures they were. Schools were businesses, and those for girls were often run by former governesses or women of some education with enough capital to start a business. Most schools were quite small, run as extended households, and often criticised as incompetent, unhygienic and morally corrupting. Whether good or bad, tutors, governesses and schools all had to meet parents' demands in order to get paid, and for over a century before Austen and for half a century after her, most parents demanded 'accomplishments' for their daughters.

'Accomplishments' included several elements. Dancing, singing and playing music displayed the young woman's body and bearing at social occasions to attract a suitor.[9] Drawing, painting, fashionable modern languages (especially French and Italian) and decorative needlework demonstrated taste and 'polite' knowledge as markers of cultural distinction, as did the social arts of conversation and letter-writing, with accompanying knowledge of the 'belles-lettres'. These comprised approved essays, drama, poetry, travelogues (the most widely read form of book after novels), perhaps the 'better sort' of prose fiction and 'elegant' learning, especially historiography (often recommended as an antidote for dangerous novel reading, which may explain Austen's antipathy to it). Similarly desirable and useful was knowledge of 'books of the day', or important and widely read contemporary publications. This fashion impelled what commentators called the 'rise of the reading public' and dated from the mid eighteenth century. Belles-lettres and books of the day constituted a common literary culture for both men and women of the upper and middle classes. The Austen family participated in this culture, as do Austen's characters, and her novels allude to belles-lettres and books of the day just as they are designed to take their place among them.

'Accomplishments' enabled marriageable and married women to display the cultural distinction that demonstrated social distinction and advanced upper- and middle-class family interests. Accordingly, 'accomplishments' were preferred to two main alternatives. A woman lacking 'accomplishments' might be merely 'notable' – the period's term for a woman who knew little more than domestic economy and was consequently incapable of cultivated socialising, though some commentators asserted the 'notable' woman's usefulness to her family, especially in uncertain times. If being 'accomplished' was set against being 'notable', both were set against being 'learned', or a 'bluestocking', supposed to unfit a woman for the marriage market, genteel society and even 'notability'. 'Learning' was accordingly condemned by female conduct books, satirised by male and female writers and excluded from most females' education. 'Learning' meant knowledge proper to male education and restricted to male participation, and included classical and Biblical languages, analytical and scientific discourses, controversial writing, theology and mathematics. The Austen sisters were not 'learned' in this sense, though they were both 'accomplished' and 'notable'.

By their day 'accomplishments', too, were increasingly criticised. This was less for subordinating women to men and family interests and more for failing to provide women with the sovereign subjectivity and intellectual resources thought necessary for their roles in family, society and nation, for independence when unmarried or widowed and for their individual spiritual salvation. Mary Wollstonecraft's *A Vindication of the Rights of Woman* (1792) argued that educating women to be 'accomplished' or 'notable' denied them the intellectual independence and moral self-discipline conferred by a professional education, thus leaving them an obstacle to social progress and reform. Jane Austen would more likely agree with Wollstonecraft's further argument that 'accomplishments' left women dependent on men's judgement and authority, consequently incapable of using God-given reason to guide desire to good rather than evil and therefore barred from spiritual salvation. In the national and imperial crisis of the day a more frequent criticism, voiced forcefully by Hannah More in *Strictures on the Modern System of Female Education* (1799), was that education in mere 'accomplishments' disabled women for their role as moral, cultural and social reformers within the home and local society and thus in the great national patriotic struggle then underway.

Like many contemporaries, including Wollstonecraft and More, Austen used the novel to illustrate these concerns; unlike them, she eschews overt didacticism and develops the theme of female education through novelistic form, especially character and plot.[10]

In *Pride and Prejudice* Mr Bennet and Mr Bingley marry women of beauty, but whereas Mrs Bennet was only beautiful and 'notable' and thus unable to govern her houseful of daughters or impress the right kind of suitors, Jane and Elizabeth Bennet have a good education thanks to their father and their relatives the Gardiners (apt name for cultivators) and both achieve proper marriages. Jane Austen does present under-, ill-, or mis-educated heroines, in Catherine Morland, Emma Woodhouse and Marianne Dashwood, but there are more poorly or wrongly educated minor female characters, such as the comically pedantic Mary Bennet and her dangerously superficial sister Lydia in *Pride and Prejudice* and the sympathetic but ignorant Harriet Smith in *Emma*. In each case, character is attributed to education, affecting the individual's, family's and even nation's destiny.

There are two further and more important differences between Austen's and her contemporaries' treatment of female education. She and they correlate education with moral and intellectual character, but, as Jane Austen told her niece Fanny Knight, 'pictures of perfection' – presumably properly educated – 'make me sick & wicked' (*L*, 23–25 March 1817) and she also excludes from her novels the 'improperly' educated and consequently 'fallen' women found in many other novels. In Austen's novels, neither 'good' nor 'bad' education guarantees anything: both the well educated Elizabeth Bennet and her badly educated sister Lydia are fallible, though in different ways; the properly educated Fanny Price is tempted by the viciously educated Henry Crawford, the viciously educated Mary Crawford loves the virtuously educated Edmund Bertram and despite his education he is attracted to Mary rather than Fanny for most of the novel. Moreover, very few of Austen's badly educated females – Maria Bertram in *Mansfield Park* is a rare exception – end in the 'ruin' that would be their fate with many another novelist. Austen does distribute novelistic justice according to a character's education, but all are fallible despite education.

Austen's avoidance of overt didacticism and extremes in her novelistic treatment of education may owe less to conscious artistry than to her religious education. Anglican theology held that human sinfulness could only be redeemed by free will exercised for good and sanctioned by divine grace. Like contemporaries from Wollstonecraft to More, Austen believed that an educated mind was necessary for this task. As a Christian and Anglican, however, Austen rejected more reformist contemporaries' view that education or 'Enlightenment' could eventually create a humanly made paradise on earth; equally she rejects the common conduct-book doctrine that education would at best help women endure the inevitable miseries of female life and at worst inspire unachievable and thus afflicting aspirations.

Finally, Jane Austen similarly aims to educate her readers, again indirectly, through novel form. Her use of the recently developed narrative technique of free indirect discourse, or reported inward speech and thought, encourages readers to sympathise, identify and agree with the heroine; when Elizabeth Bennet or Emma Woodhouse realises her error in reading her world, readers are forced to recognise theirs in reading her: all are fallible, all in need of continuing education, all awaiting grace, divine or humane. This technique makes Austen's novels, unlike most of their contemporaries, different on rereading, and a rereadable book is, if only by cultural convention, a 'classic', or canonical literature – a public institution of continuing education in which Austen's novels, as this Cambridge edition indicates, are firmly installed.

NOTES

1. D. D. Devlin, *Jane Austen and Education* (London and Basingstoke: Macmillan, 1975), p. 1.
2. Alan Richardson, *Literature, Education, and Romanticism: Reading as Social Practice, 1780–1832* (Cambridge: Cambridge University Press, 1994), part 4.
3. See Barbara Horwitz, 'Women's Education During the Regency: Jane Austen's Quiet Rebellion', *Persuasions* 16 (1994), 135–46.
4. See Edward Copeland, *Women Writing about Money: Women's Fiction in England, 1790–1820* (Cambridge: Cambridge University Press, 1995), ch. 4.
5. Michael Sanderson, *Education, Economic Change, and Society in England, 1780–1870*, new edition (London: Macmillan, 1991), p. 62.
6. See Amanda Vickery, *The Gentleman's Daughter: Women's Lives in Georgian England* (New Haven: Yale University Press, 1998), ch. 4.
7. See Christopher Martin, *A Short History of English Schools 1750–1965* (Hove: Wayland Publishers, 1979), pp. 37–41.

8. See Trev Broughton and Ruth Symes, *The Governess: An Anthology* (New York: St Martin's Press, 1997) and Katharine West, *Chapter of Governesses: A Study of the Governess in English Fiction 1800–1949* (London: Cohen and West, 1949).
9. June Purvis, *A History of Women's Education in England* (Milton Keynes: Open University Press, 1991), p. 64.
10. See Jane Nardin, 'Jane Austen, Hannah More, and the Novel of Education', *Persuasions* 20 (1998), 15–20.

Food

MAGGIE LANE

Jane Austen grew up in a household where the provision of food was not a simple matter of shopping or placing orders but of forward planning, hard work and daily contrivance. Almost all the foodstuffs consumed in Steventon Rectory were home-produced, the exceptions being luxury imported goods like tea, coffee, chocolate, sugar, spices, wine, dried fruit and citrus fruit. These items were valued and guarded accordingly: 'I carry about the keys of the wine and closet', Jane Austen wrote on one occasion (*L*, 27 October 1798) and there are several references in her letters to keeping careful watch on their stocks of sugar and tea.

The glebe lands attached to the benefice of Steventon were only about three acres, but Mr Austen also rented the neighbouring 200-acre Cheesedown Farm from his patron Thomas Knight. For nearly forty years, from the Austens' marriage until their retirement to Bath, the farm kept the rectory supplied with meat and cereals. Though Mr Austen had a bailiff to supervise the labourers in the field, he took an active part in managing the farm: Jane Austen writes very precisely of 'my father's mutton' (*L*, 1 December 1798). The dairy and the poultry-yard were her mother's province: even by the turn of the century, with a reduced household to feed, Mrs Austen had three cows in addition to ducks, chicken, guinea-fowl and turkeys (*L*, 11 June 1799). Potatoes, vegetables, herbs and fruit, including grapes, were grown in the garden. Beer, wines and mead – the latter from the honey given by their own bees – were made on a large scale: when the family came to leave Steventon their effects included '13 iron-bound casks'.[1] Fish and game were brought home on occasion by the sporting sons, and various gifts of food took place among the wider ramifications of the family and their friends: venison from Godmersham Park, fish from Southampton and apples from Kintbury are among the many commodities mentioned in the letters. Those with less ready access to foodstuffs had to be catered for: Mrs Austen cured pork for her sailor sons to take on voyages, while brother Henry in London was the recipient of gifts ranging from a pot of raspberry jam to nine gallons of mead made by his sisters.

All this produce had to be converted into meals or, very often, into supplies of preserved food which would last until the next season came round. Vast quantities not only of time but of space indoors and out were devoted to the cultivation, production and storage of food. Variety and sufficiency at table depended on just the right quantities of everything being produced and preserved in season, and then served to the family judiciously throughout the year. The household at Steventon fluctuated in numbers over the years, but including servants and boarding pupils Mrs Austen often had to feed ten or a dozen people three times a day – an enormous feat of organisation as well as of sheer labour. Though the family always kept a cook they did not aspire – as many of Austen's fictional families do – to a housekeeper to plan meals, organise stores and superintend the daily work of the kitchen. This was done first by Jane Austen's mother, later by Cassandra, with Jane herself as subordinate and sometime deputy.

When the family moved to Bath, and took lodgings at the seaside, this burden was eased; Bath had some of the best shops and markets in the country, but the cost of food then became an issue – as indeed did its wholesomeness, with no refrigeration or legislation against the adulteration of food (the first Food and Drugs Act was 1875). Settling at Chawton brought matters under their own control again, though there was never the same self-sufficiency as at Steventon, and they would never again be free of 'vulgar economy', as Jane Austen called it when wryly comparing their own home-made orange wine with the French wine invariably served at rich brother Edward's house.

Far more than her own heroines, therefore, Austen in her girl-hood and young womanhood was initiated into the arts of domestic economy. Her observations of life at Steventon would have impressed upon her consciousness the primacy of food provision among female duties and occupations. Her mother would have seen it as an essential part of her daughters' training that they could manage a home, whether they be called upon to make a small income go a long way or to preside over a full complement of servants.

At Chawton, Jane Austen's own especial duty concerned breakfast. We can imagine her insisting on sharing at least some of the housekeeping duty with Cassandra, and Cassandra's giving way over breakfast but insisting that Jane had the rest of the day free for writing. Breakfast in Austen's era was very different from the cold meat, coarse bread and ale of earlier ages, or the abundance of eggs, kidneys, bacon and so forth under which Victorian sideboards groaned. Rather it was an elegant light meal of toast and rolls, with tea, coffee or chocolate to drink, all taken off a handsome set of china. Jane's job would have been to make the toast and boil the kettle at the dining-room fire. Like many ladies, not trusting to clumsy servants, she may even have washed and dried the china, and put it away, together with the precious tea and sugar, in a dining-room closet.

The chief meal of the day was dinner, the timing of which altered considerably during Austen's lifetime, and depended very much on one's social position. It was originally a midday meal, taking advantage of natural light for cooking and eating. As the eighteenth century progressed, more fashionable people took their dinner later and later, copied by those lower down the social scale. In 1798 Jane Austen writes of half past three being the customary dinner hour at Steventon, but by 1808 they are dining at five o'clock in Southampton (*L*, 18 December 1798, 9 December 1808). There are many mentions of the timing of dinner in the novels, but none is so explicit as in the fragment *The Watsons*. Tom Musgrave knows perfectly well that the unpretentious Watson family dine at three, and times his visit to embarrass them, arriving just as their servant is bringing in the tray of cutlery. Tom compounds his rudeness by boasting that he dines at eight: the latest dinner hour of any character. At Mansfield Parsonage they dine at half past four and at Northanger Abbey at five. The effect of London fashion can be seen in the difference between the half past four dinner at Longbourn and that at half past six at Netherfield.

As the dinner hour became later, some sustenance was required between breakfast and dinner. It was some time before the name for it became genteel. In *Sense and Sensibility* Willoughby speaks of taking 'nuncheon' at an inn, and in *Pride and Prejudice* Lydia and Kitty order 'luncheon', also at an inn. But when a light meal is taken in the middle of the day at home, the characters refer simply to 'cold meat', or 'a collation'. Sandwiches appear at Mansfield Parsonage, with Dr Grant doing the honours of them. There is meat, bread and hothouse fruit at Pemberley. Except for the most formal occasions, midday food was served not in the dining-room but wherever the ladies were sitting. The meal would have occasioned the servants little trouble, leaving them free to cook the all-important dinner.

Until half-way into the nineteenth century, dinner was served in the form of 'courses' composed of many dishes placed on the table together. Cookery books of the period often include diagrams showing how the dishes might be arranged on the table to provide a pleasing balance. Depending on the number of diners and the means of the host, several large joints of meat and whole boiled or roasted fowl, sometimes garnished with a few vegetables, would occupy the central area, with a tureen of soup at one end, a whole fish at the other, and pies, cutlets and so forth in the corners. Each gentleman carved the meat nearest to him and helped his neighbours to this and other dishes within his reach. Jane Austen mentions one dinner she attended where a lady's dinner plate remained empty for some while because her neighbour neglected her, though she asked him twice for some meat.

When everyone had eaten enough of this course there would be large-scale disruption and bustle while the servants carried away the dishes and brought and arranged another complete course. A memorable moment in *Emma* occurs at the Coles' party, when conversation between Frank and Emma is interrupted at an interesting point: 'They were called on to share in the awkwardness of a rather long interval between the courses . . . but when the table was again safely covered, and every corner dish placed exactly right' private conversation can be resumed (2:8). (The Coles have never entertained Miss Woodhouse before, and one can imagine how their servants have been made nervous with instructions.)

This second course might contain lighter savoury concoctions such as fricassees and patties, together with a selection of fruit tarts, jellies and cream puddings. After this the tablecloth would be taken away and what was known as 'the dessert' set out. The word was taken from the French *desservir*, to clear the table, and bore a meaning quite different from its common modern usage. Comprising a variety of dried fruits, nuts and sweets, it was a way of prolonging the meal with titbits which could be eaten using the fingers after the servants had been dismissed. When Mrs Jennings seeks to cure Marianne's broken heart with offers of sweetmeats, olives and dried cherries she is describing a typical dessert.

Often in Austen's novels – and letters – the invitation is to 'drink tea' with neighbours. This is not the afternoon tea of the Victorians and ourselves, but a drink taken an hour or two after the completion of dinner. Sometimes visitors would come only for this drink, at other times it would be part of a dinner invitation. The gentlemen of the party, having lingered over the port after the withdrawal of the ladies, would enter the drawing room in time for tea, which was always made by one of the ladies of the house, often a young one. Fanny Price makes the tea when Mrs Norris is not at Mansfield Park; Elinor Dashwood 'presides' at the tea-table in Mrs Jennings's London drawing room, while at Longbourn, Jane makes the tea and Elizabeth pours the coffee.

Supper was the last meal of the day. It had once been a substantial repast, but now that dinner itself was becoming an evening meal, all that was required was a tray of elegant light refreshments. It is the older characters who are most attached to the idea of supper: Mrs Phillips, Mrs Goddard and Mr Woodhouse 'because it had been the fashion of his youth' (*E*, 1:3). It was at a ball, with exceptionally late hours, that supper came into its own. 'A private dance, without sitting down to supper, was pronounced an infamous fraud upon the rights of men and women' we learn in *Emma* (2:11), while Jane Austen herself reports attending a ball for fifty people at which 'we began at 10, supped at 1, & were at Deane before 5' (*L*, 20 November 1800). Soup seems to have been the essential component of a ball supper: there is soup at the Crown in *Emma* and at Mansfield Park on the night of the ball, and one of Mr Bingley's two conditions for fixing the date of the ball at Netherfield is that his housekeeper should have time to make 'white soup enough' for his expected guests.

This mention of white soup in *Pride and Prejudice* is an excellent example of the way Austen uses food to illustrate character. Based on the expensive ingredients veal stock, cream and ground almonds, white soup originated in the courtly cookery of medieval England and France, when its name was *soupe à la reine*.[2] Mr Bingley is here humorously acknowledging that only the most elegant concoctions suit the notions of his house guests Mr Hurst (who favours French cookery) and Mr Darcy (who can afford a French cook). In this most passing of remarks Mr Bingley displays the attractive qualities of wit, generosity and – slightly more questionable – carelessness about money.

When Mr Hurst scorns Elizabeth Bennet because she prefers a plain dish to a ragout, he is condemned and Elizabeth endorsed for their respective tastes by the narrator. All through the eighteenth century controversy raged in England about French food, which was at once fashionable and unpatriotic, held to be suspect and dishonest like the French character itself. In *The London Tradesman* of 1747 Robert Campbell railed against 'Meats and Drinks dressed after the French fashion' disguising their 'Native properties'. Parson Woodforde complained of a meal eaten out in 1783 that most of the dishes were 'spoiled by being so frenchified in dressing'.[3] The antithesis of French food was English roast beef. 'I have more than once been asked at table my opinion of the roast beef of Old England, with a sort of smile, and in a tone as if the national honour were concerned,' wrote Robert Southey in the guise of a foreign visitor to Britain in 1807.[4]

Of all the meals which the characters must consume in *Sense and Sensibility*, the only one of which Austen chooses to specify is Willoughby's snatched lunch at a coaching inn in Marlborough. We know that this consisted of cold beef and a pint of porter because he tells Elinor so, in order to refute her imputation that he has had too much to drink. But the menu does more than that: it has a moral dimension. He is behaving honourably and with feeling at last; he is not so foolish as to starve himself in his haste to reach Marianne before she dies, but neither will he waste time (as General Tilney, for example, does) by ordering a more elaborate dish. Elinor does not consciously reflect on this but it undoubtedly contributes to the reassessment of Willoughby's worth in her estimation and ours. Some of the sterling character associated with the roast beef of old England attaches to Willoughby now: he is reformed.

In such ways does Austen use detail sparingly to signify several things at once. Every mention of specific food and drink contributes more than mere local colour to the narrative. *Emma* is the Austen novel by far the most laden with references to food, and here they build up to show us the interdependence of the village community, where some people have more access to food, through wealth or occupation, than others. Robert Martin gathers walnuts for Harriet, Mrs Martin sends a goose to Mrs Goddard and Miss Bates is the grateful recipient of apples from Donwell and pork from Hartfield. Food in *Emma* is a metaphor for neighbourly love.

But even in this novel, the heroine and other worthy characters never talk about food in relation to their own appetites – never anticipate or remember a meal with relish. Across the oeuvre, no hero, heroine or other character who enjoys the narrator's approval ever willingly speaks about food. Elizabeth has to be pressed even to admitting she prefers plain food. Elinor and Marianne Dashwood cannot be made to choose between boiled fowls and veal cutlets on the journey from Devon to London. Catherine Morland is indifferent to the French bread at Northanger. Fanny Price is not to be consoled for her homesickness by gooseberry tart. It is left to Mr Elton to enumerate the cheeses and dessert at the Coles' dining table, or Mrs Bennet to boast about her soup and her partridges, or Dr Grant to salivate at the prospect of turkey. And the same prohibition extends to the narrator herself. With the single exception perhaps of the pyramid of fruits at Pemberley (symbolic of the social pyramid which Elizabeth must conquer), any mention of a specific foodstuff in Austen is made by a character who is thereby condemned for being greedy, vulgar, selfish or trivial. That Jane Austen herself could write very differently in correspondence ('Caroline, Anna and I have just been devouring some cold souse, and it would be difficult to say which enjoyed it most', *L*, 14 January 1796) is merely one of the disjunctions between life and art which make art the conscious process it is.

NOTES

1. Robin Vick, 'The Sale at Steventon Parsonage', *Annual Report* of the Jane Austen Society for 1993, p. 14.
2. Jane Grigson, *English Food*, repr. (London: Penguin, 1993), p. 5.
3. James Woodforde, *The Diary of a Country Parson, 1759–1802*, ed. John Beresford, 5 vols. (Oxford: Oxford University Press, 1949), entry for 18 August 1783.
4. Robert Southey, *Letters from England by Don Manuel Alvarez Espriella*, repr. (London: Cresset Press, 1951), p. 89.

24

Landownership

CHRIS JONES

Land, as Coleridge and Burke asserted, represented permanence.[1]
In law it was termed 'real' property, in contrast to personal property
and the stocks that were so volatile as seemingly to possess only
imaginary value. To own land was to be identified more physically
with the nation than to engage in commerce and a wide yet intimate knowledge of the affairs of the countryside where the majority
of the nation lived made landowners the 'natural' governing class.
Families like Austen's Tilneys and Brandons provided the officer
ranks of the army, maintaining the honour of their class and country.
They represented the law as justices and magistrates, and they regulated community affairs such as poor relief. Owning advowsons, the
right to appoint clergymen to their own parishes, they cemented the
bond between church and state, the spirit of religion and the spirit
of a gentleman. Burke's championship of the proud traditions of the
aristocracy against democratic ideas spawned by the French Revolution echoed arguments used throughout the eighteenth century
to justify their predominance, a political predominance buttressed
by the property qualification for a Member of Parliament enacted in
1710 and a property-based franchise virtually unaltered throughout
the century. If some saw ownership of a country house and estate in
the seventeenth century as a mere status symbol,[2] a view echoed by
Oscar Wilde's Lady Bracknell at the end of the nineteenth, it was
much more than this in the intervening period. 'Rotten' or 'pocket'
boroughs and local influence (or bribery and intimidation) in elections brought Parliamentary power and ministerial patronage, and
over the period owners tended to dispose of outlying estates to
concentrate their property and influence in their principal seats.
The popularity of mortgages as investments allowed landowners
to unlock the capital value of their property and further enhance it
by agricultural improvements and entrepreneurial activities. Estates
like Mansfield Park became the foundation of family prosperity and

the base for national and imperial ambitions. This survey will outline landowners' methods of maintaining their position, especially
in safeguarding the hereditary transmission of estates, their implication with commercial interests that were apparent adversaries and
the criticisms of their activities voiced in Austen's time.

In all Austen's novels arrangements covering inheritance, jointures and portions, well understood by her readers, are of major
importance to the plot and require some knowledge of the
procedure known as strict settlement. A practice almost universally employed by landowners since its inception in the late seventeenth century, this series of legal devices allowed a man to settle
his estate on a yet unborn descendant, in the reasonable assurance
that it would survive any extravagance of its immediate inheritor,
provide his widow with a specified income, or jointure, on his death
and secure the prospects of his children by portions, in the case of
daughters payable on marriage. An heir's allowance was not specified in the settlement, which enabled the owner to exert financial pressure on his life-style, influence his marriage choice and
persuade him to settle the estate in his turn. Settlement at marriage was common. Though the bride's property reverted to the
husband, her family's lawyers attended to her future security and
that of her children. Settlement by will was more controversial and
long-lasting. Once settled, the arrangements could not be altered
until the unborn child on whom the estate was entailed reached
the age of twenty-one. Even little Henry Dashwood is probably
bound by the settlement of Norland since he was alive at the time
the will came into effect, though he would inherit other property.
The immediate inheritor was a life tenant, not an absolute owner,
who could not sell or mortgage land except for purposes specified in the settlement. When landed men are introduced in the
novels as possessing or heir to a number of thousands of pounds,
this is understood as the yearly income from the estate; they usually did not command the capital. Elinor in *Sense and Sensibility*
echoes the conventional wisdom when she points to early independence as contributing to the ruin of Willoughby's character, yet
Edward Ferrars demonstrates the perils of dependence. In *Mansfield Park* similar criticism of Henry Crawford's early independence
is counterpointed by the lack of influence Sir Thomas has on his

heir. Such comparisons allow conventional wisdom and customary arrangements to be questioned. The power which settlement wields over the future of dependants, especially women, is highlighted in the novels, but criticism of the system seems often to be deflected by a focus on the moral responsibility of individuals to alleviate the hardship it causes.

Trustees were appointed to safeguard the interests of 'contingent remainders', the specified successors. If an estate was settled in tail male the contingency of the eldest son's failure to produce a male heir was covered by a long list of possible male successors, alive and unborn. Frequently a change of name was the condition for a distant branch of the family to inherit. The Knight family who adopted Edward Austen and caused him to change his name when succeeding to their property had raised much mirth by requiring Parliament to change their own name twice in quick succession for the same purpose. If a man died intestate (a very unusual occurrence) state law enforced primogeniture, though if only daughters were left it divided the estate between them. Tail male was the customary arrangement, vehemently supported by Dr Johnson, but there were other possibilities. An estate could be settled in tail general, admitting female heiresses, or even in tail female. Despite strict settlement, mortality among heirs and a lack of male offspring produced an unusual number of heiresses in the middle years of the eighteenth century. Most, however, like Mrs Ferrars, ignored the alternatives and were only too eager to re-establish a patrilinear estate. Lady Catherine de Bourgh herself, despite her criticism of male succession, destines her estate and her daughter for Darcy. It is typical of Austen's thought-provoking playfulness to put radical remarks into the mouth of a thoroughly conservative character quite as liable to misuse power as any man.

Just as tail male was not law but custom, similar unwritten rules governed the ratio between the portion that a woman brought to a marriage and the jointure settled on her (roughly 10:1 in the period). No longer was the widow entitled to the traditional third of her husband's land, even if she brought land to the marriage and shared in its improvement. The only remnant of the 'dower' system of the previous century was the dower-house on the estate where the dowager might spend her declining years unless, like Mrs Rushworth, she preferred the amenities of a fashionable town (where her join-ture might attract renewed amorous attentions). Marriage was, in the language of the time, a 'venture'. Jointures and portions settled at marriage might bear little relation to the wealth of the estate when they were payable but any supplementation was only possible by the life tenant out of income or at the resettling of the estate by an heir in tail. Hence the much criticised partiality of mothers like Fanny Dashwood for the first-born son and heir and discussions in novels about supplementing what the estate allowed in order to procure suitable marriages for the daughters and careers or wives for the younger sons.[3] The younger son, a potential inheri-tor, had to be expensively educated to the law, bought a commission in the army or set up with capital in business or by patronage in a government post. Despite its importance to the Constitution, only recently and through the frowned-on practice of pluralism was the church becoming a fittingly remunerative profession.

Settlement did provide security. If settlement commitments or mortgage repayments were prejudiced by an improvident life ten-ant the trustees could sequestrate part of the estate and arrange for its separate management. In *Persuasion* something is salvaged from Mr Smith's estate, though it takes Wentworth's efforts to extract it. A growing army of professionals, land agents, stewards and fam-ily lawyers, had a stake in the survival of estates like Kellynch and intervened in times of danger. Very few large estates came on to the market to be bought by the newly rich from commercial, manufac-turing, colonial, military and financial backgrounds despite William Cobbett's complaints against such supplanting of ancient names. New wealth, including West Indian plantations, was often incor-porated into old estates by marriage and involved owners like Sir Thomas Bertram in the moral and political issues it raised.

The security for wives and younger children given by strict settlement has been seen as a move towards middle-class sensibil-ity, testifying to new affectionate, more egalitarian family relations in the traditional patriarchal aristocratic family.[4] But such security had its limits, as we have seen. Strict settlement was adopted by an aristocracy and aspiring gentry principally anxious to preserve estates and names. The ascendancy of the feelings, in fact, did not work to the material advantage of heiresses who, on marriage,

were dissuaded from protecting their property by a separate contract because it showed an unromantic distrust of their husbands.
Many, however, like Lady Denham of *Sanditon*, were willing to
incur the accusation. Beauty was always reckoned a portion, but its
conquest of economic realities was rare enough to provoke comment. John Dashwood gives a quantitative survey of Marianne's
prospects based on this deteriorating asset and Miss Maria Ward's
luck in attracting Sir Thomas Bertram is calculated by her lawyer
uncle with a nicety that argues precise knowledge of the sisters'
portions. In a competitive marriage market it is difficult to gainsay
Mr Collins's estimate of Elizabeth Bennet's position.

Settlement restricted the life tenant, but only in certain ways.
Sir Walter Elliot cannot bar William Walter from inheriting
Kellynch except by producing a male child; Mr Bennet and Mr
Dashwood cannot sell or mortgage property to provide better portions for their daughters. John Dashwood, however, cuts down
trees, encloses a common and buys a neighbouring farm. If judged as
benefits to the estate and the future owner, many apparent violations
of the conditions of settlement were allowed. Even if he had not
been enriched by marriage and inheritance from his mother, John
Dashwood would probably have been able to finance his improvements through mortgages. New forms of credit, bonds and insurance also became available on the security of land and its improvement, even if distant. Improvement meant not only agricultural
improvement or landscape-gardening but exploitation of mineral
resources and the establishment of associated industries, the building and development of towns, ports, roads and canals. The landed
aristocracy and gentry were linked with the commercial activity that
raised the rent of their holdings but also produced alternative cen-
tres of society and sources of social distinction. In *Sanditon* the two
major proprietors developing a seaside resort engage in speculative
building and encourage commercial, professional and leisure industries. This produces comic juxtapositions of old and new thinking
as high prices are now to be welcomed, as is the fact that the working class are becoming more independent and 'good for nothing'
as servants. Highbury, part of the vast estate owned by George
Knightley, is a less extreme instance of the modern integration
of commercial, professional and agricultural enterprise. Emma is

old-fashioned and defensive in her snobbish rejection of the Coles'
social claims and her dismissal of Robert Martin as a 'yeoman',
traditionally the highest among the non-gentry but landed ranks,
is particularly wide of the mark. A substantial tenant co-operating
with an improving landlord, Martin would probably have the long
lease and capital to make his tenure secure and justify Knightley's
epithet 'gentleman farmer'. None of these improvements would
have been possible without enclosure.

Enclosure meant the disappearance of the old open field system of agriculture, in which holdings were scattered in 'strips'
among two or three large fields. They were consolidated as separate,
personal property. If commons and waste (land not used for agriculture) were also enclosed, the rights of those who used them to
graze cattle, cut turfs or gather wood were quantified and pro-
portionate land added to their entitlement. Enclosures had been
made from medieval times and in the early eighteenth century they
were usually small in scale and arranged by consent among the
landowners. Most of those in Jane Austen's Hampshire were of
this type. From the middle of the century the process became the
subject of Acts of Parliament. Parliamentary enclosures were more
comprehensive and included new roads, bridges and in some cases
draining schemes. They required only the consent of those holding
about three-quarters of the land affected and particularly targeted
commons and waste. The cost of this transformation of the landscape and the fencing, hedging or walling of enclosures was high,
which led to many smaller proprietors selling their shares to the
major 'engrossing' owners. The advantages were seen in the independence and convenience of working consolidated plots and in the
commutation of tithes into land. Above all, the rent of enclosed land
increased greatly and the high water mark of enclosures came with
the increase of agricultural prices during the French Wars. For the
agriculturalist Arthur Young and Sir Joseph Banks, president of the
Royal Society, enclosure enabled advances in agricultural practices
and increased production to feed the growing population (Young
publicised the advantages of enclosure in his *Annals of Agriculture*, 1784–1815, but from 1791 he favoured schemes that allowed
the poor villager a decent share of the commons to graze a cow).[5]
Enclosure of commons and waste, however, hit the poorest of the
village, those who could not prove a title to their rights or were

allotted a small patch of poor ground. It meant the loss of a traditional, semi-independent way of life (a temptation to laziness in the view of many moralists) and dependence on seasonal labour and the parish poor-rates. Enclosure of commons became, especially in the work of Cobbett, a sign of selfish landowners abandoning their duty of care. In a letter Jane Austen asks whether Northamptonshire is a country of hedgerows (*L*, 29 January 1813). From her brother Henry she might have received an account of the popularly resented partitions of the county most heavily affected by Parliamentary enclosure, the 'lawless laws' lamented by John Clare in his poem 'The mores'. Austen knew the business of agricultural improvement through her farming father and her landowning brother and her allusions to enclosure include both sides of the argument. Enclosing a common is appropriate to John Dashwood's unsympathetic character (it might have unbalanced the presentation of Sir Thomas Bertram's) while Knightley's concern in consulting villagers about changing a right of way reconciles improvement with social responsibility. In *Persuasion* the farmers working their enclosures firmly meaning to have spring again are a salutary contrast to Anne's despondency.

Landscape gardening was often associated with enclosure in practice and in critical discourse. It was part of a gentleman's duty to patronise the arts and many combined it with advanced farming techniques and experimental botanical introductions from America and the Empire. An equally strong motive, however, was self-aggrandising display, often of enormous extravagance and sometimes demonstrating a callous disregard for the components of the landscape. Goldsmith's *The Deserted Village* (1770) is thought to have been motivated by the resiting of a village in favour of a prospect and General Tilney shows a contracted version of this high-handedness when only Catherine's admiration of a cottage halts his plans for demolition. Landscaping as the rendering of an ideal relationship to nature was an aesthetic legitimation or 'naturalisation' of the landowner's propriety/property, and developed a more paternalistic aspect during the century. Cottages and workers are often included in the prospects designed by Humphry Repton, in contrast to the splendid isolation of the great house amidst gravel drives and parkland favoured by Lancelot 'Capability' Brown.[6] In *Mansfield Park* we might see an ironising of the aesthetic exponent of the ubiquitous 'Park' (about 400 estates in the Chilterns were 'Parks' in the eighteenth century). Its aesthetic impression is negligible compared with Pemberley, while the real business of the house is administering extended estates and patronage networks and exercising political power in London.

Austen's concern with the conduct of landowners and their influence on the community runs through all her novels and inevitably reflects some of the views of her contemporaries. Though she shows no sympathy with the comprehensive attacks on private property in land mounted by Thomas Spence and William Godwin, some similarity can be seen between her caricatured landowners, such as Lady Catherine de Bourgh and Sir Walter Elliot, and those of 'Jacobin' novelists like Robert Bage and Charlotte Smith. The criticism of inherited status when not combined with cultivated virtues of mind, which Jane Austen shares with such radical writers as Mary Wollstonecraft, has been seen as favouring the professional classes against the traditional aristocracy. But if the moral qualities of leaders of society are sought in those outside the traditional landed class, like the Crofts, their qualifications are proved in fulfilling the same traditional responsibilities. *Mansfield Park* has been seen as supporting the conservative values of the old aristocracy against modern, even Continental, corruption in a 'Tory' Burkean way or contributing to Evangelical attempts to recall the aristocracy to lost moral and religious principles (though the spiritual quality of Evangelicalism is attenuated). It has also been taken as a parody of these qualities or read in the context of Cobbett's radical reformist criticism of the neglect produced by overweening ambitions for power and profit. In *Emma* Knightley's commercial agriculture and improvements have suggested aligning Jane Austen with the 'Whiggish' modernising agrarian capitalists of the day.[7] Knightley, however, seems to demonstrate a combination of improvement with benevolence, paternalism with values of independence. Knightley was reportedly Austen's favourite portrait of a country gentleman[8] and in his unostentatious encouragement of the independence and prosperity of others, his sociability and co-operation in parish business, she attempts to unify old and new, Whig, Tory and even radical ideas of responsible stewardship of land.

NOTES

1. Edmund Burke, *Reflections on the Revolution in France*, ed. L. G. Mitchell (Oxford: Oxford University Press, 1993), pp. 51–2; Samuel Taylor Coleridge, *On the Constitution of Church and State*, ed. John Barrell (London: Dent, 1972), p. 20.

2. Kari Boyd McBride, *Country House Discourse in Early Modern England* (Aldershot: Ashgate, 2001), pp. 138–9.

3. See the debate between John and Fanny Dashwood in *S&S*, ch. 2. In *Sir Charles Grandison* (1753–4) Samuel Richardson's benevolent hero pays scant attention to customary practice or the intentions of the deceased in distributing equal portions to all children from estates falling to his administration.

4. See Lawrence Stone, *The Family, Sex and Marriage in England 1500–1800* (London: Weidenfeld and Nicolson, 1977); Randolph Trumbach, *The Rise of the Egalitarian Family* (London: Academic Press, 1978). For criticism of these ideas see John Habakkuk, *Marriage, Debt, and the Estates System* (Oxford: Clarendon Press, 1994), pp. 233–4; Amy Louise Erickson, *Women and Property* (London: Routledge, 1993), pp. 7–8; Susan Staves, 'Daughters and Younger Sons', in *Early Modern Conceptions of Property*, eds. John Brewer and Susan Staves (London: Routledge, 1995), pp. 194–218.

5. See *Arthur Young and his Times*, ed. G. E. Mingay (London: Macmillan, 1975), ch. 3.

6. Tim Fulford, *Landscape, Liberty and Authority* (Cambridge: Cambridge University Press, 1996), pp. 116–56.

7. See Gary Kelly, *Women, Writing and Revolution* (Oxford: Oxford University Press, 1993), pp. 181–3; Marilyn Butler, *Jane Austen and the War of Ideas* (Oxford: Oxford University Press, 1987), pp. 219–49; Alistair M. Duckworth, *The Improvement of the Estate. A Study of Jane Austen's Novels* (Baltimore and London: Johns Hopkins University Press, 1971), pp. 36–80; Claudia L. Johnson, *Jane Austen, Women, Politics and the Novel* (Chicago and London: University of Chicago Press, 1988), pp. 94–120; Chris Jones, 'Jane Austen and Old Corruption,' *Literature and History* 9:2 (2000), 1–16; David Spring, 'Interpreters of Jane Austen's Social World', in *Jane Austen: New Perspectives*, ed. Janet Todd (New York: Holmes and Meier Publishers, 1983), pp. 53–72.

8. Deirdre Le Faye, *Jane Austen: A Family Record*, second edition (Cambridge: Cambridge University Press, 2004), p. 233.

25

Landscape

ALISTAIR M. DUCKWORTH

In the decade in which Jane Austen was born, the English landscape garden was at the peak of its renown, and the picturesque vogue was in its early stages. The spacious park landscapes of Lancelot 'Capability' Brown (1715–83) at such places as Blenheim, Chatsworth and Harewood displayed the taste of landed gentlemen who resided on their estates. The mountains of Wales, the Lake District and the Scottish Highlands catered to a different group: prosperous but unlanded tourists mostly, women as well as men. Equipped with guidebooks, sketchbooks, maps, pedometers and Claude glasses, enthusiasts for the picturesque sought out wild scenery, preferred ruined abbeys to Doric temples and valued a native Gothic past over the classical heritage admired by those who took the European Grand Tour.

Both tastes in landscape had their champions. Horace Walpole, in his *History of the Modern Taste in Gardening* (printed 1771, published 1780), promoted the Whig view that the natural style of the English garden was an expression of liberty, whereas the geometric formality of the French garden signified political despotism. In the landscapes of William Kent (1684–1748), he found 'the delicious contrast of hill and valley', 'the beauty of the gentle swell, or concave scoop'.[1] Such descriptions might equally refer to Brown's landscapes, with their rolling lawns, grouped trees, serpentine lakes and encircling belts of woodland, and they accord with Edmund Burke's definitions of the beautiful in his *Inquiry into . . . Our Ideas of the Sublime and Beautiful* (1756). Walpole had praised Brown in passing, but it was left to Thomas Whately, in his *Observations on Modern Gardening* (1770), to provide the rationale for Brown's system. Whately criticised the devices, 'rather *emblematical* than expressive', used in earlier gardens such as Stowe and The Leasowes. Elevating gardening to a liberal art, he analysed natural materials (ground, wood, water, rocks, buildings) and encouraged designers to express the 'original' character of a place (*Observations*, 3rd edn, pp. 151, 153).

As for the picturesque, the vogue was already being promoted as William Gilpin (1724–1804) was taking his tours to various parts of Britain in the 1770s, and before he began to publish his *Observations*, beginning in 1782. Dr John Dalton in his *Descriptive Poem* (1758) and Dr John Brown in his letter describing the vale of Keswick (1767) had 'discovered' the Lake District, and Thomas West had published his *Guide to the Lakes* (1778); in the second edition (1780) Thomas Gray's journal appeared as an appendix. West and Gray not only provided much of the descriptive vocabulary of the picturesque; they also mapped a succession of 'stations' from which the tourist might appreciate picturesque views.[2] But, if Gilpin was not the first to promote the picturesque, he was its most influential pedagogue. His successive *Observations* provided leisured amateurs with verbal and visual instruction. Born in Scaleby Castle, he had a native love of the rugged scenery of Cumberland and Westmorland and preferred irregular, weather-stained ruins to modern buildings. His aquatint illustrations followed a simplified set of compositional principles. Thus, on the assumption that the picturesque signifies 'that peculiar kind of beauty, which is agreeable in a picture' (*Essay Upon Prints*, 1768, p. x), scenes should have a foreground, middle distance and background; each part should contribute to the whole; care should be taken in the distribution of light and shade; the texture should be varied and the expression animated; and the mood of the place and time captured.[3]

The works of Walpole, Whately and Gilpin, along with those of Repton, Price and Knight, which will be discussed shortly, were all to be found in the libraries of the polite. That Jane Austen knew these works is likely. She was, as her brother Henry wrote in his 'Biographical Notice' (1818), 'a warm and judicious admirer of landscape, both in nature and on canvass'; and, 'at a very early age she was enamoured of Gilpin on the Picturesque'. As a well-connected gentry woman, she would have had an interest in landscape. At Chawton, the formal gardens of the Jacobean house had been replaced with a more modern landscape between 1763 and 1785. At Godmersham, a Palladian house sat in a park between wooded downs, on one of which a Doric temple gave an Arcadian

Figure 40. 'Godmersham Park', from vol. 2 of John P. Neale's
*Views of the Seats of Noblemen and Gentlemen in England, Wales,
Scotland and Ireland* (1825).

air to the scene (fig. 40). At Adlestrop, the grounds were improved
in 1799 by Repton, who made a landscape out of the gardens of
the rectory and the great house and created a stream that flowed
down through a flower garden and over ledges of rock into a lake.[4]
At Stoneleigh Abbey, Repton was also active; his Red Book (1809)
shows the removal of walls, opening of prospects and redirection of
the river Avon. Austen knew these places and others, such as Esher,
from whose beautiful grounds (improved by Kent), she wrote to
Cassandra in 1813, 'there could not be a Wood or a Meadow or
a Palace or a remarkable spot in England that was not spread out
before us, on one side or the other' (*L*, 20 May 1813).

As her enthusiasm suggests, she was no enemy to tasteful modern landscapes. In *Pride and Prejudice*, Pemberley is a tribute to
Darcy's taste. The house stands on rising ground in a large park; the
approach road is winding; oaks and Spanish chestnuts are scattered
over the lawn; a stream has been tastefully enlarged. The landscape

is devoid of buildings (such as the Doric temple at Cleveland in *Sense and Sensibility*, or the Hermitage at Longbourn in *Pride and Prejudice*) aimed at directing the viewer's response. Instead, natural materials (Whately's water, wood and ground) are the source of Elizabeth's delight. A simple bridge is 'in character with the general air of the scene' (*P&P*, 3:1). Pemberley's landscape has been attributed to both Brown and Gilpin, which may not be contradictory if we recall that Pemberley is set in the Peak District, not far from such scenic spots as Matlock and Dovedale. If the park is Brownian, a nearby 'glen' offers Elizabeth picturesque points of view. She has joined her aunt and uncle (a prosperous London businessman) on a tour to the Lake District; the tour is curtailed, but it seems to have been based on the itinerary of Gilpin's *Observations . . . on the Mountains and Lakes of Cumberland and Westmoreland* (1786).

Having described a tasteful modern landscape in *Pride and Prejudice*, Jane Austen went on, in *Mansfield Park*, to show improvements in a bad light, and, in *Emma*, to praise a conspicuously unimproved estate. In so doing, she joined a line of writers who criticised false or extravagant improvements on both aesthetic and social grounds.[5] As the pre-eminent improver of the time, Capability Brown came in for his share of abuse as well as praise. William Chambers, in his *Dissertation on Oriental Gardening* (1772), claimed that Brownian landscapes were indistinguishable from common fields, while Oliver Goldsmith in *The Deserted Village* (1770) castigated the Brownian improvements of the 'man of wealth and pride' who 'takes up a space that many poor supplied; / Space for his lake, his park's extended bounds, / Space for his horses, equipage and hounds' (lines 275–8). A little later, William Cowper, in Book III of *The Task* (1785), viewed Brown as an 'omnipotent magician' (line 766) at whose command 'woods vanish, hills subside, and vallies rise' (line 775). Cowper deplored improvements as 'the idol of the age' (line 764) in a critique that continues the traditional complaints of country house poems from Ben Jonson to Alexander Pope against ostentatious display and neglect of hospitality. With the removal of cottages from the park, and the siting of mansions in solitary splendour, the landscape garden seemed to a range of legal, constitutional and religious writers to be destructive of traditional customs and ideas of charity.[6]

Austen does not name Brown in her novels, though she does associate his nickname with Henry Crawford's schemes for Sotherton and Frank Churchill's for the Crown Inn. She does name Repton during the debate over improvements in chapter 6 of *Mansfield Park*. As Brown's heir, Humphry Repton (1752–1818) was the target of attacks made on professional improvers by connoisseurs. Richard Payne Knight in his poem *The Landscape* (1794) and Uvedale Price in his *Essay on the Picturesque* (1794) affirmed gentlemanly taste by urging improvers to find inspiration in the landscape paintings of such artists as Claude and Salvator Rosa. In his *Sketches and Hints on Landscape Gardening* (1795), Repton defended Brown by arguing that practical considerations should outweigh picturesque ones in landscape design. The quarrel was political as well as aesthetic. Knight and Price were Foxite Whigs who believed that the new fashion introduced by Brown destroyed the distinctive character of diverse localities and betrayed Whig patriotic ideals. Against what they took to be formulaic in the Brownian landscape Knight and Price set their versions of the picturesque, elaborating ideas from Gilpin but redirecting them to the ends of estate management. Their advocacy of picturesque forest over tended lawns, rough textures over smooth and even neglect over improvement outraged Brown's defenders. Knight's proposal in *The Landscape* that Brownian parks be destroyed was particularly inflammatory in 1794; Anna Seward accused him of a 'Jacobinism of taste', and Horace Walpole claimed that he wished 'to guillotine Mr. Brown'.[7]

Price's picturesque was less libertarian than Knight's. As a conservative country Whig, he defended a paternalist rural order, rooted in landed property, against 'levelling' improvements that, in his view, weakened 'the voluntary ties' binding together the different social ranks.[8] Price's theories were consistent with the arguments of Edmund Burke who, in *Reflections On the Revolution in France* (1790), made frequent analogies between the condition of estates and of the nation at large. Price's views also accorded with those of Wordsworth, Coleridge and Southey, who took a political interest in landscape improvements (Everett, *Tory View*, pp. 153–78).

Austen's response to the debates over improvements is not recorded, and it is difficult to derive from her novels a view consistent with that of any one of the major proponents. She may have shared with Knight, Price and others concerns over the socially divisive effects of Brownian emparkment, but she would not have endorsed Knight's primitivism in *The Landscape* or Price's sentimental fondness for 'old, neglected bye-roads and hollow ways' (*Essay*, p. 19). As for Repton, Austen's association of him with dubious characters in *Mansfield Park* has posed problems for scholars who believe his ideas of improvement were close to her own. Repton increasingly departed from Brown's formulas, reintroducing terraces near the house and planting shrubberies not unlike those at Mansfield Park and Hartfield. Moreover, from being the critic of 'ancient' gardening in *Sketches* Repton turned full circle and became an advocate, in *Fragments on the Theory and Practice of Landscape Gardening* (1816), of old estates and gardens.[9]

On the other hand, Repton was a figure of controversy. George III thought him a 'coxcomb,' John Byng described him as 'Capability R.', John Claudius Loudon, in his *Treatise on Forming, Improving and Managing Country Residences* (1806), accused him of 'quackery' in his deceptive use of 'before and after' illustrations and Thomas Love Peacock in *Headlong Hall* (1816) satirised him as Marmaduke Milestone. That Jane Austen was exploiting his notoriety cannot be ruled out. It is also possible that she shared the Tory views of her Leigh ancestors and disliked the improvements Repton made at Adlestrop and Stoneleigh.[10] A critique is evident, in any case, in the parody of Repton's prose that appears in Henry Crawford's discredited proposals for the improvement of Thornton Lacey (*MP*, 2:7).[11]

Improvers like Crawford, who seek change while neglecting their social responsibilities as landowners, are criticised in Austen's novels. General Tilney's grandiose improvements at Northanger Abbey not only disappoint Catherine Morland's Gothic anticipations but identify him as an avaricious consumer capitalist. In *Sense and Sensibility*, the selfish materialism of John Dashwood is evident in his enclosure of the common at Norland, purchase of a neighbouring farm and – to his sister Elinor's dismay – removal of old walnut trees to make way for a greenhouse and flower garden for his wife. In the same novel, Colonel Brandon's Delaford, with its great garden walls, dovecote, stewponds and canal, all in close proximity to the parsonage and village, testifies to Austen's fondness for estates that have missed, or rejected, the hand of the improver (*S&S*, 2:8). Of all such places, Donwell Abbey in *Emma*, with its low and sheltered situation, 'old neglect of prospect,' irregular house, ample gardens and 'abundance of timber in rows and avenues, which neither fashion nor extravagance had rooted up', is the most chauvinistic expression of her social ideal. From Donwell's grounds, the Abbey-Mill farm can be seen: it is 'a sweet view . . . English verdure, English culture, English comfort' (*E*, 3:6). Mr Knightley takes his Christian name from England's saint, and his surname implies traditional values going back to feudal times. But, while he keeps improvements out of his gardens, he pursues them in his fields; like his tenant farmer, Robert Martin, he reads the Agricultural Reports, and with his brother discusses questions of drainage and crop-rotation. Donwell combines commitment to a traditional community (Knightley consults his neighbours before moving a path) with agricultural improvement in the manner of Arthur Young.

Somewhat later than the attacks on the Brownian garden, the picturesque also became the target of satire. For all its promotion of real nature over ideal landscapes, the picturesque had produced its own clichés. Among works that criticised its absurdities were James Plumptre's comic opera, *The Lakers* (1798), and *The Tour of Doctor Syntax in Search of the Picturesque* (1812), in which William Combe's satirical verse accompanied Thomas Rowlandson's burlesque illustrations of the eponymous tourist's mishaps amid mountain scenery. More serious critiques appeared in Wordsworth's 1806 *Prelude* and Scott's *Waverley* (1814). Wordsworth objected to appreciations of landscape that relied on comparisons with paintings, privileged the visual over the other senses and were oblivious to the affective resonance of place; Scott in his description of the village at Tully Veolan observed how the picturesque and poverty were interdependent. Gilpin himself propounded a troubling paradox, when he argued that though cultivated landscapes were pleasing in a moral light, they were disgusting to the picturesque eye. By the same perverse logic, 'the industrious mechanic' was not fit for representation, though 'the loitering peasant' was.[12]

Critics of the cult from the time of John Ruskin have been hard on its nostalgia for a harmonious rural world that supposedly existed before agrarian reform; its condescending look at peasant life; its aesthetic mystifications of rural poverty and ruins; and its avoidance of historical analysis in favour of sentimental reflections on the effects of time and accident. Austen was not blind to the ambiguities of the picturesque, but she was less concerned to expose the cult's political deficiencies than to exploit the opportunities it afforded for irony and humour. She was not a picturesque writer after the manner of Ann Radcliffe; she never invokes Claude to paint a beautiful scene in words or Salvator Rosa to paint a sublime one. As author, she seldom composes her scenes according to picturesque principles, though she does make fun of a character for doing so: Henry Tilney, responding to Catherine Morland's admission of ignorance in drawing, 'talked of fore-grounds, distances, and second distances – side-screens and perspectives – lights and shades', with such persuasiveness that Catherine rejects the city of Bath, viewed from Beechen Cliff, as 'unworthy to make part of a landscape' (*NA*, 1:14).

From her earliest works, ironic allusions to Gilpin are frequent.[13] Sometimes, they are amusingly obvious, as when Augusta in 'Love and Freindship' (1790) explains her sudden presence in Scotland as the consequence of having read Gilpin's *Tour to the Highlands of Scotland* ('Letter the 14th'). In other instances, they assume a discerning reader, as when, in *Pride and Prejudice*, Elizabeth refuses to join Darcy and the two Bingley sisters on a walk, because 'the picturesque would be spoilt by admitting a fourth' (1:10). The (insulting) joke here depends on the reader's knowledge of Gilpin's theory, expounded in words and drawings in his *Observations* on the Lake District, that three cows form a group (vol. 2, pp. 258–9). In *Sense and Sensibility* occurs the aesthetic debate between Edward and Marianne. Edward's denial of any knowledge of the picturesque is false modesty, while Marianne is perfectly aware that 'admiration of landscape scenery is become a mere jargon' and that Gilpin's taste and elegance have been depreciated by his followers. Neither speaker wins, but Edward's definition of 'fine country' as that which 'unites beauty with utility' is a traditional view (as old as Horace's *utile dulci*), while his preference for 'a troop of tidy, happy villagers' over 'the finest banditti in the world' suggests he has been reading Repton's *Sketches and Hints* (*S&S*, 1:18).

Gilpin is an unnamed presence in *Mansfield Park*. In the windows of Fanny Price's room are transparencies of Tintern Abbey and a moonlit lake in Cumberland (*MP*, 1:16; fig. 41). Fanny combines a picturesque sensibility with more practical views. She wishes to

Figure 41. 'A view of Lake Windermere', from vol. 1 of William Gilpin's *Observations on the mountains and lakes of Cumberland, and Westmoreland* (1786).

see Sotherton in its old state, quotes Cowper as she deplores Rushworth's plan to cut down the avenue and refers to Scott when the chapel is not as ancient as she hoped. But on the way to Sotherton, she observes 'the appearance of the country, the bearings of the roads, the difference of soil, the state of the harvest, the cottages, the cattle' (*MP*, 1:8), as if she were taking notes for Young's *Annals of Agriculture*.

In her late novels, Austen's attention often veers from landscape to nature, as her descriptions express her heroines' sensitivity to atmospheric conditions and seasonal moods. Fanny's response to the rural spring, 'that season which cannot, in spite of its capriciousness, be unlovely' (*MP*, 3:14), is quite different from Marianne's 'passion for dead leaves' (*S&S*, 1:16); and her response to the view from the ramparts of Portsmouth, though it may be influenced by Gilpin's account of the city in his *Observations on the Coasts of Hampshire, Sussex, and Kent* (1804), reveals her synaesthetic sensibility (*MP*, 3:11). Emma, who insults Miss Bates on Box Hill, a beauty spot praised by Gilpin in *Observations on the Western Parts of England* (1798), soon after welcomes 'the exquisite sight, smell, sensation of nature, tranquil, warm, and brilliant after a storm' (*E*, 3:13); while Anne Elliot, during her period of loss and separation, is alive to the external autumnal scene, and to the poetic associations it arouses (*P*, 1:10). In the same novel, something of the guidebook pertains to the narrator's descriptions of Charmouth, 'with its high grounds and extensive sweeps of country,' and Pinny, with 'its green chasms between romantic rocks' (*P*, 1:11). The picturesque is not merely a frame for viewing scenery, however, but a means of deepening the novel's concern with the passing of time. Typically, Austen chastens excessive introspection; Anne Elliot, sensing her self-indulgent mood on the walk to Winthrop, rouses herself. What she sees would not be picturesque for Gilpin: 'large enclosures, where the ploughs at work . . . spoke the farmer, counteracting the sweets of poetical despondence, and meaning to have spring again' (*P*, 1:10). But the scene would please Edward Ferrars and Mr Knightley, and it is a late affirmation of Austen's own belief that the art of landscape need not be in conflict with its cultivation.

NOTES

1. *The History of the Modern Taste in Gardening*, ed. Isabel W. U. Chase, in her *Horace Walpole: Gardenist* (1943), p. 26.
2. Esther Moir, *The Discovery of Britain: the English Tourist, 1540–1840* (London: Routledge & Kegan Paul, 1964), pp. 139–41.
3. Carl Paul Barbier, *William Gilpin: His Drawings, Teachings, and Theory of the Picturesque* (Oxford: Clarendon Press, 1963).
4. Humphry Repton, *Observations on the Theory and Practice of Modern Gardening* (1803), p. 161.
5. Edward Malins, *English Landscaping and Literature, 1660–1840* (London: Oxford University Press, 1966), ch. 5; Alistair M. Duckworth, 'Improvements', in *The Jane Austen Companion*, eds. J. David Grey, A. Walton Litz, Brian Southam (New York: Macmillan, 1986), pp. 223–7.
6. For anti-improvement sentiments in William Blackstone, Edmund Burke, Sir Thomas Bernard and others, see Nigel Everett, *The Tory View of Landscape* (New Haven: Yale University Press, 1994). Subsequent references are included in the text.

7. Stephen Daniels, *Humphry Repton: Landscape Gardening and the Geography of Georgian England* (New Haven: Yale University Press, 1999), ch. 3; Everett, *Tory View*, p. 116.

8. Uvedale Price, *Essay on the Picturesque*, (1794), pp. 27–9; *A Letter to H. Repton, Esq*, second edition (1798), pp. 178–9. Daniels, *Humphry Repton*, p. 115. Subsequent references to *Essay* are included in the text.

9. See ch. VI of *Sketches* ('Of the Ancient Style of Gardening') and, by way of contrast, Fragments XIX, XXVI, and XXXII of *Fragments*. For a comprehensive account of Repton's career, including attention to his political conservatism and accommodation of some of the views of Knight and Price, see Daniels, *Humphry Repton*.

10. Mavis Batey, *Jane Austen and the English Landscape* (London: Barn Elms, 1996), pp. 80–93.

11. Alistair M. Duckworth, *The Improvement of the Estate. A Study of Jane Austen's Novels*, new edition (Baltimore and London: Johns Hopkins University Press, 1994), pp. 48–55.

12. William Gilpin, *Observations . . . on the Mountains and Lakes of Cumberland and Westmoreland* (1786), vol. 2, p. 44.

13. John Dixon Hunt, 'The Picturesque', in *The Jane Austen Companion*, eds. Grey *et al.*, pp. 326–9.

26

Literary scene

RICHARD CRONIN

In 1800 a now forgotten novelist, Robert Bisset, identified the three leading practitioners of his craft: 'Were I to characterize Mrs. Ratcliffe, Mrs. Smith, and Miss Burney by one prominent feature in their works I should say that Mrs. Ratcliffe was chiefly distinguished by vivacity of fancy, Mrs. Smith by tenderness of feeling, Miss Burney by acuteness, force, and comprehensiveness of understanding.'[1] Jane Austen would surely have agreed with his ranking. By 1800 she had already drafted three of her novels. *Northanger Abbey* affectionately burlesqued the Radcliffe manner, Austen's father identified the genealogy of 'First Impressions' as it was then titled, by describing it to the publisher Thomas Cadell as 'about the length of Miss Burney's Evelina'[2] and when it was finally published its title, *Pride and Prejudice*, was taken from Burney's *Cecilia*, and the future Lady Byron confidently reported after reading it that it had been written by 'a sister of Charlotte Smith's'.[3] When Henry Tilney acknowledges that he has read 'all of Mrs. Radcliffe's works, and most of them with great pleasure' (*NA*, 1:14), he underlines his good sense, and one of Austen's earlier heroines, 'Catharine', tests the ability of a new acquaintance by engaging her in a discussion about the novels of Charlotte Smith, but for Austen, as for the forgotten Robert Bisset, it was Frances Burney who took the palm. It was one of two 'pleasing' traits in the character of a Miss Fletcher that 'she admires Camilla' (*L*, 15–16 September 1796), and Jane Austen's niece Caroline records that the only occasion on which she can remember her aunt reading aloud she had taken up 'a volume of Evelina and read a few pages of Mr Smith and the Brangtons and [Caroline] thought it was like a play' (Le Faye, *Family Record*, p. 183). It was from Burney that Austen inherited the main lineaments of the plot that was to serve her throughout her career, the misadventures of a young woman at what she, like Sir Thomas Bertram, seems to have judged 'the most interesting stage' of her life, that is, the time during which she makes her choice of marriage partner (*MP*, 1:3).

Jane Austen drafted her first three novels in the years from 1795 to 1798, but by the time that the first of them was published, in 1811, neither Smith, nor Radcliffe nor Burney had produced a novel for more than a decade. Smith was dead, Radcliffe had retired from writing and Burney had not published since *Camilla* in 1796. When a new novel, *The Wanderer*, at last appeared in 1814, it failed. Burney had come to seem old-fashioned. Austen's very first reviewer admired *Sense and Sensibility* as an 'agreeable lounge' but conceded its 'want of *newness*'.[4] The danger of cultivating too unregulated a sensibility had, after all, been an issue rather thoroughly canvassed in the 1790s, both in discursive prose, as in Wollstonecraft's *A Vindication of the Rights of Woman*, and in novels such as Radcliffe's *The Mysteries of Udolpho*. In fact none of the six novels that Austen completed seems fully engaged with more recently fashionable literary trends.

The Prince Regent's librarian, James Stanier Clarke, amused Austen by recommending that she 'delineate in some future Work the Habits of Life and Character and enthusiasm of a Clergyman' (*L*, 16 November 1815), or, failing that, try her hand at 'any Historical Romance illustrative of the History of the august house of Cobourg' (*L*, 27 March 1816). But however inappropriate his suggestions they are those of a man with up-to-date literary tastes. His first recommendation was that Austen should write a novel that would appeal directly to the Evangelical readership that had made Hannah More's *Cœlebs in Search of a Wife* (1808) so sensational a success that it ran through fourteen editions in five years. His second was that she write a novel that incorporated its domestic concerns with the life of the nation. Jane Porter's *Thaddeus of Warsaw* (1802) was to reach its tenth edition in 1819, and following in its wake was a sequence of novels, several of them like Lady Morgan's *The Wild Irish Girl* (1806) and Christian Johnstone's *Clan-Albin* (1819), subtitled 'A National Tale'. It was Jane Porter, too, who, in *The Scottish Chiefs* (1810), combined the national tale and the historical novel, giving Walter Scott the clue that was to prompt the series of Scottish novels that began with *Waverley* (1814). Scott also acknowledged a debt to Maria Edgeworth's Irish novels but Edgeworth did more than instigate the fashion for national tales. In novels such as *The*

Absentee and *Patronage* (1814) she showed how it was possibly to adapt to post-revolutionary times the kind of weighty ethical and political themes that had been addressed by the Jacobin novelists of the 1790s. The notion of writing a novel without a love interest may have remained as Charlotte Smith ruefully notices in *The Banished Man* (1794) 'the experiment that has often been talked of, but has never yet been hazarded' (vol. 2, pp. vi–vii), but novelists such as More and Porter were at least expanding the range of the novel by accommodating within it concerns other than courtship. By contrast, a novel by Austen such as *Emma* would easily merge with the standing stock of the circulating library, shelved as it would be alongside *Emma: or the Unfortunate Attachment* (1773), *Emma: or, the Child of Sorrow* (1776), *Emma Corbett* (1780), *Emma Dorvill* (1789), *Emma; or the Foundling of the Wood* (1803).

Jane Austen has often been represented as living sequestered from the literary life that in England centred so firmly on London, but all the evidence suggests that, on the contrary, she was as responsive to literary fashion as to fashion in clothing. On 5 March 1814, for example, she remarks to Cassandra that 'ribbon trimmings are all the fashion at Bath' in a letter that she begins because she has 'read the Corsair, mended [her] petticoat, & [has] nothing else to do' (*L*, 5–8 March 1814). It was just a month since Byron's poem had been published. Six years earlier she had been almost as quick to read Scott's *Marmion*, asking Cassandra whether she should be 'very much pleased' with it (*L*, 20–22 June 1808). This is not very surprising because Byron and Scott were the best-selling poets of the day, but in *Sanditon* the poetaster Sir Edward Denham, who thinks Scott '*tame*' in comparison with Burns, also points out that Wordsworth has 'the true soul' of poetry, and the only earlier reference to Wordsworth in a novel of which I am aware is in *The Antiquary* by Wordsworth's friend, Scott. Austen's interest in the novel, unlike her interest in poetry, was professional. There is an anxious urgency in her response to the emergence of a new novelist such as Mary Brunton: 'We have tried to get Self-controul, but in vain,' she writes, nervous of finding her 'own story & [her] own people all forestalled' (*L*, 30 April 1811). By October 1813, she was reading the novel for a second time, relieved to find nothing of 'Nature or Probability in it': 'I declare I do not know whether Laura's passage down the American River [a solo journey undertaken by the heroine in a canoe], is not the most natural, possible, every-day thing she ever does' (*L*, 11–12 October 1813). In August 1814, just months after its publication, Austen was already describing it as an affectation in Cassandra not to have read *Patronage* (*L*, 23–4 August 1814), and the following month Austen, while voicing her determination not to 'like Waverley if [she] can help it', shows that she is already perfectly aware of the name of its author: 'Walter Scott has no business to write novels, especially good ones' (*L*, 28 September 1814).

It is plain, then, that Jane Austen was as alert to the changing literary scene within which she worked as one would expect of any other ambitious author. It is much less clear what she thought of it. This is partly because of her habitual dryness. She notes that she has read *The Corsair* and mended her petticoat, but leaves the pairing of the two activities to make its own effect. The references to Byron in *Persuasion* and *Sanditon*, though they reveal a great deal about Captain Benwick and Sir Edward Denham, reveal very little about Austen's own opinion of him, and this is entirely characteristic. No doubt, as is always said, Jane Austen did admire George Crabbe, but Edmund's conviction that Fanny will be perfectly content alone in her room because, if ever she tires of Lord Macartney's *Journal of the Embassy to China*, she has 'Crabbe's Tales, and the Idler, at hand to relieve' her (*MP*, 1:16), tells us more about his insensitivities than Austen's tastes. The ambition that Jane revealed to Cassandra to become the second Mrs Crabbe – 'I will comfort *him* as well as I can, but I do not undertake to be good to her children' (*L*, 21 October 1813) – is so good a joke not because it expresses a passion for the poems but because it transposes onto the unlikely person of the Revd Crabbe the feelings that in 1813 Byron was inspiring in young women all over Britain. Her opinion of the new fashions in the novel might seem clearer. Mary Brunton, in making her heroine, Laura Montreville, so unyielding an exponent of the Christian virtues, was appealing to a fashion that Hannah More had done most to create. Austen was offended even by the spelling of More's title character, whom she insists on referring to as Caleb, sensing 'pedantry & affectation' in the 'Dipthong' (*L*, 30 January 1809). 'I do not like the Evangelicals,' she tells Cassandra, and this has prejudiced her against the novel: 'Of course I shall be delighted when I read it, like other people, but till I do, I dislike it'

(*L*, 24 January 1809). The only evidence as to how Austen did respond to the novel is a small alteration that she made to the manuscript of 'Catharine' in which Mrs Peterson measures her shock at seeing Catharine being kissed by Edward Stanley in the bower by recalling that she had bought two books for her niece, 'Blair's Sermons and Coelebs in Search of a Wife.' Maria Edgeworth, on the other hand, meets with her approval: 'I have made up my mind', she wrote to her novel-writing niece Anna, 'to like no Novels really, but Miss Edgeworth's, Yours & my own' (*L*, 28 September 1814). The titles of three of her novels, *Sense and Sensibility*, *Pride and Prejudice* and *Persuasion*, and the title that she preferred for her niece Anna's novel, 'Enthusiasm' ('something so very superior that every common Title must appear to disadvantage', *L*, 10–18 August 1814), serve surely to advertise them as novels of the Edgeworth kind, novels that function also as moral fables. On the other hand, when she insists to Anna that '3 or 4 Families in a Country Village is the very thing to work on' (*L*, 9–18 September 1814), and when she recommends that she does not stray beyond her own experience – 'Let the Portmans go to Ireland, but as you know nothing of the Manners there, you had better not go with them' (*L*, 10–18 August 1814) – she seems quite clearly to indicate that she has no ambition at all to write a novel such as *Thaddeus Of Warsaw*. But even this much can be assumed of Jane Austen only tentatively.

Many readers, for example, have understood *Mansfield Park* as Austen's own Evangelical novel. Fanny after all resists the blandishments of Henry Crawford in a manner that might be compared with Laura Montreville's virtuous determination in Brunton's *Self-Control* to overcome her feelings for the rakish Hargrave. Lionel Trilling detected a trace of 'national feeling' in *Emma*, the heroine of which finds in Donwell Abbey so perfect an embodiment of 'English verdure, English culture, English comfort' (3:6), and in *Persuasion* the sailors, Admiral Croft, Captain Harville and Captain Wentworth, seem charged not just with the defence of the nation but with establishing in the social manners that they cultivate an ideal of Englishness that will supplant the outmoded class-bound rigidities to which Anne Elliot's ridiculous father still adheres. In Sir Thomas Bertram's trip to Antigua in *Mansfield Park*, and in accounts of their voyages given by several of the characters in

Persuasion, Mrs Croft, for example – 'I have crossed the Atlantic four times, and have been once to the East Indies, and back again; and only once, besides being in different places about home – Cork, and Lisbon, and Gibraltar' (1:8) – the later novels even find ways to gesture towards the geographical expansiveness that many of Austen's contemporaries attempted, and that she herself seems most often to shun. But, though they may signal a familiarity with the most recent novelistic trends, Austen's novels scarcely conform to them. Fanny Price, for example, is surely saved by her duplicity from Evangelical heroism. She does not really refuse Henry Crawford because she doubts his principles, but because she is in love with her cousin. *Persuasion* may seem to be identified by its title, which may in any case have been supplied after Austen's death, as a fable modelled on novels by Edgeworth such as *Manoeuvring* and *Patronage*, but at the end of the novel it remains uncertain whether it is good or bad to be susceptible to persuasion, and even unclear whether that is the central question with which the novel is concerned. The later novels may share a concern with Englishness, but it would scarcely be appropriate to describe them as national tales. Rather, they are novels of the English counties, of Northamptonshire, Surrey and Somerset, almost as if their settings were chosen in conscious mockery of the more extravagant ambitions of Austen's contemporaries.

Hannah More, Austen suggests in her emendation to 'Catharine', tries to raise the novel to the status of a sermon; Edgeworth makes of it an exercise in practical moral philosophy; and Walter Scott and his predecessors attempt to secure the approval of serious-minded readers such as Henry and Eleanor Tilney by making the novel as instructive as the works of historians such as 'Mr. Hume or Mr. Robertson' (*NA*, 1:14). Austen seems sceptical of such efforts to raise the status of the novel by associating it with some other, more dignified form of writing, as she intimates when she playfully suggests to Cassandra that *Pride and Prejudice* might be improved by the inclusion of some 'solemn specious nonsense – about something unconnected with the story; an Essay on Writing, a critique on Walter Scott, or the history of Buonaparte' (*L*, 4 February 1813). Yet she yields to none of her contemporaries in the claims that she is prepared to make for the novel as the form 'in which the greatest powers of the mind are displayed, in which

the most thorough knowledge of human nature, the happiest delineation of its varieties, the liveliest effusions of wit and humour, are
conveyed to the world in the best-chosen language' (*NA*, 1:5). It is
just that her claims are differently based.

Austen's fifth novel, *Emma*, was published by John Murray, the
gentleman publisher, with a dedication to the Prince Regent, and
priced at a guinea. In all of these particulars it advertised its difference from the kind of novel that A. K. Newman was publishing
at the Minerva Press, which was priced at five shillings, and sold
almost exclusively to circulating libraries. Austen's writing career
coincided with the period in which the novel divided into two
sharply distinct kinds, one of which consisted, as Scott put it in his
review of *Emma*, of 'the ephemeral productions which supply the
regular demand of watering-places and circulating libraries' while
the other, amongst which *Emma* was to be placed, was made up of
works 'exalted and decorated by the higher exertions of genius'.[5] In
other words, by 1816 novels were of two sorts, one of which was
literature and the other of which was trash. Austen frankly enjoyed
novels of both kinds. She never lost her capacity to be entertained
by a novel such as *Margiana, or Widdrington Tower* by Mrs S. Sykes,
for example: 'We are just going to set off for Northumberland to
be shut up in Widdrington Tower, where there must be two or
three sets of Victims already immured under a very fine Villain'
(*L*, 10–11 January 1809). But she makes a sharp distinction between
such novels and the novels written by Burney and Edgeworth that
she praises in *Northanger Abbey*, and it is clear to which class she
believes her own novels belong.

The key distinction between the two kinds of novel is that one is
readable, whereas the other is rereadable. Readable novels might be
borrowed from a circulating library, but rereadable novels might be
purchased. Austen, who came from a family all of whom were 'great
Novel-readers & not ashamed of being so' (*L*, 18–19 December
1798), was one of those responsible for establishing this distinction. She read novels indiscriminately, but the novels she judged
best were those that survived rereading. It was on 'looking over
Self Control again' that she found it to be 'without anything of
Nature or Probability in it' (*L*, 11–12 October 1813), and it was
on a third reading that she decided that Sarah Burney's *Clarentine*
was 'without striking merit of any kind' (*L*, 8–9 February 1807).

But if Austen helped to establish this distinction as a reader, her practice as a novelist did much to secure it. The compliment paid Jane Austen by the Prince Regent when he let it be known through his librarian that he kept a set of her novels in both of his residences was delicate precisely because it placed Austen so firmly in the class to which she aspired, the class of novelists who merited rereading. She did not achieve that status by accident, but, in part at least, as a matter of calculation. The use of a free indirect style far more elaborate than anything attempted by her predecessors allowed Austen to seed her novels with ironic pleasures only fully available on rereading, prompting extravagant claims by later admirers such as Reginald Farrer, who insisted that *Emma*, the novel in which free indirect style is employed most elaborately, must be read more than a dozen times before it can be fully appreciated.[6] Austen joined with her contemporaries such as Maria Edgeworth, Hannah More and Walter Scott in a cooperative effort to raise the status of the novel. Her distinction is that, whereas they assumed that the novel was dignified by the subject matter that it accommodated, Jane Austen showed that the novel could secure its status as literature simply by the way in which it was written.

NOTES

1. Robert Bisset, *Douglas; or, the Highlander* (1800), vol. 3, ch. 9.
2. Deirdre Le Faye, *Jane Austen: A Family Record*, second edition (Cambridge: Cambridge University Press, 2004), p. 104. Subsequent references are included in the text.
3. David Gilson, *A Bibliography of Jane Austen*, corrected edition (Winchester: St Paul's Bibliographies, 1997), p. 25.
4. *Critical Review* 4 (February, 1812), 149–57.
5. Walter Scott, *The Quarterly Review* 14 (October, 1815), 188–9.
6. Reginald Farrer, 'Jane Austen', *The Quarterly Review* 228 (July 1917), 23–4.

27

Manners

PAULA BYRNE

Manners are key indicators of human behaviour in society. They can reveal social status and its vicissitudes – a matter of great interest in Austen's age, which was a time of rapid social mobility. 'Nothing has been longer observed,' wrote Samuel Johnson in essay 172 of *The Rambler*, 'than that a change of fortune causes a change of manners.' An 1807 lecture by Samuel Taylor Coleridge is the earliest recorded instance of the term 'manners-painter': the word was used with regard to Chaucer, but it could as well have been applied to Jane Austen as a portraitist of her own social world.

The word 'manners' had a variety of meanings in the late eighteenth century, ranging from 'character of mind' and 'general way of life; morals; habits' to 'ceremonious behaviour; studied civility'.[1] Austen's novels were written on this spectrum: she was always interested in 'character of mind'; she anatomised the 'general way of life', the morals and habits, of the English middling classes of her time; and she was exasperated by – and made comic capital out of – excessively ceremonious behaviour and over-studied civility.

The idea that novels as opposed to didactic moral treatises were a means to paint 'manners and morals' – a common pairing of terms – was relatively new and seriously controversial. The epistolary novel, which was formative of Austen's early art, emerged out of the genre of the conduct book through the agency of Samuel Richardson in the mid eighteenth century. Young women of middling class – newly literate, newly articulate – were the primary intended readers of both genres (though Henry Tilney in *Northanger Abbey* reminds Catherine that men too may enjoy and learn from novels).

Conduct books were considered to be the appropriate reading material for young women. Usually written by men, often clergy, they were repositories of moral and social advice. They represented a significant shift from the aristocratic ideals of civility and gallantry exemplified in earlier courtesy literature. Lord Chesterfield's

Letters to His Son (1774), often considered the last courtesy book, was famously described by Dr Johnson as teaching the morals of a whore and the manners of a dancing master. Conduct books addressed the newly emerging middle class rather than the aristocratic elite; the new watchword was 'Politeness', a code of behaviour that emphasised benevolence, modesty, self-examination and integrity. These virtues were seen as the product of nurture and education as opposed to innate superiority. 'Politeness' was the means by which social improvement could be realised, the passions regulated and conduct refined. 'Conversation' and the arts were inextricably linked; decorum, protocol and elegant ease were all linked to an ethical code of civic virtue.

Conduct books gave advice on how women should behave during courtship and marriage, and how they should be dutiful daughters, wives and mothers. One of the most popular and influential was John Gregory's *A Father's Legacy to his Daughters* (1774), which contained sections on religion, conduct and behaviour, friendship, love and marriage. His precepts included not eating in public, being silent in company and keeping one's intelligence and education 'a profound secret, especially from the men, who generally look with a jealous and malignant eye on woman of . . . cultivated understanding'. Gregory even warned against the dangers of clever words: 'Wit is the most dangerous talent you can possess. It must be guarded with great discretion and good nature, otherwise it will create you many enemies.'[2]

Austen's relationship to the conduct book tradition was complex and ambivalent. On the one hand, Emma Woodhouse does indeed discover that her wit is her most dangerous talent: when used with indiscretion at Box Hill, it leads her astray in exactly the manner predicted by Gregory. On the other hand, another conduct book author, the sermonising James Fordyce, suffers the indignity of being made the favoured reading matter of Mr Collins in *Pride and Prejudice*. The key to the paradox is the distinction between theory and practice: Jane Austen valued good manners in action, but scorned those who did not practise what they preached. That is why her chosen form was the novel, in which the code of politeness could be dramatised (and sometimes ironised) rather than reduced to a set of rules.

Nevertheless, as a realist, she ensured in her novels that her characters' conduct was commensurate with the conventions of polite society. Her concern with realistic detail can be seen in her advice to her would-be-novelist niece Anna. One of her objections to Anna's draft novel was that the hero was too predictable: 'a handsome, amiable, unexceptionable Young Man (such as do not much abound in real Life)' (*L*, 28 September 1814). But she also took issue with the more local matter of a point of etiquette that Anna has got wrong: 'Remember, she is very prudent; – you must not let her act inconsistently . . . a woman in her situation would hardly go there, before she had been visited by other Families' (*L*, 9–18 September 1814). She had previously corrected other social faux pas: 'As Lady H. is Cecilia's superior, it w^d not be correct to talk of *her* being introduced; Cecilia must be the person introduced' (*L*, ?mid-July 1814). She told Anna that she had 'scratched out the Introduction between Lord P. & his Brother, & Mr Griffin. A Country Surgeon . . . would not be introduced to Men of their rank.' She also advised her to keep her setting in England: 'Let the Portmans go to Ireland, but as you know nothing of the Manners there, you had better not go with them. You will be in danger of giving false representations' (*L*, 10–18 August 1814).

For the social historian, Austen's own novels are a fascinating repository of the manners of 'polite' society. Morning calls, for example, were part of everyday life for those in the middling ranks, especially when in town. The etiquette of calling was a firmly established ritual in society, and the calling card an essential part of introductions, invitations and visits. Sending compliments was the most basic form of polite notice and would require some acknowledgement in return. Compliments were sent to effect introductions, to enquire after health, to take leave and to decline invitations, to offer congratulation and condolence and to express gratitude for hospitality. (In *The Watsons* calls are always made to Mrs Edwards the morning after a ball.) 'Visiting and visited is the whole of a Woman's life in England,' observed one commentator.[3]

A lady would start making calls as soon as she arrived in town. She remained in her carriage while her servant took her card and it was presented to the mistress of the house, who would then decide whether or not to receive the visitor. Calls could only be made on 'At

Home days' and usually lasted between twenty and thirty minutes. If the mistress was 'not at home', it was a rejection of the visitor, though not necessarily an insult. For a first call, it was advisable to leave the card without inquiring as to whether or not the mistress was at home, leaving her to make the next step. Cards were placed on a silver salver or in a bowl. A turned down corner indicated that the card had been delivered in person, rather than delivered by a servant. It was good manners to call on neighbours who had left cards. A call should be returned with a call, and a card with a card, within one week. In *Pride and Prejudice*, Jane waits at home every morning for a fortnight for Miss Bingley to return her visit or to send a note, and, when she does finally appear, the shortness of the visit and the 'alteration of her manner' spell out that the friendship is over.

Austen's real interest, however, is not the minutiae of these conventions, but the ways in which they can be morally revealing. She could be scathing about the social cachet of the calling card. In *Persuasion*, Sir Walter Elliot and his daughter Elizabeth are highly offended that calling cards are left 'by people of whom they knew nothing', but when they are reconciled with their aristocratic relations they insist that 'the cards of Dowager Viscountess Dalrymple, and the Hon. Miss Carteret' should 'be arranged wherever they might be most visible' (*P*, 2:4). Likewise, social climber Lucy Steele in *Sense and Sensibility* 'had never been happier in her life than she was on receiving Mrs. John Dashwood's card' (2:4). Lady Middleton plans to leave her card with the new Mrs Willoughby, but only 'in the interests of her own assemblies' (*S&S*, 2:10). By contrast, in *Persuasion* Admiral Croft's disregard for etiquette is presented in a favourable light: in one of the cancelled chapters at the end of the novel, he overrules Anne's instinct to leave her card and insists that she enters his home as a friend. These distinctions are symptomatic of Austen's loathing of hypocrisy and snobbery, and her conviction that sincerely good manners are bound up with goodness of heart rather than social status.

Polite society in Austen's time was predicated upon strict standards of decorum, particularly for women. Chaperoning was of vital importance for young women of marriageable age: it was not acceptable for a young unmarried woman to be alone in the company of a gentleman (save for close family friends). Mrs Jennings agrees to chaperone the Dashwood sisters in London and Mrs Allen takes on the role for Catherine Morland. Nor was it considered proper for a gentlewoman to travel on public coaches unescorted. Lady Catherine expresses disapproval even of two women 'travelling post' by themselves. This is one reason why General Tilney 'acted neither honourably nor feelingly – neither as a gentleman nor as a parent' in dismissing Catherine Morland from Northanger Abbey, forcing her to travel seventy miles post, 'alone, unattended' (*NA*, 2:13). It was even regarded as indecorous for a woman to walk alone in a public place. Elizabeth Bennet transgresses this rule by walking to see her sister at Netherfield – in fact she even runs!

Women were discouraged from writing to men until there was a formal engagement between them. Mary Crawford and Edmund Bertram do not correspond with one another, as this would be a breach of propriety, so they use Fanny Price as a conduit. Elinor Dashwood in *Sense and Sensibility* is convinced that Marianne is secretly engaged to Willoughby, since she writes to him: 'if we find they correspond, every fear of mine will be removed'. When she sees a letter from Edward Ferrars to Lucy Steele she concludes, 'a correspondence between them by letter, could subsist only under a positive engagement, could be authorized by nothing else' (*S&S*, 1:22). The fact that Marianne is corresponding with Willoughby in the absence of an engagement indicates that she is a rebel against the constraints of decorum.

Like Catherine Morland in *Northanger Abbey*, Marianne is also guilty of the social impropriety of riding in an open carriage with a young man she barely knows. She accepts presents from Willoughby and allows him to call her by her Christian name: these forms of behaviour were frowned upon in conduct books. Elinor constantly censures her sister's social indiscretions, but it is hard not to sympathise with Marianne's comment that 'if the impertinent remarks of Mrs Jennings are to be proof of the impropriety in conduct, we are all offending every moment of all our lives' (*S&S*, 1:13). Marianne, in contravention of all conduct book rules, pointedly refuses to conform to false modesty in courtship: 'I have erred against every commonplace notion of decorum; I have been open and sincere where I ought to have been reserved, spiritless, dull and deceitful: – had I talked only of the weather and the roads, and had I spoken only once in ten minutes, this reproach would have been spared' (1:10). For Marianne, modesty in courtship is a 'disgraceful sub-jection of reason to common-place and mistaken notions' (1:11). This is a sentiment that could have come straight from the mouth of Mary Wollstonecraft. Austen's authorial voice is much more sympathetic to Marianne than some critics allow: she shares some of her character's scorn for the 'common-place and mistaken notions' of proper female behaviour.

Austen seems to have had little patience with the female ritual of 'coming out'. There was a whole literature about the complex con-ventions of this practice, which meant to be introduced to society and thus to become a commodity on the marriage market. As a girl Jane Austen wrote a very funny parody on the subject. Two sisters excitedly make their first entrée into the world, after being given solemn warnings and advice about the dangers of society, only to find themselves merely drinking tea in all-female company: '"The long-expected Moment is now arrived" (said she) "we shall soon be in the world" – In a few Moments we were in Mrs Cope's par-lour' ('A Collection of Letters'). In a letter to her niece Anna, Jane Austen shows her admiration for one of Anna's fictional charac-ters who disapproves of the ritual: 'what he says about the madness of otherwise sensible Women, on the subject of their Daughters coming out, is worth its' weight in gold' (*L*, 10–18 August 1814).

Tom Bertram in *Mansfield Park* gets into a 'dreadful scrape' at Ramsgate over a question of female protocol in regard to 'coming out'. He flirts with the younger sister who is 'not out' and ignores her elder sister who is 'out'. In *Pride and Prejudice*, much to Lady Catherine's mortification, all of the younger Bennet sisters are 'out' before the older ones are married. Elizabeth's reply kicks against the shackles of propriety: 'I think it would be very hard upon younger sisters, that they should not have their share of society and amuse-ment because the elder may not have the means or inclination to marry early' (2:6). Mary Crawford complains about the extreme changes in behaviour between girls who are 'out' and those who are not: 'manners as well as appearance are . . . so different' (*MP*, 1:5).

Convention dictated that country gentlemen of leisure concerned themselves with hunting, shooting and conversations on politics. Women of a respectable class were expected to confine them-selves to indoor activities (needlework, music, reading of improving books – hence the vigorous debate in the period about whether or not novels were acceptable matter). Female conversation turned on neighbours, frocks and balls. When Anne Elliot in *Persuasion* shows interest in current affairs, she is marking herself out as a woman prepared to push at the barrier of what was deemed acceptable behaviour. Austen was often less interested in observing the customs of the day than in showing her heroines transgressing them.

Politeness and true manners were inextricably linked with education and nurture. On 3 July 1813 Jane Austen wrote to her brother Frank about their mutual nieces: 'We have the pleasure however of hearing that they are thought very much improved at home – Harriet in health, Cassy in manners. – The latter *ought* to be a very nice Child – Nature has done enough for her – but Method has been wanting . . . She will really be a very pleasing Child, if they will only exert themselves a little.' 'Manners', then, come from a combination of 'Nature' and the careful nurture of sensible parents ('if they will only exert themselves a little'). 'Politeness', then, meant more than good external manners: it was a code of behaviour definitive of gentility, a code that could be learned through 'Method' in childhood and experience in adolescence. It was not predetermined by one's status at birth.

Austen satirised the excessively ceremonious behaviour and overstudied civility that sometimes characterised the upper echelons of the gentry. Many of her most 'well-born' characters are moral hypocrites or lacking in warmth and openness – two of her most damning charges. Mr Elliot in *Persuasion* has external polish and good breeding but Anne discovers that 'he was not open'. Like her creator, Anne 'prized the frank, the open-hearted, the eager character beyond all others' (2:5). Thus, 'Admiral Croft's manners were not quite of the tone to suit Lady Russell, but they delighted Anne. His goodness of heart and simplicity of character were irresistible' (2:1).

Notions of precisely what constituted 'gentlemanly behaviour' in the late Georgian era were complex and open to debate. Mr Woodhouse, for example, is associated with 'quaint, old-fashioned politeness' rather than 'modern ease' (*E*, 2:17). Possessing an 'easy manner' was not necessarily synonymous with true gentility. Henry Crawford and Frank Churchill have 'easy manners', but they are associated with French dandyism and affectation. The exemplar of the English gentleman is Mr Knightley. He makes his marriage proposal to Emma 'in plain, unaffected, gentlemanlike English' (*E*, 3:15) and his definition of a true gentleman includes 'English delicacy towards the feelings of other people' (1:18).

The question of whether a person's observable 'manners' in the sense of 'polite behaviour' reveal or conceal their 'manners' in the sense of 'character of mind and morals' was at the core of Austen's world. Perhaps the key question was the true nature of good breeding or 'politeness'. Characters such as General Tilney in *Northanger Abbey* and Sir Thomas Bertram in *Mansfield Park* are extremely 'well-bred' and yet their behaviour is morally culpable. To be well born was not necessarily to be well bred. Lady Middleton in *Sense and Sensibility* and Elizabeth Elliot in *Persuasion* have 'elegant' and 'well-bred manners', but they are cold and selfish. In a striking phrase, Anne Elliot refers to the 'heartless elegance of her father and sister' (*P*, 2:10). Darcy has a 'noble mien', but he is 'haughty, reserved, and fastidious, and his manners, though well bred, were not inviting' (*P&P*, 1:4). The Bingley sisters are well-bred women of fashion but proud and contemptuous, whereas 'in their brother's manners there was something better than politeness; there was good humour and kindness' (*P&P*, 1:17). Again, Austen reveals the fault-lines between theory and practice: in theory, 'politeness' embodied both elegance of manners and the virtues of 'good humour and kindness', but in practice 'manners and morals' did not always go together.

Jane Austen repeatedly ironises the term 'well-bred', nowhere more damningly than in the case of Lady Middleton: 'As it was impossible, however, now to prevent their coming, Lady Middleton resigned herself to the idea of it with all the philosophy of a well-bred woman, contenting herself with merely giving her husband a gentle reprimand on the subject five or six times every day' (*S&S*, 1:21). True good breeding comes not from birth, station or social nuance, but from the heart. It manifests itself in the gift of sensitivity and what would now be called emotional intelligence. It can come from unusual quarters, as when an embarrassing silence in *Pride and Prejudice* is broken by a walk-on bit-part player, who almost seems to be invented for the specific purpose of revealing the true nature of good manners: 'Mrs Annesley, a genteel, agreeable looking woman, whose endeavour to introduce some kind of discourse proved her to be more truly well bred than either of the others; and between her and Mrs Gardiner, with occasional help from Elizabeth, the conversation was carried on' (*P&P*, 3:3).

NOTES

1. Definitions 8–10 of 'manner(s)' in Dr Johnson's *Dictionary*.
2. John Gregory, *A Father's Legacy to his Daughters* (1774), pp. 30–3.
3. See Amanda Vickery, *The Gentleman's Daughter: Women's Lives in Georgian England* (New Haven and London: Yale University Press, 1998), p. 209.

28

Medicine, illness and disease

JOHN WILTSHIRE

Jane Austen does not give much attention to doctors. Doctoring is another matter, and plays a significant part in the novels. This entry begins by sketching the 'medical world' at the time Austen was writing, and then goes on to look at the various forms of amateur medical treatment which the novels record. The presentation of disease is uncommon in texts which are predominantly comic – though there are examples of serious fevers – but the everyday paraphernalia of illness experience – drops, powders, waters, tonics, rhubarb and court plaister – is the source of much insight and amusement. Austen is interested in illnesses' cultural aspects, in the patient's use of the body for social advantage and in the entertainment to be extracted from hypochondria in its various forms. At the same time, the novels also understand how social conditions register themselves in the body, especially in the bodies of women. Sexuality and illness being often intertwined, the entry ends with a brief look at sex and embodiment in these texts.

'The Practice of Medicine, in a comprehensive sense, is conducted in this country, by Physicians, Surgeons and Apothecaries: for, however one profession may be independent of another, the prevalence of custom has given them such a relation, as renders them constituent parts of the same structure.' This definition was given by John Coakley Lettsom, in the introduction to the second edition of William Falconer's *A Dissertation on the Influence of the Passions upon Disorders of the Body* (1791). Lettsom's inclusion of apothecaries was liberal and progressive: it was not until the Apothecary Act of 1815 that the role of these men, who did in fact provide medical care to most people, was recognised, and their profession regulated. His sketch is generous, if incomplete – midwives at least should be added – but this tripartite division was generally accepted.

Physicians were educated at Oxford and Cambridge, or, far more likely, had degrees from one of the Scottish medical faculties. They were scarce, expensive and practised largely in the metropolis as members of the London College of Physicians, though they might be consulted and give medical advice by post. Surgeons, whose status as gentlemen was compromised by their intimacy with the body, would serve an apprenticeship, as John Keats did with Thomas Hammond from 1810–1815, and perform operations, including dentistry. The Royal College of Surgeons of London was established in 1800. Apothecaries were theoretically forbidden to give advice as well as sell drugs, but often acted as doctors to the poor, and made their business out of compounding and supplying medicines. In practice, the division between surgeon and apothecary is hazy. A 'surgeon' would prescribe and an 'apothecary' would carry out surgery. A medical practitioner would set himself up in business in a town and, if successful, be known as the 'doctor' and honoured with the title 'Mr'.[1]

'Mr' Perry, the only important medical practitioner in Austen, is always known by that title, just as the doctor who treated Frances Burney's husband Alexandre d'Arblay during his last illness in Bath in 1818–19 was 'Mr' Hay. Perry (introduced as 'the apothecary', *Emma*, 1:2) attends to Harriet's 'putrid sore throat' (*E*, 1:13), Mr Woodhouse's biliousness and also (the reader might assume) delivers Mrs Weston's baby. Men like these competed for business in an overcrowded profession. It is an 'advertising Surgeon' who could 'form a separate establishment' in his burgeoning resort that Mr Heywood is in search of when his carriage is overturned at the opening of *Sanditon*. Heywood would have seen the same sort of advertisement in *The Morning Post* as that scanned by Edmund Bertram in *Mansfield Park* (3:3): 'To Parents and Guardians – WANTED an APPRENTICE, by a Surgeon and Apothecary . . . in a principal Watering Place.' Surgeons and apothecaries were thus, for all practical purposes, the same outside London – general medical practitioners. As Leigh Hunt wrote in 1817, some apothecaries 'may take rank in our estimation as physicians, sometimes above them, if they are good surgeons also . . . in a village, for instance, where there is no physician, he may be undoubtedly one of the most valuable members of society.'[2]

The title of James Parkinson's frequently reprinted 1800 handbook illuminates the medical man's role outside the big towns and cities: *The Villager's Friend and Physician, or a familiar address on the preservation of health . . . supposed to be delivered by a Village Apothecary, with cursory observations on the treatment of children, on sobriety, industry, etc., intended for the promotion of Domestic Happiness.* As this makes clear, the responsibilities of such a doctor in a smaller community extended into the ethical realm. He would be an elder to the village, dispensing helpful advice as well as drugs. Already the informal social ministry associated with the idea of the 'general practitioner' was in place, though the term itself, first used in its modern sense in 1809, took some decades to become accepted.[3] This is plain in *Emma*, too, where Mr Perry's successful rise into gentlemanly status (signalled by the possibility of his setting up a carriage) is based on his role as 'friend' to many in the community, which involves forgiving fees to those unable to pay, and listening for hours to Mr Woodhouse's conversation. The only moment in the novel in which his speech is reported – when he sympathetically suggests that Jane Fairfax's 'nervous disorder' will have been made worse, rather than better, by 'her present home' (*E*, 3:9) – fills out Perry's role as a humane and kindly man, whose expertise is as much psychological as physical. Falconer's book is one of several which suggest how widely the relation between mental state, social conditions and the body's vulnerability was understood.

Other novelists of the period, though, offer much fuller representations of 'the doctor' as repository of social wisdom than Austen. Burney's *Cecilia* (1782), praised by Austen in *Northanger Abbey*, is a good example. Dr Lyster is a physician who borrows much of his advice from Samuel Johnson, suggesting, for example, to Cecilia, the much harassed heroine, that 'Thought, after all, has a cruel spite against happiness . . . Run about and divert yourself; 'tis all you have for it' (vol. 4, bk. 8, ch. 7). To Dr Lyster, 'that sagacious and friendly man', who 'found it impossible to study the human frame, without a little studying the human mind' is given the moral: 'The whole of this unfortunate business . . . has been the result of PRIDE and PREJUDICE' (vol. 5, bk. 10, ch. 10). In the same mould is Dr Norberry of Amelia Opie's *Adeline Mowbray* (1804). Scathing and impatient with Adeline's romantic ideals, he is the unpretentious idiomatic voice of common sense, a 'blunt but benevolent man' who cuts through much fashionable talk about nerves, and 'prescribes' for the family's psychological as well as physical health (ch. 14). In Mary Brunton's *Self-Control* (1810) the outwardly rough but actually kind Dr Flint says 'I should have told your father long ago that physic was useless to him, but whimsical people must have something to amuse them, and if he had not paid for my pills, he would for some other man's' (ch. 17). The doctor in her *Discipline* (1815) has the same no-nonsense but kindly manner: '"By the time you are a little older, Miss Percy", said the doctor, "you . . . will not run the risk of being thought crazy, by showing more sensibility than other people"' (ch. 24). Thus doctors were often presented by female novelists as the down-to-earth debunkers of fashionable complaints. 'The polite system of nerves' (ch. 6) is similarly treated with robust contempt by the hospital doctor Frumpton in Maria Edgeworth's *Patronage* (1814).

Supplementing local doctors was an enormous range of folk and informal medicine. Amateurs like clergymen and even farmers with an interest in medicine sometimes functioned as a community's effective physician. The last decade of the century saw the rise of the druggist, whose shops supplied medicines to patients at a fraction of the cost of an apothecary's attendance, and thus further facilitated medical self-help (Loudon, *Medical Care*, p. 133). Though even Catherine Morland realises that 'neither poison nor sleeping potions [were] to be procured, like rhubarb, from every druggist' (*NA*, 2:10), they did supply patent medicines, like James' Fever Powder, dismissed by his friend Johnson as quite useless, but still going strong well into the nineteenth century. Like many others, a mother in *Patronage* 'dosed her children with every specific that was publicly advertised, or privately recommended. No creatures of their age had taken such quantities of Ching's lozenges, Goldbold's elixir, or Dixon's antibilious pills' (ch. 20).

In Austen, the amateur lady doctor is presented most fully in Mrs Norris. Aunt Norris enjoys her time with the gardener at Sotherton, 'for she had set him right as to his grandson's illness, convinced him it was an ague, and promised him a charm for it' (*MP*, 1:10). She affects concern about the 'poor old coachman' who is hardly able to drive the carriage, she says, 'on account of the rheumatism which I had been doctoring him for, ever since Michaelmas' (2:2) and which she claims to have cured at last; scrounging soup from the big house she hastens off to nurse a sick maid. Much medical attention is really at this folk level – the provision of lavender drops (*S&S*, 2:6) or arrowroot (*E*, 3:9) and assorted other specifics or remedies. But Austen draws her reader's attention mainly to the abuse of social power the assumption of the doctoring role allows Mrs Norris (and to a lesser extent Diana Parker in *Sanditon*). The cover of kindness allows Mrs Norris to interfere in the lives and bodies of her inferiors. One might say that in such figures the ideology of 'benevolence', so much the source of genteel self-satisfaction in this period, is scanned for its hidden virus.

Other informal medical practices in the background of the novels include the cult of cold water, and of sea-bathing, and the taking of the waters at Bath, Leamington and other spas. In 1789 George III put the royal stamp of approval on the idea of sea-bathing when he recuperated his health at Weymouth. From that time forth the resorts on the south coast of England so copiously mentioned in Austen's novels flourished. The cult was not a matter of pleasurable exercise: it involved being taken into the sea in a horse-drawn vehicle, and being 'dipped'. Johnson 'used to call Tattersall the old Dipper of Brighton, "Dr Naked"'.[4] The practice was widely supposed to deliver a salutary bracing shock which would strengthen the 'fibres'; the sea at Sanditon, claims Mr Heywood, though, is both 'relaxing' *and* 'fortifying' (*S*, 2). Even Mary Musgrove bathes at Lyme in November (*P*, 2:2). The 'chilly and tender' Creole Miss Lambe in *Sanditon* has to be accompanied in the bathing machine by Miss Parker, so fearful is she of the cold water dip. And as *Sanditon* makes clear, one result of the birth of the consumer society was a greatly increased, even obsessive, attention to the body, its supposed illnesses and needs.

Then as now, there is no accounting for some informal medical practices. But they flourished because the number of effective drugs could be counted on one hand. Much progress was made in understanding the structure of the body in the later eighteenth century, largely through the work of John and William Hunter, but pharmaceutical progress was a different matter. One important new drug was discovered – digitalis or the foxglove, which regulated the heart when carefully prescribed – but for the most part all a doctor could offer was opium in various compounded forms. The differentiation of one disease from another remained primitive; in the writings of eighteenth- and early nineteenth-century physicians, the conception of infectious fevers, their modes of transmission and the remedies proposed are 'still almost medieval'.[5] Indeed, the eighteenth century is not usually considered as a time of great medical progress. The conception of the body current was generally the same at the end as at the beginning: a hydraulic model of pressures, inputs and outputs, fluids and obstructions, in which the body was considered less as a congeries of distinct but interacting organs than as a unified system – so that gout, 'repelled' from the feet, might manifest itself as the same condition in another part of the body. Yet a comparison of Bartholomew Parr's *London Medical Dictionary* of 1809 with Robert James's *Medicinal Dictionary* of 1743–5 is illuminating.[6] James's is a ragbag of iatromechanical, iatrochymical, Boerhaavian and Galenic notions. Many entries in Parr's *Dictionary* offer a discriminating assessment of recent competing theories, are sceptical and rational in tone and make clear how much is not known.

Nevertheless, physiology in the eighteenth century did have a very significant influence on culture and the impress of this is present in Austen's novels. Experiments performed on animals to test their responsiveness to stimulation of various kinds were widely carried out, and were famously excoriated by Johnson in *Idler* 17 in 1758. But such experiments on 'sensibility' and 'irritability' seem to have coalesced with the notion of natural 'sensibility' as propagated in Shaftesbury's *Characteristics* of 1711 to initiate a new or more refined definition of the genteel. It is as if the medical understanding of sensibility offered a platform or substrate for the philosophical and cultural elevation which Shaftesbury had proposed. The discovery that sensibility, both a physiological capacity and a moral endowment, might vary among individuals allowed the quality to become a marker of superiority, and, more broadly of class difference. 'Nerves' were the lady's claim to superior social status, the mark, indeed, of her being a lady. At the same time, sensibility was not gender-specific. Thus 'sensibility' is laid claim to by Robert Ferrars as well as by Marianne Dashwood (that benevolence out of which both Mrs Elton and Mrs Norris make so much personal capital is closely allied). Sensibility is so interesting because it twists between the social and physiological realms: Marianne's natural sensitivity is heightened, and to her validated, by cultural fashion. It has both a material aspect – as a reflection of real social conditions – and a cultural aspect – as a sign of delicacy and refinement. The contempt with which Austen treats most of her characters with 'complaints' of whatever kind does not obscure her recognition of this.

Though she is most perceptive about the social and cultural aspects of patienthood and symptomatology, there are certainly 'real' illnesses in Austen's fictions. Fevers, 'continued, intermittent, and eruptive', or what we should call 'acute infective disorders . . . dominated the practice of ordinary medical practitioners of the eighteenth and nineteenth centuries' (Loudon, *Medical Care*, p. 62). This state of things is reflected in the novels: Harriet Smith's 'putrid sore throat' signals not just the common cold, but an infection, which might at the worst be typhus or typhoid. Most fully presented is Marianne Dashwood's fever, brought on by imprudence in sitting about in her wet shoes and stockings. Elinor at first acts as the home nurse, 'forcing proper medicines on her', but next day feels it necessary to call in 'the Palmers' apothecary', Mr Harris, who, 'allowing the word "infection" to pass his lips, gave instant alarm' (*S&S*, 3:7). He prescribes what are described as 'cordials' and visits every day. The fever remits for a while, but on the third day – thus a 'tertian fever' – comes on more strongly, and the high temperature leads to delirium. Meeting Willoughby in the lobby of Drury Lane, Sir John tells him abruptly that Marianne is 'dying of a putrid fever' (*S&S*, 3:8). Elinor feels Marianne's pulse (this had become common practice since the advocacy of Floyer in the early eighteenth century[7]) and is concerned enough to send for Mr Harris, who presumably has to ride across country at night, once more. Like most local surgeon-apothecaries, Mr Harris works hard: he attends this genteel patient at five in the morning, and again at eight and at four the same afternoon. Each time he instigates 'a fresh mode of treatment' (*S&S*, 3:7) Perhaps he tries quinine – one of the more effective medicines. Eventually Marianne passes through a crisis and recovers.

Tom Bertram's illness is even more serious. His fever is brought on by 'a neglected fall, and a good deal of drinking' (*MP*, 3:13). After some time in bed he is brought back to Mansfield, where his fever increases at first and then remits. But 'some strong hectic symptoms . . . seemed to seize the frame on the departure of the fever' (3:14). *The London Medical Dictionary* defines 'hectic' thus: 'by this term is meant slow, but long continued, fevers, which induce consumption, and impair the strength . . . Intemperate drinkers, and those who indulge in excesses of any kind, are very subject to it' (vol. 1, p. 734). Tom is attended by the higher-ranking 'physician', not your ordinary surgeon-apothecary, who warns Sir Thomas of the danger: 'They were apprehensive for his lungs' (*MP*, 3:14). The phrase 'to seize the frame' is perhaps a polite reference to vomiting or the spitting of blood. But since Tom does not in fact have consumption, Austen may be describing another disease. In bed, Tom has been attended only by servants, and the prolonged immobility might well be supposed to lead to pneumonia. Austen's descriptions of illness avoid the technical – they would have seemed quaint and out of date if she had not – but in these two instances she charts the progress of the disease with some care.

Her interest is really, though, in the social and cultural aspects of illness behaviour. Throughout the novels she observes the way people use physical symptoms for the purposes of social advantage. She anticipates the thinking of medical sociologists in her detection of the 'secondary gains' of illness – the advantages of power and access to services that the ill, or the sickly, can extract from their identity as sick persons, or, in the neologism of the time, as 'invalide'. Secondary gain enables Mrs Churchill, for instance, to call Frank to her side whenever she feels like it, and Mary Musgrove to exploit her sister as a nanny and servant. The comedy of hypochondria is most fully developed in the fragment of *Sanditon*, where Arthur Parker, lusty and lazy, excuses his indolence because he is 'very subject to Perspiration, and there cannot be a surer sign of Nervousness' (*S*, 10). By 1817 the invalid has become an important consumer identity: whole capitalist enterprises, like the resort of Sanditon, are generated to supply the needs and desires of people who occupy the 'sick role'.

But there is another side to this: illness in Austen's novels is not simply assumed or 'put on'. The symptoms complained of by Mrs Bennet, Mr Woodhouse and Mary Musgrove – even of Marianne Dashwood – may be heterogeneous and vague, but they are not perceived to be without meaning, or merely, in the first three instances, as comic foibles, presented for the reader's amusement. They signal, if not physiological or organic causation, certainly causation of a sort. They register, in their different ways, social conditions, and in particular the malaises, the 'nervous diseases' of a leisured class that were identified and described early in the eighteenth century by George Cheyne as 'the English malady'.[8] Mary Musgrove is a sketch of the lady with no intellectual interests and little to do, whose symptoms are a prefiguring of that recursion of vacuity and idleness into physical malaise found in many genteel figures of Victorian and Edwardian life, real as well as fictional. Mrs Bennet's 'nerves' and tremblings and faintings – through which she vainly lays claim to a fashionable heightened sensitivity – are witnessed by a daughter who must endure her mother's extravagant bodily performances, but the novelist allows the reader to deduce that they are not merely embarrassing and absurd. They signal, and are a conversion of, frustration, including sexual frustration, and the need to obtain control of some sort.

Mrs Bennet's pride in the provision of ample meals might be read as another symptom of her social and sexual quandary. In Austen medical matters are often, in fact, intertwined with the comedy of food. The bringing of nourishment or drink as comfort to the sick or bereaved must be universal, and is another source of amusement in these novels of everyday life. Mrs Jennings offers the Constantia wine that her husband found useful for the 'cholicky gout' as a cure for Marianne's broken heart (*S&S*, 2:8); the Bertrams produce gooseberry tart as a salve for the dreadfully homesick little Fanny Price (*MP*, 1:2). Mr Woodhouse's hypochondria permits him to impose his culinary tastes on his visitors, and the tussles over food between Emma and her father are a recurrent source of the novel's comedy. Arthur Parker entertains Charlotte Heywood by telling her that toast without butter 'hurts the Coats of the Stomach' (*S*, 10). On the other hand, a glass of wine (*S&S*, 2:8) is found useful on more than one occasion when a woman is suffering from headache or faintness.

Austen's interest in the body, then, extends well beyond the medical. Whilst the physiology of her characters is usually presented in generic terms, with heroes 'tall and handsome', or with 'air and countenance', sexuality is everywhere understood, understated and assumed. There are clear examples: Darcy's 'admiration' of Elizabeth Bennet when her face and eyes are 'brightened by the exercise' (*P&P*, 1:8) of running across fields and leaping over stiles. Less overt is General Tilney's interest in Catherine Morland after she tears into Milsom-street to make her apologies to the Tilneys: 'the general attended her himself to the street-door, saying everything gallant as they went downstairs, admiring the elasticity of her walk' (*NA*, 1:13) or Edmund Bertram's fascination with Mary Crawford's tripping off to play the harp, an instrument whose role in courtship not only depended on sweet music, but also on the rare display of a lady's body as she plucked the strings. Telling, too, is the sentence in *Sense and Sensibility* when the ground for Elinor's knowledge of Brandon's interest in Marianne is explained: 'She watched his eyes, while Mrs Jennings thought only of his behaviour' (3:6), a Richardsonian moment, the converse of which is Henry Crawford's sardonic dismissal of Maria's love for her fiancé: 'I could see it in her eyes, when his name was mentioned' (*MP*, 1:5).

More broadly, the novels are often structured around a contrast between healthy and unhealthy bodies. Emma, declares Mrs Weston early in the novel, is 'the picture of grown-up health' (*E*, 1:5), whereas Jane Fairfax is thought vulnerable to the tuberculosis that runs in her family. 'Bless me! poor Jane is ill!' is Miss Bates's first exclamation when reading the letter that introduces her into the text (*E*, 2:1). Elizabeth Bennet's vivacity, signalled in her sparkling eyes – which so disturbingly reproduce her mother's – is contrasted with the other candidate for Darcy's hand, Lady Anne de Bourgh, much higher in social status, but repeatedly depicted as 'sickly and cross'. The novel might thus be said to argue that Elizabeth's elevation is not merely due to her personal charm and integrity but awarded also to her healthy and replenishing vitality. In *Mansfield Park*, the Bertram and Crawford set are sporty and active, whilst Fanny Price, ill nourished as a child (as the reader might assume) is not strong. But the novelist vigilantly wards off here any assumption that a vigorous and healthy body necessarily carries moral or ethical value by putting such an idea into the mouth of Maria (*MP*, 1:7) – a warning lost on many of the novel's critics.

Like many of her contemporaries, Jane Austen was sceptical about the fashionable cults of sensibility and 'nerves'. She treated many other illnesses just as sceptically. The Heywoods in *Sanditon*, she writes, could not afford to 'indulge in' 'Symptoms of the Gout and a Winter at Bath' (2). The crusty medical men in the novels of her contemporaries may be versions of 'Dr Johnson', but

Austen's incorporation of Johnson's intellectual disposition is far deeper, realised in her pervasive alertness to affectation, and that scorn and ridicule of medical narcissism which is powered by feeling for real distress. Many aspects of medicine and sickness behaviour in her time, though, make their way into Austen's novels. She is unique among her contemporaries in the vigilant attention she gives to illness complaints, and her last three works, in particular, focus on matters of health. Village life in *Emma* is structured around its invisible centre, Mr Perry, the doctor; *Persuasion* relates a succession of injuries, and meditates on healing and recuperation; *Sanditon* is a manic satire on medical consumerism. Jane Austen does not treat much of professional medicine, but sickness and sexuality are entertainingly entwined in all her major texts.

NOTES

1. R. W. Chapman wrote that 'a medical man is nowhere, I believe called a "doctor"', 'The Manners of the Age', Appendix to *Emma*, revised edition (Oxford: Oxford University Press, 1988) p. 515: his mistake is forgivable since the only use of the term is by the ignorant Mr Price in *MP*, who calls the ship's surgeon 'the doctor'. A 'surgeon' is called 'Dr Flint' in Mary Brunton's *Self-Control* (1810); usually, as in the case of 'the worthy doctor' Barlow in Hannah More's *Cœlebs in Search of a Wife* (1809), the term is reserved for a cleric.
2. Leigh Hunt, *The Examiner*, 7 September 1813, cited in Andrew Motion, *John Keats* (New York: Farrar, Straus, Giroux, 1997), p. 48.
3. Irving Loudon, *Medical Care and the General Practitioner 1750–1850* (Oxford: Clarendon Press, 1986), p. 1, and throughout. Subsequent references are included in the text.
4. The Marquis of Lansdowne, *The Queeney Letters* (1934), p. 258.
5. Peter Mathias, *The Transformation of England* (London: Methuen, 1979), p. 271.
6. Bartholomew Parr, M. D. *The London Medical Dictionary, including under distinct heads every branch of medicine* . . . , 3 vols. (1809). Subsequent references are included in the text.
7. Sir John Floyer, *The Physician's Pulse Watch* (1707).
8. George Cheyne, *The English Malady, or a Treatise of Nervous Diseases of all kinds* (1733).

29

Money

EDWARD COPELAND

Money in Jane Austen's novels has an uncanny way of seeming so much like our own that we run the serious mistake of thinking that it is. Everything in the Austen novels seems to add up at the cash register in the usual way – the pianos, shawls, muslins, carriages and horses – so familiar that we think we are in the same world. We are not. The Austen fictional economy draws on a real economy in a state of rapid and unsettling transition: an expanding commercial sector, a rapidly developing consumer culture, an economy tied to the ups and downs of foreign wars, high taxes, scarce capital, inadequate banking and credit systems and large sums of money to be made and spent by those who never had it before. Aggressive enclosures of common lands, consolidation of neighbouring farms and the introduction of modern agricultural improvements had brought enormous wealth and power to the great landholders. These conspicuous and deeply felt changes in the distribution and management of wealth were made even more acute by an unheard of rate of inflation in prices, punctuated by periodic economic depression. In this unstable economy, marriage, Austen's narrative mainstay, was a legitimate and common means of gaining access to all-important capital.

People without money, or living on fixed incomes, or tied to older patriarchal systems of financial support were in big trouble, or so it seemed in the 1790s when Austen's first three novels, *Sense and Sensibility* (1795, 1797), *Pride and Prejudice* (1796–7) and *Northanger Abbey* (1798–9) were conceived. These early novels share a common economic vision – the danger of losing it all, the chance of hitting it rich, huge losses, huge gains, everything riding on luck and the main chance. Austen's later novels, *Mansfield Park* (1811–13), *Emma* (1814–15) and *Persuasion* (1815–16) explore much more complex economic fictions, sometimes deeply troubling morally, as Austen reflects more widely on social changes brought about by the economic upheavals of the war years and the following post-war adjustments, a time marked by a decline in agricultural profits, an expansion of the credit economy and the sense, particularly in her last work, the unfinished *Sanditon* (1817), that the movement of money was the key to the disturbing new shifts in the arrangements of power.

The money that Jane Austen would have held in her hand, besides small coin, would have been paper, not an insignificant fact. Paper money printed for the Bank of England and backed by gold had been in circulation in England from the late seventeenth century throughout the eighteenth century, at first mostly between merchants, but with increasing circulation among the public, especially in London. People actually came to prefer the small paper notes as a protection against coins whose value had been diminished by clipping or filing. Country banks, too, printed their own currency, also backed by gold, first as advertisement to attract depositors but also as a great convenience for local people. However, on 27 February 1797, a profound alteration in the status of paper money occurred. The Prime Minister, William Pitt, driven by the enormous expense of the Continental war, declared that Bank of England notes for the first time could not be redeemed for cash, that they were inconvertible, a status that remained in effect until 15 May 1821. Pitt's actions met the obvious need to prevent the withdrawal and hoarding of gold that occurred at the threat of invasion towards the close of 1796, but the news brought a profound shake to public confidence in the economy. Contemporaries lamented the disappearance of legal gold coin and the inevitable damaging effects on the economy that paper money would facilitate: false credit and fictitious capital and 'mischievous' speculation. Most particularly, there was concern for the ravages to the poor that inflation would cause in rents and in prices of 'articles of the first necessity' – clothing, provisions, even bread.[1] Paper money and its likely effects on the economy became a central topic of public discussion and remained so throughout the stoppage of payments, though, in actual fact, 'the paper pound' did not follow the feared catastrophic depreciation that accompanied the paper currencies of France and Austria. Its lowest mark never dropped below 71 per cent of its face value. Even so, paper money was a constant focus of public anxiety and discontent during the war years and beyond.[2]

Taxes, ever increasing, kept money and the economy in public view as well. To meet Pitt's need to pay for the war, there were taxes levied in 1795 on tea, wines and spirits, wood imports, salt, insurance of ships' cargoes and hair powder. In 1797, taxes on spirits and tea were increased, and new ones were added on sugar, tobacco and horses, together with additional customs and excise duties, a new house tax and a seriously afflictive 'triple assessment' tax that sharply increased taxes on such luxuries as windows, servants and carriages. In 1798 the most significant tax of the entire period was proposed, an income tax that was implemented in 1799 as a wartime expedient. This tax was to raise 80 per cent of all the tax revenues imposed by the government between 1793 and 1815. The income tax, as contemporaries admitted, fell most heavily on those people with moderate incomes of from £200 to £600 a year, incomes that provided only a marginal hold on the consumer symbols of genteel life.

Jane Austen's interest in the economy appears in her earliest works, possibly when she was only thirteen years of age, in 'Edgar and Emma', for example, which parodies the vague economic clichés of sentimental novels by introducing 'Mr. Willmot of Willmot Lodge . . . the representative of a very ancient Family & possessed besides his paternal Estate, a considerable share in a Lead mine & a ticket in the Lottery' (ch. 2). Money comes into view in Austen's novels, however, mainly through the focussing lens of her own social rank. This group of genteel professionals, situated in the country and consisting of clergymen of the Anglican church, men in the law (preferably barristers), officers in the army and navy and rentiers retired from business and of large fortune, has been called by the historian David Spring the 'pseudo-gentry', a mischievous but sharp description of the group's social position. They were, writes Spring, 'gentry of a sort, primarily because they sought strenuously to be taken for gentry'.[3] Sandwiched between commerce and the landed gentry, the pseudo-gentry made use of consumer goods to assert their claims to social consequence. Consumer power drove the value of that negotiable concept of an income that contemporaries called the 'competence'.

Adam Smith defined the term competence in its broadest social inclusion, that is, 'whatever the custom of the country renders it indecent for creditable people, even of the lowest order, to be without'.[4] But, as John Trusler, a contemporary economist, writes in his *Domestic Management* (1819), 'What is competency to one, is not so to another.' As he explains: 'Wealth is comparative: that which would make one man rich, another shall be poor with. Every man should be able to live, and make an appearance in life, equal to his station in it.'[5] The Dashwood sisters debate its meaning in *Sense and Sensibility*. 'Come, what is your competence?' Elinor asks Marianne, and can only laugh when she gets her answer: '*Two* thousand a-year! *One* is my wealth! I guessed how it would end' (1:17).

As a comparison, a common labourer at the lowest end of the economic scale would earn around £25 a year, including extra work during harvests, a sum, according to Anna Laetitia Barbauld, on which he was expected to maintain 'himself, his wife, and half a dozen children in food, lodging, clothes, and fuel'.[6] Hannah More provides an idea of the family's diet in the recipe she recommends for them in her *Cheap Repository Tracts*: a mess of garden vegetables supplemented with 'a bit of coarse beef, a sheep's head, or any such thing', with the meat to go to the father, the working man; 'the children don't want it,' she says cheerfully, 'the soup will be thick and substantial, and requires no bread'.[7] Mary Wollstonecraft wrote to her sister of a governess's position available at £25 per annum, a situation that would provide food and shelter, but not enough money, as she knew from her own experience, to cover the cost of appropriate dress for the parlour.[8] Up a step, at £40 a year, a curate with a house and garden would have almost twice the income, but also the duty of appearing like a gentleman. As Anne Plumptre explains in *The Rector's Son* (1798), 'Placed in a situation in which they are expected to sustain the rank of gentlemen, they have scarcely the means of procuring even the common necessaries of life, much less of obtaining those superfluities which are considered as essential appendages to that of rank' (vol. 1, ch. 1). Austen's published works seldom reach this far down the scale in consumer distress, except perhaps in Mrs Smith's unfortunate situation in *Persuasion*, where there is 'the absolute necessity of having a regular nurse, and finances at that moment particularly unfit to meet any extraordinary expense' (2:5), though in her unfinished pieces, *The Watsons* and *Sanditon*, Austen seems prepared to give more attention to lives lived at the lower end of the economic spectrum.

Landed estates, however, provide the most prominent unit for measuring competences in Austen's novels: Mr Bennet, for example, has an estate worth £2,000 per annum, Mr Darcy, £10,000 per annum. An heiress's fortune, in contrast, is given as a lump sum figure, which then must be calculated for the annual income it yields, the presumption being that it is invested in the government funds at an annual interest rate of 5 per cent. This holds true in all of Austen's novels, with an exception in *Pride and Prejudice*, where the question arises of a choice between 4 or 5 per cent. Mrs Bennet, who, if she does not understand entails, does understand incomes, is scrupulous in reporting Mr Bingley's potential income, using both 4 and 5 per cent multipliers to convert his known inheritance of £100,000 into its annual income from investment in the funds: 'A single man of large fortune,' she tells Mr Bennet, 'four or five thousand a year. What a fine thing for our girls!' (1:1). Miss Grey, the heiress to £50,000 in *Sense and Sensibility*, brings Willoughby a yearly income, based on the 5 per cent multiplier, of £2,500 a year. Emma, with a fortune of £30,000, has access to an annual income of £1,500. Mrs Elton in *Emma*, who has 'so many thousands as would always be called ten; a point of some dignity', brings her 'caro sposo' an alleged addition to his clergyman's income of £500 a year (2:4). The Dashwood women, who lose Norland Park, the landed estate worth £4,000 a year, must share a diminished fortune (lump sum) among them of only £10,000, which means that by calculating its 5 per cent interest, their new annual income of £500 a year is revealed.

The great question for modern readers of Austen's novels, however, concerns the consumer power of these incomes. The effort to understand the power of incomes is not idle speculation, either in Austen's time or now. Contemporaries were actively interested in knowing the incomes of their neighbours, which were scarcely private since the values of clerical livings, landed estates and great inheritances were publicly known, but also because the topic itself was not hedged with the secrecy it possesses today. Letters and diaries sent along the news of other peoples' incomes almost as a duty. Susan Ferrier, for example, reports that her friend Anne Walker has told her that Mr Knatchbull, the groom in a recent match, 'is very handsome, and has 500 *l.* a year, so for a poor *plainish* miss it is no bad match'.[9] Jane Austen confides to Cassandra information of the same kind about their brother: 'Frank limits himself, I believe, to four hundred a year' (*L*, 7 January 1807). With the instability that an expanding consumer economy inevitably brings to hierarchies of rank, it was essential to evaluate and to fix, if possible, acceptable relationships between incomes, rank and spending practices.

The lowest competence alluded to in Austen's novels is an income of £100 a year. On this amount a '*widow* or other *unmarried Lady*, may keep a *Young Maid Servant*, and a low salary; say from 5 to 10 Guineas a year', according to Samuel and Sarah Adams in their domestic guide *The Complete Servant*.[10] This is Miss Bates's exact situation in *Emma*, where we understand her income from her having only the single servant, Patty, the maid of all work, who cooks, cleans and answers the door. 'Oh!' anxiously cries Miss Bates upon hearing that the chimney needs cleaning, 'Patty do not come with your bad news to me' (*E*, 2:9). Miss Bates's cry, no surprise to a contemporary reader, is consistent with her two cramped rooms over a shop, reached by a dark and narrow staircase. When Mrs Jennings in *Sense and Sensibility* believes that Lucy and Edward are to marry on only £100 a year, she takes immediate pity on them: 'I must see what I can give them towards furnishing their house. Two maids and two men indeed! – as I talked of t'other day. – No, no, they must get a stout girl of all works' (*S&S*, 2:14).

For Austen, a competence of £300 a year is only slightly less marginal. In *Sense and Sensibility* this sum will make Edward Ferrars comfortable as a bachelor, says Colonel Brandon, but will not enable him to marry (3:3). 'The Colonel is a ninny' (3:4), says Mrs Jennings, who as a merchant's wife understands the lower range of competences better than Colonel Brandon. Mrs Jennings is certain, though mistakenly, that Lucy, the niece of a provincial schoolmaster, will be glad enough to marry on that sum. Elinor and Edward, Lucy's superiors in rank and in consumer expectations, are 'neither of them quite enough in love to think that three hundred and fifty pounds a year would supply them with the comforts of life' (*S&S*, 3:13). They postpone their marriage until better prospects arrive. James Austen, Jane's eldest brother who was married on £300 a year, quickly discovered that it would not support his ambitious notions of a competence: a close carriage for his wife and a pack of harriers for his hunting pleasures.[11]

In *Northanger Abbey*, Mr Morland offers his son James and his intended bride, Isabella Thorpe, a clerical living of £400 per annum, which, though not to Isabella's great satisfaction, is a substantial deduction from his own income for the sake of the couple and, though not grand, makes a reasonable starting income for a young family. Fanny Price's mother in *Mansfield Park* has very near this competence in Portsmouth, though she also has a drunken husband and too many children. She keeps two servants, exactly the number that John Trusler claims that £370 a year will support. Austen supplies a trail of economic indicators by which the reader can determine the family's income: by calculating that Mrs Price came to her marriage with the same dowry as her sisters, £7,000 for each, which pays £350 a year from the 5 per cent government funds, and by adding to it her husband's income for half-pay naval officers, a standard £45 a year, it approaches the £400 competence. As Fanny admits, this sum would have made a respectable competence under the management of her Aunt Norris, though for her ill-judging mother it spells a 'scene of mismanagement and discomfort from beginning to end' (*MP*, 3:8).

A competence of £500 a year is greeted in most women's fiction as a thoroughly genteel income for a single woman. The Adams' *Complete Servant* suggests that a widow with this competence could have three servants: two women and a boy, and an occasional gardener, which is the staff the Dashwood women in *Sense and Sensibility* take to Devonshire on their £500 a year and the same number that the Austens plan to employ when they move to Bath on a similar income (*L*, 3 January 1801). Fanny Dashwood's description of life on that sum presents a revealing picture of the consumer life experienced by the Austen family on Mr Austen's retirement income: 'They will live so cheap! Their housekeeping will be nothing at all. They will have no carriage, no horses, and hardly any servants; they will keep no company, and can have no expences of any kind! Only conceive how comfortable they will be!' (*S&S*, 1:2)

At the highest income levels of the Austen family's professional rank, a competence of between £800 and £1,500 a year brings significant consumer signs along with it. Trusler suggests that £800 a year will support a carriage, though the Adamses suggest that the purchase would be more prudent for incomes between £1,000 and £1,500 a year. Mrs Dashwood in *Sense and Sensibility* sells her carriage when her income falls to only £500 a year (1:5). Jane Austen's father set up a carriage when his income reached £700 a year, but soon gave it up as too expensive (*L*, 17 November 1798; *Family Record*, p. 112).

The largest incomes in Austen's novels are most frequently reserved for the landed gentry and are characterised by the degree and kind of consumer display undertaken by their possessors. Colonel Brandon's estate, according to Mrs Jennings, is worth £2,000 a year, all debts paid, and, she marvels, has 'the best fruit-trees in the country' (*S&S*, 2:8). John Dashwood's Norland produces £4,000 a year, not including the addition of his wife's dowry and a substantial inheritance from his mother, and is spent lavishly on an expensive visit to London for the season and a showy new greenhouse for Fanny. In *Pride and Prejudice* Mr Bennet's estate is worth £2,000 a year, which he just keeps within, though without making any provisions for dowries for his daughters. Mr Darcy's £10,000 a year from the Pemberley estate is spent admirably on furniture that has 'less of splendour, and more elegance, than the furniture of Rosings' (3:1). He also refurnishes a parlour solely for his sister's pleasure and makes a substantial contribution of resources for the sake of Elizabeth to retrieve Lydia's honour, such as it is. In *Mansfield Park*, Mr Rushworth's estate of £12,000 a year supports a house in an expensive, fashionable part of London, where his wife falls into an adulterous relationship with Mr Crawford. Mr Crawford, who ignores the management of his £4,000 a year estate, spends the income on the selfish pleasures of a man-about-town. The estates in *Emma* and *Persuasion*, Donwell Abbey and Kellynch Hall, reveal their economic value through gaps in the consumer spending of their owners. The loss of the season in London for Elizabeth and Sir Walter measures the condition of the Kellynch income in precise terms. The season, according to the economic historian F. M. L. Thompson, could have been managed on an income of £5,000 in the 1790s, a sum that would explain the John Dashwoods' ready engagement of this expense. But after the war, as Thompson notes, the expenses for this luxury had doubled.[12] Mismanagement and inflation take their toll on Sir Walter's pretensions to grandeur. On the other hand, Mr Knightley's infrequent use of a carriage, so deprecated by Emma, is understood by the reader to be a prudent investment in the future of Donwell Abbey on the assumption that he sensibly invests his spare capital in improvements to his estate.

In her final novel, *Persuasion*, Austen abandons the landed estate altogether to replace it with a vision of prosperity in the professions. In this novel, the heroine refuses the opportunity to become mistress of her ancestral estate Kellynch Hall in order to marry an officer in the navy on his £25,000 prize money from the war (or £1,250 a year). But it is with *Sanditon*, the unfinished last work, that Austen takes up her most ambitious review of the contemporary economy. Astringently observed, this fragment offers an appraisal of the economic conditions of 1817, its year of conception. It probes the consequences of abandoning the landed estate as the model of the British economy. The social world of *Sanditon* appears in terms of credit, speculation and the vagaries of consumer demand with the traditional landed estate falling into the hands of the commercial classes. Lady Denham, the great lady of the novel, born into a petty trade, inherits her first husband's estate and her second husband's title. Mr Parker, eldest son and heir to his family estate, mortgages the land to the hilt in order to support his investment in the seaside resort of Sanditon. Sir Edward Denham, with a baronet's title, no money and no estate, hovers about the edges of this new cash society with his equally impecunious sister like two scavenger birds on the lookout for what they can pick up. The reordering of the economy in this novel vibrates with the possibility of bank failures (Henry Austen's bank had just collapsed), undependable credit, inadequate capital and the ever-present threat of an unsteady business partner for Mr Parker in the small-minded greed of Lady Denham. Depressed agricultural prices, empty houses and a sagging consumer market present a general and prevailing sense of economic uneasiness in *Sanditon*. Characters from classes never before allowed subjective presence in Austen's novels make their appearance in *Sanditon*: a circulating library mistress idled by a failing business, a mulatto heiress just arrived from the West Indies to be exploited, a distressed family singled out for charity subscription, a local gardener whose income must be supported against the prices of the local market. The world of *Sanditon* is hopeful and depressed, principled and naive, forward-looking and uncertain, backward-looking, too, but like Adam and Eve's melancholy backward glance at their garden, there is no hope of return. As the Parkers' carriage proceeds up the hill to their new home in Sanditon, Mrs Parker catches sight of Mr Parker's ancestral home in a protected valley and sighs for an economic past that Jane Austen suggests is gone for ever: 'It was always a very comfortable House – said Mrs Parker – looking at it through the back window with something like the fondness of regret. – And such a nice Garden – such an excellent Garden' (*S*, 4).

NOTES

1. V. H. Hewitt and J. M. Keyworth, *As Good as Gold: 300 Years of British Bank Note Design* (London: British Museum Publications and The Bank of England, 1987), pp. 28–43.
2. E. J. Hobsbawm, *The Age of Revolution: Europe, 1789–1848* (London: Cardinal, 1962), p. 121.
3. David Spring, 'Interpreters of Jane Austen's Social World: Literary Critics and Historians', in *Jane Austen: New Perspectives*, ed. Janet Todd (New York and London: Holmes & Meier, 1983), p. 60.
4. Adam Smith, *An Inquiry Into the Nature and Causes of the Wealth of Nations*, 2 vols. (Chicago: University of Chicago Press, 1976), vol. II, p. 399.
5. John Trusler, *Domestic Management, or the Art of Conducting a Family, with Economy, Frugality & Method* (1819), pp. 10–11.
6. Anna Laetitia Barbauld and John Aikin, *Evenings at Home: Or, the Juvenile Budget Opened* (1846), vol. I, pp. 229–30 (written between 1793 and 1796).
7. Hannah More, *Cheap Repository Tracts Published in the Year 1795* (1795), vol. I, 'The Way to Plenty', pp. 25–6.
8. *The Collected Letters of Mary Wollstonecraft*, ed. Janet Todd (London: Allen Lane, 2003), pp. 108–9, 177–9. Nelly Weeton, with some shock, records that she had heard of a woman who paid the governess 'only £12 a year!': *Miss Weeton: Journal of a Governess: 1807–1811*, ed. Edward Hall, 2 vols. (1936–9), vol. II, p. 21.
9. *Memoir and Correspondence of Susan Ferrier, 1782–1854*, ed. John A. Doyle (1898), p. 169.
10. Samuel and Sarah Adams, *The Complete Servant* (1825), p. 5.
11. See Deirdre Le Faye, *Jane Austen: A Family Record*, second edition (Cambridge: Cambridge University Press, 2004), p. 72. Subsequent references are included in the text.
12. F. M. L. Thompson, *English Landed Society in the Nineteenth Century* (London: Routledge & Kegan Paul, 1963), p. 26.

30

Nationalism and empire

WARREN ROBERTS

Samuel Johnson expressed an eighteenth-century cosmopolitan attitude when he defined patriotism as 'the last refuge of a scoundrel' in his *Dictionary*. Laurence Sterne voiced a similar attitude when he travelled to Paris during the Seven Years' War, and said 'it never entered my mind we were at war with France'.[1] Not everyone in England shared these perspectives, which were limited to a narrow, elite stratum. There had always been a latent, sometimes overt chauvinism in England, manifested as hostility to foreign states with which England was engaged in conflict. When Captain Robert Jenkins displayed an ear that a Spaniard had cut off in the West Indies in the 1730s the clamour for war was so great that Robert Walpole, who wanted to resolve differences with Spain through diplomacy, was forced into a war he wanted to avoid. Begun in 1739, the War of Jenkins' Ear fed into the much larger war that broke out in the following year, the War of Austrian Succession. It was in the very year that Britain entered the War of Austrian Succession, 1740, that the first performance of Thomas Arne's masque, *Alfred*, was given. Its rousing chorus, 'Rule, Britannia', was a celebration in music of Britain's naval supremacy, the source of her greatness: 'Awe with your navies every hostile land / Vain are their threats, their armies all in vain / They rule the world who rule the main.' Viewed in retrospect, Arne's 'Rule, Britannia', whose verse was written by James Thomson, was prophetic. In the decades that followed the first hearing of 'Rule, Britannia' Britain emerged victorious from an all-out struggle with France, and it was through naval superiority and power that she did so.

The War of Austrian Succession, fought between 1740 and 1748, set the stage for a larger conflict that began in the American wilderness in 1754, the French and Indian War; that war escalated into the Seven Years' War two years later, waged between 1756 and 1763 in Europe, North America, India, the West Indies and

West Africa. Britain's victory over France in this global conflict was overwhelming; out of the struggle between two imperial rivals and their diplomatic allies came a British Empire that seemed unassailable. It turned out that Britain's crushing victory over France in 1763 contained the seeds of future conflict, first the American Revolution, then the French Revolution and finally Britain's epic struggle with Napoleonic France that ended in 1815. All of these conflicts were interconnected, and all can be traced back to Britain's stunning success achieved in 1763. The Seven Years' War had been expensive, and it imposed heavy demands on the British Treasury. Since the American colonies had benefited directly from Britain's victory over France, and would benefit also from costly protective measures that had yet to be undertaken, it seemed reasonable in London that the American colonies should shoulder some of the burden. In fact, resistance to every tax measure imposed by Britain was fierce and resulted in a series of collisions that led to the American Revolution. Still smarting from the crushing defeats of the Seven Years' War, France threw her support behind the revolt of the American colonies, support that in the end proved decisive. Revenge was sweet for France, but it proved disastrous. Already burdened by the cost of earlier eighteenth-century wars, the cost of supporting the American Revolution plunged France into bankruptcy. Four years after Britain's defeat in North America, France had no choice but to address fiscal problems that proved intractable, and led to the summoning of the Estates General. Thus did the French Revolution come about, an indirect outcome of the struggle for empire between Britain and France.

There was a seismic shift of public feeling in the second half of the eighteenth century, not only in Britain but throughout Western society, and within that shift the civilised cosmopolitanism of an age of classicism and Enlightenment gave way to the turbulent forces of nationalism. One way to trace the trajectory of change is through the selection of patriotic subjects in art, in which England led the way. Benjamin West won the enthusiastic support of George III with his 1770 *The Death of General Wolfe*, a painting that portrayed Britain's victory over France in the Battle of Quebec in 1759, a turning point in the Seven Years' War. Having chosen a subject of contemporary history, one that depicted a British victory, West tapped into a vein of patriotic feeling that was present not only in

England but in France as well. During the decade of the 1780s Jacques-Louis David established himself as France's leading artist by depicting scenes of patriotic sacrifice and heroism, but within a classical context. With the eruption of the French Revolution David turned, as West had earlier, from the classical past to the present, from heroes of antiquity to contemporary heroes dedicated to the nation. Swept up in revolutionary enthusiasm, David began work in 1790 on a colossal painting, *The Tennis Court Oath*, that portrayed the same patriotic devotion he had depicted in his 1784 *Oath of the Horatii*. That David never finished *The Tennis Court Oath* is one indication of the political turbulence unleashed by the French Revolution, forces that within the period of a mere five years blew away the Revolution's political leadership. The men whose patriotic dedication David extolled in his *Tennis Court Oath* were consumed by the Revolution, and David himself was imprisoned after the fall of Robespierre and fortunate to escape with his life. Taking directions that no one in 1789 could have predicted, the Revolution abolished monarchy, undertook a systematic effort to eradicate Christianity and declared war on hostile states beyond its frontiers, initiating a period of warfare that was different in kind and scale to all previous wars.

When Britain entered the war against Revolutionary France in February 1793 it was a month after the execution of Louis XVI and in response to that event, but it was also in response to French expansion in the Low Countries. The subsequent struggle between Britain and France that ended in 1815 was political and ideological; it was also a continuation of the earlier conflict between two imperial rivals. The 1801 Treaty of Amiens that resulted in peace between France and Britain was but a truce; both nations, driven by imperial ambitions, made ready for renewed hostilities. Napoleon hoped to gain control of St Domingo and vast American territories west of the Mississippi River, part of a global strategy in future conflict with Britain. When war resumed in 1803 that plan had failed, but Napoleon's imperial ambitions continued, adjusting over time to the dynamics of the ongoing struggle. It was a struggle that saw the construction of a Napoleonic empire on the Continent, achieved by military conquest over coalitions of rival powers. Napoleon repeatedly defeated the armies of coalition after coalition of European powers on Continental battlefields; what Napoleon was never able to do was overcome Britain's naval supremacy. The conflict was between two imperial powers, one global and the other Continental. It was the global empire, that of Britain, that emerged victorious in 1815.

The Britain that achieved victory over France was pushed to extreme limits; she did prevail, but in doing so she underwent deep internal change. William Wilberforce, an influential MP, wrote in 1797 that 'our national difficulties must, both directly and indirectly', be 'chiefly ascribed' to 'the decline of religion and morality'.[2] The difficulties Wilberforce referred to were bound up with the French Revolution, its impact on Britain and the ongoing struggle between the two nations. British responses to the French Revolution had been favourable initially, and resulted in the formation of a network of radical clubs, including the London Corresponding Society. Tom Paine's *Rights of Man* (1791) far outsold Edmund Burke's conservative *Reflections on the French Revolution* (1790) during the decade of the 1790s. Revolutionary ideology was taking hold in Britain, and France threatened Britain with invasion. For Britain to prevail, Wilberforce argued, she must undergo internal reform. The reform movement began before the challenges of the Revolutionary era, but those challenges gave it a new sense of urgency, as seen in the stark choice another Evangelical, John Bowdler, offered readers in his book *Reform or Ruin*, which went through eight editions in the year of its publication, 1798: either Britain undergo reform or the nation faced ruin. The Evangelical goal was first to reform the upper orders, and by that example to regenerate society as a whole. Arthur Young maintained that the lower classes would not be virtuous while the upper classes indulged in 'Sunday parties, excursions, and amusements'.[3] In 1798 the *Annual Register* said, 'It was a wonder to the lower orders throughout all parts of England to see the avenues of churches filled with carriages. This novel appearance prompted the simple country people to inquire "what was the matter"?' The Evangelical programme was not limited to moral and religious reform within Britain; it extended also to the British Empire, and particularly to the institution of slavery, one of the Empire's underlying props. Wilberforce wrote in his *Journal* that God had set before him two great purposes, the reformation of manners and suppression of the slave trade. When the House of Commons debated a measure to abolish the slave trade in 1807 Samuel Romilly compared Wilberforce to Napoleon. Napoleon was surrounded 'with all the pomp of power and all the pride of victory,' whereas Wilberforce was a man of humane and unceasing labours, whose good work was about to achieve its finest moment in a statute that would rescue countless men, women and children from unspeakable misery.[4] Wilberforce considered Parliament's abolition of the slave trade in 1807 as his finest achievement.

Jane Austen, the daughter of a country parson, grew up in the rural backwaters of southern England. With close ties to Oxford and belonging to a family that moved in polite circles, her world was that of the English gentry, a civilised, elite social group. When her father retired as rector of Steventon in 1801 she moved to Bath. Bath was a major outpost of eighteenth-century cosmopolitan civilisation but London was its principal English centre, and here too Austen spent time. Her upbringing, accomplishments, reading interests, tastes and family connections placed her within the world of a refined stratum in English society. Jane Austen was fourteen in 1789, when the Revolution unleashed forces that soon found their way into her world through her cousin, Eliza de Feuillide, to whom she was personally close. Eliza was born in India but came to England at age four and never returned to India. She went to school in France, where she acquired the sophisticated manners of elite, aristocratic, French society. As a girl she spent time with relatives in England, including the Austens; through her French manners entered the rural gentry world of Steventon. There also she helped organise a private theatrical that allowed her to flirt with Jane Austen's brothers, who also participated in the event. By this time she had married the comte de Feuillide, an impecunious noble who benefited from her £10,000 dowry. Through Eliza Austen learned first-hand about the Terror when the comte was guillotined.

Jane Austen's ties to the British Empire, and to Britain's long struggle with France, were personal and direct, through the members of her family. In India her father's half-sister formed close ties to Warren Hastings, one of the key figures in solidifying the power of the East India Company after the Seven Years' War. It was Hastings who provided Eliza, his goddaughter, with a dowry. When Hastings sent his small son to Britain he placed him in the care of Jane Austen's father. Francis Austen, one of Jane's brothers, convoyed a fleet to India for the East India Company. Cassandra, her sister, was engaged to Thomas Fowle, a regimental chaplain who died in the West Indies of yellow fever in 1797. Jane Austen's father was trustee of an Antigua estate owned by an Oxford classmate, James Langford Nibbs. Her sailor brothers, Francis and Charles, were active participants in the military struggle between Britain and France. Francis took part in the blockade of Cadiz in 1797; he joined Nelson in the Mediterranean in 1798; as captain of the *Petrel* he pursued Napoleon after the Battle of the Nile; in 1803 he raised Sea Fencibles to protect the coast of Britain from possible French invasion; he helped blockade the French fleet in Boulogne that Napoleon built to invade Britain; in 1805 he narrowly missed fighting in the Battle of Trafalgar; he participated in the Battle of St Domingo in 1806; he sailed on convoy duty to the Cape of Good Hope in 1807 and accompanied another convoy to St Helena in 1808; he took General Anstruther to Portugal in 1808 and he was at Spithead in 1809 when the battered remains of Sir John Moore's army returned to Britain after the Battle of Corunna. Jane's other sailor brother, Charles, searched American ships for British deserters and helped maintain a blockade of American trade with Europe. This blockade was a response to Napoleon's Continental System, an attempt to prevent British commerce from entering Continental ports. War between the two empires was waged on land and sea, and it was economic as well.

It is evident from Austen's correspondence that she was well informed of Britain's struggle with France. She knew about it from letters, most importantly those written by her two sailor brothers, but she also learned about it from newspapers, which kept her abreast of contemporary events. Her responses to wartime news in letters to her family were oblique and ironic, private rather than public. She heard of Napoleon's plans to invade England through her brother Francis, who helped organise coastal defences and whose ship, the *Leopard*, was part of the British fleet that blockaded Napoleon's flotilla in Boulogne that was to have invaded Britain. When she referred to Napoleon's plan to invade England in 1805 the focus was not on that episode but on how 'gentlemen of the neighbourhood' (*L*, 30 August 1805) felt inconvenienced by plans to safeguard the coast. Three years later, in 1808, she wrote a letter to Cassandra in which she described recent visits to neighbours, difficulties with servants, some illnesses, and a rug that was almost finished. Buried in this letter is the cryptic comment, 'our poor army, whose state seems dreadfully critical' (*L*, 10 January 1809). The army she referred to was the one under Sir John Moore that had marched into Spain in 1808 to join Spanish resistance to Napoleon, suffered heavy losses and fallen back to Corunna in what is regarded as one of the most harrowing marches ever. Not only did Austen know about this episode but was able to predict its outcome, the evacuation of Moore's army from Spain, in which she thought her brother Francis might participate. A different response to the struggle between Britain and France is seen in a letter written to her sister Cassandra in January 1813. She had read Captain William Pasley's *Essay on the Military Policy and Institutions of the British Empire* (1810), a blueprint for total victory over France, military, political and economic. Upon first reading Pasley's *Essay*, Austen 'protested' against it, but she ended up admiring an author who 'does write with extraordinary force & spirit' (*L*, 24 January 1813). Pasley praised the British Constitution 'that alone has preserved our independence'; he urged fellow Britons to make every necessary sacrifice to protect the Constitution from the French threat; and he said that in order to defeat France England had to 'become a military nation'. The victory he foresaw would be a 'blessing to mankind'.[5] Austen's response to Pasley's *Essay* suggests that by 1813, towards the end of the wars with France, she shared the patriotic feeling that was part of a larger British response.

In the course of the long conflict between Britain and France the members of Jane Austen's family were drawn to Evangelicalism. Francis Austen, a protégé of the Evangelical Admiral Gambier was known as 'The officer who knelt in church'. Consistent with his religious views, Francis deplored the consequences of slavery; he believed that 'slavery however it may be modified is still slavery, and it is much to be regretted that any trace of it should be found to exist in countries dependent on England or colonised by their subjects'.[6] When James Austen, a clergyman, conscientiously refused a living worth £100 in 1808 his decision was consistent with the Evangelical programme. When Henry Austen entered the clergy in 1816 he leaned decidedly toward Evangelicalism. Cassandra read Evangelical writings and encouraged her sister to do the same: after reading Thomas Gisborne's *An Enquiry into the Duties of the Female Sex* (1797) Jane Austen said, 'I am glad you recommended "Gisborne", for having begun, I am pleased with it, and I had quite determined not to read it' (*L*, 30 August 1805). It is in Austen's novels that her responses to Evangelicalism are to be found, as are her responses to Britain's struggle with France. That Francis and Charles Austen recognised themselves in their sister's naval characters suggests a direct connection between Austen's fiction and her own experience. Far from being isolated from the great events of her day she was open to them; in her novels she dramatised issues that were of central importance to the Evangelical reform programme, and she introduced naval officers as protagonists who endured hardships at sea, risked their lives, but prevailed in the long wars between Britain and France.

For Gisborne, Bowdler, Wilberforce and the Evangelical movement as a whole the reform of manners and the inculcation of a sense of moral principle in English society was the essential vehicle of national salvation, the means by which Britain, internally strengthened, would prevail in the struggle with France. In the theatrical episode with its intrigue and self-indulgence Austen incorporates the themes of Evangelicalism and patriotism in *Mansfield Park*. Opposed to the theatrical world of play and fancy is a different set of values, rooted in limit, restraint, self-denial and respect for authority, as seen in Fanny, the only person who refuses to participate. Sir Thomas's return to Mansfield Park brings the theatricals to an end. He has been to his Antigua estates to repair the family finances, weakened by disturbances in the West Indies and by the extravagance of his oldest son. Upon returning to Mansfield Park Sir Thomas wants to discuss his experiences in Antigua, and particularly slavery, but only Fanny expresses an interest in the subject. Fanny's response helps define her role in the moral struggle taking place within Mansfield Park. The positive characters in *Mansfield Park* are more serious, less brilliant, than those who represent negative choices; they are more sober, more plain, more English than the more fashionable characters, whose manners and superficiality bear the stamp of French culture. This dichotomy is continued in *Emma*, in the contrast between

Figure 42. A French satiric view of English 'stiffness': C. Vernet, *La Parisienne à Londres: Le Suprême Bon Ton No. 12* (Paris: Martinet, 1802).

George Knightley and Frank Churchill (fig. 42). Plain-spoken, forthright, not given to witticisms or repartees, Knightley is an English type, a magistrate, active in local affairs, a working farmer and closely connected to village society, a man who greets his brother 'in the true English style, burying under a calmness . . . real attachment' (*E*, 1:12). At the time of his arrival in Highbury, Churchill professes 'himself to have always felt the sort of interest in the country which none but one's *own* country gives' (*E*, 2:23), and when he visits the village he is eager to 'prove myself to belong to the place, to be a true citizen of Highbury' (*E*, 2:24). A clever manipulator, all of Churchill's patriotic claims are false, and, when his engagement falters, he wants nothing more than to leave: 'I am sick of England – and would leave it to-morrow, if I could' (*E*, 3:6). The central contrast in *Persuasion* is between the vainglorious, self-centred members of the Elliot family, obsessed with their genealogy but oblivious to the wartime combatants who have just returned to Britain after helping bring about the defeat of Napoleon. These men are naval officers who risked their lives in the struggle between Britain and France, long-time imperial combatants. In that conflict Britain's naval supremacy had been of major importance and Jane Austen's own brothers, who recognised themselves in their sister's naval characters, had played an active role in the eventual victory.

NOTES

1. Cited in Robert Darnton, 'A Euro State of Mind', *New York Review of Books* 49: 326 (February, 2002), 30.
2. William Wilberforce, *Practical View of the Prevailing Religious Systems* (1851), p. 451.
3. Arthur Young, *An Enquiry into the State of the Public Mind amongst the Lower Classes* (1798), p. 25.
4. V. H. H. Green, *The Hanoverians 1714–15* (London: Edward Arnold, 1948), p. 290.
5. William Pasley, *The Military Policy and Institutions of the British Empire*, fifth edition (1914), p. 129.
6. Cited in J. H. and E. C. Hubback, *Jane Austen's Sailor Brothers* (1906), p. 171.

31

Pastimes

PENNY GAY

A gentleman, unless he belonged to one of the accepted professions (the law, the church, the army or the navy), had a great deal of time every day to be filled with activities, some more obviously useful than others. The same can be said of the ladies of Austen's world, though the professions were barred to them. Women's pursuits and pastimes were mostly indoor and domestic, men's outdoor and sporting. But there was also time spent together – walking or driving outdoors, or the many indoors occupations described below: all of which provided opportunities for flirtation, gossip and even occasionally self-improvement.

Most houses had several sitting-rooms, in one of which the ladies of the household would gather after breakfast to 'work'. By this is meant needlework, an accomplishment which was both useful and artistic, and which was considered a necessity for women of all social classes. Jane Austen herself was a fine needlewoman, working purses and huswifes (a small cloth bag containing needles, thread and other necessities) as well as trimming her bonnets, sewing her own clothing, and making shirts for her brothers and clothes for the poor. If visitors called, it was often considered more genteel to continue with one's 'fancywork' rather than 'plain' shirt-making or mending. Fancywork included embroidery, carpet- or rug-work (on canvas), knotting (thread 'knotted at regular intervals by means of an oval shuttle . . . to form a narrow trimming – the knots resembling a string of small beads'[1]) and netting (making meshes with a shuttle, out of silk or heavier materials). 'Fillagree-work' (S&S, 2:1), making little ornaments out of slips of rolled paper, was an intricate yet pointless craft, entirely appropriate for the self-serving Lucy Steele.

When not doing needlework, women might spend hours improving their accomplishments, generally either music or drawing and watercolour painting. Music might include not only practice of an instrument (generally piano or harp) and singing, but also copying out music from published sources for later study. Several volumes of Jane Austen's own collection of music are held at Chawton, much of it copied in her own hand. She was a pianist, practising every morning before breakfast, as well as occasionally singing 'simple old songs' to her own accompaniment in the evenings.[2] Amateur singers were expected to be able to hold a part: the 'glee' that is sung in *Mansfield Park* (1:11) would have been a simple part-song for the three ladies, probably with piano accompaniment. Frank Churchill, like Willoughby, is a keen duettist, not so much (perhaps) to 'show off his voice', as Mr Knightley says (*E*, 2:8), as to engage in the heightened opportunities for flirtation that making music together supplies.

Less talented or tenacious young ladies, like Harriet Smith, might occupy themselves with making a commonplace-book by sewing together some leaves of fine hot-pressed paper, and perhaps binding it with fabric-covered board. Into this she would copy, in Harriet's case, as many riddles as she could find or persuade her friends to remember. There was a fashion for enigmas, charades, riddles and conundrums: new collections by such authors as 'Peregrine Puzzlebrains' and 'Peter Puzzlewit' were regularly published 1790–1830. *Emma* is fascinated by such word-games: the Jane Fairfax plot is its enigma, which the ingenious reader might guess; Mr Weston's riddle on 'Perfection' is technically a conundrum, i.e. 'a riddle in the form of a question the answer to which involves a pun or play on words' (*OED*). Riddles often took the form of 'charades', in which the two or three syllables of the word (e.g. *courtship*) were each represented by some rhyming lines containing the formula, 'My first/second' etc. and concluding with an enigmatic 'My whole'. An anthology of such riddles written or collected by Jane Austen's family still exists – and they are often quite cryptic: far too much for Harriet's feeble brain.[3] She might have had more luck guessing the rather easier charade on 'Courtship' offered in the collection *The Frolics of the Sphynx* (1812):

> My first to each sex adds a grace, and gives ease,
> With my next you encounter the turbulent seas;
> My whole you rejoice at, with marriage in view,
> And the longer it lasts, 'tis the better for you.

'Practical' or mimed charades were less common, and tended to represent (sometimes with costumes and props) a moral quality such as 'Pity'.

Women often spent considerable time every day writing letters, thus putting fresh local and family news in circulation. Reading was the other main indoor pastime, for both men and women. Every gentleman's house had a library, whether it was a huge and constantly growing collection like Mr Darcy's, or a few books lovingly arranged on shelves, as in Captain Harville's or even a farmer's cottage. 'Foreigners were impressed by the passion for reading and education shown by a wide cross-section of the English,' as Roy Porter noted.[4] Such collections – of classic authors, essays, sermons, novels, poetry, plays, history, travels, etc. – could be supplemented by the circulating libraries which were a feature of every sizable town. These carried the latest fashionable publications; there were, as well, newspapers and a huge variety of journals to which the master (and often the mistress) of the house subscribed. Reading aloud was a very common activity, especially after dinner, when listeners could sit in reduced light while the reader, in the strongest candlelight, entertained the circle. A good reading manner was prized: see the discussion between Edmund and Henry in *Mansfield Park* (3:3). Jane Austen herself 'read aloud with very great taste and effect. Her own works, probably, were never heard to so much advantage as from her own mouth; for she partook largely in all the best gifts of the comic muse' (*Memoir*, p. 140).

Any lady who played the piano was expected to have a good repertoire of airs for country dances (new collections were regularly published), for an 'impromptu ball' when a group of young people were gathered together. Even Mr Darcy sees the advantage of this custom, and invites Elizabeth to 'dance a reel' to Miss Bingley's after-dinner playing of 'a lively Scotch air' (*P&P*, 1:10), though she refuses him. Country dances, with the ladies and gentlemen standing opposite each other in a line or a circle, were based on a simple skipping step: the variations of each dance were the patterns formed by the dancers taking hands, crossing, twirling, and 'going down the set'. A single dance could last quite a long time if there was a large number of dancers, unless the set was subdivided into two or three dancing concurrently. In *Northanger Abbey* we are told that 'The cotillions were over, the country-dancing beginning'

(1:10): this signifies the conclusion of the more formal and complex French dances (the cotillion was a 'square' dance for four or eight people); dancers could then relax into the merriment of the simpler communal dances, with opportunities for conversation as couples awaited their turn to go down the set. The 'German waltz', requiring that the lady and the gentleman clasp each other for the whole dance, was at that time considered improper for those not husbands and wives, and is not used by Austen: Mrs Weston's 'irresistible waltz' in *Emma* (2:8) refers to a tune and time signature for a country dance, which might have included a ländler-like figure in which the lady danced under her partner's raised arm.[5]

Grand houses such as Mansfield Park had rooms big enough for formal balls, which would be planned some weeks in advance, with invitations going out to all the gentry families of the neighbourhood. Sir John Middleton, typically, organises 'numerous' private balls every winter (*S&S*, 1:7). The Crown ball in *Emma* neatly places the 'world' of Highbury: Randalls is not big enough for the Westons to invite guests to a ball; Hartfield is not offered, in deference to Mr Woodhouse's sensibilities; and neither is Donwell, which, as a much older structure, would not have had a suitable space even if Mr Knightley could bring himself to offer it. Netherfield, in *Pride and Prejudice*, a modern house, has large reception rooms suitable for balls.

As well as the ballroom, card rooms and supper rooms were needed for such an event. Those not dancing would while away the evening at cards, which was a common after-dinner alternative to reading in both grand and small establishments. People of all conditions played cards: in *Pride and Prejudice*, the De Bourghs, the Bingleys and the Philipses all sit down to cards after dinner. A comment in *Emma* notes the use of the Crown room for 'a whist club established among the gentlemen and half-gentlemen of the place' (2:6); Southey, however, notes that a pack of cards is too costly (because of the tax applied) for the pastime to be available to 'the lowest class of society'.[6] The varieties of card games were numerous, but they were basically divisible into games which required a specific number, of which whist, a game of strategy not unlike bridge, for four players, was the most common; and round games, which could be played by any number, and which tended to be the simpler and noisier games: cassino, commerce, loo, speculation, vingt-un, lottery tickets. Of these games speculation is the one given most detail in Austen's writing, where it clearly plays a symbolic role (*MP*, 2:7). As David Selwyn argues, it is 'a metaphor for the game Mary Crawford is playing, with Edmund as stake', and its demands match her brother's approaches to life.[7] A relatively new game in 1813 – it is new to Fanny as well as to Lady Bertram – its rules allegorise the idea of financial speculation, first cited by *OED* in the sense of involving 'risk on the chance of unusual profit' in 1776. Older card games included cribbage, which is played between two, three or four players, using a peg-board for scoring. Piquet is for two players (such as Mr Woodhouse and Mrs Goddard) using a thirty-two-card pack; quadrille, an old-fashioned game for four players using a forty-card pack, is the choice of Lady Catherine De Bourgh.

Gambling of small sums was a common accompaniment to many of these card games, and there was no opprobrium attached to it. Tokens, often known as 'fish', were a common alternative. Backgammon is the only non-card game mentioned by Austen, but chess, draughts and dominoes were also played. In some drawing-rooms there could be found an ingenious small table, which contained chess and backgammon boards, a reading slope and – hanging underneath – a sliding sewing-bag for the unoccupied lady.

Gentlemen's indoor activities were more circumscribed than women's: apart from reading or writing (which included attending to the business of the estate) in his library, a gentleman might play billiards if the house had a billiard-room (as Rosings, Cleveland and Mansfield Park do). Or he might retreat to his gun-room and clean his hunting equipment. After dinner he might join in dancing, card games or board games, or even undertake some knotting or other handiwork: Captain Harville 'drew, he varnished, he carpentered, he glued; he made toys for the children, he fashioned new netting-needles and pins with improvements; and if everything else was done, sat down to his large fishing-net at one corner of the room' (*P*, 1:11). Along with netting and wood-turning, Jane Austen's brother Frank (like Captain Harville, a sailor) enjoyed making knotted fringes to decorate curtains or furniture covers.

Occasionally the family would indulge in more organised activities, of which home theatricals were the most elaborate.

There had been a fashion for private theatricals since the early eighteenth century, and in the houses of the aristocracy it frequently became the full-scale extravaganza of building a private theatre and inviting an audience. 'The craze reached its climax in the 1780's, declined somewhat in the 1790's, increased again slightly in the first decade of the nineteenth century and, after that, petered out.'[8] Converting a room (such as the Mansfield Park billiard-room) to a temporary theatre was not uncommon. The Austens themselves used their dining-room, or 'fitted up' the barn, for a series of performances by the young people of the family and their friends in the 1780s. As in *Mansfield Park*, their favoured plays were the popular ones of the day (and not, for example, Shakespeare), the oldest being Susannah Centlivre's racy comedy of 1714 (presented in 1787 by the Austen family), *The Wonder! A Woman Keeps a Secret*, a play still very popular in the late eighteenth century. The other plays that we know the Austen family undertook were: a bombastic tragedy by Thomas Francklin, *Matilda* – their first effort in 1782; followed by Sheridan's comedy *The Rivals*, produced in 1784. In 1788 they presented *The Chances* (Garrick's revision of Buckingham's tragicomedy) and Fielding's ribald farce *Tom Thumb*. In 1789, Isaac Bickerstaff's *The Sultan* (a popular two-act comedy which is also the basis of Mozart's *Die Entführung aus dem Serail*) and James Townley's farce *High Life Below Stairs* were staged. All these plays have quite large casts and complex, wordy texts – quite a challenge for a group of young people, even though they were only performing for their families. As in the public theatre, the performances were furnished with a prologue and an epilogue appropriate to the occasion; several witty examples by Jane Austen's brother James survive.[9] Jane was probably too young to take a role in her own family's home theatricals, but she undoubtedly, like Fanny, watched with fascination, and used her intimate knowledge of some of these plays, and the process of putting them on, in her later writing (significantly, there is no instance cited in Rosenfeld of *Lovers' Vows* being performed privately). Although the Austen family ceased holding Christmas theatricals after 1789, the habit of taking part in sociable dramatic readings was part of Jane Austen's adult life, particularly when visiting her brother's great house at Godmersham.

Jane Austen was a favourite aunt to her nephews and nieces: telling them stories, playing expertly at such games as bilbo-catch (cup and ball), battledore and shuttlecock, ninepins and spillikins. She also helped them with less boisterous occupations, such as making paper ships, or cutting out paper and scraps of material to make collages or clothes for dolls. She might, like Emma, have made alphabet letters for an anagram game that could also be played by adults. In this period the first educational games were manufactured for children: 'dissected puzzles' (which became, a century later, jigsaws) featuring maps or the monarchs of England; and numerous board games, most based on the 'race to the finish' principle – the stops might represent, for example, the cities of the European Grand Tour, Human Life (with moral lessons), or 'Universal History and Chronology'.

'Cricket, base ball, riding on horseback, and running about the country' (*NA*, 1:1) were not confined to boys, in at least some households; and exercise was an important pastime for adults, both men and women. Austen's heroines, like the writer herself, take a substantial daily walk unless the weather is against them. Women of richer families might take their fresh air in a carriage, or even on horseback, as Fanny does at Mansfield Park until deprived of her horse by the city-educated Mary Crawford's desire to learn to ride. The daily outing might take the form of a visit to a neighbouring family, or a trip to local shops like Ford's in Highbury (or, for Jane Austen, the shops of Alton) or a wander along the lanes and in the fields of the surrounding country. Women walking substantial distances alone (as Marianne does at Cleveland) were on the whole frowned on as eccentric, unfeminine, though Elizabeth's walking with a charitable purpose, to visit her sick sister (*P&P*, 1:7), of course cannot be condemned by the right-minded. Emma, more conventional, always chooses to be accompanied, even when on charitable visits; hence the usefulness of Harriet as a companion after Miss Taylor's marriage.

In clement weather, especially in summer, organised outings were undertaken. Sir John Middleton 'was for ever forming parties to eat cold ham and chicken out of doors' (*S&S*, 1:7), to drive around the country or to go boating on a neighbour's lake. Mrs Elton's instigation of the Box Hill picnic in *Emma*, and her behaviour at the strawberry-gathering at Donwell, is an example of both the fashion for 'picnics' and their potential absurdity in the hands of those not used to a straightforward use of leisure time. Light gardening – cutting roses, gathering berries, attending to a herb-garden or vegetable patch – was an acceptable outdoor activity for both gentlemen and ladies: Charlotte Lucas positively encourages Mr Collins to spend as much time as possible in the garden. Charlotte herself has poultry to look after, as did Mrs Austen (the dirty work associated with this activity would of course be done by a servant).

For gentlemen, the principal outdoors pastime in the autumn and winter was 'taking out a gun', usually accompanied by a pointer dog or two. This could only be done on a gentleman's own property or by personal invitation of a landowner. The prey was usually birds – duck, pheasant, partridge, grouse, woodcock – or hares and rabbits. Organised hunting meets on horseback (riding to covert), with a pack of dogs, generally pursued deer, hares or foxes. Captain Benwick demonstrates his more masculine qualities to Charles Musgrove at 'a famous set-to at rat-hunting . . . in my father's great barns' (*P*, 2:10); this would have employed terriers and men with sticks, not guns. In summer the more peaceable activity of fishing provided outdoor entertainment for gentlemen.

In towns, young 'sparks' would attempt to lord it over their peers, and impress young ladies, by driving very fast in the latest and lightest two-wheeled carriage, such as John Thorpe's gig, a one-horse equipage which he insists is 'curricle hung' (*NA*, 1:7), i.e. it resembles the faster and more expensive two-horse curricle. The pursuit of novelties or bargains in carriages, horses, dogs and guns was as much a preoccupation of the average young gentleman as was the pursuit of fashion for most young ladies. One of the ways in which Austen distinguishes her heroines and heroes from their social peers is in their unconventional leisure interests: Elizabeth Bennet rarely takes up her needlework with eagerness (*P&P*, 3:11); neither she nor Anne Elliot likes card games. On the other hand, the fascinating Henry Tilney is knowledgeable about muslins.

At some point Jane Austen stopped calling what she did 'writing' and started referring to it as 'work'.[10] This marks a semantic shift away from the standard idea that women's 'work' was needlework. Women had, of course, been writing – and even publishing – for over a century (letters, verses, essays, novels); but for the quiet daughter of a country clergyman to think of herself as working to contribute to her (all-female) household's income by her writing was a revolutionary change in the idea of what a woman might do with her time.

NOTES

1. Penelope Byrde, *Jane Austen Fashion: Fashion and Needlework in the Works of Jane Austen* (Ludlow: Excellent Press, 1999), pp. 111–12.
2. *A Memoir of Jane Austen and Other Family Recollections*, ed. Kathryn Sutherland (Oxford: Oxford University Press, 2002), p. 71; subsequent references are included in the text. For Austen's music collection, see Mollie Sandcock, ' "I Burn with Contempt for my Foes": Jane Austen's Music Collections and Women's Lives in Regency England', *Persuasions* 23 (2001), 105–17, and Ian Gammie and Derek McCulloch, *Jane Austen's Music* (St Alban's: Corda Music, 1996).
3. See the examples in *Collected Poems and Verse of the Austen Family*, ed. David Selwyn (Manchester: Carcanet, 1996).
4. Roy Porter, *English Society in the Eighteenth Century*, repr. (London: Penguin, 1990), p. 233.
5. Some interesting contemporary comments on dancing can be found in *Regency Etiquette: The Mirror of Graces*, repr. (Mendocino, CA: R. L. Shep, 1997), pp. 183–7. See also *Memoir*, pp. 32–4.
6. Robert Southey also commented on the popularity of whist: *Letters from England by Don Manuel Alvarez Espriella*, repr. (Gloucester: Alan Sutton, 1984), pp. 364–6.
7. David Selwyn, *Jane Austen and Leisure* (London: Hambledon, 1999), pp. 271–5.
8. Sybil Rosenfeld, *Temples of Thespis: Some Private Theatres and Theatricals in England and Wales, 1700–1820* (London: Society for Theatre Research, 1978), p. 11. See also Penny Gay, *Jane Austen and the Theatre* (Cambridge: Cambridge University Press, 2002), ch. 5.
9. See *The Complete Poems of James Austen, Jane Austen's Eldest Brother*, ed. David Selwyn (Chawton: Jane Austen Society, 2003), pp. 18–29.
10. Jon Spence, *Becoming Jane Austen* (London: Hambledon, 2003), p. 173.

32

Philosophy

PETER KNOX-SHAW

Unions of fiction and philosophy have generally turned out for the worse, and novelists of the great tradition in its later phase are famous for having shrunk at the prospect. Lawrence colourfully described the hurt done by moral systems to his sacred genre in the imagery of crucifixion – at best the novel was able to walk away with the nail; and the mere thought of *having* a philosophy caused Conrad to groan, 'shall I die of it do you think?'[1] If Jane Austen was untroubled by these post-Romantic demurs it was not because she was a didactic novelist of an older mould, but rather that she shared the outlook of a movement that itself arose in reaction against the dogmatic.

The 'philosophical character' of Austen's work was hailed, a few years after her death, by the critic Richard Whately, who revealingly applied the term to her entire conception of the novel, even indeed to the new school of fiction which she was seen to head. Whately was not alone in distinguishing the central features of the new novel as fine observation and a deep concern for probability, but he based his high claims for Jane Austen on Aristotle's idea that mastery of the probable is a guarantee of insight into the way things work. It was from science that this idea crossed to literature in the *Poetics*, and Whately updates the scientific analogy by equating Austen's approach to human nature with the method of the naturalist who relates minute detail to a range of suppositions about function and form. Whately became an Archbishop, and his essay has been cited as evidence that Jane Austen's Christian beliefs fuelled her rising fame, but a better clue to its drift is that he was, at the time, an enlightened don, already well launched on his first career as a polit-ical economist. When the editor-to-be of Francis Bacon begins to enlarge on the philosophical character of Austen's work it is the so-called 'experimental method' of the new humanities that holds the stage.[2]

Though contemporaries widely agreed over the qualities that set Austen apart from earlier novelists, there was dissent over their value. This is reflected in Sir Walter Scott's uneasy review of *Emma* which shows him eager to praise the new realism but reluctant to relinquish faith in the tonic effects of heroic example and high romance. It is clear too in the mixed comments on her work that Jane Austen dispassionately jotted down: some of her readers find truth to ordinary life demeaning or at least no advance on the ordinary; others have only applause for an author intimately or 'experimentally' acquainted (as one has it) with the society she describes. Philosophy had a major role to play in boosting the status of day-to-day experience throughout the eighteenth century, and the tradition most relevant to this process starts in England with Shaftesbury, who insisted that morals should be founded on human nature rather than on speculative ideas about divine will or law. Hutcheson, in his turn, urged followers to 'quit the Disputes of the Learned' and observe men in their common settings,[3] but it took some time, in truth, for a discourse at all consistent with common sense to develop. When it came to morals, few philosophers had any professional reason to concern themselves with everyday life. Rationalists (like Locke) held that ethics could be deduced from first principles like algebra; out-and-out sceptics (like Hobbes) argued that there was nothing to choose between different kinds of motive; and even intuitionists (like Hutcheson) believed in a watertight 'moral sense'. For Hume and Smith, however, it was precisely in the society around them that the proof of moral activity and the key to its workings lay. In the long run, the 'experimental method' cut against both idealistic and cynical trends. It granted full meaning to the language of moral discrimination while yielding a more worldly account of sociability than had yet been current, and it led particularly to a new appreciation of the way judgement depended on specific contexts, and to a sharper sense of the difficulties faced by the subject in constructing these. If there was ever a philosophical school in search of a novelist it was surely the Scottish Enlightenment in its later phase.

Gilbert Ryle had the longer tradition in view when he proposed (on a happy day off-bounds) that Austen had a true interest in 'theoretical problems about human nature' even if her approach to them was from a sunnier aspect than the philosopher's. While he drew chiefly on the founding figures of Aristotle and Shaftesbury, later commentators have been more impressed by parallels – verbal and otherwise – between the novels and works by Hume and Smith.[4] That this rich field of inquiry remains relatively open has much to do with the divergent paths taken by studies of 'the age of reason' and of Jane Austen. Paradoxically, the historicism that led to the vogue for an anti-Jacobin and Evangelical Austen favoured a version of the Enlightenment that was strongly anti-clerical and anti-establishment. Over the last decade each of these opposing biases has been modified, however, and the receptivity of eighteenth-century Anglicanism to new ideas could hardly be better illustrated than by the household of Austen's adolescence, though no more than a glance at it is appropriate here.

The Rector of Steventon has been well described as 'a true son of the Enlightenment',[5] and his broadmindedness as a father is brought out both by the plays that the young Austens acted (some feminist, some libertine) and by what they read. Jane Austen never learned to spell the author of her Catechism, but in later life she vividly remembered Thomas Percival's 'moral tales' (*L*, 7–9 October 1808), a manual on science and liberal opinion masquerading as a conduct book.[6] Percival, a founder of the Manchester Literary and Philosophical Society, introduced his readers to Shaftesbury, Voltaire, Robertson and Smith; led them through experiments (Archimedes, Boyle, Hooke, Harvey, Newton, Franklin, Priestley); taught them to abhor slavery; and urged them, above all, to be observant and alive to the wonders of the ordinary. If it took some time for the young Jane to come round to Percival's view that stories should be 'conformable to the usual course of things', she seems to have adopted Hugh Blair's advice that writers should at all costs avoid 'the affected and frivolous use of ornament' from the moment she began *Volume the First*.[7] When Austen much later spelled out the guidelines governing her narration (in helping a niece with a novel) foremost among them were plain style, fidelity to public fact and the avoidance of anything 'so little usual as to *appear* unnatural in a book' (*L*, 10 August 1814). These norms – soon to be seen as the defining features of the 'new style of fiction' – can be traced back to Steventon days where they are attached to a cultural matrix of tell-tale origin. Whether it is Austen's allusion to Blair in her hilarious parody of opportunistic 'moral reflections' during the accident scene of 'Love and Freindship', or her brother Henry's fond salute in his direction in the course of a satiric piece on opaque language in *The Loiterer*, or the same periodical's lampoon of the old-fashioned naturalist who builds upon freak results and pours 'contempt upon the Experimentalist', the underlying ethos is one that her brother James rejoiced to call *enlightened*.[8]

Austen is, in any case, more explicit about her cultural affiliations than is often supposed. Her puff for the novel in *Northanger Abbey* (1:5) can hardly have failed to encourage talk of the new school, for it extols work that conveys 'the most thorough knowledge of human nature' (despite the joke that fellow-writers should stick together), while meting out scorn to the improbable and outdated. First drafted after the rejection of 'First Impressions', and evidently intended over a long period to be her first book, *Northanger Abbey* preserves the character of a manifesto. Its comic parade of romance and Gothic conventions brings home just how far removed popular fiction is from the stuff of ordinary experience, but the demand for a more serious, inspirational fiction is also found wanting. In his *Rambler* no. 4, Dr Johnson had notoriously called for an end to morally 'mixed' characters on the grounds that novels (aimed at the young and impressionable) 'take possession of the memory by a kind of violence, and produce effects almost without the intervention of the will'. He is answered by the ingenuous Catherine, who has her head turned by a text that deals almost exclusively in angels and fiends.

The cultural kinship of the new novel is further clarified in *Northanger Abbey* through the adoption of a sister-genre, the recently canonised 'philosophical' history represented at its 'most distinguished' (as the Tilneys have it) by the work of Hume and Robertson. A long discussion, balancing the earlier set-piece on fiction, proclaims the rewards of this challenging reading matter, and singles out the imaginative qualities that have transformed the chronicle into a form that adds the lustre of drama to analysis. Catherine's often cited objections to history (*NA*, 1:14) show her to be unaware of its recent, more social directions: her complaint about too many popes and kings echoes a famous preface by Voltaire; her charge of too few women overlooks Robertson, who constructed his popular *History of Scotland* round the story of two rival queens (as the narrator of 'The History of England' claimed for her own piece), and who urged that it was principally through 'the private and domestic situation of mankind' that social forces were felt.[9] But Catherine's ignorance of history is telling in another way, for it accounts for the naive quality of her absorption in *Udolpho*, the sixteenth-century setting of which she unblinkingly transposes to the present. High on the list of Henry's reproaches when he discovers that Catherine holds his father guilty of the murder of his wife is her failure to remember the country and the age.

Unlike Mary Bennet, whose appetite for philosophy is bookbound, Henry Tilney embodies the Enlightenment's ideal of an extrovert intellect, and his puncturing of Catherine's daydream – like so much of his social commentary – is rich in implication. Observing Catherine's suspicions, he feels his way towards her position, urging her to test her dark thoughts by looking around her and considering what is probable. This stress on the importance (and difficulty) of attuning the mind to context is highly reminiscent of Hume and Smith, and the same tradition points to the normality of the imaginative acts that go into Catherine's all-consuming pursuit of the one idea. Indeed, unlike the delusions of other quixotic heroines, Catherine's fantasies reveal a natural process of growth – one that corresponds to Hume's remarks on how an irrational and universal 'propensity to believe' generates a momentum of its own, so that 'any train of thinking is apt to continue, even when its object fails it, and like a galley put in motion by its oars, carries on its course'.[10]

In connection with the new history Henry speaks of 'human nature in a civilized state' (*NA*, 1:14), a phrase that reveals his debt to its premiss that, though human propensities have to be accepted as a given, and are relatively stable, their expression is modified by the way societies pass through different phases. The gist of his comforting remarks to Catherine is that modern, commercial England lies at some distance from the war-torn fiefdoms of Ann Radcliffe's Italy. Even present-day Italy, in fact, was then much touted by Whig zealots as a foil to English progress, and Austen was fully aware of debate on the issue, particularly of the Italophile Baretti's retort that legal regulation was a feeble curb against most human evils – a view summed up in his slogan, 'it is in your country as in all others'.[11] But if the sordid disclosures that follow swiftly on Catherine's regained faith in the security of central England go some way to support such a case and restore a measure of poetic truth to her Gothic hunches, they by no means negate the force of societal influence (which seems here a stimulus to greed). Rather they point to ordinarily hidden human depths. Because Henry is alive to these, his speech on modern society bears up well even in retrospect, and no less so for its stress on the role of institutions – churches, courts, libraries and schools. True to the liberal tradition Henry presents a social fabric woven of many strands that hold together without the starch of absolutism. But he sides with its more robust proponents when he ends with the reminder that there *are* forces to be restrained, picturing a country 'where every man is surrounded by a neighbourhood of voluntary spies, and where roads and newspapers lay every thing open' (*NA*, 2:9). Though self-sustaining, such an order is at a far remove from the painless models projected by some champions of benevolence.

Henry on 'roads and newspapers' echoes Dr Johnson, who remarked with more Latin, 'Society is held together by communication and information', while discussing *The Fable of the Bees*, to which he owned a debt so substantial that Austen had no need to read Mandeville (though she may well have done) to have come by his ideas.[12] If Hume and Smith took over the notion of founding ethics on human nature from Shaftesbury and Hutcheson, it was from Mandeville, the arch-opponent of benevolence, that they learned to grapple with what that entailed. Though the two rival heritages appear to jar in their work, giving rise to an ethics based on sympathy and an economics based on self-preservation (hence the longstanding 'Adam Smith problem'), they are in practice convincingly reconciled – largely by the insight that the workings of society are dependent on what had fallen for many moralists under the label of vice. For Hume, 'self-interest is the original motive to the establishment of justice', and the 'artificial virtues' on which social order relies evolve out of it through a spontaneous process of adjustment closely allied to Mandeville's 'joynt Labour of many Ages' (*Fable*, 2, 128). The same insight leads Smith to the idea of the 'invisible hand' in his masterpiece on political economy, though even in his earlier work on ethics (sympathy-based though it is) he does everything to redeem the concept of self-love. He not only acknowledges there that society can subsist without 'any mutual love or affection', but argues that self-love nourishes virtue because of the way it excites the desire to be approved or to be seen to excel. Though Smith balks at the word 'pride' in this context, reserving it for an inflated sense of self, Hume is only too ready to point out that the deadliest sin is the most fertile of many ambivalent energies that yield a harvest for the good.[13]

That motives are commonly as mixed as human nature itself does not prevent either Hume or Smith from grading them into high and low. And the line drawn by Hume between different grounds of self-esteem in his popular second *Enquiry* finds a parallel in *Pride and Prejudice* when Darcy, convicted first by Elizabeth of the 'worst kind of pride' (2:10), is at last declared free of all 'improper' varieties. Hume insists that 'character' is a truer object of approbation than 'rent-rolls', however much store the world sets by riches and power; and he proceeds to note that in aristocratic societies – as opposed to commercial ones whose vice it is to foster greed – a premium is placed on birth with the result that 'spiritless minds remain in haughty indolence, and dream of nothing but pedigrees and genealogies' (*Enquiry*, Section VI). *Pride and Prejudice* surveys the no man's land between these warring societies, Lady Catherine de Bourgh's estate providing a comic epitome of a backward-looking absolutism shored up, intriguingly, by 'reason' and 'humility'. Darcy, who has been taught from childhood to care for no one beyond his own family circle, and who inherits some of his aunt's horror of bad connections, renounces his pride of rank when he tracks down the disgraced Lydia in Eastcheap with the help of the city-based Mr Gardiner, who duly reports his motive – 'His character was to speak for itself'. Speak to Elizabeth it does, and while she is happy to suppose Darcy doubly inspired by 'compassion and honour' (*P&P*, 3:10), his rescue of Lydia strikes the reader as no worse for being prompted by romantic attachment also – like so many other worthy deeds in Austen's work. Sympathy and pride are again twinned as joint goads to right action when Jane exclaims of the supposed evil fathered on Wickham by Darcy, 'No man of common humanity, no man who had any value for his character, could be capable of it' (*P&P*, 1:17); and in the same context Elizabeth underlines the value of pride when she exclaims that she would at least have expected justice and honesty of Darcy from 'no better motive' (1:16). Hume complained that there was no proper word for the admirable 'sentiment of conscious worth' that he identified as pride, but this is precisely the quality that Elizabeth and Darcy so attractively embody, and which accounts for the more lived-in level of the novel's two-storied moral scheme.[14]

Though Mandeville won notoriety for his claim that pride was the human quality most beneficial to society, he also warned that it could blind understanding, and this point, much developed by the Scottish school, is illustrated by Austen when Darcy boasts that 'where there is a real superiority of mind, pride will be always under good regulation' (*P&P*, 1:11). Hume had argued that a natural propensity to over-value the self made pride offensive unless it was kept 'well-regulated'; to which Smith added that the high self-esteem of others, even when well founded, 'mortifies our own', a caveat turned by Elizabeth into epigram when she says of Darcy, 'I could easily forgive *his* pride, if he had not mortified *mine*' (*P&P*, 1:5).[15] Control of the virtuous vice is thus partly a matter of social skill, and Bingley (unlike Darcy) shows himself to be an adept in this department when he calls attention to the speed and careless rapture of his letter writing, his 'humility' on the occasion masking a proud show of what he rates as a flattering trait.

Jane Austen never let slip an opportunity to expose the motives lurking behind social concealment, no matter how habitual or necessary, and particularly rich in satiric reward were those polite affectations that seemed designed to erase all trace of egoism. A raking light is thrown on these by a *Loiterer* essay that, following a lead from Hume, treats affectation as a special feature of commercial society on the grounds that its 'mixt intercourse of ranks' has reduced reliance on external status and promoted the urge 'to make ourselves conspicuous by appearing to possess qualities in a superior degree to the generality of those around us'.[16] From 'Love and Freindship' to *Sanditon*, Austen took a delight in dealing out self-immolative creeds to the most assertive. Yet *Sense and Sensibility*, despite its send-up of cult attitudes, makes an eloquent plea for the power of sympathy and benevolence – chiefly through the central relationship between the sisters themselves – in terms that closely echo Smith. Austen's comic plots seem particularly well suited, in fact, to the celebration of the 'natural' virtues. Typically, central characters find their sympathies enlarged as their chastened pride leads them to a firmer grasp of the world around them. But there is another, less advertised, form of recognition at work in the novels, more especially the later ones. Whether it is Fanny Price discovering that she can act *in propria persona*, Emma suspending 'heroism of sentiment' to secure Knightley for herself or Anne Elliot taking command at the Cobb, expressed desires make for clarity. Nor could there be a more attractive or more social brief for the realisation of will than what Henry Tilney describes as the 'contract' of marriage.

When Mandeville paired public benefits with private *vices* in his account of the social dividends that derive from pleasure-seeking, he took a side-swipe at that self-denying ethos that Dr Johnson was to call 'monastick morality'. Austen parodies this ascetic outlook in a letter to her sister when she writes, 'It is a Vile World, we are all for Self', adding that 'though *Better* is not to be expected, *Butter* may' (a neighbour's cow was in calf, *L*, 23 January 1817). Her aim as a writer of comedy was to laugh readers into clear-eyed recognition of a self-love that had been vilified, demonised or otherwise disowned (according to creed) by a strain of lift-by-the-shoelace rationalism still active within the Enlightenment itself. In company with those latter-day sceptics, Hume and Smith, she preferred a poised and good-humoured acceptance of human frailty to a blinkered and anxious idealism; and her version of human behaviour, in keeping with theirs, restored the body and its affections to a central place. Like them, she viewed the individual as subject both to sweeping cultural change and to continuous alteration in the private life, even indeed to improvement there – thanks to an inborn capacity for correcting bias towards the self. Like them, again, she understood that society, far from being preordained, was forever evolving, and she saw the need for reform. But unlike most of her fellow-novelists (more particularly those who took themselves seriously) Jane Austen distrusted lofty motives and steered clear of elevated sentiment. True to her Scottish mentors she took the low road, confident that it was the swifter route to a good that included bread and butter as well as moral gain.

NOTES

1. D. H. Lawrence, 'Morality and the Novel', in *Selected Literary Criticism* ed. Anthony Beal, repr. (London: Heinemann, 1964), p. 110; *Letters from Conrad*, ed. Edward Garnett (1928), p. 199.
2. Richard Whately, unsigned review of *Northanger Abbey and Persuasion*, entitled 'Modern Novels', *The Quarterly Review*

24 (January 1821), 352–76. Whately's *Political Economy* (1832) is based on Adam Smith and includes a sturdy defence of Bernard Mandeville.

3. Francis Hutcheson, *An Inquiry into the Original of our Ideas of Beauty and Virtue* (1738), pp. ix–x.

4. Gilbert Ryle, 'Jane Austen and the Moralists', in *Critical Essays on Jane Austen*, ed. B. C. Southam (London: Routledge & Kegan Paul, 1968), pp. 106–22. See also Kenneth Moler, 'The Bennet Girls and Adam Smith on Vanity and Pride', *Philological Quarterly* 46 (1967), 567–9; Tony Tanner, *Jane Austen* (London: Macmillan, 1986), pp. 108–10; Isobel Armstrong, Introduction to *Pride and Prejudice* (Oxford: Oxford University Press, 1990), pp. vii–xx; Peter Knox-Shaw, '*Sense and Sensibility*, Godwin and the Empiricists', *Cambridge Quarterly* 27 (1998), 183–208, and '*Northanger Abbey* and the Liberal Historians', *Essays in Criticism* 49 (1999), 319–43.

5. Irene Collins, *Jane Austen: The Parson's Daughter* (London: Hambledon, 1998), p. 19.

6. Probably the fourth edition with its new subtitle, *A Father's Instructions, consisting of Moral Tales, Fables and Reflections* (1779).

7. Thomas Percival, *A Father's Instructions* (1776), pp. 15–16. Hugh Blair, *Lectures on Rhetoric and Belles Lettres*, 3 vols. (1806), vol. I, p. 28.

8. Blair cites Cardinal Wolsey's soliloquy in his critique of tragic 'moral reflections', see *Lectures on Rhetoric*, vol. III, p. 314; his major debt to Adam Smith's lectures of the same title was acknowledged. See nos. 35, 59 of *The Loiterer*.

9. *Works of William Robertson*, 10 vols. (1821), vol. I, p. lxxxii.

10. David Hume, *A Treatise of Human Nature* ed. David Fate Norton, new edition (Oxford: Oxford University Press, 2002), 1.3.9, p. 78; 1.4.2, p. 132.

11. Joseph Baretti, *A Journey from London to Genoa*, 2 vols. (1770), vol. I, p. 29; and *L*, 20–22 February 1807.

12. Mary Crawford's irreligious joke about the sacrifices performed by returning heathen heroes tallies well with Mandeville's scoffing account of 'the many Hecatombs that have been offer'd after Victories' in his *Fifth Dialogue*, see *The Fable of the Bees*, ed. F. B. Kaye, 2 vols. (1924), vol. II, pp. 214–17; subsequent references are included in the text. See also James Boswell, *The Life of Samuel Johnson*, ed. Roger Ingpen, 2 vols. (1925), vol. II, pp. 791–2.

13. David Hume, *Enquiry Concerning the Principles of Morals*, ed. Tom L. Beauchamp (Oxford: Clarendon Press, 1998) 9.1, p. 147 (subsequent references are included in the text); and see *Treatise*, 2.1.7, pp. 194–5, and 3.3.2, p. 383.

14. See David Hume, *The Theory of Moral Sentiments*, ed. D. D. Raphael and A. L. Macfie (Oxford: Clarendon Press, 1976), III. 3.4, p. 137; VII. ii. 4.8, p. 309; and see *Enquiry*, 6.2, p. 130; and Appendix 4, p. 177, and 7, p. 133.

15. *Treatise*, 3.3.2, pp. 381–3; *Theory*, VI. ii. 21, p. 246; see also the article by Kenneth Moler cited above (note 4).

16. *The Loiterer* 31; and see Hume's essay, 'Of the Rise and Progress of the Arts and Sciences'.

33
Politics

NICHOLAS ROE

Saturday, 16 December 1775, was Jane Austen's birthday. It was also the anniversary of a key event in English political and constitutional history: the signing of the Bill of Rights in 1689. By this Act, civil and political rights in England were guaranteed by Parliamentary authority in matters of law and taxation. The right to petition the King was established, and the maintenance of a standing army without consent of Parliament was declared illegal. The Bill also secured free elections, and freedom of speech in Parliament.

In Austen's lifetime the English Bill of Rights was a powerful influence on revolutionary changes of government in America (1774–6) and Europe (1789). From the 1760s tension between Britain's American colonies and the 'mother country' had steadily increased. Imports from Britain and Ireland were boycotted, and the Tea Act of 1773 – which was intended to secure a monopoly for the East India Company – met with active opposition across the Atlantic. On 16 December 1773, two years before Austen's birth, men disguised as Indians dumped a cargo of tea overboard, in what became known as the Boston Tea-Party. By drawing the population together, this protest helped to link the colonies in opposition to British rule. Close co-operation between the American provinces led up to the First Continental Congress held at Carpenters' Hall, Philadelphia, in September 1774. Congress resolved to halt trade with Britain and issued a Statement of Rights and Grievances on matters of government and taxation. For the moment they stopped short of an outright break, but the route to conflict and American independence had been opened. When the American Constitution was drawn up in 1787 it echoed the English Bill of Rights; in September 1789 amendments to the Constitution were ratified as the American Bill of Rights, and by this date the flame of liberty had crossed the Atlantic to kindle another revolution in France.

'What an eventful period is this! I am thankful I have lived to it.' So the French Revolution of 1789 was greeted in London by the Unitarian Richard Price.[1] In Paris the prison of the Bastille had fallen – tyranny had been overthrown. Thomas Paine, the author of *The Rights of Man* (1791–2) was jubilant: his pamphlet *Common Sense* (1776) had urged the American colonies to break with Britain, and he had helped to draft the constitution enshrining American independence. As he watched liberty spreading in Europe, Paine was convinced it was 'an age of Revolutions in which everything may be looked for'.[2] For the poet Helen Maria Williams, a resident in revolutionary Paris, the French Revolution was 'the triumph of humankind'; to the poet William Wordsworth, who visited France twice during 1790 and 1791–2, it was a 'glorious time'. The human form of that glorious, eventful era is seen in William Blake's radiant figure, 'Glad Day', arms spread wide with joy. Its musical signature is heard in Beethoven's exultant third symphony, the 'Eroica', composed in honour of his hero Napoleon. Shelley said that the French Revolution 'may be called the master theme of the epoch', and its influence continues to the present day in ideas of democracy and human rights.[3]

But not everyone joined in the jubilation, as the national political scene in Britain demonstrated. In his pamphlet *Reflections on the Revolution in France* (1790) Edmund Burke – who had supported freedom in the American colonies – attacked the revolution in France as 'evil' and predicted that it would lead to bloodshed. When war between Britain and France broke out in 1793, he seemed to have been proved right. The Church of England minister Isaac Hunt (a British loyalist at Philadelphia during the American Revolution) warned that the 'sovereign-deposing, bishop-kicking, title-levelling' Thomas Paine planned to revolutionise 'the government of England on the models of those in France and America'. That meant a 'mob assembly'.[4]

While Burke and his kind were drawn to an idealised past of nurturing customs and traditions ('the age of chivalry'), Blake, Paine, Wollstonecraft and Wordsworth all responded to the millenarian excitement of the times and looked for reform of the Parliamentary system. The majority of the population was not entitled to vote in elections, and the 'Test Acts' excluded Catholics and dissenters on religious grounds. Once the debate about the French

Revolution was underway, its repercussions would be felt in all areas of national life: in Britain, men and women were imprisoned without trial for their ideas; others were banished to Botany Bay in Australia. In France hundreds were dragged to the guillotine during Robespierre's Terror of 1793–4. Liberty and rights were contentious issues, and they would be disputed after the union of Ireland with Britain (1801), throughout the years of the Napoleonic Wars (1798–1815) and in the aftermath of the French defeat at Waterloo, 18 June 1815.

Jane Austen's lifetime spanned this Age of Revolutions. As the daughter of a Church of England clergyman in the rural village of Steventon, Hampshire, she might appear as the perfect embodiment of Burkean conservatism in an age of unprecedented and at times violent change. In her novels and letters she has little to say about the political personalities and issues of the day such as the threat of Napoleon, the Duke of Wellington or the Battle of Waterloo. The burden of heavy taxation to pay for the war effort goes unmentioned; so do unemployment, poor laws and the role of parish relief; and the vicious punishment involved in military floggings. Although she was an enthusiast for Thomas Clarkson's abolitionist writings, she gives no clues about the ongoing campaign to put a stop to the slave trade. But she was by no means ignorant of contemporary events. She knew that her cousin Eliza de Feuillide had lost her first husband to Robespierre's Terror when in February 1794 he was guillotined. Following the arrest of leading reformers in London in May 1794, the political scene in Britain became more sharply divided and it seemed as if the Prime Minister, William Pitt, was about to introduce his own system of 'British Terror' patterned on Robespierre's. It was this time that inspired Austen's scene in *Northanger Abbey* in which Catherine Morland's solemn announcement of 'something very shocking indeed [that] will soon come out in London' is understood by Eleanor as a reference to 'politics', 'the state of the nation', 'murder' and 'dreadful riot'. Henry Tilney explains the mistake – Catherine had been talking of a new Gothic novel – but Eleanor's readiness to anticipate 'horrors in London' was by no means as irrational as he suggests (*NA*, 1:14). From the 1790s Jane Austen's brothers Henry and Charles were in active service in the Oxford Militia and the Royal Navy, and throughout her life she was closely and admiringly aware of Britain's maritime exploits against the French and the booty it brought in the shape of prize money for capturing enemy ships.

Austen's novels present an England of small rural communities, farmers and the landed gentry, but this is never a sleepy, pastoral setting and the organisation of society (hotly debated in national politics throughout her lifetime) is always at issue. Mr Darcy and Mr Knightley are ideal landlords; Sir Thomas Bertram and Sir Walter Elliot fail to manage their estates and are unable to govern their households effectively. Country houses and mansions were the most visible symbols of aristocratic power in the English countryside, and the possession and maintenance of such a property expressed the continuity and stability of rule. That such a house could be mismanaged, or fall into the wrong hands, might be a matter of anxiety – especially so at a time when a French invasion was feared to be imminent. When William and Dorothy Wordsworth rented Alfoxden House at Holford, Somerset, in 1797–8, it was widely suspected that some 'French people' or 'democrats' had based themselves in the local 'mansion house' to coordinate a French landing. Although nothing so momentous is anticipated in Austen's novels, her country houses are an arena for related tensions and fears. While patriarchal authority was being championed by Edmund Burke and questioned by Mary Wollstonecraft and other early feminist writers, Austen's novels focussing on domestic authority reflected urgent debates on the national political scene.

In *Pride and Prejudice* and *Mansfield Park* we are always aware of the presence of the army – Lydia Bennet is excited by a summer visit to Brighton where there will be 'a whole campful of soldiers' (*P&P*, 2:16). Brighton was the fashionable resort frequented by the Prince of Wales (from 1811, the Prince Regent), and the military presence was appropriately conspicuous. Lydia sees 'all the glories of the camp; its tents stretched forth in beauteous uniformity of lines, crowded with the young and the gay, and dazzling with scarlet; and to complete the view, she saw herself seated beneath a tent, tenderly flirting with at least six officers at once' (*P&P*, 2:18). Red coats certainly add colour to the novels and bring the prospect of romance, although the reality was not all regimental balls. During the Napoleonic Wars, soldiers were barracked throughout England to protect against a French invasion and also to suppress domestic discontent and unrest. When John Keats visited the Isle of Wight in spring 1817 he remarked on the 'extensive Barracks' and was 'disgusted . . . with Government for placing such a nest of Debauchery in so beautiful a place.'[5] The riotous behaviour in *Pride and Prejudice* when Lydia assists in the cross-dressing of a soldier provides a hint of the kind of 'debauchery' Keats may have had in mind.

Beneath the surface appearance of unruffled calm and continuity, Austen's novels focus on families and individuals confronted with the upheavals of births, marriages and deaths; inheritance, or failure to inherit; increasing wealth, and declining prosperity; the perils and prospects of social advancement. Her novels typically focus on sections of English society that inhabit the vulnerable cusp or borderline between different groups and classes, so that we are always aware of the extraordinary mobility of English society as individuals move across that threshold. Austen's heroines usually marry (or aim to marry) 'up' – Elizabeth Bennet most spectacularly so. But her male characters are sometimes equally vulnerable to the contingencies of fortune: Willoughby's dependence on his wife's money is such that he allows her to dictate his separation from Marianne. Frank Churchill in *Emma* is all attention to his aunt who 'rules at Enscombe' (*E*, 1:14).

Austen's preoccupation with social mobility and change is most evident in *Persuasion*. From the outset we are aware that Sir Walter Elliot, Baronet, is no longer able to afford the upkeep of Kellynch Hall, his ancestral home; Admiral Croft (who moves into Kellynch Hall) and Captain Wentworth, who have made their fortunes at sea during the Napoleonic Wars, represent the 'new money' that lubricates social mobility in the years after Waterloo. As Sir Walter peruses his copy of the 'Baronetage', we see how present changes are set against a long view of 'the history and rise of the ancient and respectable family' in the mid seventeenth century; how an Elliot had represented 'a borough in three successive parliaments'; and how 'exertions of loyalty' had been rewarded with 'dignity of baronet, in the first year of Charles II' (*P*, 1:1). The 'Baronetage' is a mirror to Sir Walter's vanity, and the details Austen gives us are telling. The Elliots' rise to power came after the period of English revolution and civil war, when the family's 'loyal exertions' on behalf on the monarchy brought a reward at the Restoration of Charles

II. The Elliot family's decline at the end of the next century coincides with a new age of revolutions, and widespread social changes impelled by economic pressures and the ideas of Paine and Wollstonecraft.

Money dictates whether characters are dependent or independent of patriarchal or matriarchal rule, and in this way the jostling of generations reflects a comparable struggle in English politics. George III had been crowned in 1760, but a first attack of illness in 1788–9 had been followed by recurrent bouts of madness. When George, Prince of Wales, became Prince Regent on 5 February 1811 (with limited powers, lest his father should recover) he was expected to advance his Whig friends and associates into power. A friend in power is often a friend no longer – and it swiftly became clear that the Regent was no longer inclined to further the Whigs' policies of Parliamentary reform and civil rights for Irish Catholics.

During the Regency (1811–20) political allegiances shifted, with many Whigs withdrawing their support for the Prince, who was now a figure of 'universal distrust'.[6] Even the Regent's long-time friend and apologist Richard Brinsley Sheridan found his loyalty strained. He owed his seat in the House of Commons to the Prince's patronage, but increasingly resented attempts to influence his voting on Irish matters. In February 1812 Lord Moira's motion calling for civil rights for Irish Catholics came before Parliament, the fifth such motion since 1805. Lord Byron supported it in the House of Lords; in the Commons, Sheridan came under pressure not to vote. In the event Sheridan voted in favour of the motion, but like earlier attempts to grant Irish Catholics civil and religious liberty it was heavily defeated.[7] Jane Austen was pleased when her cousin Colonel Thomas Austen was posted to Ireland; that her novels were 'read & admired in Ireland' delighted her (*L*, 3–6 July, 3 November 1813). But otherwise the pressing cause of Ireland goes unmentioned in her books.

With the war against France in its eighteenth year, the domestic political scene looked desolate to those who, like the poet Anna Barbauld, had hitherto clung to hopes of political and social renewal. Her disturbing poem 'Eighteen Hundred and Eleven' begins with the 'deeds of blood' engulfing Europe: 'Still the loud death drum, thundering from afar, / O'er the vext nations pours the storm of war.' And then she turns to the fate of Britain:

And think'st thou, Britain, still to sit at ease,
An island Queen amid thy subject seas,
While the vext billows, in their distant roar,
But soothe thy slumbers, and but kiss thy shore?
To sport in wars, while dangers keep aloof,
Thy grassy turf unbruised by hostile hoof?
So sing thy flatterers; but, Britain, know,
Thou who hast shared the guilt must share the woe.
Nor distant is the hour; low murmurs spread,
And whispered fears, creating what they dread . . .[8]

Barbauld's poem captures the restive mood of Britain at this moment, described by the Whig lawyer Henry Brougham as 'most dangerous & unfortunate'.[9] Bankruptcies were at an all-time high; industrial unrest and 'Luddite' machine breaking spread across the north of England. The evocation of 'low murmurs' and 'whispered fears' in 'Eighteen Hundred and Eleven' tapped into anxieties lying deeper than present discontents, stirring uneasiness about the nation's future. To Unitarians like Barbauld, Joseph Priestley and Coleridge, God's purposes were being fulfilled through advances in political knowledge and a glorious dawn, the millennium, was in prospect. Coleridge struck this note of jubilant optimism in his poem of 1796, *Religious Musings*, in which his 'young anticipating heart' welcomed a 'blest future' and 'promis'd years' of unimaginable glory. But the millennium had not arrived on cue and, as years passed and the century turned, it became more and more difficult to proclaim the imminence of paradise regained. By 1811, Anna Barbauld's mood had darkened, as her poem reveals. War, the collapse of commerce, the gluttonous 'Luxury' of a few, and 'ghastly Want' of the many, all signalled Britain's imminent downfall (line 64). The theme of Barbauld's poem is the passing of empire: as earlier empires had risen, flourished and eventually faded, so now in Britain, 'enfeebled despots sway' and 'evil days portend' (lines 58, 244). The changeful 'Genius' of national prosperity had abandoned the once 'favoured shore' (line 241) to decline and disaster.

These sublime prospects of paradise regained and 'evil days' seem worlds away from Austen's novels – a kind of parallel universe where day-to-day events were understood in a framework of apocalyptic meaning. But perhaps we could think of the quiet, interpersonal discoveries and enlightenments in Austen's narratives – *Emma*, for example – as an ironic mirror of the sensational revelations of self-invented prophets such as Joanna Southcott and Richard Brothers. Instead of Shiloh, the seraph man whose birth was expected by Joanna Southcott, Emma settles for a more domesticated messiah in Mr Knightley. Austen depicts new dawns and realisations as her heroines come to fuller self-knowledge – a less 'eventful period' than the millennium expected by Richard Price but a more sustainable one.

In the radical *Examiner* newspaper, the journalist Leigh Hunt took every opportunity to attack the Regent, and in 1813–15 was jailed for two years and fined heavily for an article, 'The Prince on St Patrick's Day', in which the Regent – who no longer inclined favourably to the Irish cause – was described as a 'clencher of Irish chains'. Hunt would leave prison to become a poetic mentor to Percy Bysshe Shelley and John Keats. Austen would certainly have been aware of Hunt's political activities and his prison sentence, but she could not have known that James Henry Leigh Hunt had in fact been named after her uncle, the Hon. James Henry Leigh. Hunt's father, the loyalist Isaac Hunt, was a tutor to the young James Henry Leigh, and he had hoped to further his own ambitions with this compliment to his pupil. Austen evidently thought her own interests as a novelist were best served by dedicating *Emma* 'To his Royal Highness The Prince Regent', despite her private reservations about the Prince Regent's attempts to divorce his wife, Caroline, before his accession to the throne.

When Jane Austen died on Friday 18 July 1817 the Regency still had two and a half years to run before the death of George III. Just two days after her death the *Examiner* reported Henry Brougham's 'Address on the State of the Nation' in the House of Commons, expressing 'deep concern that the measures of his Royal Highness's advisers have neither been calculated to fulfil the hopes, to alleviate the sufferings, nor to recover the affections of the People'. It seemed that the 'costly victories' of the twenty-two year war with France had been 'thrown away', leaving a 'universal discontent'.[10] Change would come, and by 1830 the Test Acts had been repealed and Catholic Emancipation passed. The Great Reform Act passed into law in June 1832 extended the franchise, notably in the new industrial cities, although the majority of the working classes and the rural poor, who owned nothing, could not find the £10 necessary to qualify for a vote. Women were still excluded from the franchise. Further reforms were urgently needed. The nineteenth century would turn the narrative sophistication, psychological insight and social vision Jane Austen had brought to the novel to the explicitly political and social concerns of the 'condition of England'.

NOTES

1. Richard Price, *A Discourse on the Love of our Country* (1789), p. 49.
2. Thomas Paine, *Rights of Man*, ed. Henry Collins (Harmondsworth: Penguin, 1969), p. 168.
3. Letter to Lord Byron, 8 September 1816, *The Letters of Percy Bysshe Shelley*, ed. F. L. Jones, 2. vols (Oxford: Clarendon Press, 1964), vol. IV, p. 504.
4. Isaac Hunt, *Rights of Englishmen. An Antidote to the Poison now Vending by the Transatlantic Republican Thomas Paine* (1791), pp. 6, 8.
5. *Letters of John Keat*s, ed. H. Rollins, 2 vols. (Cambridge, MA: Harvard University Press, 1972), vol. I, pp. 131–2.
6. 'George IV', in *The Works of Henry Lord Brougham*, 4 vols. (1872), vol. IV, p. 24.
7. *Letters of Richard Brinsley Sheridan*, ed. Cecil Price, 3 vols. (Oxford: Clarendon Press, 1966), vol. III, p. 150. Fintan O'Toole, *A Traitor's Kiss. The Life of Richard Brinsley Sheridan* (London: Granta Books, 1997), pp. 440–1.
8. *The Poems of Anna Laetitia Barbauld*, eds. W. McCarthy and E. Kraft (Athens: University of Georgia Press, 1994), p. 154, lines 39–48.
9. British Library Add. Mss. 38108.
10. *Examiner* (20 July 1817), 451.

34

Professions

BRIAN SOUTHAM

During the second half of the eighteenth century, the traditional 'learned professions' – the church, the law and medicine – took on a new and distinctive *social* character as the 'liberal professions', 'liberal' in the sense of befitting a gentleman. Together with the army and the navy – known as the profession of arms – they came to be regarded as suitable occupations, both socially and financially, for the sons of gentlemen. Since the eldest son would inherit the family estate, this applied to younger sons in particular. As Mary Crawford points out, 'there is generally an uncle or a grandfather to leave a fortune to the second son' (*MP*, 1:9); or he might inherit money or land from his mother's side of the family. If not, along with the other younger sons, he would be left to make his own way in the world, to earn a living in one of the gentlemanly occupations that the liberal professions could provide. In the colder moral climate that arrived towards the turn of the century, employment came to be valued for its own sake as a force in character building and a safeguard against idleness, benefits available to eldest and younger sons alike. This thinking stands behind General Tilney's pronouncement. He considers 'it expedient to give every young man some employment' (*NA*, 2:7).[1]

As to which profession, the army was the favoured choice of aristocratic families; the navy offered fame and fortune; the law was well regarded for its earning power and its usefulness in a political career; the church was rising steadily in remuneration and status; while in medicine only the Fellows of the Royal College of Physicians, fewer than two hundred of them, were accepted as the gentlemen of the profession. Very often the choice was determined by family tradition. There were established medical, legal, clerical and service families; and in a society where patronage and connections counted for so much, the well-trodden family path could be the most profitable road to choose. Lowly merit, too, found its reward. Advancement in a profession enabled those who were not born of the gentry to enter its ranks, a process reinforced by the idea that since the gentry entrusted their lives and fortunes to physicians and lawyers, and their souls to the clergy, and the kingdom itself to commanders in the army and navy, so these professionals should themselves be men of standing in society. As Adam Smith put it in *The Wealth of Nations* (1776), 'Such confidence could not safely be reposed in people of very mean or low condition. Their reward must be such as may give them that rank in the society which so important a trust requires.'[2]

The importance of the professions to the world of the novels can be gauged by the prominence of professional figures: the clergymen, headed by Mr Collins and Mr Elton, Henry Tilney and Edmund Bertram, with Mr Collins ready to hold forth on 'the profession of a clergyman' (*P&P*, 1:18); the naval men led by William Price and Captain Wentworth; together with a scattering of other clergymen, soldiers, sailors, lawyers and a few medical men. Moreover, in line with the leading moral and educational writers of the time, Jane Austen makes the choice of a profession, and issues of professional knowledge, professional duty, income and the sense of vocation, topics for discussion and debate among her characters. Many of her young men are just embarked, or about to embark, upon professional careers; those around them are concerned for their success; and the structure of the professions, with their distinct hierarchies, and the ambitions of their lowlier members answer Austen's style of social comedy, with its attention to the snobberies and pretensions of rank, status and class.

Much of Austen's knowledge of the professions came from her own family connections and the circles in which she moved. On her father's side in earlier generations there was a body of medical Austens. The lawyers in the family were headed by her father's guardian and benefactor, her great-uncle Francis Austen of Sevenoaks, who prospered as agent for the Sackville estate at Knole. Her mother's father and grandfather were clergymen; and immediately around her was a wide clerical society which included her own father, two of her brothers and an extensive network of clergy relatives and friends. Jane Austen was also familiar with the profession of arms. Her sailor brothers Francis and Charles served throughout the twenty years of the French wars and beyond, and she drew upon their naval lives in the writing of *Mansfield Park* and *Persuasion*. Similarly, it was in 1796–7, at a time when her brother Henry was serving in the militia, that she first drafted *Pride and Prejudice*, giving the story a timely background of redcoats and militia camps.

In the pages that follow, I outline each of the professions as they stood during the period of Austen's lifetime (excepting medicine, which is covered by John Wiltshire in this volume). But a note of caution is in order. As much as her depiction of life and manners is detailed and accurate, it belongs to a fictional scene which is highly selective and limited in scope. With few exceptions, Austen's focus is upon the cultivated and prosperous middle gentry society of London, Bath and the southern counties, the world in which she was at home. But this was a privileged setting. The England that lay beyond this scene was very different, not least for the professions and for the conditions of professional life.

The established Church of England is the only church mentioned by Austen. The prominence of clergymen in the novels is an accurate reflection of the central place they occupied in rural society at this time. In country parishes, the rector stood alongside the local landowner or squire at the head of the community. Beyond his church responsibilities, he played an active part in the social life of the neighbourhood and in its civil administration, carrying out such duties as the registration of births, deaths and marriages, the conduct of the Poor Law, reporting on the manpower available for wartime service in the volunteers, sitting on the bench of magistrates and so on.

In about half of the country's 10,500 parishes the church livings were the property of local squires. With ownership came the right of appointment, opening the way to respectable employment for their younger sons, a niche that became increasingly attractive towards the end of the eighteenth century as livings rose in value. At one end of the scale (according to a Parliamentary enquiry in 1802) about 1,000 church livings were worth less than £100 per annum, with another 3,000 between £100–150, barely enough to live on. But it was another story for country parishes in the prosperous south. Ownership of the glebe (the church agricultural land), together with the tithes, produced an income that rose in step with the rising value of both of the land and its produce, a boom that lasted until 1814. In the 1770s, Mr Austen's two Hampshire parishes were worth about £200. Thirty years later, their value had gone up more than fourfold: the tithes were producing £600 and the glebe £300. This change in the economics of farming and land ownership had much to do with the attraction that the church increasingly held for the sons of the gentry.

Clergymen without family connections were obliged to look elsewhere for patronage. The crown, bishops, cathedral chapters, and the universities of Oxford and Cambridge together controlled several thousand livings, although these were often reserved for appointees. As for the rest, young ordinands would depend on the good will of unmarried or childless squires. And beyond the fortunate clerics remained a body of clergymen, calculated in 1805 to number up to 45 per cent of those ordained, who never found a church living and were forced into dead-end employment as penurious curates hired for as little as £50 a year, or who turned to teaching or some other occupation outside the church.

This surplus in the number of ordinands is partly explained by the fact that entry to the profession was relatively undemanding. The minimum age for ordination to deacon was twenty-three, to priest twenty-four. A candidate was required to present himself to a bishop with (amongst other papers) evidence of his degree (from Oxford or Cambridge, 60 per cent of whose graduates entered the church), a 'Certificate from the Professor of his having attended the Divinity Lectures' and letters from his college testifying to 'his learning and good behaviour' and to his worthiness 'to be admitted to holy orders'.[3] A candidate also faced examination by the bishop's archdeacon to ascertain that he was someone 'apt and meet for Learning and godly Conversation to exercise your Ministry duly, to the Honour of God and the Edification of his Church'.[4] Then followed examination by the bishop to satisfy himself that the candidate was competent in Latin and sufficiently acquainted with the Scriptures, the church liturgy and the 39 Articles. This procedure was as demanding or undemanding as his Lordship chose to make it. As the Bishop of Sarum remarked, 'a great measure of piety, with a very small proportion of learning, will carry one a great way.'[5]

Yet, as we know both from the novels and from historical evidence, in the average parish clergyman of this time one was as likely to encounter worldliness as 'piety'. There were recognised devices for a clergyman to make the best use of his time and money. One was 'pluralism', the occupancy of more than one living. If these were neighbouring parishes, a clergyman might serve both without undue strain, as Mr Austen himself managed in travelling between the adjoining parishes of Steventon and Deane. For parishes some distance apart, the clergyman might be an 'absentee' for one of them, paying a curate to fill his place. Although such arrangements were widespread – Jane Austen's brother James had three parishes and was offered a fourth – with the rise of Evangelicalism they came under increasing criticism.

Over the course of the eighteenth century, these 'wants and claims' had considerably lightened. In many parishes, the routine two Sunday services had fallen to one, with Holy Communion celebrated only once a month. Sermons were commonly borrowed or adapted from printed collections. Midweek duties were confined to occasional baptisms, marriages and funerals and visiting the sick – these 'claims' attended to according to the conscientiousness of individual clergymen, or left to the curate. At one extreme, according to Mary Crawford, was the 'slovenly and selfish' clergyman: 'His curate does all the work, and the business of his own life is to dine' (*MP*, 1:11). Then comes the clergyman in 'nominal residence', as the practice, accepted and tolerated, was termed, visiting his parish on Sundays only, or rarely more, in the manner of Henry Tilney. At the other extreme is Jane Austen's figure of the true professional, Edmund Bertram, a young man approaching ordination thoughtfully, visualising himself in prospect as a resident clergyman setting a Christian example to 'the parish and neighbourhood' by living up to 'those doctrines which it is their duty to teach and recommend' (*MP*, 1:9). However, of these doctrines themselves, and larger church matters, Jane Austen has nothing to say.

As a consequence of Parliamentary legislation and the regulation of the Inns of Court and other legal bodies, the law was the most visibly and effectively organised of the professions; and of all the professions it offered the greatest opportunities for social, political and financial advancement. A rank-and-file solicitor (usually known as an attorney) qualified by way of five years' apprenticeship in a legal office as an articled clerk, for which an annual premium was paid. London attorneys numbered about 1,800 and in a sought-after and successful practice, a placement which would attract the sons of the gentry, the premium would be as much as £500–600 a year. Regarded as inferior were country practices; in 1812, there were just over 4,300; and the premium would run to about £200. When the clerk's apprenticeship was completed, he came before a judge, to be examined (if at all, a perfunctory procedure), sworn in, admitted and enrolled as a working attorney, now qualified to practise. Beyond the fees and commissions to be earned from his bread-and-butter work – witnessing oaths, drawing up wills, deeds and marriage settlements etc. – a capable attorney could make considerable sums as agent for a landed estate. An attorney might also engage in property transactions on his own behalf, providing loans, mortgages and an informal banking service for the benefit of his clients. In addition, he might serve as an MP's election agent, distributing bribes etc., or even enjoy a small taste of power and local recognition himself as clerk to the magistrates' court and other official bodies.

The upper branch of the legal profession, its unquestioned gentlemen, were the barristers. They formed a small and highly select group – about 600 in 1810, not all of them active – the only lawyers permitted to address the courts. The path to qualification was steep. It required an income sufficient to support five years (three years for university graduates) keeping terms at one of the four Inns of Court, the London institutions with the exclusive right to admit students to the Bar. On top of this were pupillage fees paid to the barristers in whose chambers they learned their law or to the solicitors in whose offices they worked as clerks. Once called to the Bar, further money was needed to support themselves in the early years of practice when briefs could be few and far between. Alongside these serious students were fashionable young bloods who patronised the Inns of Court as a smart social and dining club, but with no intention of practising law seriously. Nonetheless, despite the slow and costly start, the Bar offered 'the surest road to riches and honour'.[6] An average yearly income for an established barrister was £4,000, with the possibility of rising to £15,000 or more. As to 'honour', the Bar was the training ground for judges and Lord Chancellors. It also opened a political path. One in four MPs was a barrister – a predominance remarked on caustically by Cobbett: 'We have been brought to our present miserable state by a lawyer-like policy defended in lawyer-like debates.'[7] Barristers were favoured for government appointments; they were prominent in the cabinet; and included Prime Ministers Pitt and Addington.

The wars with France, from 1793 to 1815, raised the prestige and popularity of the military profession and vastly enlarged its numbers. The navy more than quadrupled, from a pre-war strength of about 30,000 to a peak in 1810 of 140,000; and the army increased fivefold, from 45,000 to 250,000 by 1812. As Austen was concerned almost entirely with the officers, the two sections that follow take no account of the non-commissioned ranks.

The social composition of the officer corps of the regular army was altogether changed by its rapid wartime expansion – from 3,100 officers in 1792 to almost 10,600 by 1814. Whereas in peacetime this was a select body almost entirely composed of the sons of officers, the landed gentry and aristocracy, such was the wartime demand for new officers that 'almost any young man who wished to and was literate would have little difficulty in obtaining a commission'. Applicants had to be between sixteen and twenty-one (although this upper age was often exceeded) and carry a letter of recommendation from a major or above certifying to their 'character, education and bodily health'.[8] The junior department of the Royal Military College opened in 1802 to train gentlemen cadets aged between thirteen and fifteen. But this new route provided fewer than 4 per cent of first commissions. The other professional entry was via the Royal Military Academy at Woolwich. This admitted cadets of between fourteen and sixteen for a rigorous technical course, normally between eighteen months and two years but shortened in wartime. It concluded with an examination, the best candidates going into the Royal Engineers, the remainder into the Royal Artillery. But, again, the numbers were small and as many as 65 per cent of newly commissioned officers entered the army wholly untrained. Their military education began when they joined their regiments, as young officers, where they were drilled with the men or under the care of a sergeant, and picked up what they could from the various manuals of instruction. Only officers who had risen from the ranks (one in twenty), and those who joined from the militia (one in five), would bring any prior military knowledge or skills. During the war with France, it was easy enough to obtain a commission, and at no cost provided that the applicant declared that he was (in the official wording) 'prepared immediately to join any regiment to which he may be appointed'. For the much smaller number wanting to join an elite regiment there were barriers both financial and social. Socially, a prospective officer would have to be acceptable to the colonel of the regiment; and in addition to purchasing his commission he would need the resources to meet mess and other expenses which far exceeded his pay. According to the official price list, ensign, the lowest rank in an infantry regiment, cost £400, in the Foot Guards £600; cornet, the lowest cavalry rank, in the dragoons £735, in the Blues £1,050 and in the Life Guards £1,600. These price differentials give us an accurate measure of the relative social standing, exclusivity and expense of the different regiments. According to the regulations of 1809 – tightened since 1795 under the reforms introduced by the Duke of York, the Commander-in-Chief – after three years' service a junior officer could sell his existing commission and purchase promotion to captain, and so on after a further four years to major and a further two years to lieutenant-colonel. The price of the commission rose, according to rank and regiment, up to £6,700 for lieutenant-colonel in the Foot Guards. Although only 20 per cent of promotions were by this method, nonetheless purchase was valued as an important institution. In the eyes of its champions, Wellington among them, it brought to the army 'men of fortune and education', men with a stake in the country's welfare who could be trusted in its defence.[9] Seventy per cent of promotions went according to seniority of service; and seniority was the sole mechanism for promotion to colonel and beyond, as it was for every rank in the Royal Artillery and the Royal Engineers. The remaining 10 per cent were promotions by patronage, on the recommendation of the commander-in-chief or a general officer for merit or bravery, or to replace an officer dismissed the service.

Such was the cost of army life that even officers with free commissions could barely scrape by on their pay. An infantry ensign received 5s 3d a day, a Guards' ensign 5s 10p, a cornet in the cavalry 8s, and in the Life Guards 8s 6d. Against this came a burden of fees and deductions plus the daily cost of meals, wine, servant, the purchase and upkeep of the uniform and equipment and other minor expenses; in addition, a cavalry officer had to provide his own horse. While an infantry officer might get by with a private allowance of £50 or £100, those moving in London society in the elite regiments needed not less than £500.

Alongside, yet quite separate from, the regular standing army was the militia, an auxiliary military force formed solely for the homeland defence of the kingdom. Dormant in peacetime, it was embodied at the end of 1792 in response to the threat from revolutionary France. The appointment of officers, drawn from the county gentry, was in the hands of the county Lord Lieutenants. Their rank did not depend on military experience or expertise but on a complex system of property qualifications, on the principle that the more a man owned the greater his entitlement to command a force dedicated to the defence of the national property, the kingdom itself. So to each of the ranks, from ensign to colonel, the regulations attached a minimum property requirement. During the years of the war, however, this condition was relaxed, since such was the shortage of officers that – as with the regular army – 'anyone remotely suitable had to be taken on'.[10]

While there are a number of high-ranking army officers in the novels, including General Tilney and several colonels, we hear nothing of their military lives save for the fact that Colonel Brandon's regiment was once stationed in the East Indies; and of junior officers, no more than that Frederick Tilney was a captain in the 12th Light Dragoons (a real regiment, given the title 'The Prince of Wales's' by George III in 1768). Of the militia officers we learn slightly more: that, for example, Mr Weston was formerly a captain in the Surrey force, fired it seems not by patriotism but to satisfy his 'active cheerful mind and social temper' (*E*, 1:2). Similarly, Wickham claims that his 'chief inducement' in taking the rank of lieutenant 'was the prospect of constant society, and good society' (*P&P*, 1:16). On his marriage to Lydia, Wickham moves over from the militia to make a career in the regular army, starting as an ensign, this rank and his later promotion to unspecified higher ranks purchased for him by Darcy.

Away from the battlefield, the army seemed pleasantly social and amateur, whereas the navy offered a lifelong career, demanding and highly professional. Commissions were only granted after a lengthy period of preparation and training. The examination for lieutenant called for a minimum of six years' service at sea and candidates, aged nineteen and above, had to produce their personal journals and certificates of service. To reach this point, youngsters of between eleven and thirteen went straight to sea, designated as 'captain's servants', later 'volunteers'. In effect, they were officer cadets in a sea-apprenticeship. Under the direct surveillance of the ship's captain they were trained in seamanship, navigation, mapping, the construction of the ship and all the other areas of knowledge and skill called for in holding a command. The alternative route, taken by only 1 or 2 per cent, including Jane Austen's sailor brothers Francis and Charles, was via the Royal Navy Academy at Portsmouth. This provided a two- to three-year programme, combining naval training and school-room education, for boys aged between twelve and fifteen at the time of entry. After the Academy they joined the volunteers at sea, continuing for three or four years before presenting themselves as midshipmen for the lieutenant's examination.

'Passing for lieutenant', as it was called, did not automatically bring the rank. This only came with the commission to a specific lieutenant's post on a ship. Promotion to commander and then captain was on merit – but could also be effected by 'influence', the pulling of strings by a relative or patron, perhaps a member of the House of Commons or Lords. Equally helpful was the patronage of a senior naval officer – as Admiral Crawford intervenes to help William Price towards a commission in *Mansfield Park*. Promotion above the rank of captain was according to seniority on the captain's list. In this, longevity was the secret of success. Witness the later careers of the sailor brothers: Charles Austen promoted to rear-admiral in 1850 at the age of seventy-one and Francis at the age of eighty-nine achieving the navy's highest rank, Admiral of the Fleet.

Naval pay was modest. All lieutenants received £101 a year. Captains were paid according to the rating of their ships: for the largest three-deckers, with over 100 guns, £386 a year, down to vessels of 20–30 guns, a fraction over £200. And for the periods they were back in England between ships – this could be for a matter of months, even years – they were left to subsist on half-pay. However, there was always the hope of prize money, a share in the value of captured enemy ships. It was a complex and tightly regulated system. But broadly speaking, up to 1808 a three-eighths share went to the captain and the remaining five-eighths were divided on a diminishing scale, according to rank, amongst the other officers, commissioned and non-commissioned, and the ordinary members of the crew (post-1808, a slight change was made to the allocation of these shares). It was prize money that brings Captain Wentworth his £25,000, the small fortune that plays a crucial role in the romantic drama of *Persuasion*. There was always the hope of other material rewards too: an elaborate tariff of annuities and cash payments and pensions for those involved in great victories at sea; and, at a more routine level, freight or treasure money paid to captains for the transport of gold or silver bullion or minted coins, a perk which Francis enjoyed. As Jane Austen put it neatly to her brother, the navy was a 'Profession' that 'has its' douceurs to recompense for some of its' Privations' (*L*, 3–6 July 1813) – 'privations' that were manifold: absence from family and home; accidents at sea and fever, a toll that far exceeded death or disablement at the hands of the enemy; and a naval culture that led to drunkenness and upheld shipboard discipline of the utmost brutality.

NOTES

1. Lawrence Stone and J. C. Fawtier, *An Open Elite? England 1540–1800* (Oxford: Clarendon Press, 1984), p. 228.
2. Adam Smith, *The Wealth of Nations*, Books I–III ed. Andrew Skinner (London: Penguin, 1982), p. 207.
3. Christopher Hodgson, *Instructions for the Use of Candidates for Holy Orders* (1817), pp. 1–4.
4. Arthur St George, *The Archdeacon's Instructions for Candidates for Holy Orders*, new edition (1799), p. 1.
5. Gilbert Burnet (Bishop of Sarum) quoted in *The Clergyman's Instructor, or A Collection of Tracts on the Ministerial Duties*, ed. George Bull (1817), p. 189.
6. [Anon], *Advice to a certain Lord Chancellor* (1792), p. 7.
7. *Political Register* (4 July 1812), xxii, 9.
8. Richard Glover, *Peninsular Preparation: The Reform of the British Army 1795–1809*, repr. (Cambridge: Cambridge University Press, 1977), p. 36.
9. Quoted in Edward M. Spiers, *The Army and Society, 1815–1914* (London: Longman, 1980), p. 12.
10. J. R. Western, *The English Militia in the Eighteenth Century: The Story of a Political Issue 1660–1802* (London: Routledge, 1965), p. 311.

35

Psychology

JOHN MULLAN

Any discerning reader can relish Jane Austen's psychological discernment. From a literary historical point of view, her achievement seems the more remarkable. In her apparent vindication of her chosen genre in *Northanger Abbey*, Austen described the fiction of predecessors like Frances Burney and Maria Edgeworth as conveying 'the most thorough knowledge of human nature, the happiest delineation of its varieties' (1:5). Yet a reader who comes to Burney's or Edgeworth's novels after Austen's is likely to think that their 'human nature' often excludes psychological probability. He or she would notice, in particular, that their heroines are models of feminine rectitude. They may be placed in difficult situations, and variously tricked or misinformed, but they do not exactly have faults. One useful way of understanding Austen's psychological subtlety is as an escape from models of the heroine offered by fiction before her.

Jane Austen was an avid novel reader and well aware of how her work might compare with the fiction of her predecessors or contemporaries. Usually when she refers to other novels or novelists in her fiction or letters it is in some spirit of satire. Just before she died, the new novel on which she was working was invigorated by the follies of novel readers just as *Northanger Abbey* had been. *Sanditon* sets in motion a sub-plot involving a character's laughable susceptibility to fiction. Sir Edward Denham, we hear, 'had read more sentimental Novels than agreed with him'. He enthuses about his favourite works: 'The Novels which I approve are such as display Human Nature with Grandeur – such as shew her in the Sublimities of intense Feeling – such as exhibit the progress of strong Passion from the first Germ of incipient Susceptibility to the utmost Energies of Reason half-dethroned.' His 'fancy', we are told, 'had been early caught by all the impassioned, and most exceptionable parts of Richardson's' (*S*, 8).

Richardson had made novels morally respectable and, by his extraordinary use of epistolary form, had seemed to recreate the shifts of a character's mind. We might remember that the earliest version of *Sense and Sensibility* was, reportedly, an epistolary novel, and infer Richardson's direct influence on a novelist who wanted to get the reader into the minds of her main characters. Certainly we are assured in Henry Austen's 'Biographical Notice' of his sister that she (along with most European novelists) greatly admired Richardson. Yet we can catch in the passage from *Sanditon* Austen's sense that the high strains of Richardson's stories (predatory, enraptured men pursuing virtuously distressed young women) could seem absurd. The habit of setting her own characters and situations against those of other novelists ran deep. Her burlesque 'Plan of a Novel', probably composed in 1816, is a menu of novelistic clichés and emphasises one expectation against which she rebelled. 'Heroine a faultless Character herself –, perfectly good, with much tenderness & sentiment, & not the least Wit.' She was thinking of many heroines of many novels. 'As far as she could be perfect, considering the people she had to deal with and those with whom she was inseparably connected, she is perfect,' wrote Richardson in the preface to the third edition (1751) of *Clarissa*. His heroine 'is proposed as an exemplar to her sex.'[1] 'Pictures of perfection as you know,' wrote Jane Austen to her niece Fanny Knight, 'make me sick & wicked' (*L*, 23 March 1817).

Between Richardson and Austen, 'virtue' is invariably the leading characteristic of any novel's heroine. 'All the Good will be unexceptionable in every respect – and there will be no foibles or weaknesses,' wrote Austen in her 'Plan of a Novel'. Escaping such goodness was essential to her psychological realism. When Elizabeth Bennet and Mr Darcy banter in *Pride and Prejudice* about each other's possible deficiencies, or when Mr Knightley and Mrs Weston discuss 'dear Emma's little faults' (*E*, 1:5), we might hear in the comedy Austen's rejection of the faultlessness of the Richardsonian heroine. This is the significance of Austen's taking the title of her best-known novel from the final chapter of Frances Burney's *Cecilia* (1782). Here the 'sagacious' Dr Lyster sums up how the eventual union of Cecilia with the man she loves, Mortimer Delvile, has been impeded by their two families. '"The whole of this unfortunate business," said Dr. Lyster, "has been the result of PRIDE and PREJUDICE"' (vol. 5, bk. 10, ch. 10). The virtuous heroine and her beloved have had to overcome the pride and prejudice of others. In Austen's version, in contrast, the pride and the prejudice are distributed between the heroine and the man who is her match.

It is notable that half of Austen's completed novels have abstract nouns for their titles, all of which direct our attention to what we might call qualities of mind (there is some debate about whether the title of *Persuasion* reflected Jane Austen's own wishes or was entirely the choice of her brother Henry). There was something of a fashion for such titles at the beginning of the nineteenth century, when they were used for essentially didactic purposes. Examples included Elizabeth Inchbald's *Nature and Art* (1796), Mary Brunton's *Self-Control* (1811) and Maria Edgeworth's *Patronage* (1814). Brunton's title is most like those used by Austen, though her novel is predictably admonitory as Jane Austen's would never be. The heroine of *Self-Control*, Laura Montreville, discovers the joys of 'chastened affection' and 'tempered desires' (ch. 34). Austen was certainly aware of this work, published in the same year as *Sense and Sensibility*, for she jokes in a letter to Cassandra about Laura's escape from her would-be seducer, by canoe down a Canadian river, as 'the most natural, possible, every-day thing she ever does' (*L*, 11 October 1813).

Brunton was drawing attention to the necessity, especially for a young woman, of the habit of mind announced by her title. In the titles of her own first two published novels, Austen was being altogether more quizzical. It is no accident that she began her career as an author by interrogating the quality possessed by all Richardsonian heroines, and synonymous with inwardness in eighteenth-century fiction: 'sensibility'. 'Sensibility', which had originally referred to merely bodily sensitivities, began to stand for emotional responsiveness in the early eighteenth century, and came to designate a laudable delicacy in the second half of the century. It was a natural human faculty often displayed by characters in novels. Here, for example, is our introduction to the heroine of Burney's *Cecilia*, who is a young heiress. 'But though thus largely indebted to fortune, to nature she had yet greater obligations: her form was elegant, her heart was liberal; her countenance announced the intelligence of her mind, her complexion varied with every emotion of her soul, and her eyes, the heralds of her speech, now beamed with understanding and now glistened with sensibility' (vol. 1, bk. 1, ch. 1). Burney's paragon has just the qualities to be found in any amount of post-Richardson fiction, all somehow legible, beaming and glistening, in her very face. Emily St Aubert, the heroine of Ann Radcliffe's *The Mysteries of Udolpho* (1794), is also privileged with 'sensibility', 'observable' as 'a degree of susceptibility too exquisite to admit of lasting peace': 'As she advanced in years, this sensibility gave a pensive tone to her spirits, and a softness to her manner, which added grace to beauty, and rendered her a very interesting object to persons of a congenial disposition' (vol. 1, ch. 1).

No wonder that the physically robust Catherine Morland is said in the opening paragraph of *Northanger Abbey* to be ill suited to be the heroine of a novel. Emily St Aubert, the protagonist of her own favourite book, is physically susceptible to her feelings, just like Richardson's heroines. They have sensibilities keen enough to make them ill. They are always trembling, fainting, turning sick with feeling. The best people are so attuned to their own feelings that they can be weakened by them. As they are also laudably responsive to others' feelings, especially of distress, they can be sure that this susceptibility is virtuous. In fiction, this was sometimes true of men as well as women. The sensitive hero of Henry Mackenzie's hugely successful novel *The Man of Feeling* (1771) feels and weeps for others so much that, enfeebled by his sympathies, he wastes and dies – a man too good for an unfeeling world.

The *OED* suggests not only that 'feelings' were first identified in the later eighteenth century, but also that novels might have been where they were first explored. The word 'feelings' – used in its now most common sense to mean 'emotions' – has its first recorded use in the 1770s. The two earliest examples cited are both taken from novels: by Elizabeth Griffith and Ann Radcliffe. 'Feeling' (singular noun) dates from at least the fourteenth century; 'feelings' (plural) is an eighteenth-century coinage: a new concern or possession of refined individuals. We might say that the polite culture of novel consumers that Richardson helped to make was one whose members were learning to have 'feelings', and to value them.

Novels were where you went to have those feelings. This is why some novels (presumably enjoyed by Sir Edward Denham) began to use the declaration 'A Sentimental Novel' on their title pages (especially in the wake of Laurence Sterne's *A Sentimental Journey*, 1768). 'Sentimental' was a word for a type of text, promising an *occasion* for fine feeling. This fine feeling could be experienced by both the book's characters and its reader. A sentimental novel at once depicted sensibility and appealed to it.

It was not only novelists. To the historian of ideas, this pursuit of feelings looks like a much wider cultural preoccupation. David Hume, notably in his *A Treatise of Human Nature* (1739–40), and Adam Smith, in his *A Theory of Moral Sentiments* (1759), are the leading examples of how empiricist philosophy turned to the work-ings of feelings in the mid eighteenth century. They both set out to describe the properties of 'sympathy', the faculty by which 'the passions and sentiments of others' become our own'.[2] Like the sen-timental novelists, they were trying to understand how 'sentiments' might be both vivid emotions and moral judgements. Though the philosophical psychologists of the eighteenth century rarely noticed contemporary novelists, Smith did single out Richardson as one of those 'poets and romance writers' who are good 'instructors' because they celebrate 'that extraordinary sensibility, which we naturally feel for the misfortunes of our nearest connections'.[3] From Locke onwards, philosophers had explored the psychology of the individ-ual, his (or her) mind supplied only by experience and the activity of reason. The philosophers of sympathy elaborated a means of rescuing that individual from isolation.

By the 1790s, however, the psychological refinements of the novel of sensibility had come to seem deeply suspect to many. As Marilyn Butler was to point out, opposition to sentimental literature as being individualistic, possibly politically radical, grew up just in the period 'when the apprentice Jane Austen formed her literary attitudes'.[4] From early on there was the suspicion that the display of sensibility was artificial – at best merely fashionable, at worst deeply hypocritical. The literary cult of sensibility produced its own descant – voices like those of the respected moralist Hannah More, in her *Sensibility: A Poetical Epistle* (1782). More valued the tender effects of reading Richardson or Sterne, and readily conflated feeling with virtue.

> Sweet Sensibility! thou keen delight!
> Thou hasty moral! sudden sense of right!
> Thou untaught goddess! Virtue's precious seed!
> Thou sweet precursor of the generous deed!
> Beauty's quick relish! Reason's radiant morn,
> Which dawns soft light before Reflection's born!
>
> (lines 246-51)

Yet much of her poem is given over to complaining of the fashion for self-indulgent displays of fine feelings.

> There are, who fill with brilliant plaints the page,
> If a poor linnet meets the gunner's rage:
> There are, who for a dying fawn display
> The tenderest anguish in the sweetest lay;
> Who for a wounded animal deplore,
> As if friend, parent, country were no more
>
> . . .
>
> Alive to every woe by *fiction* dressed,
> The innocent he wronged, the wretch distressed,
> May plead in vain; their sufferings come not near,
> Or he relieves them cheaply with a tear.
>
> (lines 280-95)

As Coleridge put it more sardonically in his 1796 periodical *The Watchman*, 'The fine lady ... sips a beverage sweetened with human blood, even while she is weeping over the refined sorrow of Werter or of Clementina. Sensibility is not Benevolence.'⁵ The woman of fashion will weep with the emotionally afflicted hero of Goethe's novel *Young Werther* or the helplessly sensitive young woman in Richardson's *Sir Charles Grandison* (1753–4), but forget that the sugar in her tea comes from slave plantations.

For More and Coleridge, it was all to do with reading. Fine feelings, depicted in novels and experienced by their readers as they read, had become the guarantee that those novels were morally elevating. When a popular anthology of extracts from the writing of Laurence Sterne was published as *The Beauties of Sterne* (the first of many editions was published in 1782) it was subtitled, 'Selected for the Heart of Sensibility'. In *Sense and Sensibility*, when Marianne Dashwood identifies Edward Ferrars's lack of 'sensibility', his insufficiently animated reading of Cowper's poetry is evidence. With wonderfully foolish hyperbole, she declares that 'it would have broke *my* heart had I loved him, to hear him read with so little sensibility'. She speaks to her mother with solemn complacency. 'Elinor has not my feelings, and therefore she may overlook it, and be happy with him.' Sensibility (as More has suggested) is something you learn from books. In her first conversation with Willoughby, Marianne discovers a shared 'sensibility' in their shared tastes in reading when 'her favourite authors were brought forward and dwelt upon with so rapturous a delight, that any young man of five and twenty must have been insensible indeed, not to become an immediate convert to the excellence of such works, however disregarded before' (*S&S*, 1:3). Willoughby has quite enough 'sensibility' to respond to the right books in the right way – but also to respond to the raptures of this attractive, enthusiastic young woman. And, as far as Marianne is concerned, he has himself walked out of a book. 'His person and air were equal to what her fancy had ever drawn for the hero of a favourite story' (*S&S*, 1:9).

Sceptical responses to the cult of sensibility did not only come from conservatives. In *A Vindication of the Rights of Woman* (1792) Mary Wollstonecraft was concerned that celebrations of sensibility taught young women to be weak and ill. She convicted 'the herd of Novelists' of fostering in women 'a romantic unnatural delicacy of feeling', depicting 'sensibility' as a fashionable female weakness encouraged by men, and by bad habits of reading (ch. 2). Austen also suggests that sensibility involves sickness. When she first appears to have been jilted by Willoughby, Marianne Dashwood weeps all night and gets up with a headache, 'unable to talk, and unwilling to take any nourishment' (*S&S*, 1:16). 'Her sensibility was potent enough!' exclaims the narrator. The implication is that Marianne's susceptibilities are manufactured – that she imposes upon herself. She vaunts her sensitivity at a cost to her mother and sister: she is so busy showing how fine her nerves are that she does not notice their distress.

Sensibility is suspect because it can become an affectation. Reliant as it is on gesture and display, it can be faked. The calculating Lucy Steele weeps readily enough and dotes on children. Yet it is not merely bogus. Marianne eventually becomes genuinely, indeed dangerously, ill in the true manner of a heroine of sensibility. It has been thought that Marianne's illness is a kind of punishment. She emerges suitably chastened, speaking not in surges of enthusiasm but measured Johnsonian periods, and now quite ready to marry the flannel-waist-coated Colonel Brandon. Yet the illness also suggests that Austen believes that sensibility is something real. The influence of mind on body is evidence of its operation and roots Austen's psychology in its times.

There is a kind of reversal of what happens to Marianne in *Persuasion*, where Anne Elliot is represented as a woman whose 'youth and bloom' have fled (1:7). As much as the years, this is the consequence of her disappointment in love. As Wentworth's attentions begin to turn to her, that bloom mysteriously comes back (though we are to take it that the sea air also plays a part). Austen even makes a joke of the mystery, Anne's vain father complimenting her on her 'improved looks' (*P*, 2:4) and presuming that she must be using Gowland (a well-known contemporary skin lotion). On the evening after Wentworth declares his love for her, Anne attends an assembly, 'Glowing and lovely in sensibility and happiness' (*P*, 2:11). 'Sensibility' now seems redeemed, a state of unambiguous emotional and physical health.

So Jane Austen may satirise the cult of sensibility, but she remains intrigued by the idea. In its positive use it refers us to the self-awareness that characterises all her heroines. In *Mansfield Park*, when Edmund Bertram first begins to find Fanny Price 'an interesting object', he perceives her 'to be farther entitled to attention, by great sensibility of her situation, and great timidity' (1:2). She feels deeply (and silently). Indeed, her sensitivity weakens her. Fanny suffers from 'nerves' that become 'agitated'. She is easily tired or made faint, as if her virtue were a kind of exhausting burden. Her 'spirits' (a favourite word of Austen's) frequently 'sink'. 'Spirits', like 'sensibility', conflates the physiological and the psychological. Anne Elliot in *Persuasion* suffers in her 'spirits' when we might like to call her 'depressed'. She ails physically as well as emotionally. Originally 'spirits' were the so-called 'animal spirits', substances in the body that supposedly governed a person's state of mind. Laurence Sterne's novel *Tristram Shandy* makes much comic use of this out-of-date theory. Those Austen characters who possess some excess of vitality have 'spirits'. In *Mansfield Park*, this means Tom Bertram and Mary Crawford, who likes to describe herself as 'a woman of spirit' (2:7).

These two are dangerously unrestrained. Yet 'spirits' also invigorate Captain Wentworth and animate Emma Woodhouse.

The correlation of the physiological and the psychological is inherited from the novel of sensibility. When Elizabeth Bennet walks across the fields to visit her sick sister we are to infer something about her character as well as her physical health. It is a strictly unconventional action not only by the standards of the coldly observing Bingley sisters, but also by the standards of earlier novels. Tenderness and delicacy were the attributes associated with sensibility. Jane Fairfax in *Emma*, on the other hand, is naturally prone to physical weakness, perhaps illness. Mr Knightley comments on Jane Fairfax in a way that must compliment her, even if it registers puzzlement at her self-concealment. 'Jane Fairfax has feeling . . . I do not accuse her of want of feeling. Her sensibilities, I suspect, are strong' (*E*, 2:15). Her 'feeling', and the secretiveness into which she is forced, seem debilitating.

Having begun by escaping virtuous sensibility, Jane Austen ends her short career by returning to some of the vocabulary of the novel of sensibility. *Persuasion* seems a work designed to redeem 'feeling' and 'feelings'. The words appear on almost every page. We are told that the nineteen-year-old Anne was 'an extremely pretty girl, with gentleness, modesty, taste, and feeling' (*P*, 1:4). The last of these is a quality that will remain undimmed. Recovering from her encounter with Captain Wentworth, after their long separation, she tries 'to be feeling less'. Such self-conquest is not possible. 'Alas! with all her reasonings, she found, that to retentive feelings eight years may be little more than nothing' (*P*, 1:7). 'Alas!' is no doubt Anne's inward sigh, but also the narrator's rueful knowledge that rational precepts stop short of reality. Can 'feelings' ever before (or since) have been coupled with that adjective, 'retentive'? A reader of Austen's day would have been more likely than us to catch something like an oxymoron: 'feelings' in fiction would usually be fleeting, momentary, exquisite for this very transience.

Persuasion gives us this too, for its psychological complexity comes partly from its realisation of Anne's agitated moments, those mixed feelings – 'a confusion of varying, but very painful agitation', 'emotions so compounded of pleasure and pain, that she knew not which prevailed' (1:10) – to which it is so attentive. Brilliantly it mimics the blur of these moments. It also redeems the psychological preoccupation of fiction that Jane Austen began by repudiating. Here is a novel of 'feelings' that are properly retentive.

NOTES

1. The most widely available edition containing this preface is the Everyman edition (London: J. M. Dent, 1962), see pp. xiii–xiv.
2. David Hume, *A Treatise of Human Nature*, ed. L. A. Selby-Bigge (Oxford: Oxford University Press, 1978), p. 316.
3. Adam Smith, *The Theory of Moral Sentiments*, ed. D. D. Raphael and A. L. Macfie (Oxford: Clarendon Press, 1979), p. 143.
4. Marilyn Butler, *Jane Austen and the War of Ideas* (Oxford: Clarendon Press, 1975), p. 23.
5. *The Watchman*, no. 4 (25 March 1799).

36

Rank

THOMAS KEYMER

Mr Elliot's bland assertion that 'rank is rank' (*P*, 2:4) makes plain the gulf between Jane Austen's characters and first audience, for whom rank is an intricate but self-evident system of social organisation and signification, and modern readers, for whom the nuances and gradations of the system are often obscure. Social position is of consuming importance in the novels, with individuals and families measuring their relative standings to the finest degree while devising long-term strategies for advancement in status. Yet these concerns are articulated in terms predating the class-based language of politics that grew up among radicals such as Paine, Spence and Thelwall in the 1790s, became consolidated in the work of social theorists such as Robert Owen and David Ricardo in the 1810s and 1820s, and continues to shape modern assumptions. The term 'class' was already current by Austen's day – P. J. Corfield cites a writer of 1753 who itemised English society in 'five Classes; *viz.* the Nobility, the Gentry, the genteel Trades (all those particularly which require large Capital), the common Trades, and the Peasantry'[1] – but as an organising concept it was yet to diverge significantly from traditional specifications of rank, station or degree. 'Rank' remained the established model, and dictated conventional thought. Where 'class' would be measured in terms above all of productivity and income, locating individuals in socio-economic positions attained through material success, 'rank' placed primary emphasis on lineage, implying that social status was more or less inalienably conferred by birth and descent. Where 'class' brings with it overtones of structural antagonism and conflict, moreover, 'rank' suggested stratifications that were harmonious, orderly and stable – ranks being nothing if not serried. For Samuel Johnson, who teased the genteel republican Catherine Macaulay by inviting her servant to dinner ('She has never liked me since'), social hierarchy was guaranteed by ties of interdependence and mutual advantage, and consisted of 'fixed, invariable external rules of distinction of rank, which create no jealousy, as they are allowed to be accidental' (i.e. given).[2]

As exponents of a genre specialising in close and particular renderings of social reality, few novelists of Austen's day fail to register the defining importance of rank. Yet it is hard to think of a contemporary or precursor in whose fiction there is quite so thorough an immersion in, and calibration of, the minutiae of the system. The eighteenth-century novelist most admired by Jane Austen, Samuel Richardson, wrote innovatively about emerging fault-lines in the strata of rank, and in *Pamela* (1740) – in which a maid-servant wins her master's hand – he pioneered the plot of marital elevation that Austen was to use herself in more muted form. The self-made Richardson had no secure grasp of titles, conditions and modes of address in the gentry world, however, and in his novels frequent solecisms result from what he ruefully called 'my Ignorance of Proprietys of those Kinds'.[3] Jane Austen, by contrast, was native to this world, and writes with unfailing alertness to its codes and conventions. The premium she placed on accuracy is seen in her corrections to niceties of etiquette in a manuscript novel by her niece Anna, who had improperly shown a surgeon being introduced to a peer while also botching the form of introduction used for the peer's brother. Austen also protests, of her niece's fictional nomenclature, that 'There is no such Title as Desborough – either among the Dukes, Marquisses, Earls, Viscounts or Barons' (*L*, 10 August 1814).

Though relatively disadvantaged in financial terms, Jane Austen's family could boast aristocratic descent and ongoing connections, and if anything the lack of corresponding wealth enhanced the obsession with rank in her immediate circle. The family treasured a surviving letter to Jane's great-grandmother Mary Brydges, sister to the first Duke of Chandos, as a mark of inherited distinction, and also found in the letter (from Mary's mother, a rich merchant's daughter) consoling evidence that 'then, as now . . . rank had the power of attracting and absorbing wealth'.[4] In Austen's lifetime, rank and wealth were successfully reunited in the person of her brother Edward, who was adopted as an heir by childless cousins, the Knights of Godmersham, and thereby came into an estate of the opulence of Sotherton in *Mansfield Park*. Decades later, Edward's appalling daughter, Lady Knatchbull, wrote that Jane Austen would have been 'very much below par as to good Society & its ways' without the refinements acquired on her frequent visits to Godmersham.[5] The visits certainly afforded Jane Austen a perspective on elite life at variance with her usual viewpoint, which was that of a household similar in circumstance – a clergyman's widow with unmarried daughters subsisting in genteel poverty on £450 a year – to the Dashwoods of *Sense and Sensibility*, for whom an annual income of £500 makes maintenance of proper appearances a constant struggle. Both these perspectives inform the novels, sometimes within a single sentence.

The dedication of *Emma* to the Prince Regent takes Austen's fiction to the very apex of the social pyramid, but otherwise the highest echelons of the nobility are thinly represented. Unlike the 'silver fork' novelists who dominated the fiction market of the 1820s with their voyeuristic depictions of high society, Austen's attitude to aristocratic manners is one of general neglect, punctuated by occasional disdain. Among the nobility, the established order of precedence was as she lists it to Anna, with baron the lowest degree of the peerage, but where such ranks are specified it is typically as remote objects of social ambition. Thus General Tilney is disappointed to miss the Marquis of Longtown in Bath (*NA*, 2:2), where the Elliots anxiously cultivate the Dowager Viscountess Dalrymple (*P*, 2:4). Setting aside juvenile skits such as 'Jack and Alice', in which an ambitious girl lures a senescent peer into 'raising her to the rank of a Dutchess' (ch. 9), the character of highest rank to appear onstage in Austen is probably Lord Osborne in *The Watsons*, a stuffed shirt who does little to substantiate Mrs Edwards's confidence that 'Great People have always their charm'. Austen thus ignores a group that continued to hold the reins of political power – peers and their sons formed a majority in every government cabinet between 1783 and 1835[6] – and also the informal strings of patronage, connection and dependency that bound together the social hierarchy. Even so, aristocracy retains a teasing subliminal presence in Austen's cast. As though to inscribe the concealed noble inheritance of her mother's line, she eschews the pseudo-Norman nomenclature conventional in fiction of the day (Belmonts, Duvals, Orvilles and the like) and plays on the names of actual dynasties, extinct and surviving. D. J. Greene notes the family connection to Thomas Willoughby, first Lord Middleton, in Jane Austen's maternal line, and points to the great estate of Wentworth Wood-house in Yorkshire, where the pedigree of the incumbent family also involved Watsons, Fitzwilliams and D'Arcys.[7]

Beneath a peerage of three hundred or so families in England there ranged the graduated demographic on which Austen concen-trates her gaze: a gentry society comprising the families of approx-imately (in 1803) 540 baronets, 350 knights, 6,000 landed squires and 20,000 gentlemen, amounting in total to about 1.4 per cent of the national population and enjoying 15.7 per cent of the national income (Perkin, *Modern English Society*, pp. 18–22). It is to this rurally based society, centred on major landowning families and descending in fine gradations through non-landed professionals and moneyed rentiers of varying status, that Austen's characters refer when they speak of the 'neighbourhood'. In each novel, 'neigh-bourhood' is a feature of both the landscape and its elite population. It denotes both the hierarchy of estates and manors that revolved around the local great house, and the rural gentry who inhabited these places, where they competed for visits from, and invitations to, houses on the level above, and made seasonal forays to London or Bath in pursuit of extended connection. Though rich in rivalries and tensions, this is a hierarchy still defined and united by vertical ties of influence and dependency down to its lowest reaches, and not yet acrimoniously fragmented – as in 'condition of England' novels of the 1840s – by horizontal solidarities of class. The cities might be another story (witness Peterloo in 1819), but as late as 1824 a representative essayist could still exult that the dangerous chasm between noble and labouring classes in other nations did not exist in England: 'with us the space between the ploughman and the peer is crammed with circle after circle, fitted in the most admirable manner for sitting upon each other, for connecting the former with the latter, and for rendering the whole perfect in cohesion, strength and beauty'.[8]

At the peak of this gentry society are the baronets, the lowest hereditary titled order, whom Austen represents with uneven levels of distinction in Sir Thomas Bertram, Sir John Middleton and *Sanditon*'s Sir Edward Denham. Then there is Sir Walter Elliot, whose sense of his own distinction is reinforced by regular perusal of

Debrett's *Baronetage of England* (1808) – an authoritative dictionary of pedigree that Austen implicitly contrasts in *Persuasion* with the meritocratic *Navy List*. No fewer than 233 new baronetcies had been created between 1760 and 1800 (thereby creating the need for Debrett),[9] but most were conferred on men of established family, so that Sir Walter's own title, which dates back to the Restoration, need not be thought devalued. Next in order of precedence come the knights, whose titles differ crucially in not being heritable, so that a knighthood conveys no guarantee of ancestry: witness Sir William Lucas, who 'had been formerly in trade in Meryton, where he had made a tolerable fortune, and risen to the honour of a knighthood' (*P&P*, 1:5). Baronet and knight may be all the same to the servant in *Persuasion* who speaks of 'a baronight' (*P*, 1:12) – an eloquent malapropism that Austen may have taken from Burney's *Camilla* – but not to the socially conscious Lady Russell, whose respect for benighted Sir Walter is rooted in precedence. As Austen puts it, 'Herself, the widow of only a knight, she gave the dignity of a baronet all its due' (*P*, 1:2).

The form of Lady Russell's own title identifies it as deriving from the knighthood of her husband. Women of higher rank incorporate their Christian names in a form that distinguishes Lady Catherine de Bourgh and Lady Anne Darcy, in *Pride and Prejudice*, as titled in their own right. Regardless of their marital status or the rank (if lower) of their husbands, daughters of peers invariably used this form, which marks out both Lady Catherine, the wife of a knight, and Lady Anne, the wife of a commoner, as noble by birth (in this case, as daughters of an earl). Courtesy titles like this would survive even in spectacular cases of downward mobility, as when a member of the Watson-Wentworth dynasty, whose father was a marquis, took on the oddly conflicted name of Lady Henrietta Alicia Sturgeon on marrying her footman in 1764.

Scarcely lower in standing were the greatest of the landowning commoners, who had not been touched by – or in some cases had eschewed – the titles of their ostensible superiors. With an estate worth more, at £10,000 a year, than that of many nobles, Mr Darcy represents an important category of rural gentry in Austen's England: men of wealth and lineage for whom plain 'Mr' was a badge of honour. A conspicuous instance is the great commoner Thomas William Coke, of Holkham in Norfolk, who inherited estates worth £12,000 in 1776 and improved their yield threefold by 1816, yet during this period twice refused ennoblement – a gesture that made even a marquis congratulate him on 'such independence, portraying a dignity of mind above all heraldry'.[10] In this context, the note of regret with which Lady Catherine de Bourgh describes Darcy's paternal line as 'respectable, honourable, and ancient, though untitled' (*P&P*, 3:14) signals her distance from the Tory values often attributed to Jane Austen herself, according to which Darcy's untitled state might even be his highest distinction. Simple esquireship connotes an incorruptible aloofness from the processes of political ingratiation and meretricious reward that had characterised the Whig hegemony of the previous century – a 'peer-making age' (as one minor novelist put it) during which the House of Lords grew in size from 153 in 1688 to 224 in 1780, despite the natural extinction of titles over the same period.[11] After 1780, the younger Pitt's efforts to break the power of the Whig magnates led to increased rates of ennoblement, and brought into being a new body of parvenu peers who diluted the old equation between aristocratic rank and blue blood. Jane Austen's egregious kinsman Sir Egerton Brydges (Bart.) was among many traditionalists affronted, in this process, by Pitt's 'palpable preference of mercantile wealth, and by his inborn hatred of the old aristocracy'.[12]

Beneath a character such as Darcy, who holds his own in noble company and impresses inferiors 'as one of the most illustrious personages in this land' (*P&P*, 3:15), there stretches a long and finely graded continuum of genteel rank that was widely seen as ensuring social stability and cohesion. Though keenly hierarchical, and supervised with the almost military sense of regimentation expressed when Mrs Norris deplores 'the nonsense and folly of people's *stepping out of* their rank' (*MP*, 2:5, my emphasis), this continuum could still achieve a surprising inclusiveness of reach. Mr Knightley, with his splendid estate and handsome income, can be on visiting terms with Miss Bates, who scrimps and saves in upstairs lodgings; the obsequious Mr Collins, with only some exaggeration, can 'consider the clerical office as equal in point of dignity with the highest rank in the kingdom' (*P&P*, 1:18). Connectedness is far from constituting equality, however, and all the novels display the tensions arising from the dual imperative of nurturing community while also preserving distinction.

It is in *Emma*, where Austen's heroine is not the usual challenger of hierarchy but rather its staunchest upholder, that the fine calibrations of rank are most clearly seen. With its distinct yet interconnected 'sets of people' – the phrase recurs in *Persuasion* and *Sanditon*, and in *Emma* accommodates 'the chosen and the best', the 'second set', and more (*E*, 1:3) – the society of Highbury links, while also compartmentalising, the whole spectrum of acceptable gentility. At its peak is Knightley, the established squire whose lands have been in his family since Tudor times; near its foot are the illegitimate but connected Harriet Smith and the shabby-genteel Jane Fairfax; hanging on for dear life is the impoverished Miss Bates, whose notice was an honour, but no longer. It is worth adding that the patrician Knightley is sure enough of his standing to extend this spectrum further, preferring the company of his steward and tenant farmer, William Larkins and Robert Martin, to that of his genteel neighbours. Tellingly, however, Emma recoils from these indecorous contacts, and has no time for Knightley's unsettling idea, in Martin's case, of locating 'true gentility' in practical merit as opposed to technical rank (*E*, 1:8). She will mingle with the well born and make charitable visits to the poor, but 'the yeomanry are precisely the order of people with whom I feel I can have nothing to do' (1:4). Throughout the novel, this anxious correctness of form identifies Emma's elite status as discernibly less secure than her future husband's. Where Knightleys have owned the landscape and lived from its yield since the Dissolution, the Woodhouses are relative newcomers to their 'notch' in the Donwell estate, and live primarily from investments. The same insecurity returns when the public dance proposed by Frank Churchill arouses Emma's alarm, not so much at the temporary interpenetrations of rank involved in the dance itself, but rather at the 'difficulty in every body's returning into their proper place the next morning' – as though correct performance of social roles is itself a larger dance, strictly regulated, and not to be disrupted by the smaller. Equally alarming is what this carnivalesque proposal discloses about Frank himself, whose 'indifference to a confusion of rank, bordered too much on inelegance of mind' (*E*, 2:6) – and whose own paternity is indelibly undistinguished, we remember, his mother's great family notwithstanding.

In their relative lack of land and reliance on capital, the Woodhouses lie close to the broad category of moneyed, professional and rentier families – a category of non-landed affluence to which David Spring applies the term 'pseudo-gentry' – who deferred to, emulated and sought to enter the gentry proper. 'They devoted their lives to acquiring the trappings of gentry status for themselves and especially their children', as Spring describes the ambitions and practices of this group: 'the schooling, the accent, the manners . . . the habit of command, the large house in its own grounds, servants, carriages and horses, appropriate husbands and wives, and, last but not least, appropriate income'.[13] Yet the Woodhouses are as anxious to distinguish themselves from aspirational pseudo-gentry such as the Eltons and Westons as these families are to rise above the plain vulgarity of the Coles – an *arriviste* family who, for all their wealth, have yet to acquire sufficient refinement to erase the stigma of 'trade'. In the polite but unrelenting competition for positional advantage that results, each participant displays the one-way vision that Emma attributes to Mr Elton, whose aversions and aspirations in courtship show him 'so well understanding the gradations of rank below him, and . . . so blind to what rose above' (*E*, 1:16). When Elton finally marries Bristol money, his new wife is in Emma's eyes 'a little upstart, vulgar being' (2:14), but one who then expresses her own 'horror of upstarts' (2:18); and so the chain of upward ambition and downward condescension goes on. All subscribe to the hierarchy of rank in general while seeking to breach it in person. Social acceptance proves harder to achieve than material wealth, however, and is secured at best with the glacial pace of the Weston family, 'which for the last two or three generations had been rising into gentility' (1:2).

Yet personal mobility of status was becoming more achievable as Austen wrote, and other novels reflect the mechanisms involved. Though peopled by conservative matriarchs like Mrs Ferrars and Lady Catherine, who seek 'to have the distinction of rank preserved' (*P&P*, 2:6) and promote strict endogamy to this end, the novels deal in more than mere romance in their characteristic endings, where traditional dynastic alliances give way to modern love matches. Elizabeth is not a gentlewoman's daughter, and has an uncle in trade, but marries into the highest squirearchy; Elinor sees off a potent combination of fortune and rank in 'the Hon.

Miss Morton, only daughter of the late Lord Morton, with thirty thousand pounds' (*S&S*, 2:11). Other processes promoting the interpenetration of social layers arose from the Napoleonic Wars, which not only threw up new opportunities for trade and industry or for success in the profession of arms, but also conferred new prestige on leaders in either field. 'Mushrooms are every day starting up from the dunghill of trade', as Southey lamented in 1806, so 'undermining the distinction of ranks in society'.[14] Though Sir William Lucas remains cowed by old aristocracy, the confidence of the Bingleys in 'associating with people of rank' provides a bolder instance of entry into elite circles from the platform of trade (*P&P*, 1:4). No less firmly grounded in contemporary reality is the social as well as material advancement of Admiral Croft and Captain Wentworth in *Persuasion*. Jane Austen's brother Francis was knighted for his naval service, and early readers will have recalled Nelson (a baron) when Sir Walter deplores being leapfrogged in rank by 'Lord St. Ives, whose father we all know to have been a country curate' (*P*, 1:3). For Harold Perkin, these processes of elevation and assimilation slowed the formation of a moneyed class at odds with the landed gentry, and harnessed local dynamism in the service of larger stability: 'the result was a self-contained system of social movement which left the shape and structure of society precisely as before, a "stationary state" based on the restless movement of its constituent atoms' (Perkin, *Modern English Society*, p. 62). Bourgeois revolution is not in prospect at Highbury, to be sure. If any threat exists, it lurks instead in the hidden ranks of the labouring – or, worse, non-labouring – poor, dissevered from gentry society by the decay of rural paternalism, and ominously ruffling its serene surface in the shape of gypsies and poultry thieves.

NOTES

1. James Nelson, *An Essay on the Government of Children*, second edition (1756), pp. 365–6, quoted by P. J. Corfield, 'Class by Name and Number in Eighteenth-Century Britain', *History* 72 (1987), 38.
2. Samuel Johnson, conversation of 22 July 1763, reported in *Boswell's London Journal, 1762–1763*, ed. Frederick A. Pottle (London: Heinemann, 1950), p. 320.

3. Samuel Richardson to Lady Bradshaigh, 5 October 1753, in *Selected Letters of Samuel Richardson*, ed. John Carroll (Oxford: Clarendon Press, 1964), p. 245.

4. *A Memoir of Jane Austen and Other Family Recollections*, ed. Kathryn Sutherland (Oxford: Oxford University Press, 2002), p. 48.

5. *Fanny Knight's Diaries: Jane Austen Through Her Niece's Eyes*, ed. Deirdre Le Faye (Alton: Jane Austen Society, 2000), p. 39.

6. Harold Perkin, *The Origins of Modern English Society, 1780–1880* (London: Routledge, 1969), p. 40. Subsequent references are included in the text.

7. D. J. Greene, 'Jane Austen and the Peerage', *PMLA* 68 (1953), 1018. In Wentworth's case in *P*, the coincidence prompts Sir Walter Elliot to wonder sourly 'how the names of many of our nobility become so common' (1:3).

8. David Robinson (as 'Y. Y. Y.'), 'The Church of England and the Dissenters', *Blackwood's* 16 (1824), 397, quoted in Perkin, *Modern English Society*, p. 22.

9. Paul Langford, *Public Life and the Propertied Englishman, 1689–1789* (Oxford: Clarendon Press, 1991), p. 516.

10. Lord Townshend to Coke, 17 February 1806, quoted by A. M. W. Stirling, *Coke of Norfolk and His Friends*, 2 vols. (1908), vol. II, p. 338.

11. Charles Jenner, *The Placid Man; or, Memoirs of Sir Charles Belville*, second edition (1773), vol. II, p. 177, quoted in Langford, *Public Life*, p. 513.

12. Egerton Brydges, *The Autobiography, Times, Opinions, and Contemporaries of Sir Egerton Brydges*, 2 vols. (1834), vol. I, p. 196.

13. David Spring, 'Interpreters of Jane Austen's Social World: Literary Critics and Historians', in *Jane Austen: New Perspectives*, ed. Janet Todd (New York: Holmes and Meier, 1983), pp. 60–1.

14. Robert Southey, *Letters from England by Don Manuel Alvarez Espriella* (London: Cresset Press, 1951), p. 37.

37

Reading practices

ALAN RICHARDSON

Toward the end of the eighteenth century, England experienced a literacy crisis, though not one brought on by an appreciable spike in the number of readers. Literacy rates climbed gradually from the middle of the seventeenth century to the last decades of the nineteenth, when something close to universal literacy was finally reached. But during the period of Jane Austen's girlhood and youth – the 1780s and 1790s – the incremental growth of reading proficiency across classes and among both men and women became noticeable enough to inspire a host of pronouncements, some congratulatory, others dire.[1] For a bookseller like James Lackington, it could only be a cause for celebration that 'all ranks and degrees now READ', while the reactionary *Anti-Jacobin Review* provided a ready outlet for grimmer remarks: 'Those taught to read, to write, to reason, we now see grasping with curiosity every pernicious treatise within reach.'[2] Although probably not much more than half of lower-class males were literate by the turn of the nineteenth century, Samuel Taylor Coleridge, his radical youth now far behind him, could worry in *The Statesman's Manual* (1816) that 'Books are in every hovel. The Infant's cries are hushed with *picture*-books – and the Cottager's child sheds his first bitter tears over pages, which render it impossible for the man to be treated or governed as a child.' For Coleridge, however, as for a wide spectrum of liberal and conservative reformers, the only way forward was not to extinguish, but to manage the rise of literacy: 'Here as in so many other cases, the inconveniences that have arisen from a thing's having become too general, are best removed by making it universal.'[3] If Austen's era can rightly be seen as an age of educational innovation, expansion and reform, this may well owe less to benevolent impulses to spread literacy than to anxious schemes for controlling it.

In relation to the ever-growing number of women readers – and writers – over the course of Austen's lifetime, anxieties found equally widespread expression, especially in relation to novel reading, frequently surfacing in works of fiction themselves. When Lady Augusta, in Maria Edgeworth's 'Mademoiselle Panache,' is discovered by her worthy suitor reading an immoral French novel – and the '*second* volume' at that – he drops her immediately, an event Edgeworth does not expect her readers to take satirically.[4] Jane Austen, however, has already begun to satirise such fictive condemnations of fictionality in her juvenile work 'Love and Freindship', as the ridiculous Edward Lindsay refuses on principle to marry the woman of his choice with his father's approval ('Never shall it be said that I obliged my Father') and his flustered parent replies: 'You have been studying Novels I suspect' (Letter 6th). Novel reading, or at least the reading of all but a select few 'best' novels, finds condemnation throughout the age's extensive literature on female conduct, and any number of female writers – from the outspoken feminist Mary Wollstonecraft to the staunchly conservative Hannah More – expose the dangers of fashionable novels in their polemical and fictional works alike. Austen stands out the more, then, for including a robust defence of novel reading in her early work *Northanger Abbey*, lest readers take her satire on the Gothic novel craze as yet another sweeping condemnation of female reading habits.

Yet Austen hardly stood alone in advocating the benefits of at least some kinds of reading for girls and women: another Edgeworth heroine, the title character of *Belinda* (1801), proves attractive not least because she is 'fond of reading', rather than engaging solely in empty amusements and 'superficial' displays (ch. 1). Most writers on the question, whether their pronouncements took direct or fictional form, could agree that certain kinds of books (say, religious ones) would grace any 'middling'- or upper-class woman's chamber and help to form and discipline her mind. The disagreements largely concerned just what sorts of books might be allowed, the dangers especially of novels and other fictional works, and whether and in what contexts a woman might appropriately bring her reading into public knowledge and conversation. Along with this diversity of opinion on women's reading went a diversity of reading practices, ranging from the uncritical absorption in improbable fictions caricatured by Austen in her early works to the diverse range of methods and aims inspired by different sorts of reading material described in the journals of a historical woman reader like Anna Larpent.[5]

Historical studies of actual women readers suggest that homogenising models of the passive woman reader, however well they may correspond to influential conduct book prescriptions or stock fictional representations, do scant justice to the variety of reading styles and practices found in the historical record – and in the pages of Austen's novels. Nor does the well-known shift towards practices of reading silently and in private by the end of the eighteenth century altogether crowd out earlier practices of reading aloud and of reading as a form of social interaction. Studies of book purchasing and borrowing patterns, though again based on small samples, serve also to warn against any simplistic association between women readers and the 'rise' of the novel – not all women chose to read fiction, and some men preferred novels to other available genres. Nevertheless, both a profusion of writings on female conduct and education and any number of fictional scenes of reading reflect at least a common *perception* that women found novels seductively attractive and that young women in particular might prove liable to confuse the fictions they so greedily absorbed with the actualities of the social world they must eventually negotiate.

Two novelistic genres in particular were regularly singled out for condemnation: the Gothic, with its thematics of female constraint and persecution and its fictive indulgence in forbidden lusts and passions, and the sentimental novel, with its ideal or 'romantic' picture of life and its over-valuation of erotic love as the key to female happiness. The concern over both genres reflects a pronounced ambivalence towards the earlier genre of prose romance out of which the modern novel emerged. Gothic fiction was born, according to the first Gothic novelist, Horace Walpole, from a desire to reincorporate supernatural and sublime elements of the romance into the 'modern romance' of 'common life.'[6] Similarly, to charge a sentimental novel (or its heroine) with harbouring too 'romantic' a picture of life meant, at a time long before 'Romanticism' had become a literary historical term, to portray characters, situations and modes of behaviour that might be found in old romances but never in the real world. Austen's *Northanger Abbey* might be taken as a particularly amusing satire on the tendency to read life through the lens of improbable fictions. Its impressionable young heroine, Catherine Morland, immerses herself in Gothic novels and tales and then, to her eventual humiliation, imposes

Gothic scenarios onto the social world she is only just 'coming out' into: 'This is just like a book!' (*NA*, 2:5). But in fact, as a number of critics have noted, the Gothic proves in some ways a reliable guide to male behaviour in a social world that can grant overwhelming power to certain well-born, well-placed and well-heeled men: the stern family patriarch Catherine views as a Gothic tyrant indeed proves by the book's end to embody 'parental tyranny' (*NA*, 2:16), and despite her comically deflated suspicion that he has murdered his wife, Catherine seems finally to have 'scarcely sinned against his character' (2:15).

At once a critique and a validation of Gothic, *Northanger Abbey* also gives a more complex picture of contemporary reading practices than simply the impressionable Miss avidly reading away in the privacy of her bedroom or 'closet'. Catherine, for example, reads not only for pleasure but for social affiliation, eagerly discussing her reading with her fellow Gothic devotee, Isabella Thorpe. Isabella's boorish brother, John, exposes his shallow ignorance by affecting to despise novels like *The Mysteries of Udolpho*, although he does admire the works of Ann Radcliffe – its author (*NA*, 1:7). Henry Tilney, Catherine's eventual suitor, establishes his character as a man who appreciates women partly by his affirmation of novel reading, claiming to have read all Radcliffe's novels and 'hundreds and hundreds' more, and mocking men who routinely disparage novels when in fact 'they read nearly as many as women' (*NA*, 1:14). Here Austen herself exposes the popular consignment of novels to a largely female readership as itself a kind of fiction, and unmasks male condemnations of the novel as mere posturing. In the voice of the narrator, Austen goes still further, mocking the self-defeating practice of novelists censuring fiction reading in the very pages of their own novels, and asking rhetorically, 'if the heroine of one novel be not patronized by the heroine of another, from whom can she expect protection and regard' (*NA*, 1:5). Within the pages of *Northanger Abbey*, novel reading emerges as much more than an escapist or self-deluding pursuit: it promotes friendship, contributes to social distinction, forms a common topic and pursuit for men and women and can at best convey the 'greatest powers of the mind' (*NA*, 1:5).

Sense and Sensibility complicates stock critiques of sentimental novel reading in comparable ways. Marianne reads sentimental fiction and the poetry of sensibility – she slights her sister's love-interest for his inadequate appreciation of the poetry of William Cowper (*S&S*, 1:3) – and she falls for the more dashing Willoughby in part because he enters her world like the 'hero of a favorite story' (1:9). Yet both sisters owe their attractiveness in no small part to their refined (if, in Marianne's case, excessive) sensibilities, in stark contrast to the comparatively 'illiterate' Lucy Steele (*S&S*, 1:22), whose lack of an inner imaginative life leaves her prey to unmodified 'self-interest' (2:2). Reading promotes not simply social distinction but can constitute a kind of moral discipline, training the heart to feelings of empathy and benevolence; on the other hand, habits of sentimental self-indulgence and 'romantic' projection must be guarded against. Reading also emerges, here, as a form of courtship. Willoughby first gains Marianne's affections by adopting her favourite authors and books: 'He acquiesced in all her decisions, caught all her enthusiasm', and by the end of his first formal visit has established himself as a fellow-devotee of Cowper and an equal admirer of Walter Scott's verse romances (*S&S*, 1:10). Discussing books and authors can announce one's attainment of a certain educational level, manifest one's sensitivity to 'high' literature and to matters of the heart and help carve out a space within the significant constraints of bourgeois courtship rituals for displays of mutual enthusiasm and emotional responsiveness.

One of the more striking social changes between the end of the seventeenth century in Britain and the beginning of the nineteenth concerns the very provision of books. Changes in printing technology, in paper manufacturing, in copyright law and in the retail book trade made books far more common and readily available over the course of the 'long' eighteenth century.[7] In the world of Austen's novels, the very possession of books can serve as a marker of social pretension and intellectual attainment. The importance of a 'family library' comes in for explicit discussion in *Pride and Prejudice*, and helps to establish an initial connection between Elizabeth Bennet, who unfashionably prefers reading to card playing, and Mr Darcy, whose library at Pemberley is the 'work of many generations,' extensively augmented by himself (*P&P*, 1:8). Caroline Bingley, in contrast, demonstrates both her insipidity and her unsuitability as a wife for Darcy by failing to become caught up in reading, despite her hollow wish for an 'excellent library' such as Darcy's own (*P&P*, 1:11).

In the same novel, however, the social anxieties raised by the increasing availability of books finds voice in the fastidious horror of the fatuous Mr Collins upon discovering he has been asked to read aloud from a novel 'from a circulating library' (*P&P*, 1:14). In contrast to the home library, the contents of which might be carefully monitored by the family patriarch, the circulating library (where books could be borrowed in exchange for a one-time fee or regular subscription) represented the threat of promiscuous reading and individual autonomy of choice. Even a young woman of no great means or social standing, as Fanny Price becomes when she returns to her birth family in Portsmouth, might in this way gain access to a considerable variety of reading materials: 'She became a subscriber, amazed at being anything in *propria persona* . . . to be a renter, a chuser of books!' (*MP*, 3:9). Although frequently described as Austen's most passive heroine, Fanny actively seeks access to books, selects them herself and utilises them not only for much needed private amusement but for the 'improvement' of her bright but under-educated sister, Susan.

Reading is associated throughout Austen's novels with education in the broadest sense, that is, with intellectual and moral development. Yet not just any reading practice will result in such 'improvement'. Mary, Elizabeth's pretentious younger sister in *Pride and Prejudice*, exemplifies the error of reading for superficial knowledge and memorising set passages for the purpose of showing off. To 'read great books, and make extracts', however, does not result in genuine mental growth (*P&P*, 1:2). Darcy describes the proper method, a bit later in the novel, in completing his formula for a truly 'accomplished woman' as the 'improvement of her mind by extensive reading' (*P&P*, 1:8). Reading, for Darcy, should not involve mere acquaintance with a list of classics, much less of anthology pieces, but years of wide reading with an end to attaining habits of mental discipline as well as gaining general knowledge. Mr Knightley, in *Emma*, touches on the same ideal in lamenting the absence in Emma's life of a 'course of steady reading', in contrast to the ambitious lists of books she draws up but never gets around to reading (*E*, 1:5). Like Fanny in *Mansfield Park*, Emma devises as well a plan of mental improvement for her rather vapid protégée, Harriet, but again good intentions give way to the vagaries of an undisciplined mind, and Harriet's participation in 'this age of literature' amounts to accumulating an album of 'charades' and 'conundrums' (*E*, 1:9). Mary Bennet at least makes her own volume of elegant extracts (the title of a then-popular anthology); Harriet only collects riddles.

Poetry was still considered in Austen's time a higher and more serious genre than prose fiction, and Austen's most resolutely serious heroines, Fanny in *Mansfield Park* and Anne Elliot in *Persuasion*, both find occasion to demonstrate their intimate knowledge of poetry. Twice Fanny quotes a line of poetry to her cousin Edmund – first from Cowper and then from Scott, Marianne Dashwood's favourite poets – at moments that contrast Fanny's appreciation for nature and tradition and her religious sensibility with the urbane cynicism of Mary Crawford, her rival for Edmund's affections (*MP*, 1:6, 1:9). Fanny's internalisation of a certain poetic tradition helps establish her depth and seriousness of character, in contrast both to Mary ('She had nothing of Fanny's delicacy of taste, of mind, of feeling', *MP*, 1:8) and to Edmund's sisters ('something must have been wanting *within*', *MP*, 3:7). Anne Elliot quotes poetry silently at a moment of high stress, 'repeating to herself some few of the thousand poetical descriptions extant of autumn', as a way both of controlling her emotions and exhibiting (to the reader) her own 'delicacy' of mind (*P*, 1:10). Anne, too, however, does not confine herself to silent and private literary experiences: on getting to know Captain Benwick (with his own 'considerable taste in reading', 'principally in poetry'), Anne discusses with him the comparative merits of Scott and Lord Byron, returning to the same topic the next day (*P*, 1:11, 12). More strikingly, given the stock conduct book advice on deferring to men in conversation, Anne takes it upon herself to recommend a different, less provocative course of reading, and 'feeling in herself the right of seniority of mind', offers to put Benwick on a literary diet of prose moralists. Here the usual courtship pattern, with an older male like Henry Tilney, Mr Knightley or Edmund Bertram helping to 'regulate' the mind of a less educated young woman, gets reversed, as Anne's long-term habits of extensive reading give her intellectual and moral authority over a man close to her own age but 'younger in feeling' (*P*, 1:11).

As the reading practices represented in Austen's novels repeatedly cross the line between the private and the social, silent reading (whether alone or in a group) sometimes gives way to quotation (as with Fanny's quotations from poetry) and reading out loud.

The choice of reading material and manner of performance can be revealing: Mr Collins in *Pride and Prejudice*, for example, after rejecting the novel from a circulating library, chooses instead James Fordyce's *Sermons for Young Women*, one of the very conduct books that finds novels 'unspeakably perverting and inflammatory'.[8] Tom Bertram, in *Mansfield Park*, recalls that he and Edmund were regularly asked to recite or read out loud as boys to fit them for public discourse in later life (1:13), and Mr Elton, another fatuous clergyman, is asked to read to the young women, busy on a portrait, in *Emma* (1:6). Austen's most memorable scene of reading as performance, however, occurs when Henry Crawford reads to Fanny and her aunt from Shakespeare in *Mansfield Park*, to such effect that Fanny's reservations about his character are nearly overcome. All these readers, one notes, are males. But in the scene just mentioned, Fanny has been reading aloud to her aunt, from the same volume of Shakespeare, before Edmund has brought Henry into the room: 'She often reads to me out of those books', according to her aunt (*MP*, 3:3). Women may not read aloud to men in Austen's novels, but they read to one another.

Women may also have been expected to read Austen's own novels to their friends or families. Jane Austen herself, according to her brother Henry's 'Biographical Notice', 'read aloud with very great taste and effect'; her 'own works, probably, were never heard to so much advantage as from her own mouth'. One critic has convincingly argued that Austen's novels bear a number of marks, in the use of italics, in certain habits of sentence construction and in paragraphing, suggesting that she prepared them with successful reading aloud in mind, even by a first-time reader.[9] Austen's novels do not only represent their heroines actively choosing and defending their reading materials and bringing their reading experiences into the social arena, but may themselves have been designed to promote reading as an active female performance.

NOTES

1. For an overview of debates on literacy and education in Austen's era, see Alan Richardson, *Literature, Education, and Romanticism: Reading as Social Practice, 1780–1832* (Cambridge: Cambridge University Press, 1994), pp. 1–108.
2. Quoted in *ibid.*, p. 46.

3. Samuel Taylor Coleridge, *Lay Sermons*, ed. R. J. White (Princeton: Princeton University Press, 1972), pp. 39–40.
4. Maria Edgeworth, 'Mademoiselle Panache', Part Two, in *Tales and Novels*, 10 vols. (1893), vol. I, pp. 396–7.
5. John Brewer, 'Reconstructing the Reader: Prescriptions, Texts and Strategies in Anna Larpent's Reading,' in *The Practice and Representation of Reading in England*, eds. James Raven, Helen Small and Naomi Tadmor (Cambridge: Cambridge University Press, 1996), pp. 226–45.
6. Horace Walpole, *The Castle of Otranto* and *The Mysterious Mother*, ed. Montague Summers (1924), p. 13.
7. James Raven, 'New Reading Histories, Print Culture and the Identification of Change: the Case of Eighteenth-century England,' *Social History* 23:3 (1998), 268–87.
8. James Fordyce, *Sermons for Young Women* (1796), p. 75.
9. Patricia Howell Michaelson, *Speaking Volumes: Women, Reading, and Speech in the Age of Austen* (Stanford: Stanford University Press, 2002), pp. 180–215.

38

Religion

MICHAEL WHEELER

The moderate eighteenth-century Anglicanism that Jane Austen imbibed at Steventon from her father, the Revd George Austen, emphasised divine wisdom and atonement in theology, order and patriotism in politics and common sense and morality in private life. Most Church of England clergy steered a safe middle course between Enlightenment rationalism, with its attendant dangers of agnosticism and secularisation, and Evangelical 'enthusiasm', characterised by intense personal piety. The Established Church was thus in danger of becoming simply a quiet moral presence, rather than a dynamic body which lived out a radical gospel message. (On Easter Day 1800, there were only six communicants at St Paul's Cathedral.[1]) Nevertheless, in the tumultuous final years of the eighteenth century, religion still mattered to the majority of English men and women, and certainly mattered very much to Jane Austen, whose family bonds were strengthened by private and public devotions, and whose novels reflect the teaching and the rhythms of the Authorised Version of the Bible and the Book of Common Prayer.

The moderation that characterises both Austen's fiction and her Anglicanism flows from a pragmatic approach to moral issues and theological truths. Aspects of modernity and progress associated with the Enlightenment project may have threatened conservative Anglican values like Austen's, but an emphasis upon freedom of thought and enquiry was reassuringly Protestant. Faith in miracles may have been weakened, but the disappearance of witch-hunters was a welcome product of rationalism within the Church, and the Test Acts ensured that a small Roman Catholic, or 'Papist' minority kept a low profile in English society.

Much of the energy associated with revivalism had gone out of the Church of England by the middle of the eighteenth century, through the departure of the Wesleys and the growth of

Methodism. In the second half of the century, however, Evangelicalism gradually strengthened within the Anglican fold, through the ministries of men like John Fletcher, Henry Venn and John Newton (Cowper's friend and collaborator). At the end of the century, William Wilberforce and the 'Clapham Sect' gave fresh impetus to an Evangelical revival which was later to have a profound effect upon the private lives and public manners of the Victorians. Sydney Smith invented the name for the group, most of whom lived near Clapham and worshipped in the parish church. (Hannah More was closely associated with the group later in her life.) These wealthy Anglicans believed that their faith should be reflected in good works. They led the campaign to abolish the slave trade, founded the British and Foreign Bible Society and supported missionary work at home and abroad.

Evangelicalism, with its emphasis upon conversion and a new life in Christ, sanctification and the empowerment of the Holy Spirit, mission and acts of love (or 'charity') and a personal life set apart from worldly immorality, clearly influenced Jane Austen, but without recruiting her to its ranks. When Hannah More's popular novel *Cœlebs in Search of a Wife* first appeared in 1809, Jane wrote to her sister, Cassandra: 'You have by no means raised my curiosity after Caleb; – My disinclination for it before was affected, but now it is real; I do not like the Evangelicals. – Of course I shall be delighted when I read it, like other people, but till I do, I dislike it' (*L*, 24 January 1809). By 1814, however, she could tell her niece, Fanny Knight, that she was 'by no means convinced that we ought not all to be Evangelicals', and that she was 'at least persuaded that they who are so from Reason & Feeling, must be happiest & safest' (*L*, 18–20 November 1814). 1814 was the year of *Mansfield Park*, her most overtly Christian novel, whose pious heroine has tried the patience of many readers and critics ever since it was first published. Significantly, Fanny Price meets with Edmund's approval when she raises the question of the slave trade with her uncle (*MP*, 2:3).

The author of *Mansfield Park* would have appreciated the title of Wilberforce's *A Practical View of the Prevailing Religious System of Professed Christians, in the Higher and Middle Classes in this Country, Contrasted with Real Christianity* (1797), while reserving judgement on his emphasis upon the 'melancholy proofs of our depravity'.[2] A regular reader of sermons, Austen was closer theologically to the successors of John Tillotson, Archbishop of Canterbury in the late seventeenth century, whose sermons were a model for preachers in the eighteenth. 'Every Man', Tillotson taught, 'is sent by God into this World, and hath a Work given him to do in it, which he is concern'd vigorously to mind and to prosecute with all his Might. And tho' every Man be not sent to save the whole World, as the Son of God was, yet every Man is sent by God into the World, *to work out his own Salvation*, and to take care of *that* in the first Place, and then to promote the Salvation of others, as much as in him lies.'[3]

Among late eighteenth-century divines such as John Hey, Richard Watson and William Paley – all Cambridge men – much intellectual energy was expended upon the 'evidences' of Christianity. Revealed theology explored the relationship between the truth of the gospel and the facts of the gospels – facts concerning the life, death and resurrection of Jesus Christ. In Paley's frequently reprinted *Evidences of Christianity* (1794), he concluded that the 'truth of Christianity depends upon its leading facts, and upon them alone'.[4] Natural theology, which depends upon the operation of (God-given) human reason, focused upon evidences of God in the design of the created world and the reading of the 'book of nature' as the second 'book of God'. In the opening pages of Paley's last book, *Natural Theology* (1802), he developed the famous analogy of finding a watch in a field and realising that it must have had a maker who had a purpose in mind when he made it. This made perfect sense to pre-Darwinian generations and is reflected in Fanny's celebration of a moonlit scene in *Mansfield Park*: 'When I look out on such a night as this, I feel as if there could be neither wickedness nor sorrow in the world; and there certainly would be less of both if the sublimity of Nature were more attended to, and people were carried more out of themselves by contemplating such a scene' (1:11).

Like Fanny, Austen took more pleasure in the pre-Romantic, domestic sublime of William Cowper, hymn-writer as well as poet, than in the Romantic sublimities of Coleridge or Shelley. Austen's moderate Anglicanism also shaped her response to the Gothic sublime, as worked out in her critique of Ann Radcliffe in *Northanger Abbey*, where Henry Tilney chastises the heroine specifically for forgetting her Anglican heritage: 'Dear Miss Morland, consider the dreadful nature of the suspicions you have entertained. What have you been judging from? Remember the country and the age in which we live. Remember that we are English, that we are Christians' (*NA*, 2:9). On matters of religion, Austen avoided extremes. She can be scornful not only of selfish worldliness, as in her treatment of Mary Crawford at Sotherton (*MP*, 1:8–10), but also of intrusive pietism, epitomised in Mary Bennet in *Pride and Prejudice*. Some of the comedy in the fiction plays between these two extremes, as Austen acknowledges that human beings can be both spiritual and worldly at the same time. When Mrs Elton arrives at Highbury, she is first seen at church and the attention of worshippers is divided between their devotions and their curiosity as to her prettiness (*E*, 2:14).

Although familiar with the society pulpits of Bath and London, Jane Austen knew about the role of the Church in rural England from the inside. As Edmund explains to Miss Crawford, in the wilderness at Sotherton, 'We do not look in great cities for our best morality. It is not there, that respectable people of any denomination can do most good; and it certainly is not there, that the influence of the clergy can be most felt' (*MP*, 1:9). Ordination, all too often a rather casual private matter between a recent graduate of Oxford or Cambridge and his bishop, is a central theme in *Mansfield Park*, where Sir Thomas comments upon Edmund's living and the role of a 'parish *priest*' (Austen's only use of the word in the published novels):

Edmund might, in the common phrase, do the duty of Thornton, that is, he might read prayers and preach, without giving up Mansfield Park; he might ride over, every Sunday, to a house nominally inhabited, and go through divine service; he might be the clergyman of Thornton Lacey every seventh day, for three or four hours, if that would content him. But it will not. He knows that human nature needs more lessons than a weekly sermon can convey, and that if he does not live among his parishioners and prove himself by constant attention their well-wisher and friend, he does very little either for their good or his own.

(*MP*, 2:7)

Regular public worship and the 'weekly sermon' were, however, very important to Jane Austen and her family, who always attended

Morning Prayer, unless prevented from doing so by abominable weather. Church-going is habitual to her heroines (*P&P*, 1:12) and leads naturally to social exchange after the service (*NA*, 1:5, *MP*, 3:11). The sacred and the secular blend together organically in Austen's life and work, in a way that was also celebrated by Coleridge, himself a clergyman's son, in *Aids to Reflection* (1825), where he discusses the role of the clergy as part of England's 'clerisy' of teachers and scholars. For Austen it is perfectly natural for Elinor and her new husband, Edward Ferrars, to ensure that the parsonage reflects their future status in rural society and has a carriage drive to accommodate their guests. Temporarily based in Colonel Brandon's mansion house after the wedding, they 'chuse papers, project shrubberies, and invent a sweep' (*S&S*, 3:14).

As an Anglican clergyman, Edward is now a 'minister of religion' in the Established Church of England. In place of a medieval rood screen, the royal arms will be displayed. Instead of pre-Reformation prayers for the Pope, intercessions for the 'King and members of the Royal Family' are prescribed in the Book of Common Prayer. Thomas Herring, a successor of Tillotson's as Archbishop of Canterbury, when preaching before the House of Lords, invited his congregation to 'consider, what is the Duty of a Subject': 'Is it not, from the clearest Reason and Policy in the World, and by the strongest Injunctions of Religion, to honour the King, to pay the proper Duty and Deference to his high Character, to which he has been raised by the Order of Government, by the regular Claim of Royal Birth-right, and by the Sanction of God's Providence?'[5] Two of Jane Austen's brothers became clergymen and one of her two 'sailor brothers', Francis, who served King and Country in the Napoleonic Wars and eventually rose to be Admiral of the Fleet, was known as the 'officer who knelt at church' – something that was unheard of.

One of the few books that we know was owned by Jane Austen herself, and not simply borrowed from her father's library of 500 volumes or from a circulating library, was William Vickers's *A Companion to the Altar*, later referred to by a great-niece, Miss Florence Austen, as a 'book of devotions always used by Jane Austen'.[6] The *Companion*, a slim volume designed to slip into the pocket or the reticule, prepares the reader for the service of Holy Communion, which in Austen's time was celebrated only occasionally. Again, the *national* significance of the sacrament is emphasised, when Vickers invites the reader to reflect upon the circumstances in which it was instituted by Christ: 'From that hour they who dwelt in the *uttermost ends of the earth, strangers to the covenant of promise*, began to *draw nigh*. In that hour the light of the Gospel dawned from afar on the BRITISH ISLANDS!'[7]

Vickers's aim is to encourage religious reflection among worshippers, not only upon God's gift of grace, but also upon man's response, in the form of good works. The main text begins:

All the blessings which we now enjoy, and hope hereafter to receive from Almighty God, are purchased for us, and must be obtained, through the merits and intercession of the Holy JESUS, who has instituted the Sacrament of the Lord's Supper, for a continual Remembrance of his Death and Passion, to our great and everlasting comfort, *Luke* xxii. 19, 1 *Cor.* xi. 24. But then we must remember, that these blessings are no where promised, but on condition that we ourselves are first duly qualified for them.   (*A Companion to the Altar*, p. 13)

The 'first part' of a communicant's duty, he argues, is 'Self-Examination': 'we must search our hearts, and examine our consciences, not only till we see our sins, but until we hate them' (pp. 15–16).

Jane Austen's three extant prayers strike a similar note. They appear to have been written for family worship in the evening. Each contains some or all of the following elements: a plea for grace, a petition for mercy on the day's sins, thanksgiving for blessings, a petition for protection this night and a petition for a heightened awareness of God's grace in the redemption of the world. Each then closes with the Lord's Prayer. As in the Anglican service of Evening Prayer, which they echo, the petitions for mercy are the longest and most urgent sections of these prayers:

Almighty God! Look down with mercy on thy servants here assembled and accept the petitions now offered up unto thee. Pardon oh God! the offences of the past day. We are conscious of many frailties; we remember with shame and contrition, many *evil* thoughts and neglected duties; and we have perhaps sinned against thee and against

our fellow-creatures in many instances of which we have no remembrance. Pardon oh! God whatever thou hast seen amiss in us, and give
us a stronger desire of resisting every *evil* inclination and weakening
every habit of sin (my emphases).

To the modern ear, 'evil' perhaps seems too strong a word to
apply to Emma Woodhouse's upbringing ('The real evils indeed of
Emma's situation were the power of having rather too much her
own way, and a disposition to think a little too well of herself',
E, 1:1), or to the invalided Mrs Smith's 'power of turning readily
from evil to good' (*P*, 2:5) or to Anne Elliot's misery at the concert
in Bath, as she thinks of Mr Elliot's attentions ('Their evil was
incalculable', *P*, 2:8). The scrupulousness with which Austen sifted
the 'evils' of each day in her prayers, however, indicates that we
need to retune.

It is Mrs Rushworth's reference to the fact that her late husband had 'let off' the custom of having prayers read in the chapel
at Sotherton by a domestic chaplain, morning and evening, that
elicits such contrasting responses from Miss Crawford ('Every generation has its improvements', *MP*, 2:9) and Fanny Price ('A whole
family assembling regularly for the purpose of prayer, is fine!').
Although Austen's sympathies are clear in *Mansfield Park*, where
the Christian heroine is finally rewarded with marriage and happiness, she eschews the kind of fervent religiosity that characterised
much of the religious fiction of her day, particularly Evangelical
fiction. Again, her own position is closer to that of the Anglican divines she would have read on Sundays, some of whose
arguments are decidedly down-to-earth. Tillotson, for example,
preaching on 'The present and future Advantage of an Holy and
Virtuous Life', lists 'temporal Interest' among his six 'eminent
Advantages':

 I. It brings great Peace and Contentment of Mind.
 II. It is a very fit and proper Means to promote our outward temporal
     Interest.
 III. It tends to the lengthning our days, and hath frequently the Bless-
      ing of long Life attending upon it.
 IV. It gives a Man great Peace and Comfort when he comes to die.
 V. After Death it transmits a good Name and Reputation to Posterity.
 VI. It derives a Blessing upon our Posterity after us.

(Tillotson, *Works*, vol. II, p. 54)

Similarly, there was a 'vein of shrewd sense' in Thomas Sherlock's sermons, of which Jane Austen was 'very fond', preferring them to 'almost any' (*L*, 28 September 1814).[8]

Late eighteenth- and early nineteenth-century preachers also dwelt upon the heavenly reward for which those who strive for holiness may hope, through the atoning work of God in Christ's passion. Following Marianne's brush with death, she says: 'My illness has made me think – It has given me leisure and calmness for serious recollection . . . I wonder at my recovery, – wonder that the very eagerness of my desire to live, to have time for atonement to my God, and to you all, did not kill me at once' (*S&S*, 3:10). The four last things of eschatology – death, judgement, heaven and hell – figured prominently in the religious discourse of Austen's day, and novelists often played God in writing 'last judgements' for their characters. Austen was clearly conscious of this when throwing Mrs Norris and Maria together in a 'remote and private' place, where, 'shut up together with little society, on one side no affection, on the other, no judgment, it may be reasonably supposed that their tempers became their mutual punishment' (*MP*, 3:17). This chapter begins, however, with an important disclaimer: 'Let other pens dwell on guilt and misery. I quit such odious subjects as soon as I can, impatient to restore every body, not greatly in fault themselves, to tolerable comfort, and to have done with all the rest.' The service of Morning Prayer that Jane Austen knew so well includes the words, 'Restore thou them that are penitent.'

As in other aspects of her religious life and understanding, then, Austen is moderate in her representation of her characters' fallen state and future hope: most are 'not greatly in fault' and deserve 'tolerable comfort' (*MP*, 3:17). In the service of Holy Communion, the priest says to the congregation: 'Ye that do truly and earnestly repent you of your sins, and are in love and charity with your neighbours . . . Draw near with faith, and take this holy Sacrament to your comfort.' At the end of *Persuasion*, Captain Wentworth trusts to 'being in charity' with Lady Russell soon, adding: 'But I too have been thinking over the past, and a question has suggested itself, whether there may not have been one person more my enemy even than that lady? My own self' (*P*, 2:11). Christian doctrine, expressed in the language of the Prayer Book and the Bible, underpins the novels of one whose family included these words in the inscription on her gravestone in Winchester Cathedral: 'Their grief is in proportion to their affection, they know their loss to be irreparable, but in their deepest affliction they are consoled by a firm though humble hope that her charity, devotion, faith and purity have rendered her soul acceptable in the sight of her REDEEMER.'[9]

NOTES

1. See Stephen Prickett, 'The Religious Context', in *The Context of English Literature: The Romantics*, ed. Stephen Prickett (London: Methuen, 1981), p. 116.
2. William Wilberforce, *A Practical View of the Prevailing Religious System of Professed Christians, in the Higher and Middle Classes in this Country, Contrasted with Real Christianity* (1797), p. 24.
3. *The Works of the Most Reverend Dr. John Tillotson, late Lord Archbishop of Canterbury*, second edition (1717), vol. I, p. 326. Subsequent references are included in the text.
4. William Paley, *A View of the Evidences of Christianity, in Three Parts*, twelfth edition, 2 vols. (1807), vol. II, p. 376.
5. Thomas Herring, *Seven Sermons on Public Occasions* (1763), p. 105.
6. See David Gilson, *A Bibliography of Jane Austen*, corrected edition (Winchester: St Paul's Bibliographies, 1997), p. 445.
7. [William Vickers], *A Companion to the Altar: Shewing the Nature & Necessity of a Sacramental Preparation in Order to our Worthy Receiving the Holy Communion* (1793?), p. vi. Subsequent references are included in the text.
8. Leslie Stephen, *History of English Thought in the Eighteenth Century*, 2 vols. (London: Hart-Davis, 1962), vol. I, p. 189. See Section II, 'From the Sermons of the Right Revd Thomas Sherlock, D. D. Lord Bishop of London', in *Family Lectures; or, Domestic Divinity, being a Copious Collection of Sermons*, 2 vols. (1791–5), vol. I, pp. 266–99.
9. See Michael Wheeler, *Jane Austen and Winchester Cathedral* (Winchester: Winchester Cathedral, 2003), p. 2.

39

Trade

MARKMAN ELLIS

On first sight it might seem that Austen's novels display the same lack of interest in trade and slavery as they do in issues of contemporary politics, whether they be the French Revolution or the Napoleonic Wars. Yet the social worlds of Austen's novels evince a profound concern with trade, for almost every character is defined and determined by his or her relationship to, and distance from, commerce. To her age, 'trade' meant not only the buying and selling of goods and services, but also a set of ideas marshalled in defence of commerce and business. As such, the term 'trade' further invoked a complex set of cultural assumptions about tradesmen, merchants and the moral status of commerce.

Jane Austen wrote, and was published, in a period of profound economic transition in Great Britain, characterised by revolutions agricultural and industrial. In 1815, Britain was the wealthiest country in Europe, and its economy was the most developed. Britain was the first country to experience the transformation of its economy and society from a predominantly rural and agricultural mode to a more urban and industrialised configuration. This change was accompanied by a significant increase in population, and unprecedented annual rates of economic growth of between 2 and 3 per cent between 1790 and 1820. The wealthy elite that Austen depicted in her novels lived in county towns and rural villages, in a world of privilege and prosperity that insulated itself from these transformations. Yet the wealth of this elite was derived from, and contributed to, this transforming and industrialising economy.

Despite the important economic transformations of her age, scenes of commerce and industry are largely absent from Austen's novels. Unlike her Victorian successors, her novels do not depict factories belching smoke, and her characters express no enthusiasm for innovative industrial wonders, such as cotton mills, coal-mines and canals. Instead, Austen's novels depict a society at leisure: characters are occupied in taking tea, socialising and practising philanthropy, but they are not shown performing – and indeed do not have – the tasks and duties of any occupation, profession or trade. The novels depict a narrow echelon of society that is, by and large, without a work ethic, even though it believes in the moral importance of labour for the poor.

For the most part, characters in Austen express a profound distaste for trade. In an age deeply concerned with status and rank, to be associated with trade was categorically demeaning. Discussion about tradesmen and merchants was conducted as part of the historically enduring debate on the nature of the gentleman, and was frequently related to questions of rank. In the early eighteenth century, numerous Whiggish writers had proposed that the status of a gentleman was compatible with trade and commerce. Addison and Steele's *Spectator* essays (1710–12) discussed many examples in which mercantile and professional men acted with the virtue and propriety of gentlemen. Nonetheless, a consistent stream of conservative opinion throughout the eighteenth century continued to argue that active engagement in commerce vitiated any claims to gentility. Many poets and writers – including those that Austen identified as important to her – adopted this anti-commercial discourse in their writing. In *The Deserted Village* (1770), Oliver Goldsmith depicted destruction of the customary world of an idealised rural village in England, and laid the blame at the corrupting forces of modern commerce. In the poem, the 'unfeeling train' of trade, governed by values that perceived everything in terms of monetary value, dispossesses the happy villagers from the bucolic and sentimental village of Auburn. William Cowper – Marianne Dashwood's favourite poet (*S&S*, 1:3) – argued that in its modern form, commerce had grown cruel and corrupting in its search for profit at all cost. In *The Task* (1785) Cowper railed against merchants, who

> disclaiming all regard
> For mercy and the common rights of man,
> Build factories with blood, conducting trade
> At the sword's point, and dyeing the white robe
> Of innocent commercial justice red.[1]

In the calculating spirit of trade, Jane Austen read, the enduring virtues of the English gentlemen were narrowed, hardened and corrupted.

To the critics of commercial spirit, trade was inimical to a gentleman's virtue, which was established by his financial autonomy, and made manifest in his real property, primarily land. Each of Austen's wealthiest gentlemen is identified by and through his estate. In the case of Darcy and Pemberley or Knightley and Donwell Abbey or Rushworth and Sotherton, the estate is a synecdoche for a gentleman's virtue, and hence an advertisement of his marital eligibility. Possession of such an estate is a guarantee of a gentleman's 'independence', a key term Austen uses to describe the economic agency afforded to gentlemen by their wealth. By contrast, critics argued, a merchant, even if prosperous, lacked this essential independence. A tradesman or merchant continually relied on others, having established bonds of trust and dependence through contracts and systems of credit. A merchant did not rely on his independent wealth, like a gentleman, but on his credit. According to contemporary economic analysis, a merchant's capital was constantly circulating, as he (or rarely she) invested in raw materials, put out the work to artisans and sold the resulting product. To critics, these circles of economic dependence led also to an ethical dependence on others, and compromised the merchant's ability to act like a gentleman.

The distinction between trade and gentlemanly independence was often articulated geographically. Trade was routinely depicted as urban, existing in towns and cities, in sharp contrast to the supposedly bucolic concerns of the rural estates. Within the great metropolis of London, much distinction was made of the distance between the polite West End of the city and the more mercantile districts around the City. Almost the only overlap between these distinct zones is the shop. Though the scenes of industry and commerce are never seen in Austen's novels, her characters are concerned with shopping and conspicuous consumption. In *Pride and Prejudice*, the younger Bennet daughters take much interest in the milliner's shop and the circulating library in Meryton, but these commercial premises are generally a cover for flirtation. Shopping expeditions are not made to purchase anything for the subsistence of the family. Rather, women make shopping trips in order to demonstrate that their labour – in needlepoint or finishing bonnets – is entirely devoted to non-productive work, and their interests are precisely not in trade.

Austen herself had some knowledge of urban commerce – and perhaps the social stigma it aroused – through her experience of the banking business of her brother, Henry Austen. After establishing his bank and army agency (which made and received payments for the families of military officers employed on active duty) in 1801, Henry lived in London in the high style expected of a banker. Jane Austen visited his house in Henrietta Street on numerous occasions: in 1813 she remarked that the family were visited by one of the bank's partners from the 'Compting house' down stairs (*L*, 16 September 1813). In 1815, however, as the wartime economy began to wind down, the banking business experienced difficulties. The Alton branch failed at the end of 1815, and by 15 March 1816 the other branches, the London bank and the army agency were all insolvent, and Henry was declared bankrupt. His extended family lost the considerable sums they had secured as sureties for the bank (totalling over £30,000): even Jane Austen lost her savings of £13, the profits of *Mansfield Park*.[2] These events would have reinforced for her the ineluctable connection between prosperity and propriety in her society, underlining the double-edged lesson that position in society was established by birth and status, but was maintained by wealth.

Austen was probably familiar with the works of Adam Smith, the most distinguished writer on economics in the late eighteenth century: allusions to his writings have been detected in *Pride and Prejudice*, for example.[3] In *The Wealth of Nations* (1776), Adam Smith wrote the definitive account of a 'commercial' capitalist economy. In his argument, all men were in some respects merchants: the originary division of labour meant that 'every man thus lives by exchanging, or becomes in some measure a merchant'. Nonetheless, Smith divided 'civilised society' into 'three great, original and constituent orders': 'to those who live by rent, to those who live by wages, and to those who live by profit', and suggested that only the first two – the landed elite and the industrious labourers – had the interests of general society in mind. In Smith's argument, merchants did not have the same 'connection with the interest of the society', for their 'thoughts' were 'commonly exercised rather about the interest of their own particular branch of business, than about that of the society'. Merchants, although they were the loudest in voicing complaints about economic policy, Smith said, were in fact only protecting their 'particular branch of trade or manufactures'.[4] Actuated by self-interest, merchants' policy tended towards the restriction of competition and the advance of monopoly. Although Adam Smith is now most widely known as an apologist for capitalism, his argument here is informed by the same kind of anti-mercantile discourse as Austen's.

To contemporaries – especially from the point of view of the gentry – the stigma attached to trade meant that no one could remain active in trade and be fully acceptable in gentry society. Much of the social drama of *Pride and Prejudice*, for example, plays out the complex consequences of this shame about trade and the origins of wealth. In notorious scenes with Lady Catherine de Bourgh and Darcy, Elizabeth Bennet has to fight to establish her credentials as a gentleman's daughter, despite the contamination of her mother's background in a professional family. In the imaginary of the Austen novels, as elsewhere in eighteenth-century culture, the acquisition of landed property was the only permanent way to seal the retirement from commerce. Adam Smith took it for granted that 'merchants are commonly ambitious of becoming country gentlemen', even though he thought their economic status quite separate (*Wealth of Nations*, I, 3, iv, 3, p. 411). Historians have debated the extent to which this cultural commonplace was true, without coming to much agreement. One historian estimates that about 11 per cent of the owners of country houses in the period 1760–1819 had purchased them with new money gained from the world of business.[5]

Even so, it was certainly widely believed in the early nineteenth century that a tradesman in possession of a secure fortune must be in want of a country estate. Sir William Lucas serves as an example: having made a tolerable fortune in trade in Meryton, Lucas had been knighted during his service as mayor of the town. Emboldened by the higher status implied by the knighthood, Lucas had developed 'a disgust to his business and to his residence in a small market town' and so had removed to a more rural residence which he grandiosely renamed Lucas Lodge. While Sir William's title and wealth give him a certain claim to gentry status, the novel makes clear to readers that this claim is recent, and insecure. Lucas's trajectory undercuts that of Charles Bingley, who is less advanced along a parallel social progress. Bingley has inherited £100,000 from his father, a fortune that had been 'acquired by trade' in the north of England. With this money, Bingley intends to purchase 'a good house and the liberty of a manor', so as to establish himself as a gentleman with a landed estate (*P&P*, 1:4). Both Charles Bingley and Sir William Lucas remind us that all landed wealth has an origin, and that in a commercial society, trade is likely to figure prominently. Subsequently, both the Bingleys and Lucases express a constant and complex anxiety about their status, which manifests itself especially as disgust for their origins in trade.

Despite these stories of disgust and stigma attached to trade, historians have suggested that the activities and attitudes of the upper classes 'belie the simplistic idea of an implacable hostility between the industrial middle class and an indolent landed one'. Austen's period was one in which 'aristocratic involvement with the business of making money moved into a new gear'.[6] This was evidenced by men like the Duke of Bridgewater, who gained much renown for his entrepreneurial spirit in developing canals and coal-mines on his estates near Manchester. Ambitious landowners like John Dashwood and George Knightley expected to grow their estates through prudent management and judicious improvement. Acquiring a country estate, as Bingley proposed, was in this sense more like a change in commercial activity from mercantile trading to capital investment. A merchant's heir like Bingley does not retire from his father's mercantile concerns by acquiring a landed estate, rather he refocusses his inherited wealth in new forms of commercial activity, the agricultural production of a landed estate. Many landowners established close links with urban trade and the new industries through their landed estates, by developing mining concerns on their land or investing in new transport developments. Similar strategies were followed by landowners who invested their wealth in joint stock companies, or who retained ownership of development land in expanding industrial regions. Others maintained significant interests in the colonies: in *Mansfield Park*, the Bertram family is maintained by a 'West Indian property', presumably a sugar plantation (*MP*, 1:1). One of the key ways in which the established landed elite were connected with the new money of the mercantile elite was through marriage. Austen's novels, with their plots of marriage into superior status, have often suggested a kind of historical allegory of social aspiration.

Nonetheless, when considered in moral terms, the merchant and tradesman were understood in Austen's period to be motivated by self-interest. Nowhere was this more apparent, it seemed to contemporaries, than in the case of slavery and the slave trade. Over three million African slaves were carried on British vessels to the Americas in the eighteenth century, and at the end of this period, the slave population of the Caribbean sugar colonies stood at over half a million. The system of chattel slavery was regulated by severe legal codes, and relied on explicit racial discrimination. Despite the endemic violence of the sugar plantations, slavery was entirely legal in British colonies throughout Austen's life. Yet she would have been aware that the immense profits of this commerce were achieved at an enormous cost in terms of human misery. Although critics had long questioned the legality and morality of slavery, apologists argued that the profits legitimated the business. Both the trade in slaves between Africa and the Americas and the slave labour plantations in the American colonies, were the two most profitable enterprises known to British commerce in the eighteenth century. Historians continue to debate the size of the trade and the extent of its profits, but to contemporaries it was clearly enormous. In 1803, the Prime Minister, William Pitt, argued that the combined trade in sugar and slaves produced a quarter of the profits of all overseas English trade. Although economic historians have been unable to agree on the exact contribution of profits from the slave plantations, the expansion of colonial trade was fundamental to British economic development in the eighteenth and nineteenth centuries.

Opponents of slavery in England successfully prosecuted a test case abolishing the state of slavery in 1772, although the ruling did not extend to the American colonies. On 22 June of that year, the officiating judge of the Somerset case, Lord Mansfield, some-what reluctantly declared that 'No master was ever allowed here to take a slave by force to be sold abroad because he deserted from his service.'[7] By the late 1780s, the campaign for the abolition of the trade in slaves (but not the state of slavery itself) had gained considerable support in England, both in public and in Parliament.

Abolitionists were drawn from many circles, including a powerful group of conservative Evangelical Anglicans, including William Wilberforce and Hannah More. Outraged as much by the trade's endemic violence as its ethics, such men and women made British involvement in slavery a sentimental, moral and religious scandal. Jane Austen, like many conservative Evangelical moralists, identified closely with the Abolition Society, which finally succeeded in having a bill for the abolition of the slave trade pass through Parliament in 1807. She was not above making a joke of it, however: in *Emma*, Austen alludes to the abolition debate when joking that a governess placement agency was like an office 'for the sale – not quite of human flesh – but of human intellect' (*E*, 2:17). Nonetheless, her letters make clear that she had read, with considerable approval, Thomas Clarkson's (1760–1846) pious *History of the Rise, Progress and Accomplishment of the Abolition of the African Slave Trade by the British Parliament*, which appeared in 1808.

It is in *Mansfield Park* that Austen ventured her most suggestive engagement with the debate on slavery and the morality of commerce. In recent decades the Antigua episode has become one of the more celebrated critical debates on Austen. The case was first articulated by Avrom Fleishman in 1967, and made better known by Warren Roberts and Edward Said in later decades. The felicity of the Bertrams at Mansfield Park is disturbed when the family find themselves, most unexpectedly, in financial difficulties. The underlying cause, Sir Thomas admits, is 'some recent losses on his West India Estate, in addition to his eldest son's extravagance' (*MP*, 1:3). A sugar plantation was expected to be an extremely profitable business: J. R. Ward estimates that sugar plantations regularly made returns as high as 15 per cent a year (a rate at which estate owners doubled their investment every five years).[8] But after unspecified recent events the Bertrams' 'Antigua estate is to make such poor returns' as to make the family 'rather straitened' (*MP*, 1:3). Sir Thomas travels to Antigua to address the unstated problem with the estate. Many readers have assumed their estate was a sugar plantation: on his return, Fanny asks him about 'about the slave trade' (*MP*, 2:3). Fleishman, and after him Roberts and Said, suggest that the estate's problems stem from a political and economic crisis in the sugar colonies caused by the Abolition Bill, although there is little historical evidence for this.

Most readings of the problems in Antigua have centred on the economic dimension, especially the connection between slavery and the Bertrams' English prosperity. To Austen this problem was also a philosophical and ethical one. The abolitionists' debate on the slave trade engendered profound unease in Britain about the morality of commerce. It was clear to all that slavery was incompatible with British notions of freedom (encapsulated in the doctrine of habeas corpus): the Mansfield decision had shown that this principle extended to Africans and ex-slaves. The Abolition Bill proposed that these British principles of liberty must be extended across the Atlantic. In his 1808 history, Thomas Clarkson advertised that the abolition debate was about ethics not economics, arguing that slave-owning was evidence of moral failing. The origin of slavery, Clarkson proposed, lay in the self-interest of the commercial spirit. 'The evil [of slavery] began in avarice. It was nursed also by worldly interest.' Of the slave traders and the slave-owning planters, he asks, 'Can their feelings be otherwise than corrupted, who consider their fellow-creatures as brutes, or treat those as cattle, who may become the temples of the Holy Spirit?'⁹ Sir Thomas Bertram's journey to Antigua broadcasts his status as a slave-holder, a morally reprehensible status which is increasingly incompatible with being a British gentlemen. For Clarkson, and for Jane Austen, the question of slavery was a question of the morality of trade. Her concern is not for the political liberties of the slave (of whom she took no notice), but the corrupted morality of the English planters and slave-traders. The slave trade was not simply a commercial enterprise, it was the clearest expression of the essentially selfish nature of the commercial imperative.

NOTES

1. *The Poems of William Cowper. Volume II: 1782–1785*, ed. John D. Baird and Charles Ryskamp (Oxford: Clarendon Press, 1995), IV, lines 678–83.
2. *Reminiscences of Caroline Austen*, ed. Deirdre Le Faye (Guildford: The Jane Austen Society, 1986), pp. 47–8.
3. Kenneth Moler, 'Literary Allusion in *Pride and Prejudice*', in *Approaches to Teaching Austen's 'Pride and Prejudice'*, ed. Marcia McClintock Folsom (New York: The Modern Language Association of America, 1993), pp. 89–93.

4. Adam Smith, *An Inquiry into the Nature and Causes of the Wealth of Nations*, ed. R. H. Campbell and A. S. Skinner, 2 vols. (Oxford: Clarendon Press, 1976), I, iv, 1 (p. 37); I, xi, 7 (p. 265). Subsequent references are included in the text.
5. Lawrence Stone and Jean C. Fawtier Stone, *An Open Elite? England, 1540–1880* (Oxford: Clarendon Press, 1984), table 6.2.
6. F. M. L. Thompson, *Gentrification and the Enterprise Culture, Britain 1780–1980* (Oxford: Oxford University Press, 2001), pp. 27–8.
7. Quoted in Granville Sharp, *The Just Limitations of Slavery* (1776), appendix 8, pp. 67–9.
8. J. R. Ward, 'The Profitability of Sugar Planting in the British West Indies, 1650–1834,' *Economic History Review*, 2nd ser., 31 (1978), 197–213.
9. Thomas Clarkson, *History of the Rise, Progress and Accomplishment of the Abolition of the African Slave Trade by the British Parliament* (1808), pp. 19–24.

40

Transport

PAT ROGERS

Any appraisal of transport in Austen's day must begin with the recognition that the prime way of covering the ground for most people was still to go on foot. Men and women, young and old, urban inhabitants and country dwellers – all were accustomed to walking more regularly than we do today. Some eccentrics covered huge amounts of ground, as a sport or simply as a means of winning bets. Perhaps the best-known example of a long-distance pedestrian is John 'Walking' Stewart (1749–1822), who hoofed his way around Europe and North America. Recreational walking increased at the end of the eighteenth century, with the growth of organised tourism. However, ordinary folk made what seem by our standards extensive trips on foot in the course of their daily business. All these kinds meet in William and Dorothy Wordsworth. The couple thought nothing of trotting from Grasmere to Keswick (or back) over a hilly pass for a short visit to Coleridge, who made the return trip just as often. Dorothy routinely took long walks with Mary Hutchinson, who later married her brother; and at the age of forty-six, a year after Jane Austen's death, she undertook her first ascent of England's highest mountain, Scafell Pike, together with a friend named Miss Barker and a guide. It is the same with William, who met John Stewart: his work is suffused with what might be called the culture of walking, as well as the mere physical activity. Aptly Robin Jarvis devotes a chapter in his study of *Romantic Writing and Pedestrian Travel* to 'William Wordsworth: Pedestrian Poet'.[1]

It hardly needs saying that fine ladies and smart gentlemen were less inclined to exercise their limbs in pursuit of health or recreation – they had horses and carriages for that. Nevertheless, even well-bred young women were permitted to take a turn to approved destinations, for social or communal purposes. This can be seen in the 'lapse' of Elizabeth Bennet, when she ploughs through the muddy fields and puddles to succour her ailing sister at Netherfield Park. It is her mother who objects on the grounds that Elizabeth 'will not be fit to be seen' when she arrives at the mansion; while her prosy sister Mary offers the weary platitude that 'exertion should always be in proportion to what is required'. The narrator tells us, 'That she should have walked three miles so early in the day, in such dirty weather, and by herself, was almost incredible to Mrs Hurst and Miss Bingley', the stiff-necked châtelaines of Netherfield (*P&P*, 1:7). Obviously, the readiness with which these alternative forms of discouragement are trotted out shows how unreal they are, as a facile response of the snobbish, the lazy and the timid. In much the same way, Emma Wooodhouse is quite prepared to make her short way home from the Westons' house, and tries to allay her father's fears by saying, 'I could change my shoes, you know, the moment I got home; and it is not the sort of thing that gives me cold' (*E*, 1:15). Only a congenital fusspot like Mr Woodhouse would believe that a genteel young woman was incapable of walking the equivalent of three blocks without damaging her health or her morals. Likewise, Catherine Morland happily embarks along with her friends on a morning jaunt up Beechen cliff, and still has time for a shopping trip before lunch (*NA*, 1:14).

It is part of this same picture that amusements laid on to entice the gentry and nobility assumed a capacity, at least in the young and healthy among them, to use their legs. Spas like Bath and Tunbridge Wells featured as a prime attraction places where visitors might perambulate. Near the centre of the town were strategically located 'Walks', suitable for the kind of *passeggiata* known as promenading. Further afield lay designated spots with vistas and points of interest such as rock formations. In the case of Bath, for example, these permitted the activity of rambling, which combined 'outdoor exercise with easy exploration of [the resort's] highly picturesque, walker-friendly countryside'.[2] While she was living in Bath, Jane Austen's letters often mention such places, ranging from the hilly suburbs to the locks on the canal which was cut along the Avon valley. Even when she was stuck in town, with little obvious entertainment at hand, she wrote to Cassandra, 'We do nothing but walk about' (*L*, 8–11 April 1805).

For most British people, travel by water was seldom a regular option, unless they ventured overseas. This was true even in

London, where the Thames watermen had played an important role for centuries in ferrying residents across the town. Their role started to decline as new bridges were opened and roads replaced the river as the major arteries of traffic, although bargees and lightermen continued to exercise a key function in shipping goods to and from the docks. Moreover, boating had scarcely evolved as a recreational activity in this period. However, most heavy goods were still moved around the country by water, as improvement schemes made rivers more navigable, especially in areas where industry accelerated most rapidly in the later part of the eighteenth century. The building of the Bridgewater Canal outside Manchester in 1761 set off a frenzy of construction over the next seventy-five years, until the coming of the railways, peaking when Austen was in her twenties. She would certainly have known the Basingstoke Canal, built between 1788 and 1794, and at Bath she could witness something of the creation of the Kennet and Avon Canal in the years 1794 to 1810. Meanwhile, the coasting trade remained important, as goods were transported from port to port round the nation – thousands of tons of coal for London still arrived every year by boat from Newcastle. A symbolic fact here concerns James Cook, one of the heroes of the nation at the time of Austen's birth. He learned the seaman's trade on board a coal transport ship, plying domestic waters, and then ventured further afield in the Baltic trade. It was this experience which provided the basis for Cook's great Pacific journeys in the 1770s: moreover, the ship on which he sailed in his first voyage was itself nothing else than a converted Whitby collier of about 350 tons. The port Jane Austen knew best was Portsmouth, a deep-sea harbour primarily important as a base for the navy and for ship-building. There were large cities like Glasgow, Bristol and Liverpool whose wealth grew from international shipping, much connected directly or indirectly to the slave trade. But most of the smaller ports dotted around the coast of Britain were engaged either in fishery or in domestic trading.

There is no mystery about the continuing significance of water transport in the burgeoning economy of the Industrial Revolution. Quite simply, it was cheaper by a factor of three to twelve than land carriage, whether the goods went by sea, river, canal or a combination of these methods. In addition, it was much quicker generally. Even as the quality of highways gradually improved, horses still got stuck in the mud at regular intervals. A number were needed to drag the cumbersome wagons, and indeed one horse pulling a canal barge could do the work of several on the road. Nor were horses low-maintenance items: they needed to be tended by grooms and shod by blacksmiths, and powerful draught-horses ate a great amount. 'From four to eight acres were required to produce the hay that was necessary for every horse.'[3] Yet this most durable of animals continued to prove its worth, as its use on the canal system shows. For our ancestors, the horse served in the office of car, lorry, tractor, traction engine, moped, racing bike, pet and friend.[4] It was employed by couriers, mailmen and highway robbers. As well as hauling barges, it bore hearses, ambulances, fire-engines, state coaches; and it carried its owner's hopes on the race course and in the hunting field.

We take little notice of the horses in Austen's novels, but they are there, unobtrusive and essential, as they were in everyone's lives. A lame carriage-horse delays the trip to Box Hill (*E*, 3:6), one of a number of strategic deferrals which build up expectations in this book, while Fanny Price laments the loss of 'her valued friend the old grey poney' (*MP*, 1:4). Willoughby offers Marianne Dashwood the inappropriate gift of a horse, which she rashly accepts without thinking of the expenses incurred for a groom and stabling, and it takes delicate diplomacy on the part of Elinor to get her sister to refuse the present (*S&S*, 1:12). Today such a subdued reference may easily pass us by, but contemporary readers would have picked up subtle clues from it, since their own lives revolved around horseback travel.

This is one of the features of life in earlier times which made the improvement in the condition of roads such a significant index of social progress. The Industrial Revolution could not have occurred as it did without better carriage of goods, but the take-off depended also on quicker and easier conveyance of people. British roads had not yet equalled the level they achieved under Roman occupation: indeed, they made no startling advance from the Middle Ages until around 1700. It was only two generations before Austen's birth that a rush of turnpike acts in the second and third decades of the new century heralded a gradual opening up of major routes across the nation. Early measures covered the stretch of the London road between Bath and Box (1707) and then Box to Chippenham

(1726). Nearer Austen's childhood home, the journey from London to Portsmouth was made more accessible to travellers by turnpikes instituted in 1710, from Petersfield to Portsmouth, and in 1749 from Kingston to Portsmouth. Naturally, the spread proceeded at an irregular pace in different parts of the kingdom.[5] As early as 1726, a Swiss visitor could make high claims for the improvements which had already taken place:

The journey on the high roads of England, and more especially near London, is most enjoyable and interesting. These roads are magnificent, being wide, smooth and well kept. Contractors have care of them, and cover them, when necessary with that fine gravel so common in this country. The roads are rounded in the shape of an ass's back, so that the centre is higher than the sides, and the rain flows off into the ditches with which the roads are bordered on either side. It is not the custom here, as it is in France, for the poor peasants to be forced to make and keep up the high roads at their own expense and care. In this country everyone who make use of the roads is obliged to contribute to the expense of keeping them up. At even distances there are barriers on the roads called 'Turnpikes', where you have to pay one penny per horse . . . If you journey on foot you pay nothing.[6]

In fact, most road maintenance was still a parochial responsibility, discharged mainly by local users, until the turnpike system transferred duties to paid officials financed by tolls. Moreover, the traveller's picture is distinctly rosy, reflecting the scale of change in favoured areas only: even when Jane Austen grew up, there were many places where travel remained dirty and difficult, especially in winter. One of her earliest letters to Cassandra shows that, right at the heart of the 'improved' road system, it still look two days in 1796 to get from Steventon to London, with an overnight stop at Staines and an early start on the following morning (*L*, 23 August 1796). Two years later, Jane tells her sister of the back roads which could quickly degenerate into muddy tracks: 'There has been a great deal of rain here for this last fortnight, much more than in Kent; & indeed we found the roads all the way from Staines most disgracefully dirty. – Steventon lane has its full share of it, & I do not know when I shall be able to get to Deane.' A recent journey home had been delayed with a halt at Basingstoke, on top of which 'we were obliged to stop at Hartley [Wintney] to have our wheels greazed'

(*L*, 27–28 October 1798). Travel plans had always to be framed with care, making due allowance for unexpected obstacles. Waiting for the arrival of relatives could be an anxious affair: 'It was considerably past 4 when they arrived yesterday; the roads were so very bad! – as it was, they had 4 Horses from Cranford Bridge. Fanny was miserably cold at first' (*L*, 5–8 March 1814).

Yet things were getting steadily better. An important contribution came from a succession of legislative measures which restricted narrow wheels on carts, the main agency by which the surface of roads became rutted and impassable. Thus an act of 1753 ordained that wagon wheels on turnpike roads should be at least nine inches in breadth, on pain of a five pound fine or forfeiture of a horse. Weighing machines placed at tollgates imposed a kind of excess baggage charge, which also served to deter any unthinking use of the highway for heavy goods. (Of course local carriage moved to the side-roads, which made rural byways around towns like Basingstoke even more of a challenge to navigate.) As for road construction, this gradually benefited from developments both in surveying and in engineering. The first true highway engineer of modern time is usually identified as John Metcalf (1717–1810), a Yorkshire horse-dealer and carriage operator. Even though he had been blind since early childhood, he mastered the skills both of making roads and building bridges. He was particularly successful in meeting the problems of boggy ground by setting up an effective system of drainage and laying down a firm foundation for the roadway. He was followed by Thomas Telford (1757–1834), a distinguished Scottish engineer, some of whose bridges stand to this day; and by John Loudon McAdam, another Lowland Scot who was driven from an early home in New York by the Revolutionary War. Subsequently he began to patent his new methods of getting a durable surface, by using crushed stone bound together with gravel, placed on a base of large stones. By this date he had became surveyor to the Bristol Turnpike Trust and had as part of his responsibility some of the routes that Jane Austen knew best.

Innovation in road-building permitted technological innovation to go on with respect to the conveyances which plied the highways. Passenger vehicles of the era, like their modern equivalents, differed in construction, function, size, speed and appearance. Terms used for these vary over time in their exact significance, but the general pattern can be described. The nearest to a family saloon was the chaise, a four-wheeled carriage, for the most part low-slung and lightly made: it could be drawn by two or four horses, one of them ridden by the driver. A chariot was a more substantial affair, commonly with four horses. The coach had an extra bank of seats and could carry as many as six people; commercial stage-coaches had additional seating on the roof. Another capacious vehicle was the barouche, fitted with a hood which could be lowered: normally two couples were seated inside, facing one another. The landau, generally smaller, also featured a retractable hood. The phaeton was a low, open carriage with a streamlined look. All these normally had four wheels. Other conveyances with two wheels included the gig, much favoured by dashing young men as the sports car of its period: it was drawn by a single horse and normally carried two people side by side. Its successor was the cabriolet. Another light carriage was the curricle, drawn by two horses abreast. Smallest of all was the dog-cart, often used by persons driving alone on short trips. Less common vehicles included the vis-à-vis, a narrow coach seating just two people face to face. Coming into favour in this time span was the four-in-hand, driven by one person on the box at the front.

A prime incentive to improvement came with the push to speed up the postal services. In 1784 John Palmer (1742–1818), who owned theatres in Bath and Bristol, made a proposal to the government for the use of stage-coaches to carry mail. This led to a test run for his coach service. The trial vehicle completed an overnight trip from Bristol to London, a distance of 116 miles, in less than sixteen hours, and within a year faster, more efficient and better guarded coaches were carrying mail on the roads to Norwich, Liverpool, Leeds, Dover and Exeter. Before long the service was extended to some of the 'cross-post' routes as well as the main arterial highways. A spin-off was a considerable shortening of time for general travel. Up to this period the London–Bristol service had taken three days in the winter and two in the summer. There had been only one coach a week to Birmingham, another journey which occupied a minimum of two days. In Austen's lifetime the speed of coach travel continued to rise, and the work of men like Telford allowed much quicker passage even on arduous routes such as the Welsh section of the Holyhead road. But the flying mail coach enjoyed only a brief spell as the conveyance of choice. In Austen's lifetime the track for the Stockton and Darlington railway was already laid down, and just after she died an act was passed to permit construction and maintenance of a 'railway or tramroad'. By 1825 steam trains had begun their inexorable and (until the 1960s) unstoppable rise to pre-eminence.

Coaches of various descriptions, private or public, figure in all Austen novels. The most striking episode involves a foolish young blade, John Thorpe, one of the most horse-obsessed characters in literature. He is constantly boasting about the speed of his favourite mount: 'I defy any man in England to make my horse go less than ten miles an hour in harness.' He takes every opportunity to show off to his pretty companion, Catherine: 'Thorpe's ideas then all reverted to the merits of his own equipage, and she was called on to admire the spirit and freedom with which his horse moved along, and the ease which his paces, as well as the excellence of the springs, gave the motion of the carriage.' Like all zealots, Thorpe is impossible to shut up: 'His knowledge and her ignorance of the subject, his rapidity of expression, and her diffidence of herself put that out of her power; she could strike out nothing new in commendation, but she readily echoed whatever he chose to assert, and it was finally settled between them without any difficulty, that his equipage was altogether the most complete of its kind in England, his carriage the neatest, his horse the best goer, and himself the best coachman' (*NA*, 1:7, 9). For those who travelled the roads of England, there must have been a down-side to this story of almost unimpaired progress, and Jane Austen can be trusted to show us what it was like to meet up with the great travel bore.

NOTES

1. Robin Jarvis, *Romantic Writing and Pedestrian Travel* (Basingstoke: Macmillan, 1997), pp. 89–125.
2. Trevor Fawcett, *Bath Entertain'd: Amusements, Recreations and Gambling at the Eighteenth-Century Spa* (Bath: Ruton, 1998), p. 70.
3. W. T. Jackman, *The Development of Transportation of Modern England*, new edition (London: Frank Cass & Co, 1966), p. 405.

4. See Joan Thirsk, *Horses in Early Modern England: for Service, for Pleasure, and Power* (Reading: Reading University Press, 1978).
5. See William Albert, *The Turnpike Road System in England, 1663–1840* (Cambridge: Cambridge University Press, 1972), a detailed survey of the evolution of road building in this period.
6. César de Saussure, *A Foreign View of England in the Reigns of George I and George II*, trans. Madame Van Muden (1902), pp. 146–7.

FURTHER READING

BIOGRAPHY

Austen-Leigh, William and Richard Arthur Austen-Leigh. *Jane Austen: Her Life and Letters. A Family Record.* Boston, MA: G.K. Hall, 1989. See revised enlarged version below under Le Faye.

Fergus, Jan. *Jane Austen: A Literary Life.* Basingstoke and London: Macmillan, 1991.

Honan, Park. *Jane Austen: Her Life.* London: Weidenfeld and Nicolson, 1987.

Jenkins, Elizabeth. *Jane Austen, a Biography.* London: Gollancz, 1938.

Le Faye, Deirdre. *Jane Austen.* London: British Library Publishing Division, 1998.

Jane Austen: A Family Record. Cambridge: Cambridge University Press, 2004.

Nokes, David. *Jane Austen, A Life.* London: Fourth Estate, 1997.

Tomalin, Claire. *Jane Austen: A Life.* London: Viking, 1997.

COMPOSITION AND PUBLICATION

Garside, P. 'The English Novel in the Romantic Era', in P. Garside, J. Raven and R. Schöwerling, eds. *The English Novel 1770–1829: A Bibliographical Survey of Prose Fiction Published in the British Isles.* 2 vols. Oxford: Oxford University Press, 2000.

Gilson, David. *Bibliography of Jane Austen.* Oxford: Clarendon Press, 1982. Reprinted with additions, Winchester: St Paul's Bibliographies and New Castle, DE: Oak Knoll Press, 1997.

Southam, B. C. 'The Manuscript of Jane Austen's *Volume the First*', *The Library*, 5th series 17 (1962), 231–7.

Jane Austen's Literary Manuscripts. 1964; rev. edn, London: Athlone Press, 2001.

LANGUAGE

Burrows, J. F. *Computation into Criticism: A Study of Jane Austen's Novels and an Experiment in Method.* Oxford: Clarendon Press, 1987.

De Rose, Peter L. and S. W. McGuire. *A Concordance to the Works of Jane Austen.* New York: Garland Publishing, 1982.

Lascelles, Mary. *Jane Austen and her Art.* Oxford: Clarendon Press, 1939.

Michaelson, Patricia Howell. *Speaking Volumes: Women, Reading, and Speech in the Age of Austen.* Stanford, CA: Stanford University Press, 2002.

Page, Norman. *The Language of Jane Austen.* Oxford: Basil Blackwell, 1972.

Phillips, K. C. *Jane Austen's English.* London: André Deutsch, 1970.

Stokes, Myra. *The Language of Jane Austen.* Basingstoke and London: Macmillan, 1991.

Stovel, Bruce and Lynn Weinlos Gregg, eds. *The Talk in Jane Austen.* Edmonton: University of Alberta Press, 2000.

Tave, Stuart M. *Some Words of Jane Austen.* Chicago and London: University of Chicago Press, 1973.

LETTERS

Brabourne, Edward, 1st Lord. *Letters of Jane Austen.* London, 1884.

Chapman, R. W. coll. and ed. *Jane Austen's Letters to her Sister Cassandra and Others.* Oxford: Clarendon Press, 1932, 1952.

Le Faye, Deirdre. *Letters of Jane Austen.* 3rd edn. Oxford and New York: Oxford University Press, 1995.

LITERARY INFLUENCES

Bradbrook, F. W. *Jane Austen and her Predecessors.* Cambridge: Cambridge University Press, 1967.

Byrne, Paula. *Jane Austen and the Theatre.* London and New York: Hambledon Press, 2002.

Fergus, Jan. *Jane Austen and the Didactic Novel.* London: Macmillan, 1983.

Gay, Penny. *Jane Austen and the Theatre.* Cambridge and New York: Cambridge University Press, 2002.

Grundy, Isobel. 'Jane Austen and Literary Traditions', in Edward Copeland and Juliet McMaster, eds. *The Cambridge Companion to Jane Austen*. Cambridge: Cambridge University Press, 1997.

Harris, Jocelyn. *Jane Austen's Art of Memory*. Cambridge: Cambridge University Press, 1989.

Moler, Kenneth. *Jane Austen's Art of Allusion*. Lincoln: University of Nebraska Press, 1977.

MEMOIRS AND BIOGRAPHIES

Austen, Caroline Mary Craven. *Reminiscences*, ed. Deirdre Le Faye. Chawton: Jane Austen Society, 1986, 2004.

Austen-Leigh, James Edward. *A Memoir of Jane Austen and Other Family Recollections*, ed. Kathryn Sutherland. Oxford: Oxford University Press, 2002.

Austen-Leigh, Mary Augusta. *Personal Aspects of Jane Austen*. London: J. Murray, 1920.

Collins, Irene. *Jane Austen, the Parson's Daughter*. London: Hambledon Press, 1998.

Lane, Maggie. *Jane Austen's Family through Five Generations*. London: Hale, 1984.

Le Faye, Deirdre. *Jane Austen's 'Outlandish Cousin', the Life & Letters of Eliza de Feuillide*. London: British Library, 2002.

Le Faye, Deirdre, ed. *Fanny Knight's Diaries: Jane Austen through her Niece's Eyes*. Chawton: Jane Austen Society, 2000.

MacKinnon, Sir Frank Douglas. *Grand Larceny, being the Trial of Jane Leigh Perrot, Aunt of Jane Austen*. London: Oxford University Press, 1937.

Piggott, Patrick. *The Innocent Diversion: a Study of Music in the Life and Writings of Jane Austen*. London: Douglas Cleverdon, 1979.

Tucker, George Holbert. *A Goodly Heritage: A History of Jane Austen's Family*. Manchester: Carcanet, 1983.

Wilson, Margaret. *Almost Another Sister – the Story of Fanny Knight, Jane Austen's Favourite Niece*. Maidstone: George Mann Books, 1997.

POETRY

Austen, James. *The Complete Poems of James Austen: Jane Austen's Eldest Brother*, ed. David Selwyn. Winchester: Jane Austen Society, 2003.

Jane Austen: Collected Poems and Verse of the Austen Family, ed. David Selwyn. Manchester: Carcanet, in association with the Jane Austen Society, 1996.

CRITICAL RESPONSES, EARLY

Galperin, William H. *The Historical Austen*. Philadelphia: Pennsylvania University Press, 2003.

Hogan, Charles Beecher. 'Jane Austen and her Early Public', *Review of English Studies* n.s. 1, 1 (1950) 39–54.

Joukovsky, Nicholas A. 'Another Unnoted Contemporary Review of Jane Austen', *Nineteenth-Century Fiction* 29 (1974–5), 336–8.

Southam, B. C. ed. *Jane Austen: the Critical Heritage, Vol. 1: 1811–1870*. London: Routledge & Kegan Paul, 1968.

Ward, William S. 'Three Hitherto Unnoted Contemporary Reviews of Jane Austen', *Nineteenth-Century Fiction* 26 (1971–2) 469–77.

CRITICAL RESPONSES, 1830–1970

Babb, Howard S. *Jane Austen's Novels: The Fabric of Dialogue*. Columbus: Ohio State University Press, 1962.

Bradbury, Malcolm. 'Jane Austen's *Emma*', *Critical Quarterly* 4 (1962), 335–46.

Bradley, A. C. *Essays and Studies*. Oxford : Clarendon Press, 1910.

Booth, Wayne C. 'Point of View and the Control of Distance in *Emma*', *Nineteenth Century Fiction* 16 (1961–2), 95–116.

Cady, Joseph and Ian Watt. 'Jane Austen's Critics', *Critical Quarterly* 5 (1963), 49–63.

Chapman, R. W. *Jane Austen, Facts and Problems*. Oxford: Clarendon Press, 1967.

Fleishman, Avrom. *A Reading of Mansfield Park: An Essay in Critical Synthesis*. Minneapolis: University of Minnesota Press, 1967.

Griffin, Cynthia. 'The Development of Realism in Jane Austen's Early Novels', *ELH* 30 (1963) 35–52.

Harding, D. W. *Regulated Hatred and Other Essays on Jane Austen*, ed. Monica Lawlor. London: Athlone Press, 1998.

Hughes, R. E. 'The Education of Emma Woodhouse', *Nineteenth-Century Fiction* 16 (1961–2), 69–74.

Lascelles, Mary. *Jane Austen and her Art*. Oxford: Clarendon Press, 1939.

Leavis, F. R. *The Great Tradition: George Eliot, Henry James, Joseph Conrad.* Harmondsworth: Penguin in association with Chatto & Windus, 1962, 1983.

Lewes, G. H. *Fraser's Magazine* 36 (December 1847), 686–95; *The Leader*, 22 November 1851; *Westminster Review* 58/n.s.2 (July 1852), 129–41.

Litz, A. Walton. *Jane Austen: A Study of her Artistic Development.* New York and Oxford: Oxford University Press, 1967.

Macaulay, Thomas Babington. *Edinburgh Review* 76 (January 1843), 523–69.

Mudrick, Marvin. *Jane Austen: Irony as Defence and Discovery.* Princeton: Princeton University Press, 1952.

Oliphant, Margaret. *Blackwood's Edinburgh Magazine* 107 (March 1870), 294.

Pollock, W. F. *Fraser's Magazine* 61 (January 1860), 30–1.

Ryle, Gilbert. Jane Austen and the Moralists', *Oxford Review* 1 (1966), 5–18.

Simpson, Richard, *North British Review* 52 (April 1870), 129–52.

Southam, B. C. *Critical Essays on Jane Austen.* London: Routledge & Kegan Paul, 1968.

Southam, B. C., ed. *Jane Austen: the Critical Heritage, Vol. 1: 1811– 1870*, London: Routledge & Kegan Paul, 1968; *Vol. 2: 1870– 1940*, London: Routledge & Kegan Paul, 1987.

Stephen, Leslie. 'Jane Austen', in *Dictionary of National Biography*, 1884–1900.

Trilling, Lionel. 'Mansfield Park', *Encounter* 3.3 (September 1954), 9–19.

Watt, Ian. *The Rise of the Novel.* London: Chatto and Windus, 1957.

Williams, Raymond. *The English Novel from Dickens to Lawrence.* London: Chatto and Windus, 1970.

Woolf, Virginia. 'Jane Austen', in *The Common Reader.* New York: Harcourt, Brace and Company, 1925.

Wright, A. H. *Jane Austen: A Study in Structure.* London: Chatto and Windus, 1952; reprinted in 1961; reprinted in Penguin, 1972.

CRITICAL RESPONSES, RECENT

Armstrong, Nancy. *Desire and Domestic Fiction: A Political History of the Novel.* Oxford: Oxford University Press, 1987.

Brown, Julia Prewitt. *Jane Austen's Novels: Social Change and Literary Form* Cambridge, MA: Harvard University Press, 1979.

Butler, Marilyn. *Jane Austen and the War of Ideas*. Oxford: Clarendon Press, 1975.

Coleman, Deirdre. 'Conspicuous Consumption: White Abolitionism and English Women's Protest Writing in the 1790s', *English Literary History* 61 (1994), 341–62.

Copeland, Edward and Juliet McMaster, eds. *The Cambridge Companion to Jane Austen*. Cambridge: Cambridge University Press, 1997.

Evans, Mary. *Jane Austen and the State*. London: Tavistock Publications, 1987.

Gard, Roger. *Jane Austen's Novels: the Art of Clarity*. New Haven and London: Yale University Press, 1992.

Gilbert, Sandra and Susan Gubar. *The Madwoman in the Attic: The Woman Writer and the Nineteenth-Century Literary Imagination*. New Haven: Yale University Press, 1979.

Grundy, Isobel. 'Jane Austen and Literary Traditions', in Edward Copeland and Juliet McMaster, eds. *The Cambridge Companion to Jane Austen*. Cambridge: Cambridge University Press, 1997.

Halperin, John, ed. *Jane Austen: Bicentenary Essays*. Cambridge: Cambridge University Press, 1975.

Hardy, Barbara. *A Reading of Jane Austen*. London: Peter Owen, 1975.

Hofkosh, Sonia. *Sexual Politics and the Romantic Author*. Cambridge: Cambridge University Press, 1998.

Johnson, Claudia L. *Jane Austen: Women, Politics and the Novel*. Chicago and London: University of Chicago Press, 1988.

'Gender, Theory and Jane Austen Culture', in Nigel Wood, ed. *Mansfield Park: Theory in Practice*. Buckingham and Philadelphia: Open University Press, 1993.

Kirkham, Margaret. *Jane Austen: Feminism and Fiction*. Sussex: Harvester Press, 1983; reprinted London: Athlone Press, 1997.

Lloyd, Trevor. 'Myths of the Indies: Jane Austen and the British Empire', *Comparative Criticism* 21 (1999), 59–78.

Looser, Devoney, ed. *Jane Austen and the Discourses of Feminism*. Basingstoke: Macmillan, 1995.

MacDonagh, Oliver. *Jane Austen: Real and Imagined Worlds*, New Haven and London: Yale University Press, 1991.

Mukherjee, Meenakshi. *Jane Austen*. London: Macmillan, 1991.

Park, You-me and Rajeswari Sunder Rajan, eds. *The Postcolonial Jane Austen*. London and New York: Routledge, 2000.

Perry, Ruth. *Novel Relations: The Transformation of Kinship in English Literature and Culture, 1748–1818.* Cambridge: Cambridge University Press, 2004.

Poovey, Mary. *The Proper Lady and the Woman Writer: Ideology as Style in the Works of Mary Wollstonecraft, Mary Shelley, and Jane Austen.* Chicago: University of Chicago Press, 1984.

Sedgwick, Eve Kosofsky. 'Jane Austen and the Masturbating Girl', *Critical Inquiry* 17 (Summer 1991), 818–37.

Smith, Leroy W. *Jane Austen and the Drama of Woman.* London: Macmillan, 1983.

Southam, Brian. 'The Silence of the Bertrams', *Times Literary Supplement* (17 February 1995), 13–14.

Stewart, Maaja. *Domestic Realities and Imperial Fictions: Jane Austen's Novels in Eighteenth-Century Contexts.* Athens and London: University of Georgia Press, 1993.

Sunder Rajan, Rajeswari, ed. *The Lie of the Land: English Literary Studies in India.* Delhi: Oxford University Press, 1992.

Tanner, Tony. *Jane Austen.* London: Macmillan, 1986.

Todd, Janet, ed. *Jane Austen: New Perspectives.* New York and London: Holmes & Meier, 1983.

Trumpener, Katie. *Bardic Nationalism: the Romantic Novel and the British Empire.* Princeton: Princeton University Press, 1997.

Tuite, Clara. *Romantic Austen: Sexual Politics and the Literary Canon.* Cambridge: Cambridge University Press, 2002.

Vanita, Ruth. 'Mansfield Park in Miranda House', in Rajeswari Sunder Rajan, ed. *The Lie of the Land: English Literary Studies in India.* Delhi: Oxford University Press, 1992.

CULT OF JANE AUSTEN

Johnson, Claudia. 'Austen Cults and Cultures', in Edward Copeland and Juliet McMaster, eds. *The Cambridge Companion to Jane Austen.* Cambridge: Cambridge University Press, 1997.

Kipling, Rudyard. 'The Janeites', in Sandra Kemp, ed. *Debits and Credits.* Harmondsworth: Penguin, 1987.

Lynch, Deidre, ed. *Janeites: Austen's Disciples and Devotees.* Princeton: Princeton University Press, 2000.

Southam, B. C., comp. *Jane Austen: The Critical Heritage.* 2 vols. London: Routledge & Kegan Paul, 1968, 1987.

Wiltshire, John. *Recreating Jane Austen.* Cambridge: Cambridge University Press, 2001.

PUBLISHING HISTORY

Bowden, Jean K. *Hugh Thomson's Illustrations of Jane Austen's 'Pride and Prejudice'*. Chawton: Jane Austen Memorial Trust, 1999.

Cohn, Maggie Hunt. 'Illustrations for Jane Austen', in J. David Grey, ed. *The Jane Austen Companion*. New York: Macmillan, 1986 (published as *Jane Austen Handbook*, London: Athlone Press, 1986).

Gilson, David, *A Bibliography of Jane Austen*. Oxford: Clarendon Press, 1982, reprinted with additions, Winchester: St Paul's Bibliographies and New Castle, DE: Oak Knoll Press, 1997.

'Jane Austen's Text: a Survey of Editions', *The Review of English Studies* n.s. 53 (2002), 61–85.

Hassall, Joan. 'On Illustrating Jane Austen's Works', Jane Austen Society, *Report for the Year, 1973*. (*Collected Reports of the Jane Austen Society, 1966–75*, 1977). Folkestone: Wm. Dawson & Sons, 1973.

'Illustrating Jane Austen', in J. David Grey, ed. *The Jane Austen Companion*. New York: Macmillan, 1986 (published as *Jane Austen Handbook*, London: Athlone Press, 1986).

Parker, Keiko. 'Illustrating Jane Austen', *Persuasions: the Journal of the Jane Austen Society of North America* 11 (1989), 22–7.

TRANSLATIONS

Battaglia, Beatrice and Diego Saglia, eds. *Re-Drawing Austen: Picturesque Travels in Austenland*. Naples: Liguori, 2004.

Bickerton, David. *Marc-Auguste and Charles Pictet, the Bibliothèque britannique (1796–1815) and the Dissemination of British Literature and Science on the Continent*. Geneva: Slatkine, 1986.

Boucher, Léon. 'Le roman classique en Angleterre, Jane Austen', *Revue des Deux Mondes*, 3rd series, 29 (1878), 449–67.

Cassaigneau, Jean and Jean Rilliet. *Marc-Auguste-Pictet ou le rendez-vous de l'Europe universelle*. Geneva: Slatkine, 1995.

Chambers, Helen. 'Nineteenth-Century German Translations of Jane Austen', in Norbert Bachleitner, ed. *Beiträge zur Rezeption der britischen und irischen Literatur des 19. Jahrhunderts im deutschsprachigen Raum*. Amsterdam and Atlanta, GA: Rodopi, 2000.

Chasles, Philarète. 'Du roman en Angleterre depuis Walter Scott', *Revue des Deux Mondes*, 4th series, 31 (1842), 185–214.

Cohen, Margaret. *The Sentimental Education of the Novel*. Princeton: Princeton University Press, 1999.

Cossy, Valérie. 'An English Touch: Laurence Sterne, Jane Austen et le roman sentimental en Suisse romande', *Annales Benjamin Constant* 25 (2001), 131–60.

Duret, Théodore. 'Miss Austen', *Revue blanche* 16 (1898), 278–82.

Gilson, David, *A Bibliography of Jane Austen*. Oxford: Clarendon Press, 1982, reprinted with additions, Winchester: St Paul's Bibliographies and New Castle, DE: Oak Knoll Press, 1997.

Jaquier, Claire. 'L'idylle sensible', *Annales Benjamin Constant* 18–19 (1996), 107–15.

L'Erreur des désirs, in *Romans sensibles au XVIIIe siècle*. Lausanne: Payot, 1998.

Nemoianu, Virgil. *The Taming of Romanticism: European Literature and the Age of Biedermeier*. Cambridge, MA and London: Harvard University Press, 1984.

Parent-Lardeur, Françoise. *Lire à Paris au temps de Balzac, Les cabinets de lecture à Paris 1815–1830*. Paris: Editions de l'Ecole des Hautes Etudes en sciences sociales, 1981.

Pictet, Edmond. *Biographie, travaux et correspondance diplomatique de Charles Pictet de Rochemont . . . 1755–1824*. Geneva: Georg, 1892.

Southam, Brian C., ed. *Jane Austen: the Critical Heritage*. London: Routledge, 1968, vol. I.

AGRICULTURE

Arnold, Dana, *et al. The Georgian Country House: Architecture, Landscape and Society*. Stroud: Sutton Publishing, 1998.

Chapman, John and Sylvia Seeliger. *A Guide to Enclosure in Hampshire, 1700–1900. Hampshire Record Series*, volume 15. Winchester: Hampshire County Council, 1997.

Clark, J. C. D. *English Society, 1688–1832: Ideology, Social Structure and Political Practice during the* ancien régime. Cambridge: Cambridge University Press, 1985.

Collins, Irene. *Jane Austen and the Clergy*. London: Hambledon Press, 1994.

Eastwood, David. *Governing Rural England: Tradition and Transformation in Local Government, 1780–1840*. Oxford: Clarendon Press, 1994.

Eden, Sir Frederic Morton. *The State of the Poor, or, An History of the Labouring Classes in England, from the Conquest to the Present Period*. London: J. Davis, 1797.

Martins, Susanna Wade. *Farmers, Landlords and Landscapes: Rural Britain, 1720–1870*. London: Windgather Press, 2004.

Poynter, J. R. *Society and Pauperism: English Ideas on Poor Relief, 1795–1834*. London: Routledge, 1969.

Virgin, Peter. *The Church in an Age of Negligence: Ecclesiastical Structure and Problems of Church Reform, 1700–1840*. Cambridge: James Clarke, 1989.

Williamson, Tom. *The Transformation of Rural England: Farming and the Landscape, 1700–1870*. Exeter: University of Exeter Press, 2002.

Young, Arthur. *A General Report on Enclosures, Drawn up by Order of the Board of Agriculture*. London: Macmillan, 1808.

BOOK PRODUCTION

Blakey, D. *The Minerva Press 1790–1820*. London: Oxford University Press, 1939.

Cross, N. *The Common Writer: Life in Nineteenth-Century Grub Street*. Cambridge: Cambridge University Press, 1985.

Eliot, S. *Some Patterns and Trends in British publishing 1800–1919*. *Occasional Papers of the Bibliographical Society*, 8, 1994.

Feather, J. *A History of British Publishing*. London: Croom Helm, 1988.

Fergus, J. and J. F. Thaddeus. 'Women, Publishers, and Money, 1790–1820', *Studies in Eighteenth-Century Culture* 17 (1988), 191–207.

Finkelstein, D. *The House of Blackwood: Author–Publisher Relations in the Victorian Era*. University Park: Pennsylvania State University Press, 2002.

Garside, P., J. Raven and R. Schöwerling, eds. *The English Novel 1770–1829: A Bibliographical Survey of Prose Fiction Published in the British Isles*. 2 vols. Oxford: Oxford University Press, 2000.

Gettmann, R. A. *A Victorian Publisher: A Study of the Bentley Papers*. Cambridge: Cambridge University Press, 1960.

Griffin, R. J. ed. *The Faces of Anonymity: Anonymous and Pseudonymous Publication from the Sixteenth to the Twentieth Century*. New York and Basingstoke: Palgrave Macmillan, 2003.

Harris, M. 'The Management of the London Newspaper Press during the Eighteenth Century', *Publishing History* 4 (1978), 95–112.

Hunt, A., G. Mandelbrote and A. Shell, eds. *The Book Trade and its Customers 1450–1900.* Winchester: St Paul's Bibliographies and New Castle, DE: Oak Knoll Press, 1997.

Knight, C. *The Printing Machine.* London, 1834.

Mumby, F. A. *Publishing and Bookselling.* London: Jonathan Cape, 1930.

Myers, R., M. Harris and G. Mandelbrote, eds. *Under the Hammer: Book Auctions since the Seventeenth Century.* London: British Library and New Castle, DE: Oak Knoll Press, 2001.

The London Book Trade: Topographies of Print in the Metropolis from the Sixteenth Century. London: British Library and New Castle, DE: Oak Knoll Press, 2003.

Pollard, H. G. and A. Ehrman. *The Distribution of Books by Catalogue.* Cambridge: Cambridge University Press, 1965.

Raven, J. 'The Book Trades', in Isabel Rivers, ed. *Books and their Readers: New Essays.* New York: Continuum, 2001.

'The Promotion and Constraints of Knowledge', in M. Daunton, ed. *The Organisation of Knowledge in Victorian Britain.* London: British Academy, 2005.

The Commercialization of the Book: Booksellers and the Commodification of Literature in England 1450–1900. Cambridge: Cambridge University Press, 2006.

Rose, M. *Authors and Owners: The Invention of Copyright.* Cambridge, MA and London: Harvard University Press, 1993.

St Clair, William. *The Reading Nation in the Romantic Period.* Cambridge: Cambridge University Press, 2004.

Smiles, S. *A Publisher and his Friends: Memoir and Correspondence of the late John Murray.* 2 vols. London, 1891.

Suarez. M. F. and M. Turner, eds. *History of the Book in Britain*, vol. V. Cambridge: Cambridge University Press, 2005.

Weedon, A. *Victorian Publishing: The Economics of Book Production for a Mass Market, 1836–1916.* Aldershot and Burlington: Ashgate, 2003.

CITIES

Ackroyd, Peter. *London: the Biography.* London: Chatto and Windus, 2000.

Burford, E. J. *Royal St James's: Being a Story of Kings, Clubmen and Courtesans*. London: Hale, 1988, 2001.

Hembry, Phyllis. *The English Spa 1560–1815: a Social History*. London: Athlone Press, 1990.

Hughes, Penelope. *The Immortal Dinner*. Harmondsworth: Penguin, 2001.

Lewis, Wilmarth Sheldon. *Three Tours through London in the Years 1748, 1776, 1797*. New Haven: Yale University Press, 1941.

Neale, R. S. *Bath 1680–1850: A Social History, or A Valley of Pleasure, yet a Sink of Iniquity*. London: Routledge & Kegan Paul, 1981.

Rendell, Jane. *The Pursuit of Pleasure: Gender, Space and Architecture in Regency London*. London: Athlone, 2002.

Rudé, George. *Hanoverian London 1714–1808*. London: Secker and Warburg, 1971.

St Aubyn, Fiona. *A Portrait of Georgian London: Based on Ackermann's 'The Microcosm of London', with the Original Illustrations by Architectural Draughtsman, Augustus Pugin, in Collaboration with Caricaturist, Thomas Rowlandson*. Ware, Herts.: Wordsworth Editions, 1985.

Sheppard, Francis. *London 1808–1870: The Infernal Wen*. London: Secker and Warburg, 1971.

CONSUMER GOODS

Davis, Dorothy. *A History of Shopping*. London: Routledge & Kegan Paul, 1966.

Guest, Harriet. *Small Change: Women, Learning, Patriotism, 1750–1810*, Chicago: University of Chicago Press, 2000.

Hart, Roger. *English Life in the Eighteenth Century*. London: Wayland, 1970.

Kowalski-Wallace, Elizabeth. *Consuming Subjects: Women, Shopping, and Business in the Eighteenth-Century*. New York: Columbia University Press, 1997.

Mui, Hoh-Cheung and Lorna H. *Shops and Shopkeeping in Eighteenth Century England*. Montreal: McGill-Queen's University Press and London: Routledge, 1989.

Porter, Roy. *English Society in the Eighteenth Century*. London: Allen Lane, 1982.

Porter, Roy and Marie Mulvey Roberts, eds. *Pleasure in the Eighteenth Century*. London: Macmillan, 1996.

Selwyn, David. *Jane Austen and Leisure.* London: Hambledon Press, 1999.

DOMESTIC ARCHITECTURE

Girouard, Mark. *Life in the English Country House: A Social and Architectural History.* New Haven and London: Yale University Press, 1978.

Grey, J. David. 'Houses', in J. David Grey, ed. *The Jane Austen Handbook.* New York: Macmillan, 1986 (published as *Jane Austen Handbook*, London: Athlone Press, 1986).

Hart, Francis R. 'The Spaces of Privacy: Jane Austen', *Nineteenth-Century Fiction* 30 (1975), 305–33.

Hunt, John Dixon. 'Architecture/Buildings', in J. David Grey, ed. *The Jane Austen Companion.* New York: Macmillan, 1986 (published as *Jane Austen Handbook*, London: Athlone Press, 1986).

Lamont, Claire. 'Jane Austen's Gothic Architecture', in Valeria Tinkler-Villani, ed. *Exhibited by Candlelight: Sources and Developments in the Gothic Tradition.* Amsterdam and Atlanta, GA: Rodopi, 1995.

Lane, Margaret. Untitled address (on Austen's use of the domestic interior) in *Report for the Year*, 1962. Alton: Jane Austen Society, 1963, 14–17, 19–24; reprinted with alterations in her *Purely for Pleasure.* London: Hamish Hamilton, 1966, entitled 'Jane Austen's Sleight-of-hand'.

McBride, Kari Boyd. *Country House Discourse in Early Modern England.* Aldershot: Ashgate, 2001.

Nicolson, Nigel. *The World of Jane Austen.* London: Weidenfeld and Nicolson, 1991.

Parissien, Steven. *Regency Style.* London: Phaidon, 1992.

Pevsner, Nikolaus. 'The Architectural Setting of Jane Austen's Novels', *Journal of the Warburg and Courtauld Institutes* 31 (1968), 404–22.

Reid-Walsh, Jacqueline. 'Mistress of All She Surveys: Elizabeth Bennet Claims Pemberley as Her Own', *The Female Spectator* 8 (2003), 16–19.

Schneider, Lucy. 'The Little White Attic and the East Room: Their Function in the Mansfield Estate', *Modern Philology* 63 (1965–6), 227–35.

Tristram, Philippa. *Living Space in Fact and Fiction.* London and New York: Routledge, 1989.

Wellesley, Gerald (later 7th Duke of Wellington). 'Houses in Jane Austen's Novels', *Spectator*, 135 (1926), 524–5; reprinted in *Report for the Year, 1960*. Alton: Jane Austen Society, 1961.

DRESS

Ashelford, Jane. *The Art of Dress*, London: National Trust, 1996. *Care of Clothes*, London: National Trust, 1997.

Brummell, Beau. *Male and Female Costume*, ed. Eleanor Parker. New York: Benjamin Bloom, 1932.

Buck, Anne. *Dress in Eighteenth-Century England*. London: Batsford, 1979.

Byrde, Penelope. *Jane Austen Fashion. Fashion and Needlework in the Works of Jane Austen*. Ludlow: Excellent Press, 1999.

Ribeiro, Aileen. *The Art of Dress. Fashion in England and France 1750 to 1820*. New Haven: Yale University Press, 1995.

EDUCATION AND ACCOMPLISHMENTS

Broughton, Trev and Ruth Symes. *The Governess: An Anthology*. New York: St Martin's Press, 1997.

Copeland, Edward. *Women Writing about Money: Women's Fiction in England, 1790–1820*. Cambridge: Cambridge University Press, 1995.

Devlin, D. D. *Jane Austen and Education*. London and Basingstoke: Macmillan, 1975.

Frantz, Sarah S. G. '"If I Loved You Less, I Might be Able to Talk about It More": Direct Dialogue and Education in the Proposal Scenes', in Bruce Stovel and Lynn Weinlos Gregg, eds. *The Talk in Jane Austen*. Edmonton: University of Alberta Press, 2002.

Horwitz, Barbara. 'Women's Education During the Regency: Jane Austen's Quiet Rebellion', *Persuasions* 16 (1994), 135–46.

Jerinic, Maria. 'In Defense of the Gothic: Rereading *Northanger Abbey*', in Devoney Looser, ed. *Jane Austen and the Discourses of Feminism*. New York: St Martin's Press, 1995.

Martin, Christopher. *A Short History of English Schools 1750–1965*. Hove: Wayland, 1979.

Mooneyham, Laura G. *Romance, Language and Education in Jane Austen's Novels*. New York: St Martin's Press, 1988.

Nardin, Jane. 'Jane Austen, Hannah More, and the Novel of Education', *Persuasions* 20 (1998), 15–20.

Purvis, June. *A History of Women's Education in England.* Milton Keynes: Open University Press, 1991.

Richardson, Alan. *Literature, Education, and Romanticism: Reading as Social Practice, 1780–1832.* Cambridge and New York: Cambridge University Press, 1994.

Sanderson, Michael. *Education, Economic Change, and Society in England, 1780–1870,* second edition, London: Macmillan, 1991.

Vickery, Amanda. *The Gentleman's Daughter: Women's Lives in Georgian England.* New Haven: Yale University Press, 1998.

West, Katharine. *Chapter of Governesses: A Study of the Governess in English Fiction 1800–1949.* London: Cohen and West, 1949.

LANDOWNERSHIP

Burgess, Miranda. *British Fiction and the Production of Social Order, 1740–1830.* Cambridge: Cambridge University Press, 2000.

Burke, Edmund. *Reflections on the Revolution in France,* ed. L. G. Mitchell. Oxford: Oxford University Press, 1993.

Coleridge, Samuel Taylor. *On the Constitution of Church and State,* ed. John Barrell. London: Dent, 1972.

English, Barbara and John Saville. *Strict Settlement: a Guide for Historians.* Hull: University of Hull Press, 1983.

Erickson, Amy Louise. *Women and Property in Early Modern England.* London: Routledge, 1993.

Habakkuk, John. *Marriage, Debt, and the Estates System: English Landownership 1650–1950.* Oxford: Clarendon Press, 1994.

Harte, Negley and Roland Quinault, eds. *Land and Society in Britain, 1700–1914.* Manchester: Manchester University Press, 1996.

Hubback, J. H. and Edith C. Hubback. *Jane Austen's Sailor Brothers.* London: John Lane, 1905.

McBride, Kari Boyd. *Country House Discourse in Early Modern England.* Aldershot: Ashgate, 2001.

Mingay, Gordon E. *Land and Society in England 1750–1980.* London: Longman, 1994.

Parliamentary Enclosure in England. London: Longman, 1997.

Mingay, Gordon E., ed. *Arthur Young and his Times.* London: Macmillan, 1975.

Neill, Edmund. *The Politics of Jane Austen.* London: Macmillan, 1999.

Sales, Roger. *Jane Austen and Representations of Regency England.* London: Routledge, 1994.

Spring, Eileen. *Law, Land, & Family: Aristocratic Inheritance in England, 1300–1800.* Chapel Hill and London: University of North Carolina Press, 1993.

Staves, Susan. *Married Women's Separate Property in England, 1660–1833.* Cambridge, MA and London: Harvard University Press, 1990.

Todd, Janet, ed. *Jane Austen: New Perspectives.* New York: Holmes and Meier, 1983.

Trumbach, Randolph. *The Rise of the Egalitarian Family: Aristocratic Kinship and Domestic Relations in Eighteenth-Century England.* London: Academic Press, 1978.

Tuite, Clara. *Romantic Austen.* Cambridge: Cambridge University Press, 2002.

Turner, Michael. *Enclosures in Britain 1750–1830.* London: Macmillan, 1984.

LANDSCAPE

Andrews, Malcolm. *The Search for the Picturesque.* Aldershot: Scolar Press, 1989.

Barrell, John. *The Dark Side of the Landscape: the Rural Poor in English Painting, 1730–1840.* Cambridge and New York: Cambridge University Press, 1980.

Batey, Mavis. *Jane Austen and the English Landscape.* London: Barn Elms, 1996.

Bermingham, Ann. *Landscape and Ideology: The English Rustic Tradition, 1740–1860.* Los Angeles: University of California Press, 1986.

Copley, Stephen and Peter Garside. *The Politics of the Picturesque: Literature, Landscape and Aesthetics since 1720.* Cambridge: Cambridge University Press, 1994.

Daniels, Stephen. *Fields of Vision: Landscape Imagery and National Identity in England and the United States.* Princeton: Princeton University Press, 1993.

Humphry Repton: Landscape Gardening and the Geography of Georgian England. New Haven and London: Yale University Press, 1999.

Duckworth, Alistair M. *The Improvement of the Estate: A Study of Jane Austen's Novels.* Baltimore and London: Johns Hopkins University Press, 1971, 1974.

Everett, Nigel. *The Tory View of Landscape.* New Haven and London: Yale University Press, 1994.

Fulford, Tim. *Landscape, Liberty and Authority: Poetry, Criticism and Politics from Thomson to Wordsworth.* Cambridge: Cambridge University Press, 1996.

Helsinger, Elizabeth. *Rural Scenes and National Representation 1815–1850.* Princeton: Princeton University Press, 1997.

Hemingway, Andrew. *Landscape Imagery and Urban Culture in Early Nineteenth-Century Britain.* Cambridge: Cambridge University Press, 1992.

Hunt, John Dixon. *Gardens and the Picturesque: Studies in the History of Landscape Architecture.* Cambridge, MA and London: MIT Press, 1992.

Hunt, John Dixon and Peter Willis, eds. *The Genius of the Place: The English Landscape Garden 1620–1820.* 1975; reprinted Cambridge, MA and London: MIT Press, 1990.

Hussey, Christopher. *The Picturesque: Studies in a Point of View.* 1927; reprinted London: Frank Cass, 1967.

Janowitz, Anne. *England's Ruins: Poetic Purpose and the National Landscape.* Oxford: Blackwell, 1990.

Malins, Edward. *English Landscaping and Literature, 1660–1840.* London: Oxford University Press, 1966.

Moir, Esther. *The Discovery of Britain: The English Tourist, 1540–1840.* London: Routledge & Kegan Paul, 1964.

LITERARY SCENE

Butler, Marilyn. *Jane Austen and the War of Ideas.* Oxford: Clarendon Press, 1975.

Johnson, Claudia L. *Equivocal Beings: Politics, Gender and Sentimentality in the 1790s: Wollstonecraft, Radcliffe, Burney, Austen.* Chicago: University of Chicago Press, 1995.

Tompkins, J. M. S. *The Popular Novel in England 1770–1800.* London: Constable, 1932.

Waldron, Mary. *Jane Austen and the Fiction of her Time.* Cambridge: Cambridge University Press, 1999.

Yeazell, Ruth Bernard. *Fictions of Modesty: Women and Courtship in the English Novel.* Chicago: Chicago University Press, 1991.

MEDICINE

Loudon, Irving. *Medical Care and the General Practitioner 1750–1850*. Oxford: Clarendon Press, 1986.

Porter, Dorothy and Roy. *Patients' Progress: Doctors and Doctoring in Eighteenth-Century England*. Oxford: Polity Press, 1989.

Wiltshire, John. *Jane Austen and the Body: 'The Picture of Health'*. Cambridge: Cambridge University Press, 1992.

MONEY

Copeland, Edward. 'Money Talks: Jane Austen and the Lady's Magazine', in J. David Grey, ed. *Jane Austen's Beginnings: the Juvenilia and Lady Susan*. Foreword by Margaret Drabble. Ann Arbor, MI and London: UMI Research Press, 1989.

Women Writing about Money: Women's Fiction in England, 1790–1820. Cambridge: Cambridge University Press, 1995.

English, Barbara and John Saville. *Occasional Papers in Economic and Social History, No. 10, Strict Settlement: A Guide for the Historians*. Hull: University of Hull Press, 1983.

MacDonagh, Oliver. *Jane Austen: Real and Imagined Worlds*. New Haven and London: Yale University Press, 1991.

Ruoff, Gene. *Jane Austen's 'Sense and Sensibility'*. New York: St Martin's Press, 1992.

Thompson, F. M. L. *English Landed Society in the Nineteenth Century*. London: Routledge & Kegan Paul, 1963.

NATIONALISM AND EMPIRE

Colley, Linda. *Britons: Forging the Nation 1707–1837*. New Haven: Yale University Press, 1992.

Ferguson, Moira. '*Mansfield Park*: Slavery, Colonialism, and Gender', *Oxford Literary Review* 13 (1991), 118–39.

Fraiman, Susan. 'Jane Austen and Edward Said: Gender, Culture, and Imperialism', *Critical Inquiry* 21 (Summer 1995), 805–21.

Gibbon, Frank. 'The Antiguan Connection: Some New Light on *Mansfield Park*', *The Cambridge Quarterly* 11 (1982), 298–305.

Guest, Harriet. *Small Change: Women, Learning, Patriotism, 1750–1810*. Chicago: University of Chicago Press, 2000.

Roberts, Warren. *Jane Austen and the French Revolution*. London: Macmillan, 1979.

Said, Edward W. 'Jane Austen and Empire', in *Culture and Imperialism*. New York: Knopf, 1993.

PASTIMES

Altick, Richard. *The Shows of London*. Cambridge, MA and London: Harvard University Press, 1978.

Malcolmson, Robert W. *Popular Recreations in English Society 1700–1850*. Cambridge: Cambridge University Press, 1973.

Mingay, Gordon E. *Mrs Hurst Dancing, And Other Scenes from Regency Life 1812–1823*. London: Victor Gollancz, 1981.

Piggott, Patrick. *The Innocent Diversion, Music in the Life and Writings of Jane Austen*. London: Douglas Cleverdon, 1979.

Selwyn, David. *Jane Austen and Leisure*. London: Hambledon Press, 1999.

PHILOSOPHY

Griswold, Charles. *Adam Smith and the Virtues of Enlightenment*. Cambridge: Cambridge University Press, 1999.

Hundert, E. G. *The Enlightenment's Fable: Bernard Mandeville and the Discovery of Society*. Cambridge: Cambridge University Press, 1994.

Knox-Shaw, Peter. *Jane Austen and the Enlightenment*. Cambridge: Cambridge University Press, 2004.

Norton, David Fate. *David Hume: Common-Sense Moralist, Sceptical Metaphysician*. Princeton: Princeton University Press, 1982.

Porter, Roy. *Enlightenment: Britain and the Creation of the Modern World*. Harmondsworth: Penguin, 2000.

Todd, Janet, *Sensibility: An Introduction*, London: Methuen, 1986.

POLITICS

Butler, Marilyn. *Jane Austen and the War of Ideas*. Oxford: Clarendon Press, 1975.

Evans, Eric J. *The Forging of the Modern State*. 2nd edition. London: Longman, 1996.

Roberts, Warren. *Jane Austen and the French Revolution*. London: Macmillan, 1979.

Rudé, George. *Hanoverian London, 1714–1808*. London: Secker and Warburg, 1971.

Sales, Roger. *Jane Austen and Representations of Regency England.* Revised edition. London: Routledge, 1996.

Todd, Janet. 'Jane Austen, Politics and Sensibility', in Susan Sellers, ed. *Feminist Criticism: Theory and Practice.* Toronto: University of Toronto Press, 1991.

Williams, Raymond. *The Country and the City.* New York: Oxford University Press, 1973.

The Long Revolution. Reprinted, London: Hogarth Press, 1992.

PROFESSIONS

Carr-Saunders, A. M. and P. A. Wilson. *The Professions.* Oxford: Clarendon Press, 1933.

Collins, Irene. *Jane Austen and the Clergy.* London: Hambledon Press, 1993.

Corfield, Penelope J. *Power and the Professions in Britain, 1700–1850.* London: Routledge, 1995.

Edgeworth, Richard Lovell. *Essays on Professional Education.* London: J. Johnson, 1808. Second edition, 1812.

Glover, Michael. *Wellington's Army in the Peninsular 1808–1814.* Newton Abbot: David and Charles, 1977.

Habakkuk, John. *Marriage, Debt, and the Estates System. English Landownership 1650–1950.* Oxford: Clarendon Press, 1994.

Lavery, Brian. *Nelson's Navy: The Ships, Men and Organisation 1793–1815.* London: Conway Maritime Press, 1989.

O'Day, Rosemary. *The Professions in Early Modern England, 1450–1800.* Harlow: Longmans, 2000.

Perkin, Harold. *The Origins of Modern English Society 1780–1880.* London: Routledge, 1969.

Stone, Lawrence, and Jean C. Fawtier Stone. *An Open Elite? England, 1540–1880.* Oxford: Clarendon Press, 1984.

PSYCHOLOGY

Ellis, Markman. *The Politics of Sensibility.* Cambridge: Cambridge University Press, 1996.

Mullan, John. *Sentiment and Sociability. The Language of Feeling in the Eighteenth Century.* Oxford: Oxford University Press, 1988.

Pinch, Adela. '*Strange Fits of Passion': Epistemologies of Emotion; Hume to Austen.* Stanford, CA: Stanford University Press, 1996.

Todd, Janet. *Sensibility: An Introduction.* London: Methuen, 1986.

Van Sant, Ann Jessie. *Eighteenth-Century Sensibility and the Novel: the Senses in Social Context.* Cambridge: Cambridge University Press, 1993.

RANK

Austen-Leigh, Joan. 'Forms of Address and Titles in Jane Austen', *Persuasions* 12 (1990), 35–7.

Burrows, J. F. '*Persuasion* and Its "Sets of People"', *Sydney Studies in English* 2 (1976–7), 3–23.

Corfield, Penelope J. 'Class by Name and Number in Eighteenth-Century Britain', *History* 72 (1987), 38–61.

Delany, Paul. '"A Sort of Notch in the Donwell Estate": Intersections of Status and Class in *Emma*', *Eighteenth-Century Fiction* 12, 4 (2000), 533–48.

Greene, D. J. 'Jane Austen and the Peerage', *PMLA* 68 (1953), 1017–31.

Lovell, Terry. 'Jane Austen and the Gentry: A Study in Literature and Ideology', in Diana Laurenson, ed. *The Sociology of Literature: Applied Studies.* Keele: Sociological Review Monographs, 1978.

McMaster, Juliet. 'Class', in Edward Copeland and Juliet McMaster, eds. *The Cambridge Companion to Jane Austen.* Cambridge: Cambridge University Press, 1997.

Spring, David. 'Interpreters of Jane Austen's Social World: Literary Critics and Historians', in Janet Todd, ed. *Jane Austen: New Perspectives.* New York: Holmes and Meier, 1983.

Terry, Judith. 'Seen But Not Heard: Servants in Jane Austen's England', *Persuasions* 10 (1988), 104–16.

READING PRACTICES

Altick, Richard D. *The English Common Reader: A Social History of the Mass Reading Public, 1800–1900.* Chicago: University of Chicago Press, 1957.

Jones, Vivien, ed. *Women and Literature in Britain, 1700–1800.* Cambridge: Cambridge University Press, 2000.

Michaelson, Patricia Howell. *Speaking Volumes: Women, Reading, and Speech in the Age of Austen.* Stanford, CA: Stanford University Press, 2002.

Pearson, Jacqueline. *Women's Reading in Britain, 1750–1835*. Cambridge: Cambridge University Press, 1999.

Raven, James. 'New Reading Histories, Print Culture and the Identification of Change: the Case of Eighteenth-Century England', *Social History* 23, 3 (1998), 268–87.

Raven, James, Helen Small and Naomi Tadmor, eds. *The Practice and Representation of Reading in England*. Cambridge: Cambridge University Press, 1996.

Richardson, Alan. *Literature, Education, and Romanticism: Reading as Social Practice, 1780–1832*. Cambridge: Cambridge University Press, 1994.

St Clair, William. *The Reading Nation in the Romantic Period*. Cambridge: Cambridge University Press, 2004.

RELIGION

Collins, Irene. *Jane Austen and the Clergy*. London: Hambledon Press, 1993.

Giffin, Michael. *Jane Austen and Religion: Salvation and Society in Georgian England*. New York: Palgrave Macmillan, 2002.

Rivers, Isabel. *Reason, Grace, and Sentiment: A Study of the Language of Religion and Ethics in England 1660–1780*. Cambridge: Cambridge University Press, 2000.

TRADE

Corfield, Penelope J. 'The Rivals: Landed and other Gentlemen', in Negley Harte and Roland Quinault, eds. *Land and Society in Britain, 1700–1914*. Manchester: Manchester University Press, 1996.

Davis, David Brion. *The Problem of Slavery in the Age of Revolution: 1770–1823*. Ithaca, NY: Cornell University Press, 1975.

Ferguson, Moira. '*Mansfield Park*: Slavery, Colonialism, and Gender', *Oxford Literary Review*, 13, 1–2 (1991), 118–39.

Floud, Roderick and Donald McCloskey, eds. *The Economic History of Britain since 1700: Volume I: 1700–1860*. 2nd edn. Cambridge: Cambridge University Press, 1994.

Grossman, Jonathan. 'The Labor of the Leisured in *Emma*: Class, Manners and Austen', *Nineteenth-Century Literature* 54, 2 (1999), 143–64.

Jones, E. L. 'Fashion Manipulators: Consumer Tastes and British Industries, 1660–1800', in L. P. Cain and P. J. Uselding, eds. *Business Enterprise and Economic Change.* Kent, OH: Kent State University Press, 1973.

McVeagh, John. *Tradefull Merchants: the Portrayal of the Capitalist in Literature.* London: Routledge & Kegan Paul, 1981.

Morgan, Kenneth. *The Birth of Industrial Britain: Economic Change 1750–1850.* Harlow, Essex: Longman, 1999.

Rule, John. *The Vital Century: England's Developing Economy, 1714–1815.* London: Longman, 1992.

Said, Edward. *Culture and Imperialism.* New York: Knopf, 1993.

Smith, Adam. *An Inquiry into the Nature and Causes of the Wealth of Nations,* eds. R. H. Campbell and A. S. Skinner. 2 vols. Oxford: Clarendon Press, 1976.

Thompson, F. M. L. *Gentrification and the Enterprise Culture, Britain 1780–1980.* Oxford: Oxford University Press, 2001.

Ward, J. R. *British West Indian Slavery, 1750–1834.* Oxford: Oxford University Press, 1984.

TRANSPORT

Albert, William. *The Turnpike Road System in England, 1663–1840.* Cambridge: Cambridge University Press, 1972.

Barker, T. C. and Dorian Gerhold. *The Rise and Rise of Road Transport, 1700–1990.* Cambridge: Cambridge University Press, 1995.

Fawcett, Trevor. *Bath Entertain'd: Amusements, Recreations and Gambling at the Eighteenth-Century Spa.* Bath: Ruton, 1998.

Jackman, W. T. *The Development of Transportation in Modern England.* 1916. 3rd edition. London: Frank Cass & Co., 1966.

Jarvis, Robin. *Romantic Writing and Pedestrian Travel.* Basingstoke: Macmillan, 1997.

Thirsk, Joan. *Horses in Early Modern England: for Service, for Pleasure, and Power.* Reading: University of Reading, 1978.

INDEX